SANTAYANA,

PRAGMATISM, AND THE

SPIRITUAL LIFE

SANTAYANA,

PRAGMATISM, AND

THE SPIRITUAL LIFE

HENRY SAMUEL LEVINSON

The King's Library

The University of North Carolina Press / Chapel Hill and London

© 1992 The University of North Carolina Press
All rights reserved
Manufactured in the United States of America

The paper in this book meets the guidelines for permanence and
durability of the Committee on Production Guidelines for Book
Longevity of the Council on Library Resources.

96 95 94 93 92   5 4 3 2 1

Library of Congress Cataloging-in-Publication Data

Levinson, Henry S.
Santayana, pragmatism, and the spiritual life /
Henry Samuel Levinson.
p.   cm.
Includes bibliographical references and index.
ISBN 0-8078-2031-8 (alk. paper)
1. Santayana, George, 1863–1952.
2. Pragmatism.   3. Spiritual life.   I. Title.
B945.S24L48   1992
191—dc20   91-50785
CIP

Frontispiece: George Santayana in 1897. Charcoal sketch by Andreas Martin Andersen
(Houghton Library, Harvard University).

FOR MY PARENTS,

MIMI AND JOE LEVINSON

CONTENTS

ACKNOWLEDGMENTS

Conversations at Stanford with Bill Clebsch about the Cambridge pragmatists initially led to my interest in Santayana. I remain deeply saddened that those conversations—and more broadly, a grand friendship—were cut short by Bill's untimely death.

By awarding me a Mellon Faculty Fellowship for 1982–83, Harvard University enabled me to begin satisfying that interest. I started research on this book during that superb academic year, made especially productive by the staffs of the Widener Libraries, the Houghton Rare Books and Manuscript Reading Room, and the Harvard Archives. The same year, I received great help from the staff of the Rare Books and Manuscript Reading Room in Butler Library, Columbia University.

After I was appointed to its faculty in 1982, the University of North Carolina at Greensboro helped generously by letting me go to Harvard before settling in the Old North State and, then, by awarding me Excellence Foundation Summer Research grants in 1984 and, again, in 1987.

Then too, in 1985–86, UNC Greensboro gave me leave to become a Mellon Fellow at that disneyland for academics, The National Humanities Center. The same year the National Endowment for the Humanities awarded me a Fellowship for Independent Scholarship. The uncommonly fine fellowship, the unstinting staff support, the provocative daily conversations and weekly seminars, and Wayne Pond's jokes, all made the NHC everything a research center should be.

Discussions with students and colleagues following lectures on Santayana at Pittsburgh University (Tony Edwards), the University of Syracuse (Amanda Porterfield), Stanford University (Hester Gelber, who suggested I read Kundera in connection with this study), and Oberlin College (Mike Michalson), as well as at the Frontiers in American Philosophy Conference at Texas A&M in June 1988 (Herman Saatkamp and Angus Kerr-Lawson), the Conference on Pragmatism at Colorado University in November 1989 (Jeff Stout, Richard Poirier, Giles Gunn), and a meeting of the Society for the Advancement of American Philosophy in Buffalo in March 1990, all were quite helpful; so too my incessant conversation with Luther Zeigler at Stanford and, then, with Mark Cladis (now teaching at Vassar) and John Sopper, in Greensboro.

I am grateful to Joanne Creighton (now provost at Wesleyan) who, as my friend and dean at UNC Greensboro, let me remain an active scholar and teacher while I spent 1987–90 writing administrative memos, dreaming institutional dreams, and concocting institutional schemes as her sidekick associate dean.

For twenty years Mike Michalson and Jeff Stout have delighted and inspired me with the erudition, wit, practical wisdom, and good humor they bring to the study of religion, not to mention the rest of life. But let me give credit where credit is due. Thanks Susanah, Clark, Sally, Sana, Noah, and Livy.

Just as I was starting to investigate Santayana's religious naturalism, multiple sclerosis began stealing insidiously into my body and, hence, into a lot of people's lives. So far I've been luckier than many people living with chronic illness, but still, I get by with a little help from my friends; and in the case of Jonathan and Sarah Malino nearby, and Dick Ransohoff, Mimi and Joe Levinson, and Max and Ethel Kaplan farther away, I receive a lot of help rather than a little.

But how to say "a lot more than a lot of help"? My daughters and bride have been there, caring, stumbling step by wobbly walk, helping me over and over again to get *Beyond Rage* (as Joanne LeMaistre has put it in a memorable book by that name). In *Winds of Doctrine*, Santayana wrote that religion is the love of life in the consciousness of impotence. I think that, together, Sarah, Molly, Cathy, and I have made that sort of love a daily discipline. In the midst of such affection, I'm left speechless, except to say to Sarah Kate Levinson and Molly Rebecca Levinson: Thanks for asking, routinely, "Hey, Pa; enough articles; where's the *book*?" And to Cathy Kaplan Levinson: Without you, nothing.

Having come many collegial miles with me already, Jeff Stout and Herman Saatkamp went more than a few extra by reading my manuscript in full, offering me invaluable advice about both its broader narrative sweep and its details—the kind of counsel that collapses the difference between substance and style by requiring an author to say what's clearly important.

My thanks to my editors at the University of North Carolina Press, Lewis Bateman, Ron Maner, and Brian MacDonald, for their advice and assistance. Thanks also go to Beth Eddy for proofreading and Patricia Mutch for making the index.

A shorter version of chapter 1, "Pragmatic Naturalism and the Spiritual Life," is reprinted by permission from *Raritan: A Quarterly Review* 10, no. 2 (Fall 1990), copyright 1990 by *Raritan*, 31 Mine Street, New Brunswick, NJ, 08903. Portions of "Santayana's Contribution to American Religious Philosophy" are reprinted by permission from the *Journal of the American Academy of Religion* 52, no. 1 (March 1984) in chapter 2. Portions of "What Good Is Irony?" are reprinted by permission from *Overheard in Seville: Bulletin of the Santayana Society* 8 (Fall 1990) in chapter 4. Portions of "Religious Criticism" are reprinted by permission from the *Journal of Religion* 64, no. 1 (January 1984), The University of Chicago Press, in chapter 5. Portions of "Meditation at the Margin" are reprinted by permission from the *Journal of Religion* 67, no. 3 (July 1987), The University of Chicago Press, in chapters 6 and 7. Portions of "Santayana and the Many Faces of Realism" are reprinted by permission from *The Proceedings of the Frontiers in American Philosophy Conference*, forthcoming, copyright by Texas A&M University, in chapter 6. Portions of "Santayana's Pragmatism and the Comic Sense of Life" are reprinted by permission from *Overheard in Seville: Bulletin of the Santayana Society* 6 (Fall 1988), in chapter 7. In addition, a photo of an 1897 charcoal drawing of George Santayana by Andreas Martin Andersen, appearing as the frontispiece, is reprinted by permission from Houghton Library, Harvard University.

ABBREVIATIONS

ACF   John Dewey. *A Common Faith*. New Haven: Yale University Press, 1934.

COUS   George Santayana. *Character and Opinion in the United States: With Reminiscences of William James and Josiah Royce and Academic Life in America*. New York: Charles Scribner's Sons, 1920.

CP   *The Complete Poems of George Santayana: A Critical Edition*. Edited with an introduction by William G. Holzberger. Lewisburg, Pa.: Bucknell University Press, 1979.

DL   George Santayana. *Dialogues in Limbo*. New York: Charles Scribner's Sons, 1926.

"DNM"   George Santayana. "Dewey's Naturalistic Metaphysics." In *Dewey and His Critics*, edited by Sidney Morgenbesser, pp. 343–58. New York: Journal of Philosophy, 1977.

DP   George Santayana. *Dominations and Powers: Reflections on Liberty, Society, and Government*. New York: Charles Scribner's Sons, 1951.

E   George Santayana. Introduction to *Ethics* and *De Intellectus Emendatione*, by Benedict de Spinoza. New York: Dutton, 1910.

GSA   *George Santayana's America*. Edited by James Ballowe. Cambridge, Mass.: Harvard University Press, 1968.

ICG   George Santayana. *The Idea of Christ in the Gospels; or, God in Man: A Critical Essay*. New York: Charles Scribner's Sons, 1946.

IPR   George Santayana. *Interpretations of Poetry and Religion*. Critical edi-
          tion by William G. Holzberger and Herman J. Saatkamp, Jr., with an
          introduction by Joel Porte. Cambridge, Mass.: MIT Press, 1990.

L   *The Letters of George Santayana*. Edited by Daniel Cory. New York:
          Charles Scribner's Sons, 1955.

LP   George Santayana. *The Last Puritan*. New York: Charles Scribner's
          Sons, 1936.

LR   George Santayana. *The Life of Reason: Or, The Phases of Human
          Progress*. 5 vols. New York: Charles Scribner's Sons, 1905–6.

LSP   George Santayana. *Lotze's System of Philosophy*. Edited with an intro-
          duction by Paul Grimley Kuntz. Bloomington: Indiana University
          Press, 1971.

LTT   George Santayana. *Lucifer: A Theological Tragedy*. Chicago: Herbert
          S. Stone, 1899.

"MSB"   George Santayana. "Moral Symbols in the Bible." In *The Idler and His
          Works, and Other Essays*, edited by Daniel Cory, pp. 152–78. New
          York: George Braziller, 1957.

NHS   *Naturalism and the Human Spirit*. Edited by Yervant H. Krikorian.
          New York: Columbia University Press, 1944.

PAP   George Santayana. *Persons and Places: Fragments of Autobiography*.
          Critical edition by William G. Holzberger and Herman J. Saatkamp,
          Jr., with an introduction by Richard C. Lyon. Cambridge, Mass.:
          MIT Press, 1986.

PGS   *The Philosophy of George Santayana*. Edited by Paul Arthur Schilpp.
          Evanston, Ill.: Northwestern University Press, 1940.

"PH"   George Santayana. "Philosophical Heresy." In *Obiter Scripta: Lec-
          tures, Essays and Reviews*, edited by Justus Buchler and Benjamin
          Schwartz, pp. 94–107. New York: Charles Scribner's Sons, 1936.

POP   William James. *The Principles of Psychology*. 3 vols. Critical edition
          by Frederick H. Burkhardt, Fredson Bowers, and Ignas K.

Skrupskelis, with introductions by Gerald E. Meyers and Rand B. Evans. Cambridge, Mass.: Harvard University Press, 1981.

PSL George Santayana. *Platonism and the Spiritual Life*. New York: Charles Scribner's Sons, 1927.

RB George Santayana. *Realms of Being*. New York: Charles Scribner's Sons, 1942.

SAF George Santayana. *Scepticism and Animal Faith: Introduction to a System of Philosophy*. New York: Charles Scribner's Sons, 1923.

SB George Santayana. *The Sense of Beauty: Being the Outlines of Aesthetic Theory*. Critical edition by William G. Holzberger and Herman J. Saatkamp, Jr., with an introduction by Arthur C. Danto. Cambridge, Mass.: MIT Press, 1988.

SELS George Santayana. *Soliloquies in England and Later Soliloquies*. New York: Charles Scribner's Sons, 1922.

SWE *Selected Writings of Emerson*. Edited by Donald McQuade. New York: Random House, 1981.

"TIDL" George Santayana. "The Two Idealisms: A Dialogue in Limbo." In *Obiter Scripta: Lectures, Essays and Reviews*, edited by Justus Buchler and Benjamin Schwartz, pp. 1–29. New York: Charles Scribner's Sons, 1936.

TPP George Santayana. *Three Philosophical Poets*. Cambridge, Mass.: Harvard University Press, 1910.

TT William James. *Talks to Teachers on Psychology and to Students on Some of Life's Ideals*. Critical edition by Frederick H. Burkhardt, Fredson Bowers, and Ignas K. Skrupskelis, with an introduction by Gerald E. Meyers. Cambridge, Mass.: Harvard University Press, 1983.

"UR" George Santayana. "Ultimate Religion." In *Obiter Scripta: Lectures, Essays and Reviews*, edited by Justus Buchler and Benjamin Schwartz, pp. 280–98. New York: Charles Scribner's Sons, 1936.

VRE   William James. *The Varieties of Religious Experience*. Critical edition by Frederick H. Burkhardt, Fredson Bowers, and Ignas K. Skrupskelis, with an introduction by John E. Smith. Cambridge, Mass.: Harvard University Press, 1985.

"WA?"   George Santayana. "What Is Aesthetics?" In *Obiter Scripta: Lectures, Essays and Reviews*, edited by Justus Buchler and Benjamin Schwartz, pp. 30–40. New York: Charles Scribner's Sons, 1936.

WD   George Santayana. *Winds of Doctrine: Studies in Contemporary Opinion*. New York: Charles Scribner's Sons, 1913.

SANTAYANA,

PRAGMATISM, AND THE

SPIRITUAL LIFE

Where the spirit of comedy has departed, company becomes constraint, reserve eats up the spirit, and people fall into a penurious melancholy in their scruple to be always exact, sane, and reasonable, never to mourn, never to glow, never to betray a passion or a weakness, nor venture to utter a thought you might not wish to harbour forever.—George Santayana

If we are in a balloon over an abyss, let us at least value the balloon. If night is all around, then what light we have is precious. If there is no life to be seen in the great emptiness, our companions are to be cherished; so are we ourselves.—Lionel Trilling

1

PRAGMATIC NATURALISM

AND THE SPIRITUAL LIFE

Santayana's Pragmatism and the Pragmatists

Many historians have argued that Santayana's writings played an extremely prominent role in inaugurating philosophical naturalism in the United States. Next to none, however, have highlighted the fact that crucial works of his were hailed, more specifically, as fashioning a sort of pragmatic naturalism. Arthur Kenyon Rogers, for one, called Santayana's *The Life of Reason* the first comprehensive presentation of pragmatism.[1] To my mind, this portrayal makes a good deal of sense because Santayana characterized knowledge as nonfoundational inquiry; reason as nontranscendent or immanent criticism; every sort of language as expressive, imaginative, or poetic; every part of existence as contingent or historical; and philosophy as reflection on problems of human finitude rather than as a search for first principles or for the really real. What is more, as I hope to show, Santayana never quit positing any of these views even when, after he left the United States and started poking fun at it, his critics stopped calling his philosophy pragmatic—even when he himself criticized "the pragmatic school," mainly associated with the writings of John Dewey, and distanced himself from it.[2]

So what did the pragmatic Santayana and Deweyan pragmatists disagree about; and do these disagreements matter? In a rough-and-ready way, I think the answer is this: Santayana's pragmatic naturalism was religious in ways that mainline pragmatists in the period from World War I at least up through World War II could not abide; and the pragmatic naturalism developed by

Dewey, and disciples like Sidney Hook and Joseph Ratner, often boiled down to a moralism too strenuous to suit Santayana.

To be sure, this picture of Santayana and other pragmatists is somewhat laden by caricature and overstatement, because Dewey, especially, paid a lot of attention to aesthetic experience along with morality and society, and even claimed that aesthetic experience had a religious quality. But I still think, in the end, that the biggest bone of contention between Santayana and other pragmatic naturalists lay in his attention to religious or spiritual life understood as something different from moral or civic virtue and as something less vague than a sense qualifying aesthetic experience.

Differences

There are six overlapping ways to think through this tension—six differences that focus my reflections in this book. First, by and large, the pragmatists, especially after James, were preoccupied with social life. They were social critics or, sometimes, culture critics. But one of the most remarkable characteristics of their culture criticism is something that was missing: There was little or no reflection on the pleasures or problems of solitude. For Santayana, spiritual life was concerned both with life alone and life together, with the question of solitary equanimity and personal well-being in the face of human extremity as well as with the issue of social solidarity.[3]

The pragmatists criticized Santayana for his interest in human solitude: He was an old-fashioned individualist, an escapist, a romantic, a mystic. For his part, Santayana criticized the pragmatists for their inability to see that critical thought extended beyond social policy formulation to problems of personal well-being that no social policy or social relationship could solve. There were not only lots of lonesome valleys that people had to walk through but solitary disciplines that brought individuals profound satisfaction as well.

Second, in the pragmatists' view, life was no laughing matter, because it was beset by tragedy. Pragmatism, as Hook put it, was informed by a tragic sense of life, by the recognition and analysis of conflicts between good and good, good and right, and right and right, and by an overriding commitment to resolve them. Their social criticism waxed prophetic, as it called readers to this duty, chiding them for their inability to live up to the social promise embodied in the symbol of "America," in its democratic institutions, and in its motto, *e pluribus unum*.

Santayana saw things somewhat differently, noting that "prophets are constitutionally incapable of a sense of humour" and advising his readers that "the young man who has not wept is a savage, but the old man who has not laughed is a fool." Human life had its compensations. In his view, people should turn to the task of resolving conflict as best they could. He said that tragedy was "not to be denied or explained away, as is sometimes attempted in cowardly or mincing philosophies." But, he suggested, there was no necessity demanding that people be consumed by it. People "not too much starved or thwarted by circumstances," and prepared to engage in spiritual disciplines, could take joy just as seriously as meanness (WD, 55; DL, 57; SELS, 140–41). Pragmatists criticized Santayana for fiddling while Rome burned. Santayana retorted by suggesting that if human life was no laughing matter, it was probably just deadly and not worth living.

Third, while the pragmatists undercut the Enlightenment's quest to find a way to ground knowledge on itself, they tended to endorse an Enlightenment commitment to the project of human self-assertion. Here is Dewey: "Faith in the power of intelligence to imagine a future which is a projection of the desirable in the present, and to invent the instrumentalities of its realization, is our salvation. And it is a faith that must be nurtured and made articulate; surely a sufficiently large task for our philosophy."[4] Santayana, to the contrary, pictured human self-assertion as indispensable but as inevitably falling short of realizing its aims, salvation as coming with "the love of life in the consciousness of impotence," and philosophy as providing disciplines for such affection (WD, 43).

Fourth and following, the pragmatists tended to construe philosophy as socially and politically engaged, a kind of inquiry that prepared citizens or their leaders for concrete social action. Indeed, they identified philosophy as a profession offering politicians, technocrats, and other professionals synoptic blueprints on which to base their social planning.

Santayana, most emphatically after writing *The Life of Reason*, inclined toward portraying philosophy as a suspension of such business, an interruption of normal social action, a disengagement from policy and politics, a disintoxication from the particular values that happened to shape up this or that society or polity, a holiday from statesmanship. Philosophy, he suggested, let people enjoy time out for intellectual festivity, celebration, worship, religious meditation, as well as cognitive or imaginative free play.[5]

The pragmatists took Santayana's characterization of philosophy this way as "hard, complacent, inhumane, and frivolous," a holdover from an Old World theological distinction between this-worldly and otherworldly concerns.[6] Santayana, on the other hand, scolded pragmatists for their shortsightedness, for their fixation on what he called the political and economic "foreground." He asked what good political and economic systems could serve if they did not afford opportunities for (oftentimes extrapolitical) spiritual well-being.

Fifth, pragmatists found little that was good to say about distinctively religious narratives, practices, or institutions, which they pictured as draining energies away from "the problems of men" while fueling superstition and fanaticism. They followed Dewey's lead by distinguishing between "religion" and "the religious." "Religion," Dewey said, amounted to fixed and differentiated creeds and cults that were indelibly supernatural in content and were socially exclusive to boot. "The religious," to the contrary, was an aesthetic quality of "any activity pursued in behalf of an ideal end against obstacles and in spite of threats of personal loss because of conviction of its general and enduring value" (ACF, 27). Suspicious of differentiating religions from other parts of culture, Dewey tried to displace them by underscoring the religious quality of aesthetic experience—for example, in the creation and enjoyment of works of art:

> We are, as it were, introduced into a world beyond this world which is nevertheless the deeper reality of the world in which we live in our ordinary experience. We are carried out beyond ourselves to find ourselves. I can see no psychological ground for such properties of an experience save that, somehow, the work of art operates to deepen and to raise to great clarity that sense of an enveloping undefined whole that accompanies every normal experience. This whole is then felt as an expansion of ourselves. . . . Where egotism is not made the measure of reality and value, we are citizens of this vast world beyond ourselves, and any intense realization of its presence with and in us brings a peculiarly satisfying sense of unity in itself and with ourselves.[7]

From Santayana's vantage point, this talk of getting beyond ourselves to find ourselves by way of a "sense of an enveloping undefined whole" amounted to the last thin gasp of Hegelian idealism, truncating religious traditions to a point that was laughable. He attempted, to the contrary, to make cultural space for religion and ridiculed the idea of some generically religious quality that could inform any activity. He argued that "the attempt to speak without speaking any particular language is not more hopeless than the attempt to have a religion that shall be no religion in particular" (LR, 3:5). And he prized particular religions for providing "another world to live in" (LR, 3:6).

In Santayana's view otherworldliness, indeed, did have a function, but it was strictly cultural, not transcendent or postmortem. Religions provided people with "another world to live in," a world in which they could practice disciplines that let them suspend the order of their normal social world, particularly the differentiations and hierarchies of social, economic, and political life. There, people got training in religious virtues like piety or devotion to the sources of their lives, spirituality or devotion to their ultimate concerns, and charity or appreciation of what was good for others as they understood themselves. Religions gave people these disciplines both to let them imagine things that bonded human beings together no matter what their social, political, or economic roles or circumstances happened to be, and to form routines allowing personal contentment.

Santayana argued that these disciplines, the religious narratives in which they were presented in exemplary ways, and the religious institutions responsible for crafting those narratives were not inevitably to blame for superstition and fanaticism. Rather, supernaturalism, or the confusion of ideals and powers, was accountable for these things. But the narratives and disciplines that constituted religious traditions could be understood or explicated in naturalistic ways without destroying either their particularity or the differences they made for people's lives.

Finally, pragmatists pictured democracy American-style as the divine way of doing things. They urged people to pour all the fervor and enthusiasm they may once have had for religious traditions into a devotion to political and social democracy. Santayana demurred, unwilling to call any one form of political life divine, and willing to note all the ways in which modern democracies, whether socialist or capitalist, had ended up pitting equality, homogeneity, and mass life against excellence. A good government, "government for the people," he claimed, "turns the forces of nature, as far as possible, from enemies into servants and the pressure of society into friendly cooperation and an opportune stimulus to each man's latent powers" (DP, 430).[8] Universal suffrage, which he construed (wrongly, I think) as the hallmark of political democracy, was one but by no stretch of the imagination the sole means to that end. In principle if not in fact, Santayana argued, timocracy was probably a better arrangement, demanding equal opportunity but permitting unequal achievement along with government by people who merited their assigned offices by the breadth and depth of their accomplishments in economic and political arts (DP, 151).

Precursors

I hope to show that these six conflicts between Santayana and "the pragmatists" had a history. They were textually inspired most immediately by themes in the writings of Ralph Waldo Emerson. Indeed I emphasize *in* because these were not conflicts between Emerson and his critics but between Emerson and himself. Society and solitude; the tragic and the comic; impotence and assertion, or fate and freedom; prophetic reform and spiritual contemplation; the grace of communion and the cant of religion; American democracy as divine life at first hand and as the land of "the dead alive" condemned to life at second hand—all these conflicts are Emersonian.

In fact these Emersonian anxieties are themselves grounded in older dialectics that inform the thought and practice of Emerson's Protestant forebears, whether republican or theocratic. The tensions I am thinking about descend from Reformed Christian preoccupations with grace and law, with the view that moral practices, while indispensable, do not circumscribe personal life in its most divine moments; that personal equanimity, in some sense, requires letting go of moral propriety understood as exclusively definitive of human life at its best; that genuine spirituality calls for some sort of solitary new birth or re-creation that reveals simultaneously the limitations and genuine functions of the social conventions we inherit, on the one hand, and the lovely and lovable character of mortal life on the other; that doing well neither adds up to nor secures being well; that personal well-being can occur, but it cannot be achieved, because its happening is gratuitous.

These views, drawn with great precision, say, by traditional Reformed Christian thinkers like Jonathan Edwards, outlasted the original supernatural and Christological context in which they emerged. They remained central when Edwards himself dropped supernatural and Christian language for aesthetic discourse in his battles with British Benevolists over the nature of true virtue. They were still the crux of the matter for Emerson's post–Christian Protestant efforts, as Clebsch put it, "to respiritualize a natural outlook that had become despirited."[9] We will see, indeed, that they remained at the heart of William James's quest to satisfy what he called "the religious demand" by searching for supernatural powers at work in the world.[10] More to the point, I will describe how they shaped Santayana's utterly naturalistic understanding of the stresses and strains between moral and spiritual practices. For that matter they also haunted Dewey's equally naturalistic vision of the ways in which aesthetic experience outstrips, as he put it, moral "consecrations of the *status quo*."[11]

Prospects

But now I want to ask explicitly who cares about these tensions anymore? Or, to put it more personally and assertively, why do I care about the prospects for a religious naturalism like Santayana's, and is my concern simply self-indulgent and atavistic? I care because I share the following views with Santayana. First, if we are concerned with the problems and promise of human finitude, we had best attend to society and solitude, because it is impossible to reflect very broadly on human joy and the things that impede it without coming to grips with both. Second, if by "the promise of human finitude" we mean the realization of such happiness, we had better make room for comedy as well as tragedy when it comes to our sense of life, because it is comedy, not tragedy, that takes joy as seriously as meanness. Third, that comic sense requires our acceptance of finitude and ultimate impotence along with our commitment to disclosing the pretensions of self-assertion. Fourth, accompanying a devotion to human solidarity, and often in its service, philosophers in the West have traditionally broken away from social policy formulation to meditate on such things, and our culture would be better off if they continued to do this. Fifth, stripped of false explanatory accounts that turn ideals into powers—accounts that let people pretend that the universe works "for truth and right forever,"[12] or that empower "us," whoever we are, so that we can dominate "them," whoever they are—traditional religious institutions, narratives, and disciplines may continue to serve their properly moral and festive cultural functions. Finally, democracy American-style is not the divine way of doing things, and the spiritual exceptionalism that suggests that it is, by collapsing eschatology and nationalism into one another, has fostered more than a modicum of cruelty. American democracy is a handy way—in my view, if not Santayana's, probably the handiest way—to structure life politically. But that is the case in great part insofar as it has permitted and continued to maintain a culture that is eclectic, thriving on a diversity of moral and religious traditions; a culture endangered by homogeneity and uniformity, whether unbearably light or weighty. Indeed, in my view, democracy's worth as a political system is to be measured not simply by its commitment to self-determination, or by its economic facility, but more by its ability to sustain this diversity of traditions that discipline imaginations in ways that give point to human life.

To my way of thinking, these six areas of inquiry constitute an agenda of study for current religious naturalists to pursue. In the pages that follow, I hope—through coming to critical grips with Santayana's writings—to begin suggesting, broad-stroke, the prospects for religious naturalism now. So finally, with this last task in mind, let me briefly tip my own hand regarding the six issues I have identified.

Society and Solitude

Strong liberal democrats like me are committed to human solidarity. But we know that there are lines, some fine, some coarse, separating concord, cooperation, and fellowship from the sort of mass or bulk or uniformed life where, as Milan Kundera has put it, "unity of mankind means: No escape for anyone anywhere."[13] We maintain mutuality as a superordinate goal to keep in mind when shaping up social attitudes, but we reject oneness, unanimity, and the deterioration of private life. Why is this so? Why do the stories of, say, Franz Kafka and Kundera that explore "the violation of solitude" strike home to us with such force? Is it because we are socially dysfunctional, politically naive, misanthropes, incurably romantic, or mystic dilettantes? No. It is because we think that moral bonding and personal well-being or joy depend as much on things that go on when people are in private and voluntary association with their families, friends, colleagues, and religious fellowships as when they are engaging issues of public policy. But more, personal contentment depends as much on things that go on in people when they are alone as on things that happen in their interactions with other people, as much on personal, even solitary, transformations as on social justice.[14]

I say "go on in people" because, more than anything else, what is at stake is imaginative life. It is important, however, not to read old epistemological or metaphysical presumptions into this phrase. The way I turn it, anyhow, there is nothing epistemologically private or asocial about imaginative life, nothing metaphysical about it.

I am, for example, writing this book not only for myself but for you; and my capacity to do so is the outcome of a lot of socialization and training. My effort, as all effort, is experienced and observable as plainly physical. But I have also turned aside from normal social routine, and asked people not to disturb me, so that I might work out this way of thinking, work on myself, play with variations on old themes concerning human joy and the things impeding it. In the doing, I am, as James or Wittgenstein would say, experiencing the practice of imagination *as* solitary. Cultural arrangements and disciplines make this possible, disciplines that involve letting go of old conventions so as to propose new ones, and my performance plays a cultural role, exhibiting some character. Moreover, I am given leave to do so by way of political and economic legitimation. But it is the performance, my solitary attention to an interest, my practical competence, not social relationships or policy per se, that is at risk and is the site of whatever agony and joy or sense of beauty goes on. The performance may or may not be good for anything else in particular. It may or may not contribute to human solidarity. Nonetheless, it may bring me, or somebody else, some sense of well-being.

There is something right, then, about Richard Rorty's suggestion that "the old tension between the private and the public remains"; right that there are no necessary connections between private hopes and social justice, but only contingent, practical ones; and, so, right to abandon a quest for some *theory* revealing an essential human core, safe beyond time and change, linking up such things.[15] On the one hand, personal well-being may occur no matter how societies are composed, decomposed, or recomposed. On the other, the realization of well-oiled democratic practices and institutions, along with the most supportive private associations imaginable, will still leave individuals yearning for solitude and having to manage the personal difficulties accompanying loss and change, suffering, absurdity, evil and death.

Tears and Laughter

There is no escaping these things, so pragmatists would do well, as Cornel West has suggested, to retain a "sense of the tragic [that] highlights the irreducible predicament of unique individuals who undergo dread, despair, disillusionment, disease, and death *and* the institutional forms of oppression that dehumanize people."[16] But it is not enough to catalog West's six horrid "d's." The problem still remains how to display suffering's meanness and then transcend it by celebrating "passing joys and victories in the world"—which is a problem that comic vision seeks to resolve.[17]

When essentialism still saturated thinking in the West, critics often explicated comic episodes as events in which conventional social distinctions or pretensions separating people from one another got undercut, disclosing a "core" humankindness or community in which everybody could take some joy. Viewed this way, the inversions of carnival where kings and paupers exchange clothes, the subversions of jokes where, say, the well-dressed lady slips on a banana peel, and the reversions from self-conscious and constrained adulthood to playful or spontaneous childhood, prominent in texts like *Alice in Wonderland*, let us abandon, imaginatively at any rate, conventional social differences for participation in delightfully "real" human unions or communions that are acultural and ahistorical in nature.

For pragmatists, this explication of comedy cannot work, because nature is historical and human history is cultural and because, as Santayana put it, "in this world we must either institute conventional forms of expression or else pretend that we have nothing to express. The choice lies between a mask and a fig-leaf . . . and the fig-leaf is only a more ignominious mask" (*SELS*, 139). But comedy surely survives essentialism. Abandoning such language does not disrupt our capacity to explore things that let us laugh, both at the absurdity of our own pretensions and at the fortuitous bonds that are forged with others who are really different (including, I suggest, our own old personalities). Embracing pragmatic naturalism does not purge happy endings. Comedy is contingent on incongruity and affinity, not appearance and reality. But both incongruity and affinity depend on the occurrence of variation, change, continuity, and coherence—things that characterize finite beings living in a world that is historical all the way along.

Thank goodness that, after years of nearly unexceptional blindness to comedy, pragmatists like West and Giles Gunn are once again exploring its critical and imaginative functions.[18] Gunn, building on the works of Kenneth Burke and Mikhail Bakhtin, reaches for a culture criticism that reflects bonds strong enough to include, in Burke's words, "our own fundamental kinship with the enemy."[19] This sort of criticism, Gunn has argued, "requires the development of a critical language that not only challenges the privileging of its own terms but also seeks to undermine such symbolic activity everywhere by revealing the strategies in which we are all implicated. For this purpose, only a comic language will do, one that thrives on the possibility of comic reversals and absurd, or at least unexpected and unlikely, linkings and comparisons."[20]

West is developing a "prophetic pragmatism" out of the fundamentally tragic idioms found in such precursors as Hook, Lionel Trilling, Reinhold Niebuhr, and Raymond Williams.[21] But speaking as an African American Christian, he has begun to celebrate "the radically comic character of Afro-American life—the pervasive sense of play, laughter, and ingenious humor of blacks" that, on his reading, emerges out of the Gospel as blacks read and act themselves into it.[22]

Self-Assertion and Impotence

That sense of play, laughter, and ingenious humor, I suggest, is misread if it is construed exclusively as an expression of power, the way West does. To be sure, humor can imaginatively disarm the dominant and empower the oppressed. But radical comedy is not simply a contest of wills. Rather, it involves an admission that, in no small part, what links people is the powerlessness and mortality that they share; it is an acceptance of things that resist or defeat self-assertion. Radical comedy occurs, as Santayana put it, when "everybody acknowledges himself beaten and deceived, yet is the happier for the unexpected posture of affairs" (*SELS*, 141). It is a performance, he suggested, that leads to forgiveness, acceptance, and understanding, showing us "the innocence of the things we hated and the clearness of the things we frowned on or denied" (*SELS*, 263).

But if this sort of radical comedy cuts ice, then Rorty's recent emphasis on private self-assertion truncates extrapolitical life. On Rorty's counsel, the old Christian idea of law gets naturalized when responsibility to God becomes responsibility to one another. Democracy, as he puts it (after Nietzsche, but without his sneer), is Christianity made natural.[23] Similarly, though Rorty does not say this, the old Christian idea of grace gets romanticized when new personal creation through divine encounter becomes "self-creation" through strong poetry. Emerson's life at second hand becomes Harold Bloom's "horror of finding himself to be only a copy or a replica"; and his life at first hand becomes the authoring of some difference that makes "his I different from all the other I's."[24]

This, certainly, is one way to naturalize the life of the spirit. But Rorty appears to dismiss the Western tradition that pictures tension between self-assertion and spirituality, the tradition of self-surrender still prominent in William James's religious demand for a sort of well-being that well-doing obstructed, in Santayana's advice that spirituality is constituted by the "willingness not to will" that is ingredient in radical comedy, and, more recently, for example, in Richard Poirier's reflections on "writing off the self."[25] This is so because, in Rorty's view, agonistic self-assertion is the only route to personal well-being worth recommending in a world without any supernatural powers in it. He argues that the tradition of self-surrender requires a metaphysics of transcendence unavailable to naturalists. Moreover, he cannot imagine a creative individual finding self-assertion "hardly satisfying."[26]

But to my mind this tells us more about the limits of Rorty's temperament than it does about the varieties of personal well-being. Even if the point of self-surrender once seemed woven into the need to worship a deity that escaped natural constraints, something new can be made of it that permits equanimity in light of natural contingencies rather than despite them. We do not require any essential or transcendent "otherness" to appreciate the wonder and beauty of other things and people, or to find well-being not in an "I different from all the other I's" that seems sure to be defeated, but there instead, where our personal dissolution is accepted. Rather, we require a particular temperament.

Judgment and Understanding

We may require a temperament, as Poirier puts it, "in favor of relaxation rather than self-assertion, of drift rather than aggressive deployments," of "contemplative receptivity" rather than active projection.[27] But it is not clear to me why we need to exhibit one temper rather than the other. They are contrary, not contradictory. Cannot both be present, sometimes even together? Are not the tensions between assertion and reception, action and contemplation, judgment and understanding better to live with than to resolve one way rather than the other?

I am persuaded that they are. It seems to me, however, that most pragmatic naturalists still suspect that diversion, meditation, and discernment are decadent in a world sufficiently wretched to demand constant contention, judgment, movement, and decision. They write to mandate action and they tend to picture contemplation and understanding as gestures that delay. But delayed reaction is the better part of wisdom when people rush to judgment, or even worse, when trained functionaries react according to convention without understanding the role they are playing. Then there is no difference that makes a difference, as Hans Blumenberg has put it, between "delayed reaction [and] 'conscious' action."[28]

Kundera has written that the modern era dawned twice over, once with Descartes, who launched the quest for certain truth, and then again with Cervantes, who introduced the art of the novel, an art that presumed the loss of such certainty. The novel became the "territory where no one possesses the truth . . . but where everyone has the right to be understood."

"The novel's wisdom," Kundera has said, "is different from that of philosophy. The novel is born not of the theoretical spirit, but of the spirit of humor. . . . [It] does not serve ideological certitudes, it contradicts them. Like Penelope, it undoes each night the tapestry that the theologians, philosophers, and learned men have woven the day before."[29]

But the distinction that Kundera has drawn between the wisdom of the novel and that of philosophy has been challenged more than once and, not least effectively, by Santayana. It presumes that philosophy inevitably must be theory, that it must be concerned with discovering the necessary or the essential or the certain. It supposes that critics like Kundera himself, full of insight about human predicaments and prospects, must be discounted as philosophers.

Indeed, interestingly enough, Kundera's distinction between novelistic and philosophic wisdom comes very close to the line that Santayana drew between moralistic philosophy, searching for ideological certitude, and spiritual life, where people learn to suspend judgment and "identify themselves not with themselves" in order to understand and appreciate others who are different (*RB*, 741). As we shall see, for Santayana, spirituality is "a second insight . . . detaching us from each thing with humility and humour, and attaching us to all things with justice, charity, and joy" (*RB*, 741, 745).

To my mind, the risk moralism runs is fanaticism; the peril in spirituality is quietism. Santayana knew this. That is why, meditating on the idea of Christ in the Gospels, he commended a passage, narrow and steep, between such extremes—a way to maintain both commitment and spiritual openness, judgment and understanding, assertion and reception, assurance and doubt, attachment and detachment, equanimity in the midst of moral or political combat.

Religion and Supernaturalism

Suppose some of us pragmatic naturalists aim to embrace disciplines and attitudes like these. Is this reason enough to engage in traditional religious practices and to meditate on canonical religious books? Surely, as Jeffrey Stout has recently argued with great effect, these practices do not depend on avowing any traditional *theological* view. We need not, as he puts it, "postulate divine purposes, let alone divine intentions" in order to engage in "wonder, awe, and even gratitude—a kind of piety in short, for the powers that bear down upon us, for the majestic setting of our planet and its cosmos, and for the often marvelous company we keep here."[30] We can, Stout notes, "keep our confidence, loyalty, hope, and love proportioned to their objects" and never "make the merely finite our ultimate concern" without invoking some "Ultimate Other who deserves our ultimate concern" instead.[31]

I accept all of this. But the religious virtues—piety, confidence, loyalty, hope, and love—that Stout avows have a history. They have been articulated by particular religious traditions, taught and learned in particular religious communities, exemplified in the books that give shape to them, and sustained as disciplines by particular religious institutions. If we want to maintain the practice of particular virtues, I believe we need to maintain traditions, communities, books, and institutions that shape up lives that way. At least, it is not clear to me what other alternatives we have.

Does it matter that the central narratives that render these particular religious virtues intelligible and practically formative are legends, as religious naturalists suggest, rather than revelations of the "really real"? Yes. It matters because it shows the profound role transparent fictions play for us, whether for good or ill, by giving us codes or ciphers that must be learned in order to practice distinctive ways of life.

Can the practices we learn, say, as Christians, Jews, Zunis, Confucians, or Moslems survive this switch? We will have to see. But of course we will fail if we do not try. We know that we need not take the stuffing out of tradition by doing so. We have seen the successes, for example, of Reconstructionist Judaism, thick with liturgy, rituals that emphasize the willingness not to will, training in moral virtues, and Torah and Talmud study. We have seen practitioners in this movement not only keep commandments but experience the wonder and joy of self-surrender. But we also know that the sociology of religions in the West may make it well nigh impossible for many adherents of those traditions to approach religious naturalism as a live, much less appealing, option.

Pragmatic naturalists like me no longer have any interest in questions like "What is the meaning of the whole of history?" or "What happened before anything else happened?" or "What will happen after everything else happens?" or "How do we make direct contact with the really real?" We do not confuse ideals with powers. So our traditions change their shapes; in fact we hold ourselves responsible for helping along the transformations. But we can still learn, practice, and give witness to them in ways that maintain continuity and coherence with our predecessors. Our Christianity or Judaism, for example, may remain culturally thick, though varied, without any semblance of supernaturalism.

Religions in Liberal Democracies

One of the things pragmatic naturalists cannot reasonably claim, to be sure, is any incontrovertible warrant for their own beliefs or practices. But if their understanding of belief is adequate, nobody can. This frightens some people who look for One Right Way to glue everything and everybody together and who are repelled by cultural plurality and eclecticism. People like this hold on, as Kundera has put it, to the Western "dream of paradise—the age-old dream of a world where everybody would live in harmony, united by a single common faith and will, without secrets from one another."[32]

But Kundera and many others have recognized that, for centuries, this dream has wreaked a lot of havoc. The historical record seems fairly clear. As Kundera, again, has reminded us: "Once the dream of paradise starts to turn into reality, here and there people begin to crop up who stand in its way, and so the rulers of paradise must build a little gulag on the side of Eden. In the course of time this gulag grows ever bigger and more perfect, while the adjoining paradise gets ever smaller and poorer."[33]

To my mind, Stout is right to argue that the liberal tradition and modern democratic institutions emerged together, in great part, in order to circumvent this scenario or, as he puts it, "because people recognized putting an end to religious warfare and intolerance [was] morally good—[was] rationally preferable to continued attempts at imposing a nearly complete vision of the good by force."[34] He is right to suggest that this is why we school our kids "not to press too hard or too far for agreement on all details in a given vision of the good."[35]

People who fault liberal democracies for permitting plural intellectual, religious, and moral traditions claim that this drains us of concerted moral purpose and spiritual vitality; they say that something verging on complete agreement about moral or religious truth is just the elixir we need to cure the social diseases that ail us. But such assertions, in my view, are silly. Moral and religious pluralism are not responsible for poisoning the earth and its atmosphere, gutting education, colonizing the urban poor, permitting rampant illiteracy, or letting the marketplace ration health care. These problems stem from amorality and immortality, including political apathy, not plural traditions—from habits like private greed and public thoughtlessness. We simply do not have to agree on grand designs to consent to functionally adequate moral details; we do not even need to agree to every detail to be genuine friends and compatriots engaged in common civic activities. Indeed our very eclecticism is a marvelous check on the pretensions of grand designs, which brings me to one last introductory reflection.

Listen to William of Baskerville, the learned Franciscan hero of Umberto Eco's *The Name of the Rose*: "Fear prophets . . . and those prepared to die for the truth, for as a rule they make many others die with them, often before them, at times instead of them. . . . Perhaps the mission of those who love mankind is to make people laugh at the truth, *to make the truth laugh*, because the only truth lies in learning to free ourselves from insane passion for the truth."[36]

It is a good thing that the Abramic traditions have their Baskervilles, Heschels, and Sanais, because they also have their Guis, Kahanes, and Khomeinis. If the first three made the truth of their traditions laugh, bringing joy to the world, the latter made it insane, prepared to make others die. All too often election theologies in the West have spelled privilege rather than responsibility and have meant joy for us and terror for them.

The good news is that, being human, we normally have the chance to make something new out of something old. Our traditions have had their dark sides. But they have also done a great deal to shape our lives at their best. We see ourselves as part of their stories, which have left us with unforgettable visions of good and evil, and even more pointedly, of delight and despair; they have instructed us in how to make life a little more divine.

Whether we admit it or not, we are always reweaving these stories. This was surely the case with Santayana and his religious naturalism. To my mind, certainly, Santayana's handiwork had gross faults. He labored under fairly crude and hurtful, if culturally normal, prejudices about blacks, women, Jews, and blue-collar workers. He hung on to aspects of Platonism that rendered his vision of spiritual life too precious and actually fought against many of his own spiritual insights. His account of society and government lacked any clear view of political judgment, decision, or activity. But his aim, unexceptionably, was to try to revise his traditions in ways that would help make the truth laugh, so that the world would not be driven insane. My point in reflecting on his work is to join him in this effort.

2

GRACE AND LAW

Santayana's Solitude

According to conventional wisdom, Santayana's writings appear to go against the grain of much twentieth-century philosophy and religious thinking seriously considered by American intellectuals. Santayana is occasionally singled out as a stranger in a strange land, a Catholic in a Protestant world, and a contemplative in an intellectual community predisposed to emphasizing activity. In addition, much is made of the fact that Santayana's apparently solitary career—or, better, career in solitude—does not adhere to the tendency of twentieth-century intellectuals to construe philosophy as a cooperative enterprise best placed at the center of culture, where it can have a realistic effect on social policy formulation. The current standard history of philosophy in America, for example, calls its chapter on Santayana "The Exile at Home" and goes on to assert that he "belongs to no American tradition."[1]

I have little quarrel with the notion that Santayana's texts stand counter, in a variety of ways, to others that have been celebrated as exceptionally American. But very few other twentieth-century writers are more preoccupied with the symbolics of America or more indebted to American predecessors, or more directed to American audiences, than Santayana. His whole career bespoke preoccupation with the tensions of thought associated with the names of William James and Josiah Royce; his seventy-year-long bibliography reverberates with Emersonian themes; one of his central philosophical concerns lay in giving a characterization of the nature of true virtue in aesthetic terms much like ones that Jonathan Edwards had used in the eighteenth century to evade various theological controversies.

In any case, it is true that Santayana celebrated and came to represent, for many learned people, solitary philosophy at just that time in American history when philosophers became signatory to this or that philosophical manifesto, whether on behalf of the new realism, critical realism, humanism, neo-orthodoxy, naturalism, or the like.[2]

All in all, however, there is great irony in the suggestion that Santayana's peculiarities made him "an exile at home" and, therefore, part of no American tradition. This is so because the solitary "exile at home" is a very traditional part of the American cultural landscape.

Anyone familiar with the writings of such predecessors as William James, Ralph Waldo Emerson, or Jonathan Edwards will recall a similar preoccupation with the soul in its solitude, embarking from society for the sake of spiritual fulfillment. James urgently told his readers and listeners to break away from social convention in order to take delight in the diverse ways of being human in the world. But more significantly, perhaps, he defined religion as "the feelings, acts, and experiences of individual men in their solitude, so far as they apprehend themselves to stand in relation to whatever they consider the divine" (VRE, 34). Emerson not only recommended that people leave the city for the wilderness, take off their shoes to feel the ground, and dare to look at the sun, but he also told them to go it alone, become self-reliant, and gather the courage to listen to themselves listening to divine nature. With Stanley Cavell, they could reflect on the fact that Emerson pictured solitary individuals having their "original relation with the universe" in exile from the conventions of social breeding. Edwards's "covenant of grace" had amounted to "a consent of being to being in general" that came about in solitary inwardness—a bond apart from and opposed to the so-called Halfway Covenant manifested in ecclesiastical and civic cooperation.

So Santayana's celebration of solitude, if not exceptional, is at least unexceptionably American. The preoccupation with solitude that Santayana shared with these remarkable (and remarkably) American precursors is indelibly wrapped up with the philosophical concern for "the life of the spirit" that was so commonplace then and, for many at least, so outlandish now. The figure of the soul in its solitude stood counterpoised to society, helping to establish a kind of tension between the hope of spiritual fulfillment (something finally personal) on the one hand and moral convention (something definitively public) on the other.

Santayana, like Edwards, Emerson, and James before him, emerged out of traditions that taught that individuals had primary responsibility for their own spiritual destiny. But more to the point, the Christian practices and patterns of thinking that shaped Santayana's religious philosophy made solitude and exile from society *cultural locations* of primary positive significance, not just personal idiosyncracies.

In contemporary culture, especially American high culture, "solitude" and "exile" are still intimately related themes. But these things often connote failure or punishment, maladjustment or banishment: It is no coincidence that, for mainline contemporary imaginations, solitary confinement is pictured as the earthly equivalent of hell. The two towering intellectual figures surviving (perhaps demanding) the end of modernity and the emergence of its successors, Freud and Marx, *both* construed solitude as pathological and characterized it, along with exile, as punishing. For Freud, solitude was in fact a form of self-punishment. For Marx, it signaled the end of distinctively human life. But, then, it is Freud and Marx who belong to no particularly American tradition.

For Santayana and his precursors things were different. They recognized, to be sure, the dangers and anxieties of solitude as well as the extremity of exile. But for them, solitude and exile were not solely locations of dread. They were also locations of profound creativity, vitality, and well-being. Indeed Santayana and his precursors *expected* that, if these good things were to be experienced at all, solitary exile from the virtues and conventions that shaped life together was inevitable. The fact is that they yearned for it.

They presumed, as expositors or inheritors of Reformed Christian culture, that well-being, as distinct from well-doing, required the practice of solitary disciplines. For Edwards and his puritan saints, solitary exile was the locale for conversion, the receptive posture permitting that "divine and supernatural light" to shine palpably through their souls. For Emerson and his romantic originals, it was the point of transection between "circles," the place necessary for fate's limitations to be overcome, where nature taught individuals their natural selves, where human creation went on (*SWE*, 263–75). For James and his religious geniuses, it was the arena for divine encounter, the moment when they were enabled to let go of self-consciousness and conscience sufficiently to experience what he called the "wider self," the "MORE of the same quality, which is operative in the universe outside of [them] and which [they] can keep in working touch with, and in a fashion get on board of and save [themselves] when all [their] lower being has gone to pieces in the wreck" (*VRE*, 400).

Unlike these precursors, to be sure, Santayana held no truck with the notion of supernatural powers at work in the world. He acknowledged no monarchial God, no Over-Soul, no supernatural more. Indeed, in ways that Edwards, Emerson, and James could not, Santayana was able to see the *ritual* character of solitude and exile. He could see the role that "solitary exile" had played and continued to play in a process of spiritual transformation that Christian culture had articulated and reiterated throughout virtually all its variations. In other words, Santayana was able to appreciate the fact that the call to solitary exile from the normal rules, roles, and relationships constituting social life was *itself* a cultural convention of long standing—a convention, in fact, more durable than the supernaturalism that had given birth to it.

The Memory: Two Covenants

If Santayana's concern with solitude along with society distinguishes him from many contemporary naturalists, so then does his preoccupation with "spiritual grace" along with "moral law." This preoccupation ties him to a Christian convention that outlasted supernaturalism and, in some cases, Christianity itself. It links him to the trope of two covenants—the covenants of grace and law. According to a traditional Christian vision of things, God had established two separate covenants with creatures made in his image, one succeeding and fulfilling the other. First, he had established a covenant of the law with the children of Israel. According to the Christian construal of this covenant, if the House of Israel kept its promise to God to exemplify the life of moral responsibility to one another, God in turn would keep his promise to let the House of Israel flourish. This was a national covenant, a relationship between God on the one hand and an entire nation on the other, a covenant that made social justice the key to genuine human life.

This Christian picture of covenant between God and the House of Israel is culturally insulting and viciously polemical, among other reasons, because it suppresses the indispensable role grace plays in Jewish spirituality, which permits no sharp break between well-being and well-doing, joy and responsibility, or, for that matter, personal and public good. As Jews understand the story, "Israel was not awarded the covenant because of previous sinlessness or special merit. Neither is subsequent sinlessness a condition of the covenant. God is constant where man is not, and though he demands perfection, he does not expect it: much of his Torah teaches ways to repent, atone, and make restitution after sin. The election of Israel is a mystery, something God did graciously, 'for his name's sake.'"[3] For Jews, divine covenant at Sinai is freely given by God and freely accepted, not only by "the nation" but by each and every individual in it. Covenant for Jews is not a quid pro quo. As Fredricksen notes, it is avowed, "a permanently binding relationship of love and reciprocal obligation, a prototype of the marriage covenant." Moreover, this marriage covenant is inalienable: "God's promises to Israel are irrevocable. He will always redeem, because of the nature of his covenant."[4]

But, in traditional Christian narratives, Jewish covenant became "the covenant of law," which came to no good end. According to the Christian story, the people that God had chosen to give witness to his ways were stiff-necked. Israel, at best, followed the letter of God's law but not its spirit. The Jews typically carried out their responsibilities the way oxen took to yokes: without joy, feeling oppressed, dispirited. The whole point of the covenant had been to achieve well-being, to overcome the things impeding human joy. But hanging well-being on a quid pro quo relationship—the vow to meet righteousness with reward—had run amok. Righteousness *per se* did not bring joy to the world.

It was the love of Christ crucified, so the Christian story went, that brought joy to the world. That was the word announced by the Gospels, which declared a new covenant, a covenant of grace. This new covenant, first of all, opened up the possibility of relations with God to gentiles. But secondly, it articulated the boundary conditions of that relationship in new ways. On the one hand, it announced that there was no way for people to *earn* the well-being they desired, because being human was naturally full of sin. Nothing people did changed their kind of being, and that kind of being was sinful, anxiety-ridden, full of dread. People, therefore, stood in need of salvation from themselves; they required supernatural help to fulfill their desire for well-being because their natures were helplessly sinful. On the other hand, the Gospel announced God's gratuitous acceptance of humankind despite humankind's natural unacceptability. Mankind's sin was more than matched by God's grace.

According to the traditional Christian vision, the event of divine incarnation in Christ was understood to do a number of things. First, it made divine covenant basically, at least, an immediate relationship between deity and individuals rather than one mediated through nationhood—primarily a matter for the soul in its solitude. Second, it revealed that the path to well-being was a God-engendered love between or among individuals that neither could be commanded nor met with any external reward without being undercut. Genuine human life could not be described exhaustively in terms of social justice alone because such justice might be loveless. Third, it declared that this love was engendered when people, as solitary individuals, came into direct contact with its supernatural source embodied in Christ Jesus. As a result, such individuals died to their natural selves and were reborn as "new beings." Solitary encounter with deity transformed death-haunted creatures floundering in dread into eternally vital ones flourishing in love. Such individuals, consequently, were enabled to return to society and to the life of moral responsibility, now gifted with a new, exhilarating spiritual well-being. Fourth, it made this spiritual possibility doxastic and specifically Christological by excluding anybody who failed to acknowledge Christ Jesus as Lord.

The Aesthetic Tradition of Spirituality in America

To be sure, it is a long way from the world of biblical and patristic Christian supernaturalism to the Emersonian America into which Santayana, at least past his ninth year, was bred and began to define his vision of things. But two New World variations on Christian covenantalism played a prominent role in shaping the contours of Santayana's religious thought. The first variation is *the aesthetic tradition of American spirituality*.[5]

This high cultural tradition emerges in the works of Jonathan Edwards, gets revised romantically by Ralph Waldo Emerson, and, as Santayana is being schooled at Harvard, receives further, essentially pragmatic revision by William James. The story of the emergence of this tradition in the works of Jonathan Edwards is complex. But the point is this: Beginning with Edwards's celebrated work on *The Nature of True Virtue*, America's most brilliant puritan divine developed an unorthodox language of beauty to capture the character of God's creation, the Christian saintliness of some of God's creatures, and the majesty of God's gracious sovereignty. For Edwards in the 1740s, the solitary encounters that individuals had with God in Christ transformed them into lovely, lovable, and loving beings divinely enabled to discern and consent to the beauty of others and, more, to being in general. People might naturally do well without divine and graceful intervention, but those who did lacked well-being in some observable way. They seemed divided against themselves, against their fellows, against the world, indeed against the Being in which they lived and moved. This was so even as they were dutiful, just, benevolent, and righteous. In other words, thinking and acting ethically did not, of itself, result in the sense of beauty that was spiritually renewing.

As Norman Fiering has put it, Edwards's position was "that conscience and the virtue of the heart function independently, even adversely, not in tandem."[6] The do-gooder might concur "with the law of God," Edwards wrote. Such intellectual and even practical agreement, however, could result from the love of self. The natural person did good and avoided evil out of fear of God's retribution. But the fact remained, Edwards insisted, that true virtue was involuntary and spontaneous, not the result of human will; it was free of any kind of calculation from self-interest. It resulted from "a certain spiritual sense given of them by God," and in the exercise of a disinterested goodwill.[7] This will consisted in an appreciation of the beauty, or a love of the loveliness, of the unity between any particular consenting being and being in general.

For Emerson in the 1840s, Christ played no crucial role in such spiritual transformations. But Emerson, too, used the language of beauty to characterize the solitary and surprising encounters with Nature that let people feel at home in it. For him, beauty was not just a sensation or feeling; the point was not just that there is a "general grace diffused over nature" that permits "the simple perception of natural forms [to be] a delight" (SWE, 9). It was more, because beauty also characterized goodwill: "Beauty is the mark God sets upon virtue. Every natural action is graceful," "unsought, unearned, lovely, fitting, harmonious" (SWE, 11). And even more, because beauty characterized the spirit in which people lived and moved and had their being: "Nothing is quite beautiful alone; nothing but is beautiful in the whole. A single object is only so far beautiful as it suggests this universal grace" (SWE, 13–14).

In Emerson's view, religious experiences—immediate solitary encounters with Nature's own being—made all the difference between a life of vital fulfillment and one of vacuous and slavish morality. It was in these "best moments of life" that "we are susceptible to the beauty that fills and overflows nature," and that we realize that imperfection, "the ruin or the blank," is "in our own eye."[8] Embarkations from settled society to an immediate perception of the process of creation revealed both the delight of living and the hellish qualities of conscience apart from such joy in loveliness.

Such moments of grace, Emerson preached, displaced pessimism with thankfulness. Their beauty swallowed whole the puritan charge of human depravity and spat it out with a laugh. Priestly Unitarian moralism was no better than the trinitarian orthodoxy it had rejected because both eventually left no place for grace. The highest aspiration surpassed righteousness for palpable joy as the bleakest condition descended well below bad judgment and immoral conduct to feelings of mortal and morbid despair. The joy felt in direct contact with Nature could displace consuming anxiety when people let themselves receive what divine Nature alone could give: a sense of the beauty of being naturally human.

For William James in the 1880s, an unearned, unsought sense of beauty or delight, welling up in solitary religious experiences with a plurality of deities, marked the difference between saints and moralists. Spiritual life could not be reduced to moral life because the moralist felt essentially oppressed by conscience, leaving a lasting impression of dissonance or alienation. He did not, as saints did, take and display delight in overcoming the bifurcations of human life.

Like his Protestant predecessors, James's religious thinking began by recognizing the desperate nature of nature and the ultimate impotence of humankind in the face of suffering, absurdity, evil, and death. Like them, he continued to search for supernatural (or natural supernatural) powers who might help people when they could not help themselves overcome their own desperate condition. Like them, he identified grace with beauty and searched for reasons to warrant the belief that deities bestowed beauty to human life.

For all of these precursors to Santayana, then, *beauty was to duty as grace was to law.* For each of them, moral responsibilities could be understood and met with or without grace, within or without the realm of spirit, with or without a sense of beauty and delight. Duty, for each, was concerned with commensurable or comparable values and could be satisfied, without any grace or display of delight, through the right employment of some moral calculus or through habits of virtue. But for each, the sense of duty did not circumscribe excellent human life because it was randomly related to the discovery and acceptance of the incomparable qualities things presented. The sense of beauty did that.

For Edwards, conscience alone missed the invaluable quality of being-in-general, but a God-gifted sense of beauty captured it. For Emerson the cold hard world of moral convention obscured the self-justifying excellence of nature; the sense of beauty highlighted it. For James, the world of practical responsibilities blinded people to the things that lent life priceless joy and made it worth living for humanity in its plurality. Only a kind of practical irresponsibility or aesthetic discipline could pierce through the scales blinding the eyes of the righteous.

This intuition that beauty is to duty as grace is to law saturated Santayana's writing as well. We see it in his early poetry—writing that he was to call his "philosophy in the making," in virtually all of his philosophical work, and in his novel, *The Last Puritan*. To be sure, the languages of beauty deployed by Edwards, Emerson, and James each ran piggyback on religious discourse that was fundamentally supernatural. They were all committed to the notion that god or divinity was a power at work in the world; indeed, they all identified divinity as the power or powers that gracefully displaced despair with delight in the lives of individuals. Santayana, to the contrary, used the language of beauty to capture the essence of graceful life for an intellectual community that had come to believe that the notion of deity-as-power was built on a tissue of confusions or deceptions, resting on diseases of language. His work challenged intellectuals to take spiritual disciplines seriously not just despite but in light of the fact that the problems of theism no longer haunted them.

It should not surprise us, therefore, to find Santayana posturing himself critically as an exile, a stranger, a pilgrim, a solitary soul on the margins of society. These had been stock characters in Christian spiritual drama, whether in the Old World or in the New. There is nothing particularly Latin about them, at least nothing more Latin than would have been expressed at the Boston Latin School where Santayana trained to go to Harvard. They are the expected, conventional roles for critics to play when they want to be protestant, when they want to protest against graceless conventions and discern the beauty of things, or break wornout moral tablets, or reveal the dispirited ways in which normal social life is going on. The striking thing is that these roles and the notions of grace, law, spirit, and world on which they depend, survive even when encounter with Christ and acknowledgment of Christ as Lord drops out as *the* crucial element in spiritual transformation. In this sense, Protestantism outlasts the Christianity that gave birth to it.

Santayana's First Sonnet Sequence

Santayana's early poetry quite specifically rejects the role that Christ has traditionally played in spiritual transformation, all the while continuing to rehearse rituals of grace. A crucial piece of work displaying this is his first sonnet sequence, written for the most part during his years as a student at Harvard. These poems are meditational, presenting an interior pilgrimage. The reader listens to the voice of somebody who takes no small comfort in having separated himself from normal Christian life, in becoming an exile who is socially marginal. He complains that realistic and active social life is saturated by sadness; moreover, traditional strategies for displacing sadness with joy are no longer live options:

> Now ponder we the ruin of the years,
> And groan beneath the weight of boasted gain;
> No unsung bacchanal can charm our ears
> And lead our dances to the woodland fane,
> No hope of heaven sweeten our few tears
> And hush the importunity of pain. (*CP*, 92)

This is the voice of a death-haunted creature without any apparent way to take joy as seriously as meanness, a mortal who seems to himself to have, or be, a double consciousness, from one angle sleepwalking from the cradle to the grave, from the other conscientiously searching for some theological or metaphysical "greater wakening" (*CP*, 93). This solitary individual finds solace neither in traditional Christianity nor in the notion of "self-realization" that currently underpins the work of neo-Hegelians like Santayana's teacher, George Herbert Palmer. He has come

> down from Golgotha to thee,
> Eternal Mother. . . .

He exhorts nature to

> let the sun and sea
> Heal me, and keep me in thy dwelling-place. (*CP*, 91)

But "healing" is not, here, tantamount to romantic self-realization. To the contrary, Santayana's "I" yearns to forget his paltry little self, his oppressive self-consciousness, his conscience and conventional sense of duty:

> I would I might forget that I am I,
> And break the heavy chain that binds me fast. . . .
> Happy the dumb beast, hungering for food,
> But calling not his suffering his own;
> Blessed the angel, gazing on all good,
> But knowing not he sits upon a throne;
> Wretched the mortal, pondering his mood,
> And doomed to know his aching heart alone. (*CP*, 94)

The "I" of this first sonnet sequence is what William James is calling at the time a *grübelsuchter*, a personality oppressed by "the questioning mania" or the immobilizing anxiety that can attend metaphysical speculation and is in need of spiritual revitalization. He is a rather adolescent thinker who, posturing, muses that "some are born to stand perplexed aside / From so much sorrow— of whom I am one" (*CP*, 96). He sees himself fated, perhaps chosen, to stand on the outside looking in, reminding those at home that normal social life is sad, perhaps absurd, morally and spiritually weightless.

The *grübelsuchter*'s calling is rhythmic and ritualistic. He must confess that conventional life is spiritually hollow because it obstructs the sense of well-being that people religiously crave. So he exiles himself to the margins of society, both to recover in solitude from spiritual discord and to serve as a lamp shining up ways of spiritual recovery to others.

There is an antimetaphysical thrust to these early, platitudinous poems. The traditional theological or philosophical approach to spiritual recovery was to pursue answers to metaphysical questions about the what, why, and whence of being. But the "I" of Santayana's first sequence, taken with naturalistic strands of James's *Principles of Psychology*, questions tradition, suggesting that the old cure really may be a disease:

Why this inane curiosity to grope
In the dim dust for gems' unmeaning ray?
Why this proud piety, that dares to pray
For a wider world than the heaven's cope?
Farewell my burden! No more will I bear
The foolish load of my fond faith's despair,
but trip the idle race with careless feet.
The crown of olive let another wear;
It is my crown to mock the runner's heat
With gentle wonder and laughter sweet. (CP, 97)

Why pursue metaphysical knowledge, the sonnets ask, when that activity inevitably leads to despair?

It is not wisdom to be only wise,
And on the inward vision close the eyes,
But it is wisdom to believe the heart. (CP, 92)

The reason metaphysical questioning may damn its practitioners to despair, the poems imply, is that the better they discipline themselves to appreciate their situation, the more the goal of metaphysical speculation escapes them. But if they drop metaphysics or theology as a cure, the sonnets suggest, then they will also drop the despair that comes when they discover that the cure never works. The thing to do is to react satirically, or "mock the runner's heat," voicing the pretensions of metaphysics and suggesting other, more adequate ways to take joy in being a human in the world.

Here, surely enough, there occurs an ironic turn in Santayana's sonnets. So far, the poems appear to be setting up the reader for some romantic outcome. We are still presented with the need to depart from a normal practice (in this case, metaphysical speculation) for some experience (in this case, the experience of heart) that will restore our lives to lost significance by allowing us to make direct contact with its source. Imagination will gain for us what thinking too much has lost. This appears to be unexceptionably romantic.

Formerly, however, romantic voices had exiled themselves from taking sole interest in a natural world because of their felt need to cure nature's sick joke, that is, the eventual death of the most excellent or beautiful things. They had sought a "wider world," one unavailable to "understanding" but directly intuited by imagination, that might render an ultimately insignificant natural world spiritually complete and eternally vital. But the *grübelsuchter* in the sonnets exiles himself from this romantic pursuit. He returns to seek a meaning that the natural world might give itself, not despite but in the clear light of inevitable death.

Santayana's turn, then, even in these early poems, is not simply a reiteration of Wordsworthian or Coleridgean or even Emersonian romanticism, for the "I" who is an exile in the poems tries to find a way of flourishing in the world that neither proceeds from nor leads to any conventional romantic sense of salvation or promise of utter bliss. He does not simply transpose an orthodox Christian sense of outward salvation inward, nor just displace the Creator-Creature connections permitting salvation with a Nature-Mind relation provisioning it. Even here, he is reaching for a graceful naturalism rather than a natural supernaturalism. The sense of hope that is established in the sonnets is the aspiration to live in a place that may be—just may be—gifted with *sufficient* beauty or loveliness to let us take joy in life, so long as it lasts. But it is also a place that inevitably misses the perfection that it suggests.

By the end of this poetic series, the *grübelsuchter*'s "angel is come back"; his sense of delight is restored but "more sad and fair" (*CP*, 99). There is hope, but hope, as Paul Fussell has put it, abridged. Delight wells up spontaneously in the presence of lovely and lovable and loving things that, as thought, are indestructible, and because this is so the truth about the natural world can lend people a sense of significance or worthiness that may suffice. But the older assumptions of Christian or romantic providence (much less eschatological fulfillment) are just not there.

Avowing toward the end of the sequence that "the soul is not on earth an alien thing," in fact, meant becoming an exile in a "home" where convention required belief in providence or eschatological fulfillment. It meant standing far enough away from traditional religious philosophy, including religious romanticism, to get critical leverage on its pretensions.

But this itself followed a traditional strategy in a religious culture used to criticizing worn out spiritual ways and means as "moralistic." Santayana knew that his readers knew this. He knew his readers expected his spiritual voice to signal departure from normal thinking in light of the fact that it obscured joyful life; to engage in a kind of abnormal, exceptional, or preternatural or dreamlike mental play that turned convention on its head and led to a sense of creative anxiety, sublimity, or spiritual rebirth; and finally to signal return to normalcy, changed and revitalized through exile or pilgrimage.

It is simply that, by the time Santayana writes these poems, *romanticism is normal*, so it is romanticism that stands in need of criticism for the sake of spiritual revitalization. But he reiterates the tension between grace and law, spirit and world, in the doing.

Santayana's first sonnet sequence ends with a request that signals concern for an older and prevailing philosophical tradition: one that demands that people search for nature's own language. The *grübelsuchter* wakes up from his musing in a way that underscores the abnormal and ritual character of his imaginative pilgrimage or exile. His tongue has been loosened, his thought strewn, in ways that have permitted him to stop grieving. But even so, he hardly has a clue about provisions for spiritual happiness. His imagination has let go of some older cures for spiritual disease but has not revealed better ones. So he asks Mother Nature:

Teach thou a larger speech to my loosed tongue,
And to my opened eyes the secrets give,
That in thy perfect love I learn to live,
and in thine immortality be young. (CP, 100)

His heart bets that earth holds her own "immortal" meaning, articulated in her own language, a "speech" he must learn if he is to flourish. But no interior move he has made has led him to understand earth's secrets or has taught him the larger speech he thinks he requires to achieve or receive some adequate sense of well-being. He hopes, in grand American fashion, for some "greater awakening." But that is all he can do in the first sonnets—hope.

The Second Sonnet Sequence

What then? The hope for some "greater awakening" that is announced in Santayana's first sonnet sequence becomes the pretext for his longer second sequence—poems that reiterate themes of spiritual pilgrimage. Here we learn that the journey will be arduous, because nature does not hold the promise that romanticism has held out. It does not reveal, as Emerson said it had, "that against all appearances the nature of things works for truth and right forever." To the contrary, it reveals "irretrievable" losses along with "indestructible" gains.

> Long is thy winter's pilgrimage, till spring
> And late home-coming; long ere thou return
> To where the seraphs covet not, and burn. (*CP*, 106)

Santayana's "nature" here departs from romanticism by explicitly *failing* to reveal any *meaning of the whole of history or whole of things*. The presumption is that that question leads to a dead end. So here, already, Santayana signals that the philosophical demand to learn nature's own language may be fruitless. Nature, apart from humankind, does not carry the sort of commentary that motivated people to learn such a language in the first place. It does not articulate "whole" what people could only partially and variably understand.

But does that imply for Santayana that life, therefore, is not worth living? No. Pilgrimage is marked not only by exile but also by return. The recovering *grübelsuchter* separates himself from nature understood romantically, dies not only to the romantic answer to the question about the meaning of the whole of history but also to the question, and returns to encounter nature unencumbered by the weight of natural supernaturalism.

In particular, encounters with "the loveliness the world can see" promise that

> After grey vigils, sunshine in the heart;
> After long fasting on the journey, food;
> After sharp thirst, a draught of perfect good
> To flood the soul, and heal her ancient smart. (*CP*, 118, 119)

This pilgrim in Santayana's second sonnet sequence exemplifies the sort of figure William James was concurrently characterizing as "twice-born," because he despairs, he lets go of despair, and he experiences a gratuitous revitalization or spiritual rebirth in his encounters with "the loveliness the world can see."

But what sort of spiritual triumph is a live option for somebody who claims that the denial of death is a lie and that providence is not simply improbable or unreasonable or incredible, but not even alluring? No traditional Christian or mainline romantic triumph. The sense of beauty, Santayana claims here, makes a difference. He says it permits episodes of human joy that are "indestructible," that cannot be undercut or taken away (L, 14). It cannot be destroyed, in Santayana's view, because the sense of beauty reveals meanings that are "eternal" in the sense that they are randomly related to questions of material genesis and eventual disposition.

This doctrine of meanings, or "essences," will turn out to be vexing and, I think, more trouble than it is worth. But Santayana's sense of beauty, even in these early poems, is no simple translation of orthodox supernaturalism into aesthetic language. People are no more "saved," in the old supernatural sense of the term anyhow, from suffering, absurdity, and evil by the sense of beauty than by traditional philosophy or theology. The sense of beauty does not turn death into life, evil into good, absurdity into comprehension; it does not eradicate pain: "Every loss is irretrievable" (L, 14).[9] The traditional quest for salvation is vain and desperate; but so much the worse for the traditional quest:

A perfect love is nourished by despair.
I am thy pupil in the school of pain;
Mine eyes will not reproach thee for disdain,
But thank thy rich disdain for being fair.
Aye! the proud sorrow, the eternal prayer
Thy beauty taught, what shall unteach again?
Hid from my sight, thou livest in my brain;
Fled from my bosom, thou abidest there.
And though they buried thee, and called thee dead
And told me I should never see thee more,
The violets that grew above thy head
Would waft thy breath and tell thy sweetness o'er,
And every rose thy scattered ashes bred
Would to my sense thy loveliness restore. (CP, 111)

Santayana's second sequence suggests that this is the best sort of commentary we can make: Beauty is to duty as grace is to law. The lovely things that are naturally given people to love will naturally die. But what has happened cannot unhappen; and memory, as well as hopes provoked by memory and current practice, may be spiritually restorative: "Hid from my sight, thou livest in my brain." Encounter with lovely things to love, he is saying, determines and defines how we mind about things that matter—and renders life worth living. "Heaven it is to be at peace with things" (*CP*, 119).

All this suggests that Santayana is still well within the high tradition of aesthetic spirituality in America in his early poetry. His solitary poetic voice breaks away from social convention, finds its promise of fulfillment vain, experiences despair over his own ability to make right what is wrong, is gifted with a sense of beauty that restores him to spiritual health, and is enabled to return to society and its responsibilities revitalized. But he has broken with both supernatural expectations and supernatural indictments. Gratuitously encountering lovely things is divine because it leaves individuals with a sense of the fitness or harmony of things that may remain part and parcel of their imaginations even when they are lost materially; because it reveals the promise of actual experience; because it displays a joy that cannot be robbed (so long as imagination is at work, anyhow). Santayana does not identify such encounters as divine on the grounds that they are supernaturally engendered; or because they reveal something otherwise hidden about the whole of history or about the whole cosmic order; or because they make apparently evil things really good. He claims they are divine because they engender a sense that the world carries its own gratuitous beauty.

We will have to explore just how adequate this interpretation is to Santayana's own demand for human well-being. But it is surely removed from the sort of romantic sublimity present in Emerson's experience of universal grace displayed through a single object: Universal grace becomes passable grace. It is distant from the Emersonian confidence that, appearances to the contrary, history marches on toward truth and right forever: History is not marching any one place in particular. People are marching lots of contrary places. Just as important, the sense of beauty sides more with acquiescence than assertion. Finally, Santayana's interpretation is just as remote from James's witness to "the varieties of religious experience" supposedly warranting belief in supernatural powers at work in the world, just as far away from James's vision of humankind cooperating with the gods to bring about heaven on earth.

The Exceptionalist Tradition of Spirituality in America

One thing that distances the "larger speech" that Santayana is groping for in his early poetry from his precursors' discourse is his active resistance to a second variation on Christian covenantalism, namely, *the broad tradition of American spiritual exceptionalism*. This is a tradition that predecessors like Edwards, Emerson, and James had embraced but that Santayana flatly rejected.[10]

Edwards, Emerson, and even James had deployed aesthetic language in ways that complemented the idea, so central to the puritan errand into the American wilderness, that being an American was tantamount to engaging in a spiritually exceptional vocation. Everywhere else in the world, the puritans had told themselves, God had displaced that older Hebraic covenant of law between himself and one particular nation, with the covenant of grace between himself and individual believers. Everywhere else in the world, laws governing the city of men were subject to spiritual criticism. Everywhere else, God's punishment for sin was destructive. But not so in America, where the people constituting the nation had each and all come into direct contact with Christ Jesus and thus constituted a communion of saints. In America, man's city was God's, grace and law fully complemented one another, spiritual identity demanded moral conformity, and God's punishments were corrective, not destructive, a sign of love for his righteous new nation.

The *broad* tradition of extraordinary spiritual errand in America that emerged out of Calvinist Protestantism but ultimately encompassed many other varieties of American religion overlapped with the *high* tradition of aesthetic spirituality in some critical ways: Edwards, Emerson, and James used essentially aesthetic language to legitimize the notion that the American people constituted a "New Israel," an exceptional vehicle of spiritual fulfillment. For each, to be an American was to participate in a pilgrimage or crusade to bring God's kingdom home, to plant the seeds of a bountifully divine New World. For each, America's promise lay in the realization of a nation of people remarkable for their selfless beauty; for each, the thing most lamentable about the nation was its difficulty fulfilling this promise.

Edwards's saints, Emerson's representative men, James's strenuous souls were all distinguishable by their palpable beauty, by the delightful and joyous and exhilarating ways they participated in the processes of salvation. Edwards's divine commonwealth, Emerson's "Columbia of thought and act," and James's "Pluralistic Universe" modeled on a "federal republic" were not construed simply as politically handy ways of organizing diverse social interests. They were pictured as divinely fitting, graceful, harmonious, and proportionate orders of social life.

Indeed, the American precursors who had emphasized links between beauty and spirit, before Santayana, had used specifically aesthetic language to revise the boundaries of sacred American identity. Bercovitch has shown that Edwards "inherited the concept of a new chosen people, and enlarged its constituency from saintly New England theocrats to newborn American saints. In fact, if not in theory, theocracy had meant tribalism, the literal and exclusive continuity from elect father to (presumably) elect son. Revivalist conversion opened the ranks of the American army of Christ to every Protestant white believer."[11] Then again, Emerson had opened the doors of sacred American identity to any middle-class Caucasian actively participating in America's continuing spiritual, and inseparably material, revolution. And once more, James had broadened the sacred constituency, ironically, to anybody, anyplace in the world, so long as they actively engaged in bringing the divine American principle, *e pluribus unum*, to fruition.

When Edwards characterized the surprising conversions that, functionally speaking, revised the boundaries of the "New Israel," he used the language of beauty to praise the new beings, and the language of moralism to castigate "Pharisaic" tribalism. Emerson and James repeated the same tactic, distinguishing the moralistic confines of the old order from the indefinite aesthetic possibilities of the new.

But Santayana used his aesthetic language of spirit to break away from American spiritual exceptionalism altogether. He found attractive ways to present America as neither the be-all and end-all of spirit, nor as exceptionally antispiritual. America has its spiritual promises and problems on the view he developed, but they are not intrinsically greater or smaller than those of any of the other nations of the world.

There is no better presentation of Santayana's attitude toward the broad tradition of spiritual exceptionalism in America than his satirical response to ritual laments over the U.S. invasion of the Philippines in 1899. President McKinley himself had exemplified one strain of the exceptionalist tradition by describing his venture in imperialism as part of America's efforts to evangelize the world in his generation. But William James had exemplified another when he proclaimed to Santayana that "he felt he had lost his country" because America had betrayed the spiritually exceptional principles on which it was founded (*PAP*, 402).

"As for me," Santayana recalled in 1945, "I couldn't help resenting the schoolmaster's manner of the American government, walking switch in hand into a neighbor's garden to settle the children's quarrels there, and to make himself master of the place. Yet that has been the way of the world since the beginning of time, and if anything could be reasonably complained of, it was the manner of the intrusion rather than the fact of it. For me the tragedy lay in Spanish weakness rather than in American prepotency" (*PAP*, 402–3).

Santayana employs somewhat different figures of speech when he writes "Young Sammy's First Wild Oats: Lines Written before the Presidential Election of 1900." There America is pictured as adolescent, not as an adult authority. In the poem, "Deacon Plaster" is mortified, as James was, by America's foreign invasions. He takes it as a sign that his country has turned to wicked sin as a way of life. Doctor Wise, on the other hand, reminds the Deacon that

We were marked at birth and smitten
    Whom the Lord had chosen out;
Picked to found a pilgrim nation,
    Far from men, estranged, remote,
With the desert for a station
    And the ocean for a moat;
To rebuke by sober living,
    In the dread of wrath to come,
Of the joys of this world's giving
    The abominable sum.
Yet all passion's seeds came smuggled
    In our narrow pilgrim ark,
And unwatered, grew and struggled,
    Pushed for ages through the dark,
And when summer granted pardon,
    Burst into the upper air,

Till that desert was a garden
  And the sea a thoroughfare.
Thus the virtue we rely on
  Melted 'neath the heathen sun;
And what should have been a Zion
  Came to be this Babylon. (*CP*, 238–39)

In the space of these passages the pendulum swings from the construal of America as a holy vessel to a view of it as a wicked lot. But the thrust of Santayana's message is this: If we place America's forays in the context of a natural history of nations (deploying metaphors of birth, youth, adolescence, maturity, old age, and death), the significance of America's imperialism changes. To be sure, it remains possible to hold American leadership in contempt. America is not to be spared criticism for its handling of the Philippines:

First he bought her, then he kicked her;
  But the truth is he was drunk,
For that day had crowned him victor,
  And a Spanish fleet was sunk. (*CP*, 241)

But it is one thing, in Santayana's view, to be drunk with power, something all nations are prone to, and quite another to be the devil's very roost: "Nature made the hearty fellow,"

Lavish, clever, loud, and pushing,
  Loving bargains, loving strife,
Kindly, fearless-eyed, unblushing,
  Not yet settled down in life.
Send him forth; the world will mellow
  His bluff youth, or nothing can. (*CP*, 241)

The point is that nature, not deity, sets the stage for the theater of events in United States history. Indeed the major problem standing in the way of interpreting American culture is the old interpretive solution of exceptionalism. "Doctor Wise" advises the Deacon that "Cousin Sam" had better

 . . . look up from his standard
  To the older stars of Heaven,

Seaward by whose might and landward,
   All the tribes of men are driven;
By whom ancient hopes were blasted,
   Ancient labors turned to dust;
When the little that has lasted
   Borrows patience to be just:
And beholding tribulation,
   Seeing whither states are hurled,
Let him sign his declaration
   Of dependence on the world. (CP, 242)

The anxiety of Emersonian influence shadows this poem just as much as it does the sonnets exploring the loveliness that makes life worth living. The poem warns us that we cannot declare our independence from the world the way Emerson's American Scholar had demanded. We cannot strike an exceptionalist pose without losing the critical distance on ourselves as individuals and as a people that our solitary encounters with nature permit. Santayana, therefore, urges his readers to turn away from identifying themselves as constituting the first new, or spiritually renewed, nation in order to declare its dependence on the world.

Just such a return, Santayana thinks, may let people judge the activities of their country far more realistically and more adequately than spiritual exceptionalism ever could. This is so because such a declaration of dependence diffuses the explosive combination of eschatology and nationalism that he finds both self-deceiving and the cause of vicious conduct toward other peoples. Undercutting exceptionalism creates room for an older kind of religious criticism that varies from the ideological course set by any of the nations of the world. It lets Santayana return to revise that older tradition which was capable of evaluating law from the standpoint of spirit or grace, a tradition whose adherents were disciplined to challenge any and every social norm for the sake of spiritual regeneration.

A Culture in Transition

Within the context of his own time, then, it is fairly easy to understand Santayana's concern for "the life of the spirit" as a young man with intellectual interests. "Spirit" is, at that time, the cultural location for solitary, personal revitalization, a cultural space for the sense of beauty to resolve moral cramps; it is spiritual practice or aesthetic discipline that lets people distance themselves from socially funded moral propriety and national arrogance and get critical leverage on such limitations and pretensions. In the face of intimations of personal insignificance, oppressive moralism, cultural dislocation, and national arrogance, anybody with Santayana's cultural breeding would turn to reflections on grace and law.

The situation in the United States in the 1880s and 1890s is this: Things are changing rapidly. Christian supernaturalism is losing its appeal to many, inebriated by a new industrial and consumer capitalism, impressed both with the gains that natural scientists have made in explaining events without reference to deity, and with the realization that people have the ability, if and when they have the courage, to assert responsibility for life together. The country is beginning to swell with alien immigrants who are crowded into newly created, newly blighted urban centers, taxing an older sense, partly nostalgic illusion, of social solidarity and natural beauty. The rise, first of industry, then of consumer-capitalist ventures, is widening the gulf between rich and poor. The new economic order is determining new possibilities for men, women, and children, and closing the door on older ones: Work no longer goes on at home; men go to offices and factories; middle-class women are consigned to domestic life that is more and more vapid or officious, more and more determined by needs newly established by corporate invention and advertisement; children are bred to fit this new order. An older Christian republican emphasis on personal and public virtue competes, less and less successfully, with a newer preoccupation with self-realization (which, not coincidentally, is well suited to the new economic order). Ever in search of cheaper labor and expanding markets, the United States is testing its power to colonize other worker and consumer populations and to spread its political message that its own democratic republicanism is divine.

The culture in which Santayana lives, in other words, is undergoing an identity crisis, a culture largely born of puritan reformed Christian assumptions, expectations, and hopes; one that seems in various ways to be reaching the end of its tether. Both privately and socially, traditional narrative accounts of life are falling apart, or coming under severe criticism. Individuals who have been trained to give sense to their personal lives by preparing to make solitary and immediate encounter with the supernatural source of significant being, whether God, or Christ, or nature, now find this instruction less and less credible. Many seem to themselves to be left with the exhausting, more or less joyless, routines of social and economic functions. Thoughtful Americans bred to think of themselves socially as God's newly chosen people are finding it more and more difficult to distinguish divine triumph from imperial power and material plunder.

As T. S. Eliot would eventually put it, the world appears to many in this era to be "no place of grace."[12] In this culture, people generally know what is expected of them; they have a keen sense of moral and social duty; they know what they should believe and what they should do. But often enough, when they stop to reflect, they find that they have no idea what they *do*, rather than should, believe. They are no longer certain what makes life worth living. On the one hand, distinctively Christian supernaturalism appears to be reaching collapse; on the other, a newer emphasis on self-realization and technical rationality is failing to give sufficient weight to spiritual and moral life. It occurs to them that their voluntary, dutiful lives impede, rather than foster, the sense of well-being or excellence, the sense of significant fulfillment, that they crave. This is no place for spontaneous affirmation or avowal, no place for gratuitous acts, no place for appreciating whatever is lovely and lovable, no place in which moral life is either grounded in or aiming toward the satisfaction of felt desires, and so, no place of grace.

Philosophy in Transition

Because I want to pursue Santayana's philosophical effort to make a place for grace in a world without any supernatural powers at work in it, I need to come to grips with the profession of philosophy during these years of cultural confusion in the United States. For one thing, it is important to note that Santayana's education in philosophy at Harvard took place at a time when every profession in the United States, including every academic one, was undergoing very significant changes.

Within the context of the Christian republican synthesis that had maintained cultural hegemony in the United States through the mid-1870s, being a professional meant being some sort of civic servant, some sort of figure—

specifically, either a cleric, teacher, physician, or lawyer—that donated his abilities and energies to public life in ways that were geared to redound to its benefit.

In this sense, Christian republican professionals identified themselves as disinterested, engaged in callings that were not intended, first and foremost anyhow, to be conducive to personal gain. Indeed, Christian republican spokesmen in the United States pictured their nation as defending liberty from the menacing clutches of economic greed and military might. As they understood things, public virtue—untiring commitment to action beneficial to the public good—was the one thing needed to withstand the forces of tyranny, defined in terms of economic and military interests. Professionals were pictured as distinctive exemplars of public virtue.[13]

But as the older republican synthesis began to break down, replaced by an emerging liberalism that was articulated economically, politically, and ideologically in terms of diverse and conflicting interests, a new notion of professionalism became prominent, one that highlighted special and distinctive knowledge at least as much as public service. Professionals began to identify themselves more by the disciplines in which they were trained than by the civic services they provided.

To be sure, professionals of any kind had always been schooled in ways to achieve characteristic skills that relied, to some extent, on special information. But professional know-how, terms of art, and information had all been construed as instrumental, subserving republican life. In the late nineteenth century, however, the technical guildlike aspects of professional careers began to thrive quite apart from issues of civic concern.

This transition in the professions received both support and articulation from the reorganization of elite colleges in the United States into universities melding German and British curricular and administrative models. Harvard was first among them. Charles Eliot's administration at Harvard, 1869–1909, never abandoned the traditional British vision of the college as an institution that trained the nation's next generation of public men. But it promoted the sort of disciplinary professionalism already salient in Germany by the schools of divinity, law, medicine, and business that it opened and generously endowed; by the organization of the college faculty into autonomous departments vying with one another for funds and prestige; and by the displacement of an undergraduate curriculum, hierarchically ordered to outfit the republic with virtuous public leaders, with one that was elective, letting students outfit themselves for competition in a diverse and open market.[14]

Santayana studied and taught in the Harvard that Eliot wrought, and his career there exemplifies many of the stresses felt by professional philosophers during this period of transition from civic to disciplinary self-understanding. In this regard, he is often pictured as a traditionalist at Harvard in open and constant revolt against cultural and political liberalism, the democratization of knowledge, and, in particular, the transformation of philosophy from a set of liberal arts into a technical discipline.

But this view of Santayana's Harvard career is a half-truth, a caricature. As an undergraduate, Santayana took full advantage of Eliot's elective curriculum. His mature efforts to break down disciplinary barriers separating philosophy from other arts and sciences mirrored rather than denied an elective and eclectic organization of study. He was only the fifth student in Harvard's history to be awarded a Ph.D. in philosophy, signifying his acceptance of this sort of study as a professional discipline.

Certainly, Santayana was just as ambivalent as many but less than most such students about their personal decisions to become professors of philosophy.[15] As a graduate student and young instructor in Harvard's philosophy department, Santayana was highly critical of schools that subordinated the demands of liberal investigation and reflection to the fortification of traditional republican values. As a graduate student, he eagerly accepted his department's offer to let him share a Walker traveling Fellowship with Charles Strong (who had been the actual winner), which practically signaled his willingness to engage the set of technical or disciplinary problems that interested his teachers, problems that were specifically epistemological and metaphysical.[16] So it would be silly to suggest that Santayana rejected new notions of professionalism from the start of his career even though, twenty-three years down the line, he quit his Harvard position to become an independent writer of philosophical prose.

In many ways Santayana not only embraced but celebrated Harvard philosophy's departures from a simply civic understanding of itself as a profession. He criticized the older professional identity, so long as it went unmodified, as provincial and tribal. The outstanding question in this regard is not how Santayana managed to circumvent his profession during his Harvard years, because he did not. The question, rather, is how professional philosophy provided an institutional context for his specific academic and personal interests, because it did.

Intellectually, Santayana's superordinate interests came to focus on championing a vision of things that secured a prominent naturalistic place for the life of the spirit as well as for morality. Institutionally, Eliot's Harvard and its philosophy department let him pursue these interests in ways that would have been practically unthinkable at virtually any other elite university in the United States at the time. But one thing they did not do was let him unequivocally embrace the solitary life he eventually came to live and advertise.

"Is Life Worth Living?"

From the standpoint of undergraduate student-faculty encounters in Harvard classrooms and studies during the 1880s, the philosophy department certainly permitted and even fostered spiritual preoccupations in its students. The department had nothing to do directly with the poetry Santayana was writing as an undergraduate, or with his work as a cartoonist for The Lampoon and as an essayist for The Harvard Monthly. It did, however, provide the context for writing papers like "The Problem of Will in Relation to Ethics," "The Ethical Doctrine of Spinoza," and "The Optimism of Ralph Waldo Emerson." Each of these papers asked what makes life significant (the title of one of James's most popular essays), criticized the view that morality alone secured a sense of meaning, and espoused various renditions of aesthetic spirituality in response.[17]

Santayana's senior essay, "The Optimism of Ralph Waldo Emerson," is exemplary in this regard. An unsuccessful submission for the 1886 Bowdoin Prize, it is nonetheless telling as a historical document revealing the academic preoccupations, assumptions, motives, and aims of a student in philosophy typically impressed with the teachings of professors like Francis Bowen, George Herbert Palmer, Josiah Royce, and William James. It also reveals Santayana making his own first effort to come to grips in prose with Emersonian romanticism.

The first thing that Santayana establishes in this undergraduate piece is the sense of threat that is being repeated ritually in the lectures, essays, and books written by his teachers—the sense that life might *not* be worth living; the sense that many people have that their lives are morally weightless and spiritually vapid.[18]

But Santayana's second step is equally typical of Harvard College philosophy in the mid 1880s. He asks the question that must have informed many of the lecture series that he attended: Given that natural experience seems to be haunted by meaninglessness, melancholy, or grief, what can philosophy, in particular transcendental idealism, do to restore the belief that human life matters and that well-being or joy is really possible?

This question did not even emerge among Harvard philosophers until the late 1870s. Up until then, orthodox Unitarian doctrine had done well enough to answer questions about the conditions of significance in human life without raising the specter that life might be *meaningless*. But by the time Santayana entered Harvard as a freshman in 1882, Darwinian naturalism had become a preoccupation, perhaps especially its picture of the inescapability of death along with its utter historicism; and varieties of idealism appeared to be the most adequate way of maintaining the view that there was something eternal and transcendent about human life and enveloping history.[19]

Santayana asks: How does Emerson handle the question whether life is worth living? In particular, how does he go about squaring empirical finitude and idealistic infinitude; and how successful is he in this effort? Emerson, Santayana argues, solves the problem of finitude, but not by establishing a sufficient set of philosophical reasons. He is able to take joy in human life, in other words, but not because there are good reasons to characterize human life as particularly divine or happy. In Emerson's view, Santayana writes, there are no good reasons to believe that people live in the best of all possible worlds, as philosophical theodicies since Leibniz's had argued; nor are there good reasons to believe that virtuous people, at least, will experience joy in life after death, as traditional Christianity had promised. Emerson simply admits that grief clings to experience; that suffering, absurdity, and evil are inevitable; that individual experience is subject to melancholy; that social progress will always be attended by darker "compensations."

Thus, as the undergraduate Santayana reads him, Emerson abandons the three dominant optimistic theories of destiny in his time: that people live in the best of all possible worlds; that this grievous life can be displaced eschato-logically with a joyous one; or that history is providential in the sense that it is on its way toward making life utterly and completely joyful.

Then what, Santayana asks, makes life worth living according to Emerson? His first and approximate answer is this: Emerson claims that everything, suffering, absurdity, evil included, "is beautiful seen from the point of view of intellect, or as truth. But all is sour, if seen as experience. . . . In the actual world, the painful kingdom of time and place, dwell care, canker, and fear." The sense of duty felt by many is a response to such anxieties, an essentially defensive and constraining reaction to threat. However, "with thought, with the ideal, is immortal hilarity, the rose of joy" (*GSA*, 72). Every given experi-ence, no matter how hard, may in turn give rise to a vision of something, or some event, that is perfectly lovely and lovable. Any experience of lack or imperfection carries with it the implication of well-being, a vision of joyful harmony that is desired, an intuition of the beauty of being that is missing.

This reading of Emerson, influenced no doubt by cognate studies of Schopenhauer, Spinoza, and Goethe, leaves the actual world and our experi-ence of it just as it is, without consolation for evil. At best, it suggests an attitude of Neoplatonic indifference, not optimism. On Emerson's grounds, Santayana argues, "we must expect evil and be armed against it. It is not a wanton infliction; it comes in the natural and necessary order of things" (*GSA*, 73).

If this is optimism, if recollecting actually horrid experiences in ideally beautiful ways makes life worth living, Santayana asserts, it is practically the same as pessimism. The difference between optimism and pessimism makes no realistic difference. To be sure, Santayana points out, Emerson departs from the simple idealist view that the world as idea includes all experience. To the contrary, Emerson holds that as events occur, they remain "immersed in our unconscious life." Only subsequently, "in some contemplative hour," do they detach themselves "from the life like a ripe fruit, to become a thought of the mind." Then, such events become transfigured: "The corruptible has put on incorruption. Henceforth it is an object of beauty, however base its origin and neighborhood" (*GSA*, 76).

Santayana writes that in Emerson's view, finitude presents people with inescapable horrors, but infinitude, or the process of soul, thoughtful trans-figuration, reconfiguration, or reconstruction, presents them with compensating joy by way of a palpable sense of beauty. Emerson's emphasis falls on presentation as distinguished from representation. People feel hurt, anxious, imperfect, grievous. But they also feel a sense of beauty when they comprehend the parts that suffering, absurdity, and evil play in the creation and recreation of things that come about as thoughtful action, whether in people's lives or in the course of nonhuman natural events.

Far from making evil disappear, Santayana argues (in a weak misreading) that Emerson teaches that evil is "the foundation of the good" (*GSA*, 73). If this is meant to be an empirical and causal claim, Santayana goes on, it is trivial. The experience of illness, of course, may provoke people to study medicine. But being physically well does not require being physically ill. Thus, if it is not simply an empirical claim but a metaphysical one, making the being of good depend on the being of evil as a matter of logical necessity, it is just wrong. People may well sense the grandeur of the tempest that causes some ship to go down and, repressing sympathy, find such a storm fitting, perhaps even lovely as a natural event. But that does not make the nature of drowning lovely, except by sleight of mind.

Emerson's transcendental idealism, Santayana concludes, is just that: sleight of mind. His aesthetic spirituality relies on a picture of the world as a perfect whole that envelopes all imperfections, in much the same way that the monistic metaphysics of Spinoza or Schopenhauer had suggested. He is closer to Schopenhauer than to Spinoza, to be sure, because his Over-Soul parallels Schopenhauer's Will. The ideal transformation of imperfection into perfection is a power at work in the world, not simply a conceptual structure of significance. But nobody is silly enough to call either Spinoza or Schopenhauer optimists. Why call Emerson one? Santayana asks.

In fact, Santayana argues, Emerson's efforts to persuade people of the harmonious oneness of things is mystical, not philosophical. His monism relies on identification or avowal, not on systematic rationality. Either we share Emerson's intuition or we do not. Either we see the beauty of the whole or we do not. And if we do share Emerson's mysticism, we also share his category mistakes: We confuse the logical relationship obtaining between "good" and "evil" (if we claim that good somehow depends metaphysically on evil, or somehow includes it) with the possibility that good deeds or characters may emerge in response to experiences of evil.

The thing that makes Emerson optimistic, Santayana concludes (in imitation of James), is finally his temperament, his form of life, or his character, rather than his thought: If things march on toward truth and right forever for Emerson, it is because he aims himself in that direction and encourages everybody else to do likewise. Although Emerson thinks he is making a critical point, actually it is his gratuitous affection for any and all things natural, his way of living rather than a theory or way of thinking per se, that makes the difference. Emersonian optimism is something that has to be shown or exemplified biographically, not vindicated metaphysically or epistemologically.

In many ways it is difficult to tell where the influence of one of Santayana's teachers begins and the other stops in this undergraduate essay. The philosophers whom Santayana uses to gain leverage on Emerson figure in Royce's understanding of "the canon," at least as he articulated it in the lectures he published as *The Spirit of Modern Philosophy* (1892). But the point Santayana makes is rather Jamesian: The question whether life is worth living can only be answered by looking at personal experience in a biographical way, not by engaging in metaphysical or epistemological projects.

The slice of student philosophizing presented by Santayana in his effort to win the Bowdoin Prize is truly undergraduate because it sheds very little light on the increasingly disciplinary tone being set by the younger and brighter lights in the department, especially Royce and, more ambivalently, James. The piece is dotted with metaphysical and epistemological allusions and talk about the relationship between theory and practice. It does not present, however, any metaphysical or epistemological analysis. Moreover, it ends on an antitheoretical note: If interpreters want to understand Emerson's optimism, they had better turn from philosophy to biography, from theory to character.

Emerson has a spiritual character, Santayana asserts, not so much because of propositions he holds as because he identifies himself as socially marginal, as an inspired solitary critic searching for the joy too often missed by people living conscientious social lives. Spiritually minded characters, the undergraduate suggests, feel "the insignificance" of "social cares and ambitions" (*GSA*, 83). Emerson fits the bill. He claims to stand apart from the practical affairs of men, highlighting ways in which, beneath and behind the social conventions that turn people into differentiated functions, any man can encounter nature face-to-face and realize that he is beautifully or harmoniously bonded with everything that is, literally bound to live for goodness's sake. This Emerson does not engage in formulating social policies about what to believe.

In fact he reminds his readers not to "set the least value on what I do—as if I pretended to settle anything as true or false. I unsettle all things" (*GSA*, 86). Where society accords privilege, Emerson finds pretension; where it despises profanity, he discovers innocent aspiration. To Santayana's mind, the outstanding question about Emerson's spiritual optimism—a "philosophic habit of mind" that permits social indifference—is whether it amounts to insensible self-indulgence or, rather, to a continually disciplined effort to give witness to the beauty of natural beings (*GSA*, 83). The senior, however, has no way to settle the issue and says so: He lacks the requisite biographical information.

If we are naturalists, if we accept the finite, contingent, material, and mortal character of humankind and the universe surrounding it, does it still make sense to explore the solitary spiritual life that so captured the interest of the young Santayana and his teachers? I think it does, because in light of inevitable suffering, absurdity, and evil, Is life worth living? and What makes life significant? remain compelling questions; and they are questions that social thought alone does not answer.

Santayana's teachers distinguished the spiritual life from moral conduct and the conventions of society because they still hoped to discern some way that people escaped the constraints of time and chance in order to secure their significance. Hoping for a key to universal well-being, Royce sought to discover nature's own language. James sought some supernatural "MORE" that made personal life flourish when people could not do so on their own. Santayana, as we will soon see, continued to toy around with the idea that an "eternity" naturally available *in* time provided enough solace to permit a sense of personal well-being in the clear light of loss.

But even supposing, as I do, that the quest for something infinite, immortal, or (metaphysically) necessary about human life is a dead option, Santayana's emphasis on the importance of spirituality is still worthy of reflection. This is so because Santayana continued to make a compelling claim that, disregarding the quest for eternal life and transcendent infinitude altogether, both public and private well-being hang on a gracious "love of life in the consciousness of impotence," which, in turn, is grounded in a sense for the lovely and lovable character of the life that chance has thrown our way.

3

WISTFUL MATERIALISM AND

THE SENSE OF BEAUTY

The Question of Systematicity

From Royce's point of view, Santayana's undergraduate preoccupation with Emerson was not all that promising. Royce, director of Santayana's dissertation, took the view that the task of the philosopher was to establish systems of thought that were metaphysically and epistemologically complete. Philosophers, on the Roycean view, should be widely read as a matter of course, and might engage in other kinds of writing besides systematic theory—but not as philosophers. It was important to distinguish visions of things, which could be articulated well enough as histories, poetry, drama, essays, or novels, from the theories that vindicated them as rational and true. Character might be an important issue. But the philosopher's task was not to fill out the biographical details of character. It was to show how the ways of the world and our knowledge of those ways vindicated or impugned claims people made; the point of philosophical work, in other words, was to know the philosophical truth. In particular, Harvard philosophers at this time followed Kant's determination, as Murray Murphey has shown, "to construct an epistemology adequate for both science and religion and one which would insure the active, constructive role of the mind while yet affording a solid basis for empirical knowledge."[1]

To Royce's mind, Emerson was a visionary, a man of letters, an orator and provocateur who read some theory and wrote some remarkably intuitive essays. Indeed, he was the intellectual whose vision best represented his historical epoch.[2] But he was no philosopher because he lacked the technical disciplines required to attend to theoretical issues that professional philosophers patiently pursued.

By 1889, when Santayana handed in his dissertation on Rudolf Hermann Lotze and was awarded a Ph.D. for that work, he had turned to the theoretical issues that were beginning to define the profession of philosophy at Harvard in a disciplinary way. He had taken his Walker Fellowship to Göttingen, had heard lectures from Paulsen, Ebbinghaus, Gezycki, and Simmel, as well as from Wagner, Lasson, and Deussen. With these professors he had studied in Greek ethics, Kant, Spinoza, Fichte, Schopenhauer, classical Indian texts, and political economy (*PAP*, 240–43, 259–60). His march forward into professional philosophy, certainly, was accompanied by doubts. He was tardy about reporting his studies and wrote James that he had faith neither in idealism nor in "psycho-physics, and all the other attempts to discover something momentous." Philosophers, at least in Germany, "seemed to be working along so merrily at problems that to me appeared essentially vain" (*L*, 31). But he did march on.

Had he written his dissertation on Schopenhauer, as he later claimed he had wanted to do, he might have retained a sharper focus on issues of spiritual discord, relief, and satisfaction that had been instanced in both his poetry and student papers in the 1880s. Schopenhauer's work provided great opportunities for theoretical reflection on the tradition of aesthetic spirituality, especially on the claim that beauty was to duty as grace was to law.

But according to Santayana, Royce told him that Schopenhauer was not a suitable subject for a doctor of philosophy; writing about him might do for a master's degree. On the other hand, Royce considered Lotze's writing important (*PAP*, 389). Lotze was the darling philosopher of liberal Protestant communities of intellectual discourse in Germany and had followers in Britain as important as T. H. Green, Bernard Bosenquet, and James Ward. At Harvard, he was being touted by James as a hard-minded analyst in the good company of Renouvier and Hodgson, one of the few "Verstandesmenschen" who brought winning criticisms to bear against absolute idealism and, simultaneously, aimed to show that "the character of Being"—the order of things—was ultimately personal.[3] His work afforded an opportunity to consider conflicts between materialism and idealism in metaphysics and between rationalism or formalism and empiricism in epistemology. These were starting points for most of the theoretical conversations going on among the Harvard philosophers, especially those between Royce and James.

At the same time, Lotze's understanding of philosophy as a discipline provided a viable model for academic professors who no longer taught a subject that stood, as not long before it had, at the pinnacle of a hierarchical curriculum. This was so because, on the face of it anyhow, Lotze claimed that philosophy had no privileged status among the arts and sciences but, to the contrary, served the function of mediation or interpretation. Philosophy did not so much award seats of intellectual authority to this or that party in cultural dispute (as Kant, for example, had pictured it), as it showed how and why such parties could contribute to an overall understanding of things without entering into damaging conflict. In Lotze's view, Santayana asserted, philosophy provided "a neutral spot where rival pretenders may parley, compare their claims, and attempt a reconciliation" (*LSP*, 225).

Lotze's Moral Idealism and
Santayana's Wistful Materialism

In his dissertation on Lotze, Santayana places high value on Lotze's integrity as a thinker. He questions, however, the adequacy of his construal of philosophy, most of the premises in his metaphysical argument, and various parts of his epistemology. It is one thing, Santayana argues, to give philosophy the office of academic, intellectual, or cultural mediation and another to insist that each interest has some power to veto whatever adverse claims other interests make. Lotze presumes that "science" and "sentiment" constitute "the conflicting tendencies in our time" (*LSP*, 113), and pictures philosophy as providing a set of principles that can "furnish a basis for negotiation" resolving disputes between them.

In the dissertation, Santayana agrees with Lotze that "philosophy should be a social product; it should coordinate and interpret all those impressions that life makes upon mortals" (*LSP*, 225–26). But then philosophers should not assume that an utter reconciliation of conflict is inevitable. That is, however, the fundamental assumption that Lotze makes, thus presuming what he should have to demonstrate.

So Santayana disagrees with Lotze's "method of mutual correction" (*LSP*, 114) that more or less enforces a peace between "science" and "sentiment." Such a policy, the graduate student argues, can be sound only "if the axiom on which it is founded is true." But, if "the laws of nature were irreconcilable with our emotional demands, this method would be in danger of leading to a misrepresentation of both." "Nor," Santayana suggests as graciously as he can, "does Lotze seem to have wholly escaped this danger" (*LSP*, 114–15).

In fact, Santayana argues, Lotze's "conclusion" that science and sentiment are harmonious is rigged by definitions and principles of explanation that are, at least partly, unacceptable. With regard to scientific investigation, for example, Lotze simply rules out of court all theories that challenge the purposive character of nature, by giving a negative twist to empirical observation. Much like Baconian realists who defended the varieties of Protestant orthodoxy in the United States throughout the first half of the nineteenth century, Lotze claims that science, by definition, establishes what is naturally going on. But Lotze also claims that scientists have no procedures for discovering why things are going that way. This, Lotze argues, can only be established by introducing principles of moral and aesthetic justification.

On the view that Lotze develops, Santayana points out, philosophers have to approach the task of mediation committed to three basic principles. The first of these is fate. Lotze insists, in other words, that there are various sorts of facts that everyone, including every sort of scientist, may encounter. These facts cannot be reduced to one type. Rather, they constitute a sort of catalog of being that cannot be derived, either from natural laws or from moral and aesthetic demands, or from categories of consciousness; they just are. Santayana claims that this is the sense in which Lotze is a strong realist and at least an empirical pluralist: He insists that there are many sorts of facts that exist independently of consciousness.

"Natural law" constitutes the second Lotzean principle that Santayana explicates: If people must contend with fate, they may still understand this fate because given facts are subject to various kinds of natural law that people can discover. Lotze characterizes these natural laws as mechanical and argues that they are not causes but, to the contrary, methods of operation. What is the difference? Natural or mechanical laws, Lotze argues, do not cause the facts that people are fated to encounter to come into being. On the contrary, they account for the effects that some of these given facts, mechanically related, have on some others. In other words, natural or mechanical laws clarify what is going on, but not why such processes are at work or how they emerged.

This leads to Lotze's third principle, a variation on the law of final causality. We cannot understand why things proceed as they do or how they come to be by exclusive reference either to data or to the mechanical laws governing their relations to one another, or to both of those principles together (contrary to what Darwin, for example, had argued). As Santayana explicates Lotze's view, order is to be found ultimately "not in any law of evolution empirically discovered, but in the sense and moral purpose of the world" (LSP, 122–23). According to Lotze, in other words, a principle of value or providence has to be invoked in order to explain the order of things.

In Lotze's system, Santayana suggests, this principle of value is not "absolute" for at least three reasons. First, value is not a principle of the causes of origin of being. Second, and consequently, the principle of value or providence does not undercut the principle of fate. Fate and providence are two independent variables. Third, and incidentally, value does not necessarily or inevitably encompass all of being. To the contrary, there is some order of valuable being, or person, at work in the world that is able to respond to or contend with prevailing conditions, or fate, in ways adequate enough to cause happiness, at least happiness for that postulated "person," to result. But this order or person is not the creator god of orthodox Christianity; it is a governmental process or officer capable of re-creation but not creation.

Santayana appreciates Lotze's vision in bits and pieces, and fairly grudgingly, but he also challenges him every step of the way. First he argues that Lotze's restrained empiricism, virtually limiting scientific investigation to sheer description, undercuts science's accomplishments, which are explanatory rather than simply explicative. For example, Lotze's negative empiricism disallows the explanatory power of Darwin's theory of evolution by natural selection, which does not just describe what is going on geologically or zoologically, but tells us how and why things have come to be the way they are.

Contrary to Lotze, Santayana invokes a pragmatic interpretation of science and asserts that the point of scientific theories is to attain explanatory power. By circumventing explanation, Lotze undercuts the very point of engaging in scientific investigation. Moreover, Santayana argues, explanatory power is gained by reduction, that is, by clarifying the order of things that people experience as disordered through causal accounts. Lotze's "desire to retain a very complex system of unexplained objects as the starting point of natural science" as well as his insistence that the natural sciences can never be unified, betray moral, aesthetic, and even theological prejudices (*LSP*, 121).

Santayana then argues that Lotze surely has no test by which to "decide where the simplification of natural processes should stop" (*LSP*, 123). His objection "to reduce all causation to one type . . . becomes an objection to the ideal of science" (*LSP*, 123). His reason for denying the possibility of methodological monism is not scientific but aesthetic: He does not *want* the world to be monotonous. But even here, Santayana asserts, Lotze is confused. "The variety of nature does not derive its aesthetic value from the multitude of physical laws; but each principle of explanation requires dignity in proportion to the value of the phenomena it explains" (*LSP*, 124).

Thus Lotze misrepresents the interests of scientific investigators for the sake of the cultural reconciliation he wants his philosophy to enforce. The thing that lets Lotze picture science in the restrictive and inappropriate way that he does, Santayana argues, is his idiosyncratic interpretation of post-Kantian critical philosophy. Lotze accepts the Kantian doctrine that mind or consciousness determines the possibility of experience, giving people no clue to the nature of any reality that might stand beyond their experience. But he departs from Kant by accepting the view that experience does, in fact, correspond to a mind-independent world. Finally, he goes on to argue that experience is fundamentally evaluative, inadequately pictured without reference to intentions, wants, needs, desires, aims, and goals.

But from a Kantian point of view, Santayana argues, Lotze's method of mutual correction looks more like mutual mutilation. This is so because it permits flagrant category mistakes. Kant would never have condemned a scientific doctrine, say, the principle of the conservation of energy, for moral or aesthetic reasons. But Lotze's method tickets such judgments. His position is more like Fichte's and Hegel's because he pictures the universe, at bottom, as a theater of moral action.

In this regard, Santayana points out that, while Lotze ridicules Hegel's absolute idealism for its formalism and for its dismissal of fate, his own picture of things ultimately relies on vague, formal analogies between natural processes in general and those specific processes that people experience that result in happy emotions. To be sure, Lotze does not claim that formal order alone constitutes the value and justification of nature (but neither did it for Hegel). He claims, rather, that the "condition and means of producing conscious and happy life," always momentary if repeatable and sustainable, gives value to "the scheme of things" (*LSP*, 138).

But Santayana argues that this means that "the only addition Lotze makes to Hegel's theory is to materialize it a little by regarding the universal Idea as a source of universal delight" (*LSP*, 140). The trouble is that Lotze has no better set of reasons for granting his synoptic vision of things ontological status than Hegel had articulated. Both idealists failed to convince anybody in need of persuasion that special metaphysical or dialectical reflection results in an assurance of the existence of any personal being (or, for that matter, some impersonal order) ordering the universe in ways that satisfy moral, aesthetic, or emotional demands.

In a remarkable preview of Santayana's own mature naturalism, the graduate student spells out some alternative readings of Kant's achievement, one of which calls into question any transcendental turn.[4] Metaphysical idealism and metaphysical skepticism, he asserts, provide the two major readings of Kant, but neither of them is a suitable reading.

Metaphysical idealists like Lotze follow Kant's construal of the possibility of experience as requiring the form of consciousness; but they renounce his notion that there is a real world standing behind the one we experience in terms of our categories of mind. They assert, rather, that the real world *is* the world we experience as conscious and valuable. Metaphysical skeptics, on the other hand, claim that an objective but unknowable reality lies beyond the subjective and human world articulated by such categories of mind as space, time, causality, and personhood.

In contrast to both metaphysical idealism and metaphysical skepticism, Santayana introduces something he calls "wistful materialism," a view that is explicitly nontranscendental: Suppose, Santayana suggests, that

> when all our spontaneous assumptions are criticized and exposed we fall back in practice on the most inevitable of them; some working hypothesis, some conventional expression for the reality, we must employ; and if we are convinced that all are equally doubtful assumptions, full of logical difficulties, we shall undoubtedly employ that which usage and necessity most impose on us; we shall be materialists. The world of matter and of

history is the world of language and human society; its final and absolute reality is ordinarily assumed by believers in other deeper entities. And if criticism has discovered to us the equal arbitrariness of all metaphysical conceptions, we shall retain those we cannot surrender, and make our thought and conversation intelligible to the world. (*LSP*, 140)

For its time and place, I think, this is a truly remarkable passage of thought. This is 1889, nine years before James's public inauguration of pragmatism in his Berkeley address on "Philosophical Conceptions and Practical Results"; indeed, one year before publication of James's *Principles of Psychology*. But here we have the announcement of a nonreductive, nonfoundational pragmatic naturalism. The message is clear: We may *defuse* the raging battle between metaphysical idealists, metaphysical materialists, and metaphysical skeptics, by falling back on beliefs that we find we cannot do without or "retain those we cannot surrender," beliefs we inevitably use, beliefs that are practically, rather than logically, necessary in *the world of matter and history, which is the world of language and of human society*. Whatever metaphysical discourse accomplishes, it is embedded in the world of language and human society, which is unexceptionally a material and historical world.

This "wistful materialism" stands opposed to Lotze's system not simply because it acknowledges things as material all the way down but because it does not let philosophers make much of metaphysics or epistemology. Metaphysics amounts to a conventional picture of how things hang together. Principles of criticism are natural and practical. Knowledge is instrumental. Whenever beliefs are challenged, people retain those that they cannot practically surrender, along with those that their experience warrants and that help them to manage their difficulties and solve their problems well enough (or better than others).[5]

Santayana points out that Lotze did not have to contend with either skepticism or nonmetaphysical materialism in his own time. Rather, Lotze had self-consciously opposed Johann Friedrich Herbart, who certainly tended in the direction of the kind of nonreductive materialism that Santayana now wants to tout. Lotze's strategy was to show that the universe was basically governed by a process of consciousness. Herbart, Lotze's most influential post-Kantian predecessor, had threatened this strategy by arguing, in effect, that consciousness did not exist except as the function of more basic, substantial or material stuff.

Herbart had claimed that conscious life was epiphenomenal, a function of material transactions; it signaled material efficacy or represented changes in material states; but in any case, it constituted no power apart from changes in material states.

Here, Santayana suggests accepting Herbart's epiphenomenalism and asserts that only a few, historically accountable things separate this position from "a modern materialist interpretation of consciousness" (actually the view of consciousness that Santayana interprets James as providing in *The Principles of Psychology*). Fearing the moral and theological implications of Herbart's view, Lotze had tried to turn it on its head by arguing that material substance was not a basic term. He had argued that substance was itself a function of process; a "thing" was, as Santayana paraphrases Lotze's notion, "the historical unity of its own successive modifications" (*LSP*, 150). If this was the case, Lotze went on, then "substance" or "matter" was not a primitive term but a function of "process."

Lotze had claimed that critics might retain the notion of substance to characterize their experience of certain processes that appeared as bodies. But "what produces the idea of substance is a series of unsubstantial states" (*LSP*, 153). These states, Lotze finally suggested in a rather ad hoc way, were too analogous to the moments of a personal life to call them anything else.

But Lotze's reduction of matter to mind, Santayana argues, is a self-fulfilling solution to an artificial problem. What Lotze was investigating, Santayana demonstrates, was "whether body must be composed of things that are not body" (*LSP*, 164). No "unsophisticated inquirer" ever has to raise this issue. Investigators without metaphysical or theological agenda inquire about the composition of material objects because they observe that such objects actually have parts and decompose from time to time. "To ask, then, what matter is composed of, is only to ask for the complete series of its transformations." But if this is the case, then the "existence of a problem about the composition of bodies is therefore no proof of the existence of a problem about the possibility of body at all. The second problem is invented by metaphysics, while the first is suggested by common experience."

Santayana argues that Lotze does not present nonreductive materialists with good reasons to give up the view that the universe is matter or body all the way down. Contemporaries, he suggests, can accept "such answers as the state of science at the time warrants" and leave metaphysics out of the picture (*LSP*,

165). On Santayana's reading, Lotze's criticism of the idea of body, crucial to his argument for idealism, is based on a misinterpretation of "a harmlessly physical expression" (LSP, 165). It is based on the assertion that extended things are indivisible. But all that working scientists mean by this phrase is that "where, in the process of nature, decomposition ceases, there, in the system of our science, indivisibility begins" (LSP, 167). They can readily admit that atoms may be split into something else again. This would involve a transformation of scientific theory; but the processes of nature "would still consist of individual particules and their aggregates" (LSP, 167). The upshot of the infinite divisibility of extension, Santayana concludes, is that "we must be satisfied with the units of matter that observation discovers to us" and avoid unedifying metaphysical projects (LSP, 172).

Indeed, Santayana argues, whenever Lotze's argumentation becomes distinctively metaphysical, it is artificial. Actually, he shows, Lotze does not base his vision on his argument against Herbart but, rather, on an acceptance of his own moral and religious affections as evidence testifying to the ways of the world in general. His claims rely on the notion that his sense of beauty provides privileged access to fundamental reality. For Lotze, then, aesthetic experience is the avenue to metaphysical disclosure.

Indeed, on Santayana's analysis, the line of thought that really undergirds Lotze's moral idealism is constituted by three assertions. First, aesthetic experience discloses a kind of order that lets people unify many, discrete moments in a harmonious way. Second, it carries with it an emotion of perfect satisfaction or happiness. Third, the happiness that characterizes it comes in response to perfectly fitting objective conditions.

As regards the issue of order, Lotze argues that the coherence of aesthetic objects like songs or stories or, most importantly, biographies, cannot be captured by the sort of numerical identity that governs standard logic as well as the natural sciences. Songs and stories and biographies, for example, unfold in light of all the changes they undergo; parts and wholes are inseparable. No one note in a song means anything except as strung along with other ones; the whole song is constituted not simply by adding various notes together, but by stringing them along concatenously with some total effect in mind. The same sort of order holds for the story of a life (and the suppressed assumption, of course, is that life is a story).

Santayana has no particular quarrel with this view of melody, story, or biography. But he finds no good reason, apart from wishful thinking, to construe the ways of the world as analogous to such order. It is surely possible to construe people as thrown into gratuitous circumstances, pursuing happiness, acting morally, and making dramatic differences, without giving any metaphysical backing to this picture.

At the same time, Santayana has no difficulty accepting the notion that people can take delight in various things, activities, and episodes, in ways that bring a sense of lasting value to their lives. But this view, he argues, can be held quite apart from the claim that there is a process governing the universe analogous to the ways in which (some) human characters maintain continuity and coherence in lovely or delightful ways. As a matter of fact, he asserts, people do experience pleasure under certain conditions, especially ones that they characterize as harmonious or fitting or proportionate to their best desires. But there is no way to extrapolate from these experiences to any certitude about how things—physically, much less metaphysically—are arranged, or are going to turn out in the long run.

Santayana's thesis on Lotze's system of philosophy is plain enough: Lotze's vision of things is attractive because it pictures a powerful deity hammering away at fate in happy ways through his instruments of natural law, helped along by the conscientious activities of some of us creatures whom he finds on hand. But the metaphysical nuts and bolts for this vision are no more secure than Emerson's; they are illusory and Lotze is, in the end, a mystic. To be sure, Santayana suggests, it makes a kind of sense to limit providence to some sort of activity that must contend with fate. Otherwise deity, if there were such a thing, would have nothing to do. As Lotze pictures his deity, however, the only evidence people have for its being is their own aesthetic experience. Deity, then, only grants "to men what their life actually supplies," hurt, heartache, gracelessness, and all (*LSP*, 224). Thus Lotze's religion sanctions "the judgements of the world." It offers people no other world to live in when they find life in this one intolerably empty.

The fact that Lotze's vision sanctions the judgments of the world, Santayana concludes, makes him a "pagan" religious naturalist. For Santayana, this amounts to paying his subject a compliment. But it is backhanded. If Lotze is a pagan (that is, nontranscendental) naturalist—which is what Santayana himself aims to be—his vision still does not hold up, either the way he wants it to or the way liberal Protestant followers, like James Ward in England or Bordon P. Bowne at Boston University, think it does. Lotze has not accomplished what he set out to do. He has not articulated a "new theory of the universe" in philosophically satisfactory ways. Far from securing his own personal idealism, he has failed to establish why anyone should accept any sort of idealism. His "compromise between sentiment and fact" is contrived, misrepresenting science, morality, and spiritual life.

Liberal Naturalism

The "wistful materialism" or naturalism that Santayana presents in *Lotze's System of Philosophy* is inchoate, but so far as he spells it out, I find it defensible. The reason Santayana calls his materialism "wistful" is to distinguish it from *metaphysical* materialism of the nineteenth century. His desire is to return to a pre-Socratic physicalism of sorts. Metaphysical materialists claimed to doubt the full reality of nonmaterial or nonphysical being (as metaphysical idealists doubted the full reality of nonmental being). They developed arguments to show that reality was constituted strictly by physical or material states of affairs (as metaphysical idealists argued that reality was constituted strictly by psychical states of affairs or states of consciousness).

In Santayana's view, metaphysical idealism is bankrupt, even malicious, *but so is materialism construed as idealism's metaphysical opposite*. His own naturalism or materialism, he claims, is not a system; indeed, he claims it is constituted by the convictions that he confesses he cannot get along without as a distinctively human animal. These convictions, in his view, are practically indispensable, but not logically necessary. They are "natural" in the sense that they go without saying. They go without saying because they spell out the discourse that makes it possible for him to understand distinctively human life. They do not, however, do what modern philosophers in the Cartesian tradition required "first philosophy" to do. They do not refute radical skepticism by establishing the firm grounds on which to build, and the principles of construction by which to build, unshakable knowledge of reality.

Strawson has recently distinguished the sort of naturalism that Santayana had in mind. He has noted that the notion of naturalism has had at least "two faces" in the history of Western philosophy, one reductive, the other liberal.[6] Those "two faces" partly recapitulate Santayana's distinction between metaphysical and wistful materialism.

The "face" of naturalism that Santayana characterizes as metaphysical is, in Strawson's terms, "reductive." Reductive naturalists try to overcome the modern skeptical problem about the external world by arguing that, in fact, there is really no internal world: They argue that the only things (states, processes, dispositions) that count as real, or at least as really real, are physical things. Perhaps ironically, they pay for victory over one sort of skepticism by accepting others. They exchange the problem of the external world for the problems of mind, meaning, morality, and, I would add, spirit.

Reductive naturalists do this by admitting that such apparently nonphysical things as moral obligations, minds, and thoughts or meanings play a role in ordinary discourse about human beings in the world. But these naturalists distinguish between the phenomenological status of such things and the real status of the physical world; and they doubt whether any satisfactory argument can be given in defense of the claim that such things as minds and moral obligations really exist. Indeed, they argue that references to nonphysical things are only nominal and reducible to physical states. Reductive naturalists, in other words, are skeptical about the reality of things like moral obligations, "the world as it appears," or mentality; they attempt either to identify such things outright with physical states or to reduce them to functions of such states.

But, Strawson notes, there are nonreductive naturalists as well, philosophers like Hume, Wittgenstein, and himself who do not try to *refute* skepticism and do not free themselves from one sort of skepticism by committing themselves to other sorts. On the contrary, they simply stop responding to skeptical challenges. They *reject* skepticism or *diffuse* it. They do so, first, by showing that commitment to the things modern skeptics call into question—for example, the material world, minds, or thoughts—"is prerational, natural, and quite inescapable, and sets, as it were, the natural limits within which, and only within which, the serious operations of reason, whether by way of questioning or of justifying beliefs, can take place." "Serious" here means something like "actually making a difference."[7]

Moreover, some nonreductive naturalists make a second, relativizing move (thereby showing, perhaps, naturalism's third and pragmatic face). We will see, as Santayana's naturalism unfolds, that it fits here. Naturalists like this admit that, as solitary and social actors, they cannot help but suppose that there are minds that perceive, thoughts, moral obligations, objects, objectives, and the like. But they are able to develop (for certain purposes, to be sure) "a conception of the world as, so to speak, morally and literally colorless."[8] They go on to point out, however, that (as Strawson puts it) they "lack reason for saying either that the scientific-objective standpoint or that the human-perceptual-and-moral standpoint gives us the exclusively correct type of conception of the real nature of things. We could have such a reason only if there were a standpoint we could occupy that is superior to either. But there is no such standpoint."[9] We keep both, they claim, in all seriousness: The two standpoints are different in ways that make for differences. Strawson says: "One is the point of view of the diarist or biographer, recounting the history of [say] John as a person. The other is the point of view of a physical scientist, recounting the history of John as an electrochemical-physical organism."[10]

One thing that makes Santayana's writing so interesting in his own time is his commitment to this "third face" of naturalism, on the one hand, and his insistence, on the other, that such a commitment renders engagement in spiritual life all the more valuable. Recalling the development of his views, Santayana claimed in 1940 that his naturalism had been

an everyday conviction which came to me, as it came to my father, from experience and observation of the world at large, and especially of my own feelings and passions. It seems to me that those who are not materialists cannot be good observers of themselves: they may hear themselves thinking, but they cannot have watched themselves acting and feeling; for feeling and action are evidently accidents of matter. If a Democritus or Lucretius or Spinoza or Darwin works within the lines of nature and clarifies some part of that familiar object, that fact is the ground of my attachment to them: they have the savor of truth; but what the savor of truth is, I know very well without their help. Consequently there is no opposition in my mind between materialism and a Platonic or even Indian discipline of the spirit. The recognition of the material world and of the conditions of existence in it merely enlightens the spirit concerning the source of its troubles and the means to its happiness or deliverance; and it was happiness or deliverance, the supervening supreme expression

of human will and imagination, that alone really concerned me. This
alone was genuine philosophy; this alone was the life of reason. (*PGS*,
12–13)

Placing Grace in Culture

So Santayana's dissertation leaves him distanced from both Royce and James
on the issue how to square science and sentiment. Royce had studied under
Lotze in Göttingen, and thought of Lotze's system as the most significant sort
of metaphysical idealism competing with his own more absolute variety. Royce
was a strong proponent of the notion that philosophy could and should
develop in transcendental and architechtonic ways. Philosophy, on his view,
was an *Urwissenschaft* that established the objective conditions that made any
and every experience possible. It was to be rigorous and exacting work that
depended on pushing through to the frontiers of symbolic logic and mathematics. It was inadequately executed so long as it was pursued in piecemeal
ways that circumvented this sort of work.[11] Santayana's devastating criticisms
of Lotze's eclectic metaphysical approach would have been welcomed by
Royce, while his "wistful materialism" simply would not have been taken
seriously by the absolute idealist.

James, on the other hand, thought that Lotze's personal idealism was the
most plausible post-Kantian German philosophy going, because it gave man
and god things to do and circumvented Royce's efforts to transform philosophy into transcendental epistemology. But if James liked Lotze's vision better
than Royce's, he remained suspicious of idealism altogether.

When it came to the issue of spiritual well-being, James claimed that "abstract considerations about the soul and the reality of a moral order will do in a
year what a glimpse into a world of new phenomenal possibilities enveloping
those of the present life, afforded by an extension of our insight into the order
of nature, would do in an instant."[12] In other words, James thought that the
issue of spiritual well-being would be resolved far better by showing evidence
of supernatural powers transforming natural life. That was his motivation for
studying "exceptional mental states" and testimony reporting "the varieties of
religious experience." To James's mind, Lotze's idealism was too abstract, be-

cause it did not present any new "physical facts and possibilities" that let well-being triumph over spiritual discord in lasting ways.[13]

So James would have found Santayana's overtures toward philosophical naturalism refreshing, his criticisms of Lotze's metaphysics telling, and his focus on aesthetic experience helpful. But he surely would have been disappointed that Santayana showed no interest in "widening" his naturalism to include nonhuman powers who could help people become their best selves when they could not go it alone.

In any case, coincident with receiving the Ph.D., Santayana was hired as an instructor in Harvard's department and his early essays written in this position strike a distinctive note. While Royce aims to vindicate the significance of human life by establishing an epistemology that will reveal that the real is ideal, and while James engages in psychical research hoping to find evidence of such things as preternatural sources of power and life after death, Santayana reflects on parts of human culture that provide space for graceful life to go on.

If, as we have seen, Santayana had written James from Spain in 1888 wondering out loud whether he "had made a mistake in taking up philosophy at all, since all the professors of it seem to be working along so merrily at [metaphysical and epistemological] problems that to me appeared essentially vain" (L, 31), his dissertation on Lotze had done little to change his mind. Indeed, if, as his understanding of James's *Principles of Psychology* suggested, knowledge is best construed in a functional way, there is no need to establish any privileged method or sort of discourse for getting at the really real.

On Santayana's reading, the upshot of Kant's "Copernican Revolution" is this: "Pictures of the world and of human nature" are "conventional and hieroglyphic in the extreme" (L, 32). Efforts to mirror nature with any verisimilitude are hopeless, actually comical, because thought signifies things without copying them or being them. The epistemological quest to come face-to-face with nature is a vestigial remain of that "great bane of philosophy . . . the theological animus which hurries a man toward final and intolerant truths as towards his salvation" (L, 28). Santayana's colleagues, he thinks, still labor under this theological animus. They continue to search for the underpinnings of vital moral life by trying to discover objective realities—meaning transhistorical, acultural, and/or supernatural conditions—that make life worth living.

Santayana tries, on the contrary, to persuade his readers that grace can be found in historical cultures, traditions, and institutions. In the early 1890s, he calls this view "paganism" in contrast to Christianity of any sort. He pictures Protestant culture in the United States as caught on the horns of an avoidable dilemma. In their attempt to avow literal truth, Protestant poets, essayists, and philosophers swing between moralism on the one hand and antinomial or playful aestheticism on the other.

Some—for example, the academic moral philosophers who still present an old guard in American colleges—voice their belief that their moral conscience or sense of duty reveals God's truth directly. Others, like Whitman, revolt against Protestant moralism only to glory in a sort of instinctive affection for things, a love that knows no moral boundaries (a celebration that is unwittingly Protestant as well). Santayana claims that for writers like Whitman, the heart, sentiment, or instinct opens them up to the power in which they live and move and have their being.

Pagan Good and Protestant Culture

Santayana argues that graceless moralism and chaotic aestheticism are both based on Protestantism's "false moral interpretation of life," one that claims that "actual goods are worthless and fictitious and imaginary goods—in which is no enjoyment, no peace, and no loveliness,—are alone valuable" (L, 35). Both moralists and aesthetes look for significance and self-esteem outside the bounds of culture, first in private conscience, then in sensuality. It is no wonder that they come up short.

Santayana writes his friend Henry Ward Abbot in 1889 that "the world may have little in it that is good: granted. But that little is really and inalienably good. Its value cannot be destroyed because of the surrounding evil. But the greatest of all evils is surely that lunacy that convinces us that this little good is not good, and subverts natural standards in favor of unnatural and irrational standards" (L, 35). Writing to a student friend, Guy Murchie, in 1894, he sums up his paganism in this alternative way: "We have to begin to love the imperfect for the beautiful things it contains, and that takes discipline. The alternative is to mistake the imperfect for the perfect, which to my mind is a much sadder fate" (L, 38–39).

Supernaturalists like James searched for "psychical" evidence of something better than nature could supply. Natural supernaturalists like Royce argued that divinity logically required the experiences of suffering, absurdity, and evil that people had (and vice versa). Santayana flatly rejects both alternatives. To his mind, death-haunted creatures subjected to experiences of all kinds of bad things have every motive to cry. But they also can experience episodes of memorable joy as natural, historical, and cultural beings. The task is to point this out, and to point out how, in a culture inhabited by many people who continually suppress recognition of the importance of nature, history, and culture in their lives.

This is what Santayana tries to do in the series of essays he published in *The Harvard Monthly* during the years 1890 to 1894. He argues that cultural activities and institutions make life significant, not direct contact with something above, below, or beside culture. Whitman's diagnosis of the spiritual malaise in the United States is more or less on target: Social and economic conventions have throttled human feelings so effectively that people feel helpless and indifferent. But Santayana is clearly ambivalent about Whitman's vision. Whitman's cure is no less diseased when, on Santayana's reading anyhow, he preaches a gospel of nearly random sensuality and sentimentalism. Whitman, sometimes at least, fails to distinguish between hollow standards and values on the one hand and vital ones on the other. He fails to indicate ways for moral life to be graceful (*GSA*, 284–91).

Santayana asserts that Americans suffer from "life-at-second-hand," as Emerson had already argued, because they have lost their habits of perception or let their senses be muffled. They are led around by the nose in their submission to conventional maxims. Their imaginations have been dried up by the habits of "abbreviated thinking" inculcated by a consumer-capitalist economy whose managers have taught them to pay attention to cost as a way of indicating desirability. They have become "Philistines" whose lives are "a stolid response to successive stimulations" void of felt joy and, consequently, of any complex sense of significance (*GSA*, 131–41).

In an essay prepared for the Harvard Divinity School–based *New World*, Santayana holds a moralistic and iconoclastic Protestant culture responsible for severe constraints on both feeling and imagination that result in life at secondhand in the United States. Protestantism emphasizes conscience or duty, he asserts, in ways that bolster capitalist rationalization along with the military preparedness to support economic expansion as well as nationalist adventures. Rather than distinguishing passions that support humane life, in society and solitude, from those that do not, it suppresses passion altogether in the name of virtue.

At the same time, Santayana argues, Protestantism has been so wary of deviance from the sectarian truth it proclaims that it discourages the very kind of imaginative power that has given birth to its own traditions and structured its institutions. Its iconoclasm has tended to curb imagination without remainder. Its theology of the cross, especially in the United States, discounts the importance of institutions, even while depending on them. Its biblical literalism renders its communicants blind to traditional development, even though literalism is itself an interpretive tradition.

To be sure, Santayana continues, there is no going back to Roman Catholicism. The only way any sort of supernatural Christianity can retain its strength as an intellectual system and social force is to "present itself as a divinely established and authoritative church capable of feeding the imagination and directing the conscience." That, he asserts, is not a live option for thoughtful people on the contemporary scene. "The monstrous unreality of the whole thing is too obvious," Santayana claims; "never can such elaborate inventions survive our habit of criticism or satisfy our need of conscientious belief." Catholicism is the "dream of an age and a society childish both in their susceptibility and in their assurance." There is no going back to the denial of death, the assurance of providence, papal supremacy, economic feudalism, or the Holy Roman Empire; and it is hardly possible to tear one of these elements away from the others without rending the whole fabric.[14]

But, Santayana points out, the current nostalgia for the church and its medieval world that is prominent in contemporary constructions of medieval church architecture, in the popularity of chivalrous romance, in high church theological movements, in renewed Protestant interest in the Virgin, in the return to more elaborate ecclesiastical rituals and liturgies, and in festivities like carnival, are all signs that people yearn for an imaginative spiritual life that has been squelched by mainline Protestantism. These things indicate cultural needs that simply are not being met by liberal Protestantism or its declension into an ideology of utilitarian self-realization. Here again, cultural activities, a grounding in historical tradition, and imaginative activities make all the difference. They are the things that foster the sense of beauty that makes for graceful life.

Finally, Santayana argues that higher education in the United States is far from least among the institutions that ground people in their historical traditions, encourage their perception of excellence, train them in moral virtues, and celebrate graceful life. Colleges like Harvard and Yale may not school the people, but they can train the next generation of public leaders in common traditions. They can teach them the principles of criticism with which to transmit those traditions selectively. They can help shape characters of conscience and celebrate the sorts of excellence that leave people feeling not just constrained by duties but delighted and delightful as human beings (*GSA*, 48–67).

The liberal arts, Santayana suggests, may help serve as a spiritual antidote both to the old moralism and the new commercialism—the twin demons that threaten to turn higher education into another link or instrument in a workaday world that appears to go on automatically and senselessly. Liberal inquiry into the things that bring joy to human life, he argues, is not instrumental but consummate—a good activity that is good for nothing in particular. It is disciplined but not work in the sense of action that has to be done in order to accomplish something practically necessary. Rather, it is serious play, or action done for its own sake under conditions that have freed people "from the stimulous of necessity" in order to let them express excellence "in beautiful and spectacular forms" (*GSA*, 123). The liberal arts, he asserts, form "a background of comparison, a standard of values, and a magnet for the estimation of tendencies without which all our thought would be perfunctory and dull" (*GSA*, 121–30).

"Industrial supremacy," Santayana warns, is "the curse of our time" because it sacrifices "every spontaneous faculty and liberal art to the demands of an overgrown material civilization." It distinguishes life from imaginative activity in a way that leaves the former servile and the latter frivolous entertainment. "When the stress of life and the niggardliness of nature relax a little and we find it possible to live as we will, we find ourselves helpless" because American culture has stripped itself nearly clean of public spaces set aside for the exercise of "spontaneous and imaginative will." Santayana fears that higher education is no exception; the academy is now "overgrown with the thistles of a trivial and narrow scholarship." It is beginning to mirror mediocrity rather than engender excellence (*GSA*, 121–30).

The Sense of Beauty

Santayana's efforts to show the cultural significance of graceful life, along with some of its locations, provided a pretext for writing the lectures that were revised for publication as *The Sense of Beauty: Being the Outline of an Aesthetic Theory*, in 1896.[15] By this time his papers, dissertation, and essays have indicated a number of things.

First, Santayana has accepted the Edwardsean and then Emersonian principle that beauty is to duty as grace is to law. Genuine moral life is both grounded in a sense of joy that is ultimately gratuitous and it is aimed at overcoming the things that impede that joy. The sense of beauty discloses things that make life worth living.

Second, Santayana's precursors, he thinks, have misunderstood the sense of beauty by characterizing it as something that lets people make direct or culturally unmediated contact with the source of value in human life. They have been blinded from, or positively suppressed, the cultural context in which people value things as beautiful and have sought transcendent, rather than immanent, sources of such experiences. Immanent or "finite" experiences of perfection or beauty, Santayana claims, happen.

Third, Santayana has asserted that the search for "the" transcendent source of value still informs the work of post-Kantians like Lotze, who characterize the sense of beauty as the key to metaphysical disclosure, or as the privileged mental function that reveals the structure of things in general. In an effort to warrant a theistic vision of things that pictures divinity battling successfully with fate in order to establish humane life, Lotze has attempted to force inferences from natural aesthetic experiences to conclusions about the ways of the world. His reasoning amounts to wishful thinking.

Fourth, Santayana has argued for "wistful materialism" and he has claimed that the role played by the sense of beauty in lending significance to life can be interpreted adequately enough without raising unnecessary metaphysical or epistemological issues. Wistful materialism is, fundamentally, a denial of the need to make any transcendental turn in philosophy or criticism. It is the view that whatever makes life worth living is to be found in "the world of matter and history." We can account naturalistically—materially and historically—for parts of spiritual life that matter to us, even though spiritual life has traditionally (and mistakenly) depended on a supernatural or metaphysical explanation.

Fifth, Santayana has argued that there are good reasons for criticizing contemporary American culture as no place of grace. But this crisis is not due to a loss of belief in supernatural powers at work in the world. Rather, it is the result, in large part, of gains in Protestant iconoclasm along with the emergence of an "industrial supremacy" or commercial "tyranny" that Protestantism has permitted and even fostered. The utilitarian organization of both life and thought that has accompanied the rise of industrial capitalism has all but completely crowded out practices of "intrinsic value" or activities done for their own sake and informed by internal standards of excellence.

In Santayana's view, rationalization of social life has brought a clearer understanding of economic and institutional rules, roles, and relationships. Indeed, he thinks that this has been beneficial because it has rendered the tasks that people must do under the force of necessity (for example, feed, clothe, and house themselves) more efficient. But its focus on wealth and power, the traditional vices accompanying Christian republican virtues, has overshadowed activities that foster human excellence. Moreover, the tendency in industry to reduce thought to calculation has placed a stranglehold on the imagination, and with it "the value of a rounded and traditional life" (*GSA*, 126). It has led to a kind of "abbreviated thinking," "a mental process [that] is all algebra" (*GSA*, 137–38).

Santayana asserts that the "world" is governed so inclusively by instrumental reason that resuscitating a life worth living requires "what we call unworldliness"; it requires the kinds of activities that discipline people "to live in sight of the ideal" (*GSA*, 139). Instrumentalism has emphasized thinking as efficacious; capitalism has produced a plethora of new interests or desires that now need to be satisfied. But few people hold fast any longer to any detailed vision of the good life. Means have run amok, with no clear end, or set of ends, in mind.

The Sense of Beauty is written in the context of these perceptions, claims, and arguments. Arthur Danto has captured the audacity of the work by recalling that

> it was a time when a treatise on beauty would have been expected to be celebratory and edifying, and beauty itself widely accepted as "the manifestation of God to the senses." Instead, Santayana addresses himself to "the nature and origin of beauty" in human sensibility, and diagnoses the myth of its objective existence as "a curious propensity of the mind." And this had to be a radical move. It was radical in the two ways of first psychologizing something held to be divine, treating it as a subject for science, bringing beauty down to earth, and then, secondly, giving a far more central place to feeling in the economy of human conduct than the preceding intellectualist tradition would have countenanced. The exaltation of emotion and the naturalization of beauty—especially of beauty— imply a revolutionary impulse for a book it takes a certain violent historical act of imagination to recover. (SB, xxvii–xxviii)

The Sense of Beauty focuses on ways that aesthetic experiences reveal "intrinsic values" that give ballast to solitary and social life. In it, Santayana turns the metaphysical claim that "beauty is the manifestation of God to the senses" on its head, arguing to the contrary that "it is . . . from the experience of beauty and happiness, from the occasional harmony between our nature and our environment that we draw our conception of the divine life" (SB, 10).[16]

The question Santayana poses in *The Sense of Beauty* is "to ask what are the conditions and the varieties of this perfection of function, in other words, how it comes about that we perceive beauty at all, or have any inkling of divinity" (SB, 10). His answer is written "under the inspiration of a naturalistic psychology" (SB, 3), in particular the one he had learned from William James.

Santayana's reading of James's *Principles of Psychology* shapes his account of the sense of beauty in five ways. First, James had argued in his 1890 masterpiece that it was possible to proceed with psychological inquiry without raising metaphysical or epistemological puzzles. James asserted that "Psychology assumes that thoughts successively occur, and that they know objects in a world that the psychologist also knows. *These thoughts are the subjective data of which he treats, and their relations to their objects, to the brain, and to the rest of the world constitute the subject matter of psychological science*" (POP, 1:196). Santayana accepts this view as the basis for his investigation of experiences of beauty.

Second, Santayana appropriates James's "natural history" model of psychological life. Psychological states or processes are not free-floating but characteristic of people; and people are populational animals situated in, and interacting with, environments. These environments are somewhat plastic or modifiable by populations of organisms. But if these populations are to survive, they must accommodate themselves to determinable environmental demands (POP, 2:1098–1192).

Third, Santayana follows James's understanding of the role played by emotion in conscious life. Emotion makes the difference between anaesthetic and aesthetic life. Without it, animals are inert, without care, apathetic, and, if intelligent, literal and detached. With emotion, animals are active, goal-directed, desiring, and, if intelligent, imaginative and able both to empathize and to sympathize. Emotion is part of the normal process of intelligence, not something to be accounted for in addition to normal intelligence or apart from it.[17]

Fourth, Santayana accepts James's view that the sense of beauty is emotional or affectional and, so, a characteristic of active, goal-directed, desiring, imaginative, sympathetic, and empathetic animals interacting with the various environments in which they live. In particular, aesthetic judgment signals the ways people divide up those environments into parts they welcome because they satisfy desires and parts they reject because they do not (so Kant and his followers are wrong to align beauty with disinterest).[18]

Fifth, and perhaps most significantly, Santayana takes the Jamesian position that many human emotions, desires, interests, and goals cannot be accounted for adequately as simple responses to environmental demand. There are local emotions that environments do not produce, even if environments maintain or dispose of them once they are there.

In Darwinian language that both James and Santayana use explicitly, some elements of human consciousness are "spontaneous variations" that people bring to their environments. Most aesthetic and moral affections count as spontaneous variations (so Kant and his followers are wrong to align either beauty or duty with universality): "If we were sure of our ground, we should be willing to acquiesce in the naturally different feelings and ways of others, as a man who is conscious of speaking his language with the accent of the capital confesses its arbitrariness with gayety, and is pleased in the variations of it he observes in provincials; but the provincial is always zealous to show that he has reason and ancient authority to justify his oddities" (SB, 29).

Santayana claims that duty and beauty are often elements of consciousness that motivate people to reconstruct their situations rather than simply accommodate to them as they are. More often than not, both philosophers note, aesthetic and moral experience open up people to environmental dangers that, otherwise, might have been avoided. Many people risk their lives for the things they perceive to be beautiful, excellent, lovely, or good.

On the basis of these psychological views, then, Santayana attempts to give a naturalistic defense of the notion held by his precursors that beauty is to duty as grace is to law—"that aesthetic satisfaction comes to perfect all other values [which] would remain imperfect if beauty did not supervene upon them." When that happens, Santayana claims, "the reign of duty gives place to the reign of freedom, and the law and the covenant to the dispensation of grace" (SB, 19).

Radical Empiricism

In order to succeed at this critical task, Santayana startles his readers by arguing that beauty is "value positive, intrinsic, and objectified. Or, in less technical language, Beauty is pleasure regarded as the quality of a thing" (SB, 33). This recalls Lotze's characterization of aesthetic experience as an instinctive acknowledgment of things as appreciable, both as an emotion of pleasure in us and as a perception of something that is delightful quite apart from us. But, even more, it prefigures James's "radical empiricism," especially James's attempt to place "affectional facts in a world of pure experience."[19]

Santayana's position on the matter is far closer to James's than Lotze's because, as his mentor will eventually try to do, Santayana attempts to defend the actuality of natural aesthetic experience without carrying along the excess conceptual baggage of Lotze's personal idealism or theism. It is one thing to acknowledge and even celebrate experiences of pleasure objectified and quite another to draw inferences about powers governing the universe or about the destiny of spirit. *The Sense of Beauty* tries to accomplish the first sort of deed in a way that discounts the second.[20]

Indeed, the thing that most distinguishes Santayana's view from Lotze's is this: Lotze claims that aesthetic experiences are both subjective and objective. A (subjective) emotion of pleasure receives (objective) warrant because it corresponds to something that is really there. Santayana, on the other hand, claims that, as experienced, the sense of beauty is neither subjective nor objective. Beauty as experienced is not located subjectively in the mind or objectively in the external world; it just is there, as Santayana puts it, "all prior to the artifice of thought by which we separate the concept from its materials, the thing from our experiences," subjective mentality from objective materials (*SB*, 32). It is an "instinctive and immediate" appreciation of something (*SB*, 14). In other words, it is an intuitive affection, an experience that goes without saying, an acknowledgment of something going on that takes place prior to, or apart from, reflections that might classify it as merely subjective or certifiably objective. It is what James would eventually call a pure experience. The outcome of "conscientious training," it is nonetheless "radical" in the sense that it is "not based on reflection" (*SB*, 23). Moreover, it is "the survival of a tendency originally universal to make every effect of a thing upon us a constituent of its conceived nature," a tendency to acknowledge things that delight us as themselves delightful (*SB*, 32).[21]

Santayana argues that this sense of beauty can be a vestigial throwback when it is used, as Lotze had used it, to causally explain the ways of the natural world. The tendency to make every effect that a thing has on a person a constituent of the thing makes for bad science. Investigators can explain natural events well enough in terms of matter and energy in space and time.

But, invoking a distinction between explanation (something appropriate to the natural sciences disclosing facts) and interpretation (not only the task of the humanities but the heart of ordinary discourse concerned with judgments of value), Santayana argues that the sense of beauty still plays an indispensable role in human life. It does not explain anything. It expresses feelings of value or desire that are intrinsic, or maintained no matter what the consequence. This is the twist Santayana gives to the notion, held by James, Emerson, and Edwards before him, that the sense of beauty is "spontaneous" rather than "deliberate" (*SB*, 11), the sense in which it is both "the root of all excellence," and eventually should supervene upon all other values (just as grace had been construed as both rooting law and supervening upon it in supernaturalistic Christian culture).[22]

Beauty and Duty

As a perception of value, Santayana goes on to argue, the sense of beauty is related to conscience. But, he claims, aesthetic and moral experience can be distinguished in a number of ways. First, while moral worth results from making utilitarian calculations, the sense of beauty spontaneously marks intrinsic values, or values that go without saying because they signal situations in which desires are perfectly satisfied. Second, conscience is basically negative and preventative. It orders social life, constrained by suffering and evil, by issuing sets of don'ts or negative commandments that, among other things, curb pleasurable experiences. The sense of beauty, on the other hand, is basically consummate. It marks moments of "unalloyed happiness" in which people are free *from* the suffering and evil that make moral obligations indispensable and free *to* fulfill desires more or less perfectly (*SB*, 22).

Santayana asserts that "death, hunger, disease, weariness, isolation, and contempt" are "spectres" standing behind "every moral injunction." But "the appreciation of beauty and its embodiment in the arts are activities which belong to our holiday life, when we are redeemed for the moment from the shadow of evil and the slavery to fear, and are following the bent of our nature where it chooses to lead us" (*SB*, 19).

By 1900, Santayana will have publicly rejected the very idea of aesthetic theory that subtitles *The Sense of Beauty*. One of many reasons why will be his recognition that this analysis of the relationship between beauty and duty does not hold up. Construing conscience as constituted by extrinsic and negative values and beauty as constituted by intrinsic and positive ones is forced and artificial. For one, there are positive moral commands, for example, "help that person," "tell the truth," or "be kind." For another, people may well avow such moral virtues as helpfulness, truthfulness, and kindness to be intrinsic, as something to hold no matter what. In other words, they may acknowledge the loveliness of such virtues. Moreover, in light of them, they may come to impugn other judgments of beauty they already may have made.

But the thrust of Santayana's own project carried its own motive for drawing a sharp line between aesthetic and moral value in 1896. Doing so sustained the principle that beauty is to duty as grace is to law in a particularly Christian way. As many traditional Christians read their Old Testaments, the covenant of law upheld by Israel fell spiritually short because it was grounded in fear rather than love, because it placed far more emphasis on prudential issues like escaping danger than on intrinsic moral goods, and finally because it organized life around largely negative commands rather than the positive virtues exercised by Jesus and Christian saints.

But, even aside from the fact that putting this Christian spin on the Hebrew Bible is either the result of sloppy reading, ignorance, malice, or a political will to domination, or some combination of these things, Santayana's principal claims about grace and law or beauty and duty are obscured by construing morality as constituted by negative commands ordered toward prudential ends. To his mind, there are two main points. First, moral practice is done gladly and has personal, though not necessarily private, point when it is grounded in a sense of beauty; but moral practice is onerous and personally pointless when it is not. Second, the practice of moral virtues is ordered toward the public good, but does not inevitably satisfy the religious demand for individual well-being that comes with disciplines permitting a love of life in the consciousness of impotence.

I think both of these primary points make sense. The claim that vital moral life is grounded in shared affections aligns Santayana with a tradition of moral thinking that ranges from Shaftesbury through Emerson and James. This heritage commits him to a view neatly captured by David Bromwich: "It is by coming to know the passions, affections, and sentiments we share with others that we recognize our relationship of mutual attachment to others in a society; by such attachment, in turn, that we are able to see the good of the duties we impose on ourselves as obligations; and by this whole picturing of our selves within the scene of other people's thoughts, feelings, and condition of life that we start to be moral beings and so are humanized."[23]

But this idea of morality as formed by common affections subordinates the individual to the community and leaves open questions about how to respond with any degree of affirmation to uncommon, deviant, or alien affections. These are difficulties Christian republican culture assigned to spiritual rather than moral disciplines—to virtues or habits of mind, heart, and will instituted to meet the religious demands both for personal well-being in the face of intractable finitude and to extend the range of solicitude as broadly as possible to include elements beyond one's own community.

It is just here that Santayana gives his characterization of aesthetic spirituality what he calls a "pagan" or Neoplatonic twist by aligning it with festivity and symbolic play and, in the doing, risks the charge of aestheticism. His point in identifying spiritual life and the sense of beauty this way is not to suggest that they are frivolous. To the contrary, the claim is that spiritual disciplines belong to "holiday life" because they provide for "spontaneous and delightful occupations" that are "not carried out under pressure of external necessity or danger" (SB, 20). From Santayana's standpoint, work or "what is done unwillingly and by the spur of necessity" is pointless unless it clears the way for activities done spontaneously and for their own sake. "Play, in this sense," he argues, "may be our most useful occupation," because it gives point to moral life and economic work (SB, 21). It makes life something more than an endless process of obligations and servile labor that it appears to be to many reflective and literate people who feel dignity and purpose slipping away in their American culture.

Most important, Santayana's association of "the sense of beauty" or "grace" with play characterizes the life of the spirit as a part of human culture, not some nonhuman reality set apart from it. It suggests that people need not embark from culture to achieve spiritual regeneration or to regain a sense of moral weight, but that they do need to expand the bounds of culture by constituting it as something more than an engine of labor, production, distribution—even equitable distribution—and consumption. Permitting and fostering the kind of playful imagination that can picture intrinsic values make all the difference.

To my mind, there is great appeal in Santayana's characterization of spirituality as playful and festive in ways that distinguish it from normal social responsibilities and from life in the workaday world. Spirituality is playful, in Gadamer's words, because it is a kind of exuberant and superabundant "excess that flows over into the realm of freely chosen possibilities."[24] But what sort of excess? Not only a freedom from normal constraint, but freedom to institute or present novel, often "unexpected and unfamiliar," ways of understanding ourselves, means of representing "what we are, what we might be, and what we are about."[25] This sort of play is symbolic in the sense that we do not look somewhere else to unpack what it means but look to it to understand or interpret the point or significance informing our own lives. Moreover, spirituality is festive because it is meant for everyone, breaks away from the regimentations that separate and divide us, and enacts a celebration of the common human lot.

Tragedy, Comedy, Sublimity, and Good

Santayana's discussion of cultural institutions fostering the exercise of spiritual disciplines remains both inchoate and schematic in *The Sense of Beauty*. The most telling instance of it comes in his analysis of tragic, comic, and sublime narratives or dramatic performances. These texts or performances are playful, symbolic, and festive. Moreover, Santayana claims, they are important for two reasons: First, they show that people can experience varieties of "finite perfection" without stepping out of culture or encountering deity. Second, and just as significant, they show that "no aesthetic value is really founded on the experience or the suggestion of evil" (*SB*, 161).

Both of these claims are important for Santayana's effort to naturalize the tradition of aesthetic spirituality that is his inheritance. The variants of natural supernaturalism articulated by Emerson, Lotze, and Royce, among others, all claim that finitude deprives people of perfection. They all argue that people naturally participate in some process of infinite spirit (whether they know it or not). More particularly, they all argue that there is a process of infinite spirit that involves people in overcoming the pockmarks of finitude: suffering, absurdity, and evil. On this view, every aspect of the process of infinite spirit, including these miseries, makes up the way of providence: The things that make life desperate are all part of a beautiful whole.

But Santayana shows, first, that finitude is marked by joys like love, equanimity, and exultation, as well as by sorrows, and second, that the only motive for claiming that evil has aesthetic value is to safeguard an untenable theology. He claims that tragic, comic, and sublime dramas clearly display this. People, he asserts, take great interest and much delight in narratives that catch both the extremity and the joy of being human. They are partly interested in such performances or episodes for the truths they reveal, whether lovely or unlovely, partly attracted by the beauty of their forms of expression, and partly interested for the pleasures, understanding, or recognition they permit or even provoke. They also are made happier by empathizing with characters in unhappy situations.

But this, Santayana suggests, provides no warrant for the paradoxical view that suffering plays a logically necessary part in a perfectly happy life. Art does not even "seek out the pathetic, the tragic, and the absurd." "It is life," Santayana notes, "that has imposed them upon our attention, and enlisted art in their service to make the contemplation of them, since it is inevitable, at least as tolerable as possible" (SB, 138). Artists render suffering sufferable, Santayana claims, by provoking complex emotions containing "an element of pain overbalanced by an element of pleasure" (SB, 141). The thing that makes a tragedy like Othello beautiful is the charm of the medium, not only such things as meter, rhyme, melody, and flights of allusion, but "the continual suggestion of beautiful and happy things" (SB, 142). Tragic characters and events delight people by letting them identify themselves with images of perfection that they approach but miss. Such promise of perfection is the thing that wins sympathy and makes an audience "all the more willing to suffer with our heroes, even if we are at the same time all the more sensitive to their suffering" (SB, 143). Comic characters delight audiences by their release from convention and their joy in spite of impropriety: People take no pleasure in the hurt occurring when somebody slips on a banana peel; they enjoy the fact that such discombobulation leaves a fellow no worse for wear. In both tragedy and comedy, pleasure is easily distinguished from pain.

But is this the case with the sublime? Aristotle had claimed that sublime exultation depends on fear. But Santayana, following Lucretius, disagrees. "The suggestion of terror," Santayana claims, "makes us withdraw into ourselves: there, with the supervening consciousness of safety or indifference comes a rebound, and we have that emotion of detachment and liberation in which the sublime really consists" (SB, 149). But this feeling of liberation is not the terror that sometimes causes people to seek it. True, Santayana argues, some people clearly delight in "the glorious joy of self-assertion in the face of an uncontrollable world" (SB, 149). Hostility to evil may well stimulate people to achieve a gratifying separation from "hopeless foreignness" (SB, 150). But the thing that such people find intrinsically valuable or aesthetically pleasing is not their hostility to evil. It is the integrity and calmness that comes from disinterest in it.

More important, Santayana argues, Stoic or agonistic self-assertion is not the only avenue to sublime detachment or liberation. He notes that Epicureans had argued long before that sublimity may emerge "when we forget our danger, when we escape from ourselves altogether, and live as it were in the object . . . [passing] into what comes before us, to live its life" (SB, 152). Santayana's examples are these: Imagining shipwreck, we "fail to sympathize with the struggling sailors because we sympathize too much with the wind and waves. . . . [W]e can so feel the fascination of the cosmic forces that engulf us as to take a fierce joy in the thought of our own destruction" (SB, 152). From this point of view, actually more indebted to Schopenhauer than Lucretius, a sublime sense of equanimity occurs not when people are self-assertive but when they are self-forgetting and accept or acquiesce in natural necessities. Sublimity then results from a disciplined, so willful, relaxation of will; and in this self-losing, as Schopenhauer put it, one becomes "*pure*, will-less, painless *subject of knowledge*."[26]

If sublimity can emerge out of self-erasing comprehension, understanding, appreciation, or affection, then, Santayana claims, the view that evil has no intrinsic or positive value for human life stands vindicated. Sublime joy does not inevitably, or logically, depend on evil or hostility. "What charms us in the comic, what stirs us in the sublime, and touches us in the pathetic is a glimpse of some good; imperfection has value only as an incipient perfection." Comic, sublime, and tragic narratives please in spite of evil, not in light of it. If they gladden, it is because they afford the pleasure of "recognition and comprehension, the beauty of the medium, and the concommitant expression of things intrinsically good . . . for the pure and ultimate value of the comic is discovery, of the pathetic, love, of the sublime, exaltation"—all varieties of delight available to finite creatures (SB, 161).

"Awed by the magnitude of a reality that we can no longer conceive as free from evil," Santayana writes at the rhetorical pinnacle of his book, "we try to assert that its evil is also a good; and we poison the very essence of good to make its extension universal. We confuse the causal connexion of those things in nature which we call good or evil by an adventitious denomination, with the logical opposition between good and evil themselves; because one generation makes room for another, we say death is necessary to life; and because the causes of sorrow and joy are so mingled in this world, we cannot conceive how, in a better world, they might be disentangled" (SB, 162).

Santayana concludes that this conceptual confusion results, at least partly, from the desiccation of disciplined imaginative activities in American and, perhaps, all of modern culture. The acolytes both of scientism and iconoclastic moralism decry too much imagination. Santayana, to the contrary, claims that the problem with contemporary life is far too little imaginative activity. If turn-of-the-century America is no place of grace, this is not because people now find supernaturalism a dead option. It is because of an "incapacity of the imagination to reconstruct the conditions of life and build the frame of things nearer to the heart's desire." This incapacity constitutes "a failure of moral imagination" far more terrible than any atheism: "We surrender ourselves to a kind of miscellaneous appreciation, without standard or goal; and calling every vexatious apparition by the name of beauty, we become incapable of discriminating its excellence or feeling its value" (SB, 162).

Such standards of excellence, Santayana argues, are no more fixed than human nature, but neither are they any less stable. When they are not insuf-ferably artificial, they articulate demands for well-being that people share or commend sharing—demands on themselves, on others, and on the natural environments with which they interact. These demands, to be sure, are as variable as humankind and its environments. But "the ideal is immanent in them; for the ideal means that environment in which our faculties would find their freest employment and their most congenial world." Feelings of such well-being, passing but memorable, constitute the source, the character, and oftentimes, the consequence of engaging in arts that function to recall people "from the distractions of common life to the joy of a more natural and perfect activity" (SB, 162).

Such feelings, Santayana argues, are just another name for the sense of beauty, "an affection of the soul, a consciousness of joy and security, a pang, a dream, a pure pleasure . . . a pledge of the possible conformity between the soul and nature, and consequentially a ground of faith in the supremacy of good" (SB, 166–67).

"The Art and Function of Criticism"

Does Santayana's aesthetic construal of spiritual life in The Sense of Beauty make him an aesthete? No. Aesthetes abandon or become indifferent to moral

virtues in order to revel in artistic creativity. They indulge in escapism, spell-
bound by works of art, or by their own work at art, in ways that deaden them
to other virtues, especially social virtues like justice. But as Santayana con-
figures things in his first book, moral obligations emerge out of shared affections, the exercise of moral virtues can not only gladden but feel delightful to
the people practicing them, and their loveliness can appeal to others. To his
mind, moreover, people practice the moral virtues in order to overcome things
impeding human joy—an aesthetic end.

Lois Hughson has argued that *The Sense of Beauty* is "anti-aesthetic . . .
dedicated to the destruction of the artificial isolation around art."[27] Her claim
is only half true. Santayana is an anti-aesthete, not anti-aesthetic. He does want
to destroy any artificial isolation around art. But he also wants to cultivate both
the natural links and the natural tensions between moral and aesthetic experience, on the intuition that, apart from the hard work involved in organizing
public life equitably, human joy demands the celebration that comes with the
hard play of imagination and experimentation that not only extends the common affections that bind people, but also opens them up to delights of both
individualized and impersonal life.

What emerges in *The Sense of Beauty* is neither aestheticism nor moralism,
but a self-imposed imperative that informs most of the great writing that
Santayana was to publish during his years as a Harvard professor. This is the
obligation to make *representation* the crucial criterion of critical judgment.
Political, rather than visual, representation provides the model. The *assumption*
is that philosophers are engaged in intellectual reform or redescription because "the human mind is a turbulent commonwealth" of interests requiring
constant reorganization. The claim is that "every human reform is the reasser-
tion of the primary interests of man against the authority of general principles
which have ceased to represent those interests fairly, but which still obtain the
idolatrous veneration of mankind" (*SB*, 23). The standard of representation
rules out both aestheticism and moralism because each holds on to single
interests without regard to the demands of any other.

Santayana will eventually belittle *The Sense of Beauty* by calling it a "potboiler,"
published under the duress of a tenure decision. He will write in 1904 that the
very idea of aesthetic *theory*, even of some "special discipline called 'aesthetics,'"
is a sham and that what counts for the moral philosopher is "the art and function
of criticism." But his naturalistic characterization of beauty and duty, as well as

the philosophical ideal of representation, will continue to shape his work. "Aestheticism," he asserts in "What Is Aesthetics?," is "dubious and inhuman" because it is arrogant, lording one interest among many over all the others. But aesthetic satisfaction, nevertheless, is the thing that makes life graceful. The discipline of philosophical aesthetics is a wheel-spinner. And yet, beauty and duty complement one another: "Aesthetic satisfaction . . . comes to perfect all other values; they would remain imperfect if beauty did not supervene upon them, but beauty would be absolutely impossible if they did not underlie it. For perception, while in itself a process, is not perception if it means nothing and has no ulterior function; and so the pleasures of perception are not beauties if they are attached to nothing substantial or rational, to nothing with a right to citizenship in the natural or in the moral world ("WA?," 39).

The "right to citizenship in the natural or in the moral world," Santayana claims, is warranted when one interest "is favorable to all other interests and is in turn supported by them all" ("WA?," 35). According to this line of thinking, the point of philosophy is to celebrate and guard the "commonwealth" of human interests, by providing a "comprehensive synthesis" of them all. This, indeed, is the critical posture that Santayana attempts to defend during the first decade of the twentieth century, starting with his publication of *Interpretations of Poetry and Religion* in 1900.

4

POETIC RELIGION

Illusion and Disillusion

The thing that sets Santayana's religious philosophy most apart from his more influential colleagues, James and Royce, is his insistence that religion is good poetry if it is good for anything.[1] This is the point of view Santayana begins to fashion in lectures like "Moral Symbols in the Bible," in his lyric play, *Lucifer: A Theological Tragedy* (1899), and in the essays he publishes as *Interpretations of Poetry and Religion* (1900).

Two themes dominate these works: illusion and disillusion. Other philosophers and theologians at the time presume that religious disciplines or experience lead to well-being by disclosing or engaging metaphysical or supernatural realities. Santayana argues, instead, that religion "initiates us, by feigning something which as an experience is impossible, into the meaning of the experience which we have actually had" (*IPR*, 168–69). In this way, religion is *imaginative*, *unrealistic*, seriously *playful*, and *symbolic*.

But quite precisely because this is so, embracing religion requires the practice of disillusion, especially for Reformed Christians who suppose that religion is realistic, literal, obligatory, and explanatory. Santayana's contention is this: Poetic illusions may well enrich human life, but people need not deceive themselves and others by claiming that these illusions are literally true. Religion is better off religiously when it is accepted as poetry. Poetry can inform lives in supremely important ways *as* poetry. But poetry passed off as the literal truth is debased. It is superstition. Indeed, in all likelihood it is superstition at work on behalf of fanaticism, empowering some people at the expense of others, who are made to suffer undeservedly. This, Santayana contends, is surely the case with many varieties of Christian literalism.

To Santayana's mind, this vicious or vain confusion between poetic illusion and literal statement, whether deliberate or not, necessitates untangling the actualities and aspirations that Western philosophers, theologians, and religious people have normally left confused. Indeed, the religious sensibility that Santayana recommends instead of the varieties of theological literalism begins by letting

> the worst of the truth appear, and when it has once seen the light, let it not be immediately wrapped up again in the swaddling clothes of an equivocal rhetoric. In such a disingenuous course there is both temerity and cowardice; temerity in throwing away the opportunity always afforded by the recognition of fact, of cultivating the real faculties of human nature; cowardice in not being willing to face with patience and dignity the situation in which fate appears to have put us. That Nature is immense, that her laws are mechanical, that the existence and well-being of man upon earth are, from the point of view of the universe, an indifferent incident—all this is in the first place to be clearly recognised. (IPR, 148)

Whatever theological or religious dogmas obscure the truths of naturalism are spiritually damning because they distort the conditions, methods, and practical possibilities of well-being. But naturalism is just what both Royce and James are simultaneously disputing, Royce in his Gifford lectures on *The World and the Individual*, delivered during 1899–1900, and James in his Gifford lectures on *The Varieties of Religious Experience*, given in 1901–2. To recapture what Santayana meant in 1900 by "a religion of disillusion," it is helpful to compare *Interpretations of Poetry and Religion* with these two sets of very influential lectures.

The similarities and differences between *The World and the Individual* (1899–1900), *Interpretations of Poetry and Religion* (1900), and *The Varieties of Religious Experience* (1901–2) are truly telling. The likenesses holding among them are their common rhetoric of intellectual statesmanship; their common drive to establish representative authority; and their overt concern with articulating visions that address the question, What makes life worth living for humanity in its plurality? All three philosophers are basically preoccupied with religious issues, especially with articulating the relationship between moral and spiritual life. But Royce, James, and Santayana are addressing these questions in strikingly different ways.

Royce is lighting up an objectivist path that most American philosophers of religion eventually will take during this century. Royce asserts, humorlessly, that his Gifford Lectures constitute "the effort of my life. If I cannot do them rightly . . . I shall be a false servant of Harvard. . . . I shall be false also to the friends who have obtained for me this high trust, and to the cause of serious thinking on Religion and to the public concerned. . . . [A] very sacred task has been put upon me."[2] He claims that if people want to know what makes life significant, they require a way to disclose metaphysical reality; he asserts that metaphysical disclosure demands the establishment of principles of knowledge that let people break through the conditions of their own finitude to "the contemplation of Being as Being," or, in other words, to some "insight into the true nature of Reality."[3]

If individual people seek to satisfy their religious craving for well-being, Royce asserts, they must learn how their ideas or plans of action fit into the whole scheme of things. Royce claims that the whole scheme of things, or "Absolute Idea," or absolute will, is what epistemology can reveal in a way that garden-variety arts and sciences cannot (and, also, that "mysticism," like Emerson's, cannot).

Indeed, in Royce's view, no art or science besides philosophy can ever attain representative authority. This is so because the central issue involved in representation is the problem of the one and the many, the problem of relating the interests, intentions, or desires of individuals to the purpose of the whole. This, he claims, is the problem of religious metaphysics, which works to establish the relationship between discrete spiritual lives and the Spirit in which those "particulars" live and move and have their being.

Royce claims that the key to true significance and well-being is the establishment of the objective relations that obtain between individuals and Absolute Spirit. He contends, further, that this is a relation that only epistemology and metaphysics can adequately account for. Giving a pragmatic twist to idealism by equating "ideas" with "plans of action," he aims to show first, as previous idealists had, that religion, or belief in Absolute Spirit, or belief that there is a purposive whole that gives point to our individual lives, is a necessary fact of consciousness; it is something without which moral life, personal identity, or claims to truth make no sense. Then, he tries to persuade his readers that recognition of this necessary fact is the essence of every sort of philosophical or religious conception of being: It ultimately characterizes the essence of every sort of realism, mysticism, critical philosophy, and idealism. Third, he ventures to demonstrate that this essential idea has been realized historically in an irreversible, unidirectional evolutionary way. Finally, he attempts to show that his own Absolute Idealism is its adequate embodiment, thereby securing representative authority by establishing pragmatically indispensable grounds for settling disputes among conflicting interests.

Santayana does not refute Royce's philosophical absolutism in *Interpretations of Poetry and Religion*, but he rejects it, along with "mysticism." Both absolutism and mysticism come, he claims, with the flights from tradition that religion and philosophy in modern, Western, Protestant cultures take. For Santayana, absolutism and mysticism are two sides of the same fantasy. They both depend on the mistaken thought that there must be some one standard of knowledge and will and spirit that is independent of human opinion, desire, and aesthetic sensibility. On Royce's view, either this standard must be outside of human cultures and apart from the material world in which they are situated, or the significance of the human endeavor is just a muddle, because human claims are inevitably plural and conflictual.

But Santayana disagrees. It is true, Santayana says, "that every idea is equally relative to human nature and that nothing can be represented in the human mind except by the operation of human faculties" (*IPR*, 12–13). Knowledge is built out of human opinions, will out of human desires, spirit out of human sensibilities. But such *relativity* is not mysticism or relativism. Relativity, per se, does not preclude learning, criticism, argument, or agreement across cultures. Nor does it block the assertion that certain opinions are true ones, certain desires good, certain sensibilities more conducive to well-being than others. Mysticism, on the contrary, is the hapless view that, without any one standard external to human cultures, there simply is no way to adjudicate disputes among them, or for people to criticize or learn from one another in ways that are not question-begging, or for truths to be asserted.

This false view, Santayana argues, results from the presumption that we ought to be able to discover judgments that, somehow, are not human opinions. Mysticism throws over "all human ideas because they are infected with humanity." But, in fact, with both absolutism and mysticism, "all human ideas are being sacrificed to one of them—the idea of an absolute reality" (*IPR*, 13). Mysticism results in a "civil war of the mind" that ends "in the extermination of all parties" (*IPR*, 15). Absolutism then tyrannously steps in to claim that superhuman Spirit resolves the disharmonies that people cannot. But Santayana's contention is that insofar as "absolute reality" is expressed, it is expressed as a human opinion, or as a human desire, or as a perceptual judgment. In any case, it fails to carry the force that both absolutists and mystics require of it.

James develops a different strategy for dealing with "the religious demand" for "well-being" in *The Varieties of Religious Experience*. Santayana thinks that it, too, promotes religious superstition, by seeking some literal truth about supernatural powers at work in the world. In *Varieties*, James plays the statesman attempting to "offer mediation between different believers, and help to bring about consensus of opinion" by discriminating common and acceptable beliefs and patterns of religious activity (*VRE*, 359). His aim is to contribute to a "science of religions" that may eventually "command as general a public adhesion as is commanded by a physical science. Even the personally nonreligious might accept its conclusions on trust, much as blind persons now accept the facts of optics—it might appear as foolish to refuse them" (*VRE*, 360).

In this effort, James flatly rejects Royce's view that, together, metaphysics and epistemology provide people with the requisite tools to solve their spiritual problems. The whole point of the work, he claims, is to defend the view that "experience," rather than "philosophy," discloses what people need to learn about the conditions of spiritual well-being.

From Royce's standpoint, James's approach in *Varieties* is profoundly off-track: James just stops asking what the essence of every conception of being is, and studies historical religions for the sake of creating grounds for religious harmony in culture. Instead of assuming that some "idea" of Spirit requires pure realization in some evolutionary ascent, he tries to account for the actual descent of religions from varieties of solitary religious experiences. He pays no attention to the problem of establishing some religious philosophy as absolutely true, but tries to establish beliefs about divinity and salvation that will carry the weight of representative authority.

To this end, James first gathers the testimony of diverse individuals who have reported solitary encounters with divinity—indeed experiences they have reported to be spiritually transforming. He then tries to show that he can transform this testimony into evidence that will warrant a theological claim.

His aim is to persuade his listeners that there are supernatural powers at work in the world, which, on occasion, change desperate people into ones whose lives are lovely, lovable, and loving.[4]

In light of his survey of religious testimony, James asks, "is there, under all the discrepancies of the creeds, a common nucleus to which they bare their testimony unanimously?" (VRE, 399). The answer, he claims, is "affirmative."

> The warring gods and formulas of the various religions do indeed cancel each other out, but there is a certain uniform deliverance in which all religions appear to meet. It consists of two parts:
> 1. An uneasiness; and
> 2. Its solution.
> 1. The uneasiness, reduced to its simplest terms, is a sense that there is *something wrong about us* as we naturally stand.
> 2. The solution is a sense that *we are saved from the wrongness* by making proper connection with the higher power. (VRE, 400)

But is this "sense" true, according to James, and does it confirm belief that supernatural powers exist? Once again: His answer is affirmative. First, there are many examples of people who, once despairing, have become saints, or have experienced the requisite sort of fulfillment—the sort that lets people attend to their moral responsibilities with a sense of delight rather than exhaustion. Second, and more significant from the standpoint of casuistry, there is a psychological theory of subconscious activity that provides a plausible, confirming account of the reports, commonly made by such people, that their personal transformation results from their encounters with powers that are quite distinct from themselves—powers to which they "surrender themselves" and which, consequently, deliver them from despair to happiness.

According to the theory of the subconscious that James endorses, there is a region of the psyche in which other powers may be at work besides the person in question. These powers, he claims, are supernatural because they are both *other* than natural selves—that is conscious, reasoning selves—and *more powerful* than natural selves because they bring about transformations that conscious, reasoning selves are unable to effect: "Starting thus with a recognized psychological fact as our basis," which preserves a "contact with 'science'" which the ordinary theologian lacks," James concludes that "the religious man is moved by an external power" and "*the fact that the conscious person is con-*

tinuous with a wider self through which saving experiences come" is *"literally and objectively true as far as it goes"* (VRE, 403–5).

From the perspective Santayana establishes in *Interpretations of Poetry and Religion*, James's line of thinking in *Varieties* is wrongheaded on a number of counts. First and foremost, James still supposes that grace or the achievement of well-being is an event that occurs outside cultural life, indeed, on the margins of natural life. He still is attempting to vindicate the view that the achievement of well-being hangs on supernatural inspiration—on an immediate encounter with deity. But his argument for divine power, for all its apparent complexity, rests either on wishful thinking or on a simple confusion or both.

Even supposing that James has explicated the testimony concerning personal transformation or conversion accurately, from Santayana's vantage point James gives no sufficient set of reasons to vindicate a theological explanation of the changes he has shown to take place. James provides no adequate way to transform testimony into evidence. Granted: Spiritual transformations occur. But it is far less jolting, conceptually, to presume that whatever permits spiritual transformation to happen is just as natural or material as the rest of human behavior. It may be true that the people undergoing such transformations seem to themselves to be helped by coming into immediate relation with powers not themselves. But such reports are question-begging, because "coming into immediate relation with deity" is an inherited, traditionally theological description that is currently under dispute, that cannot warrant itself, and that receives little aid from a concept as ambiguous as James's "subconscious."

Indeed, James's use of the theory of the subconscious to vindicate theology appears to rest on a confusion that he repeatedly criticizes others for making in his *Principles of Psychology*: the confusion of consequences with origins. Some people experience personal transformations that are divine in the sense that, subsequently, they exemplify human excellence; they flourish. Santayana has no quarrel with this claim. But to infer from such experiences that there is some discrete divine power at work in subconscious psyches that causes such excellence is no more explanatory nor revealing than the inference from the experience of sleep to the existence of a discrete antecedent or correlative dormitive power.

Indeed, from Santayana's point of view, James overemphasizes psychology when it comes to his account of religious or spiritual life. By focusing so exclusively on the psychology of exceptional mental states, including solitary religious experiences, James suppresses (wittingly or unwittingly) the traditional, cultural role that spiritual solitude has played in religious life. By suggesting that religious institutions and cultic or ritual practices *descend* from the varieties of religious experience, James remains blinded to the sense in which spiritual solitude *is* a religious ritual practice that people are bred to go through, or at least to hope to go through. In traditional Christian cultures, perhaps especially Protestant ones, children are trained or disciplined as a matter of course, day in and day out, for spiritual transformations that involve "letting go" of normal wishes and will; and an intrinsic part of that cultural training includes the teaching that makes supernatural grace explanatory in the requisite way.

Once again, Santayana has no quarrel with the notion that solitude may play an indispensable role in spiritual transformation in cultures that have been traditionally Christian. He champions this notion. His quarrel is with James's view that such spiritual solitude is better understood once the rest of full-blooded traditional religious life is stripped away from it. To the contrary, in Santayana's view, the practice of spiritual solitude only makes sense within the context of very specific traditional narratives, institutions, and practices.

The Varieties of Religious Experience gives every appearance of rich observation, because James lets so many religious individuals speak for themselves about the remarkable spiritual changes that they recall having taken place in their lives. But Santayana argues that James suffers from the disease of theological liberalism. He is so eager to give a persuasive case for *some* literal truth vindicating theology, so driven to establish some supernatural matter of fact, that he is willing to sacrifice the complexity of practices and institutions that bring spiritual well-being to life. He is part of that "liberal school that attempts to fortify religion by minimizing its expression, both theoretic and devotional," thereby "impoverishing religious symbols and vulgarizing religious aims" (*IPR*, 4).

In this respect, from Santayana's vantage point James's religious investigations cause the same debility as Royce's metaphysics and epistemology. Each boils down whole ways of imaginative human life to doctrines that are no longer than a sentence. They subtract "from faith that imagination by which faith becomes an interpretation and idealization of life, and [retain] only a stark and superfluous principle of superstition. For meagre and abstract as may be the content of such a religion, it contains all the venom of absolute pretensions. . . . In such a spectral form religious illusion does not cease to be illusion. Mythology cannot become science by being reduced in bulk, but it may cease, as a mythology, to be worth having" (*IPR*, 4).

The strategy of canceling out religious differences for the sake of establishing some more or less acceptable theological claim does not work. Worse, it voids religion of its pragmatic significance, which is not to *add* supernatural matters of fact to natural ones, but to lend meaning to the natural lives people have been given to live.

Tradition and the Crisis of Imaginative Life

If people suffer from spiritual malaise at the turn of the century, Santayana suggests, it is not because philosophers have yet to resolve the technical issues plaguing the projects of metaphysical disclosure, or because individuals are failing to make direct contact with supernatural powers at work in the world. To the contrary, efforts like these contribute to spiritual debility by mistaking imagination for explanation and by diverting attention from the operative difficulty which is this: The culture is letting its traditional religious inspiration, embodied in quite material institutions, practices, and myths, dry up— disciplines of spiritual transformation included.

Intellectual statesmen as thoughtful and influential as James and Royce are suggesting that people slough religious myth, ritual, and institutions altogether for some "core" belief that can be reasonably affirmed apart from full-blooded tradition. In Santayana's view, critics like this make a very dire mistake by implying that these material forms of religious imagination amount to "secondhand" religion that must be repressed because they have brought culture nothing but divisiveness, superstition, and fanaticism.

To the contrary, Santayana claims, it is not *too much* religious imagination that has led to religion's shady side. *It is the failure to realize that there is such a thing as a religious imagination at all!* It is the mistake that people make (even when they are as sophisticated as James and Royce) when they confuse the function of religious imagination with other things like scientific explanation and metaphysical disclosure.

Santayana's vision is this: Religious myths or narratives interpret the point or the significance of the conditions of human life, but they do not reveal what happened before anything else happened, or show how human life or its conditions came to be the way they are now, or predict how things will turn out after everything else has happened. The figures of divinity whose characters are plotted in sacred texts embody the things that people find invaluable or intrinsically valuable, but those deities are not powers; they are ideals or models. If they matter, it is because people embodying or inspired by them make them matter. Scientific explanations account for the patterns that govern the behavior of material things; and the only things that exist are material, humans and all. The religious rituals and disciplines in which people engage are rather more symbolic than instrumental, giving their practitioners a sense or understanding for their cultural location and status as both social and solitary creatures in the world, but not efficacious in any other sense. This is the lesson to be learned by studying such things as the Bible, Greek religion, Christian dogma, Renaissance Christian humanism, and the romantics.

Interpretation and Explanation

Is Santayana asserting as, say, Kant and Schleiermacher had, that religious interpretation and scientific explanation are fundamentally disconnected? Is he saying that one can have no impact on the other? In one sense he is and in another he is not. He is certainly saying, for example, that religious tales of bodily resurrection cannot properly lead to revisions in our natural understanding of morbidity and mortality. He is also claiming, to take an instance of religious practice, that praying for rain is no analogue to seeding clouds. On the other hand, scientific accounts of dying and death need not lead Christians to stop reading their Gospels, even the parts narrating bodily resurrection. Rather, Christians must ask themselves what significance that story has for their lives, self-consciously mortal beings that they are. Nor should efficacious technologies like seeding clouds necessarily provoke people to stop praying for rain, because the point of such prayer, on Santayana's reading, is to maintain equanimity, humility, and courage until rain comes, not to bring it about. So, in this sense, religious interpretation and scientific explanation (and technological control) have no impact on one another. They have different functions. Scientific explanations work to account for events or predict and control what is going to happen. Religious narratives schematize the predicaments and aspirations of death-haunted creatures seeking personal well-being and social justice.

But religious interpretation and scientific explanation both contribute to public discourse, and so they must, as Jeffrey Stout now puts it, remain *conversable*, taking their place among the variety of reasonable human voices, "as often to be corrected as to correct."[5] Santayana, then, is not arguing that religion or any other variety of human imagination is immune from critical jeopardy. The whole point of *Interpretations of Poetry and Religion* is to persuade readers that a "religion of disillusion" must be accepted as carrying the weight of representative authority: A religion of disillusion is a religion that accepts the boundaries of its imaginative status, claiming neither scientific authority nor absolute moral propriety, in great part *because* it has been corrected by inquiry.

Moreover, Santayana does not embrace the claim, often associated with the work of Wilhelm Dilthey, that there is a sharp distinction to be made between studies of human culture (because humans are subjective and self-reflexive) and studies of nature (construed as objective and determinate). For one, Santayana endorses expressivism in *Interpretations of Poetry and Religion*: In other words, he claims that science, religion, and morality are all kinds of human imagination; they do not present different spheres of mind; they serve different functions. Thus:

> Common sense and science live in a world of expurgated mythology, such as Plato wished his poets to compose, a world where the objects are imaginative in their origin and essence, but useful, abstract, and benefi-cent in their suggestions. The sphere of common sense and science is concentric with the sphere of fancy; both move in virtue of the same imaginative impulses. The eventual distinction between intelligence and imagination is ideal; it arises when we discriminate various functions in a life that are dynamically one. Those conceptions which, after they have spontaneously arisen, prove serviceable in practice, and capable of ver-ification in sense, we call ideas of the understanding. The others remain ideas of the imagination. (*IPR*, 9)

Santayana is attempting to forge just that sort of "catholic naturalism" that Strawson now champions, only his manifest image of human life is furnished not only with minds and moral practices but also with religious affections, narratives, institutions, and disciplines that add important activities to the human repertoire. There are functional distinctions to be made between the way we study comets and the way we study comedy or communion. There are even sharper functional distinctions to be made between the aims and styles of writing scientific studies, of enacting comedies, and of participating in communions. But such things do not suggest three different minds or kinds of mind at work; they suggest different kinds of activity.

The crisis of imaginative life at the turn of the century has come about, Santayana argues, partly because its diverse voices have arrogated too much to themselves. "The dignity of religion," Santayana asserts, "lies precisely in its ideal adequacy, in its fit rendering of the meanings and values of life, in its anticipation of perfection; so that the excellence of religion is due to an idealization of experience which, while making religion noble if treated as poetry, makes it necessarily false if treated as science. Its function is rather to draw from reality materials for an image of that ideal to which reality ought to conform, and to make us citizens, by anticipation, in the world we crave" (IPR, 3).

Santayana is well aware that this constitutes a radical revision in his culture's understanding of the role religion properly plays, a revision that would seem outlandish not only to people who had yet to be educated to differentiate the voices of religion and science, but also to theologians or critics of theology in his own time who had. "The mass of mankind," he asserts,

> is divided into two classes, the Sancho Panzas who have a sense for reality, but no ideals, and the Don Quixotes with a sense for ideals, but mad. The expedient of recognizing facts as facts and accepting ideals as ideals,—and this is all we propose,—although apparently simple enough, seems to elude the normal human power of discrimination. If, therefore, the champion of any orthodoxy should be offended at our conception, which would reduce his artful cosmos to an allegory, all that could be said to mitigate his displeasure would be that our view is even less favorable to his opponents than to himself. (IPR, 4)

Here, Santayana claims that "positivists," or reductive materialists, denude culture of imaginative religious practices even more indiscriminately than do liberal religious philosophers or "scientists of religion" like Royce and James. If these liberals truncate the religious imagination by severing its ties from the myths, rituals, and institutions that constitute the bulk of spiritual life in order to remain factual, apathetic naturalists mistake observation, explanation, and prediction for all of human intelligence or thinking in their quest for objectivity and, in the doing, overlook the natural status and function of imaginative and poetic activities, including religious ones.

Indeed, apathetic naturalists fail to understand the cultural role science has to play. Properly practiced, Santayana asserts, scientific investigation becomes "the starting point for a creative movement of the imagination, the firm basis for ideal constructions in society, religion, and art. Only as conditions of these human activities can the facts of nature and history become morally intelligible and practically important. In themselves they are trivial incidents, gossip of the Fates, cacklings of their inexhaustible garrulity" (IPR, 5).

The option between liberal theology and apathetic naturalism, Santayana argues, presents a false either/or, because the stuff of religion is symbolic activity, not literal assertion. Both liberal theology and reductive naturalism do great injustice to "the world of human interests" by suppressing symbolic practices conducive to human joy. Both sides share, in the end, some form of epistemological objectivism in equally unsuccessful efforts to prove to doubters that their beliefs are not only justified but literally and objectively true.

Religious Poetry and Its Corruptions

To Santayana's way of thinking, the basic question to pose about religion understood as part of culture in 1900 is this: Must people suffer from "the natural but hopeless misunderstanding of imagining that poetry in order to be religion, in order to be the inspiration of life, must first deny that it is poetry and deceive us about the facts with which we have to deal" (IPR, 71–72)? Must religion engage in sleight of mind in order to be effective? Does religion have to be embraced realistically in order to play the cultural role he thinks it should? Is it not possible to foster the communion religion brings without the cant from which it suffers? The historical track record, Santayana contends, is clear enough: In Christendom at any rate, the more realistically religious myths and rituals have been taken, the more they have shaped the cultural ethos. It may be, Santayana suggests, that the Greeks approached their own myths and rituals ironically, self-consciously recognizing their legendary and festive character, just as he commends. But there is no hint of irony, as he reads them, in the histories of Judaism or Christianity. There, on the contrary, world view and ethos, dogma and practice, worked to lend one another realistic authority. Santayana gives no definitive answer to the question whether religious people can engage wholeheartedly in religious life and maintain the disillusioned and ironic posture he proposes. Rather, he takes the view that "the future alone can decide" (*IPR*, 72).

But *Interpretations of Poetry and Religion* is surely an effort to persuade the future that such disillusion and irony are spiritually healthy. To this end, Santayana argues, first, that every human claim and practice is imaginative: Common sense, science, art, and religion are all matters of human construction, criticism, and reconstruction. There is no good reason to neglect religion, or a part of religion, on the grounds that it is imaginative. The question is whether the religious imagination helps or harms social and personal good.

Then Santayana goes on to show that "pagan," "Hebraic," and "Christian" religious constructions are utterly comparable, because they are all institutions of "relevant" legend and festivity. If modern people in Christendom read Greek myths as literature, as fables isolated from actual conditions of life, this is the case because they have no understanding of the role those myths played *for* the Greeks themselves. They have not done their homework in "the archaeology of passions," so they do not know the ways in which those myths both informed and reflected social, political, and festive practices (*IPR*, 73). The Greek myths are legends, but for the Greeks they were applicable legends, shaping such things as "ancestral worship . . . social unity and . . . personal conscience" (*IPR*, 21). The Homeric hymns, for example, are loaded with allusions to matters of local knowledge and concern. They are "fragments of narrative in Ionic hexameter recited during the feasts and fairs at various Greek shrines"; tales conceived to give "form and justification" to the cultus of a temple; or to endorse the patriotic piety of an island people; or to honor the delight and anger that Greeks felt in awesome confrontation with natural happenstance; or to celebrate gods that modeled human endurance and success in the face of "mortal destiny"; or to figure virtues like courage, honor, generosity, and strength; or to display the social costs and benefits of irresponsible humor. None of these myths were simply matters of "poetic frivolity" for the Greeks themselves (*IPR*, 28). They were examples of intervening illusion quite precisely because they attached "themselves to realities in the world of action" (*IPR*, 21). They made a practical difference by identifying the gods with "objects of actual experience, with the forces of Nature, or the passions and conscience of man or . . . with written laws or visible images" (*IPR*, 38).

Moreover, Santayana argues, if modern Christians suppress the practical contexts that helped to render the Greek myths practically decisive for the Greeks, they repress the illusive textuality of the Gospel message and the festive character of practices like communion, the more deeply their religion is sewn into daily life. Christian gospels, no less than Homeric hymns, are poetic transformations of experience. For both,

> the interpretation was spontaneous, the illusion was radical, a conscious-
> ness of the god's presence was the first impression produced by the
> phenomenon. Else . . . poetry would never have become superstition;
> what made it superstition was the initial incapacity in people to discrimi-
> nate the objects of imagination from those of the understanding. The
> fancy thus attached its images, without distinguishing their ideal locus, to
> the visible world, and men became superstitious not because they had
> too much imagination, but because they were not aware they had any.
> (*IPR*, 67–68)

In each case "the authors of doctrines" were "the first dupes to their own intuitions" (*IPR*, 67). But to recognize this fact is simply to note how "natural" or normal it is to misconstrue religious poetry by taking it, spontaneously or unreflectively, to reveal gods as powers at work in the world.

Santayana argues that Christianity, like Greek religion, was born in the articulation of affectional experiences that churched people actually had. It provided a "fable," "a new poetry, a new ideal, a new God," which transcribed "the real experience" of people who found nature faulty, who configured the human reach for perfection to be self-deceptive and vain, and who yearned for redemption from the natural world in order to experience a divine well-being that eluded their own achievements. It was a poem that gave form to an entire way of life, another world to live in, "a whole world of poetry"

> descended among men . . . doubling, as it were, their habituation, so that
> they might move through supernatural realms in the spirit while they
> walked the earth in the flesh. The consciousness of new loves, new duties,

fresh consolations, and luminous unutterable hopes accompanied them wherever they went. . . . The longer the vision lasted and the steadier it became, the more closely, of course, was it intertwined with daily acts and common affections; and as real life gradually enriched that vision with its suggestions, so religion in turn gradually coloured common life with its unearthly light. In the saint, in the soul that had become already the perpetual citizen of that higher sphere, nothing in this world remained without reference to the other, nor was anything done save for a super-natural end. Thus the redemption was actually accomplished and the soul was lifted above the conditions of this life, so that death itself could bring but a slight and unessential change of environment. (IPR, 56–57)

So religion, on Santayana's account, is poetry that is "relevant" because it pictures what "life in the ideal" or human well-being looks like, depicts the "conditions" or the things that support or impede it, and evokes a "method" or a set of practices that achieve, approximate, or prepare for it ("MSB," 168). Religion, as Clifford Geertz now puts it—very much indebted to Santayana— is "a cultural system" providing both a world view and an ethos.[6]

Religion persists, Santayana claims, because more distinctly than any other institution it contributes "moral symbols" to culture that give people a way to live joyfully with the events that threaten meaninglessness: physical extremity or suffering, the limits of intellect or absurdity, and the dark edge of moral comprehension or evil.

"Is the spiritual experience of man the explanation of the universe?" Santayana asks. "Certainly not . . . [because] the existence of things must be understood by referring them to their causes, which are mechanical." But "their functions can only be explained by what is interesting in their results, in other words, by their relation to human nature and to human happiness"; and a religion, for instance Christianity, is "a magnificent poetic rendering of this side of the matter" (IPR, 58–59).

Invoking the same sort of Darwinian model of historical transmission James was to use in The Varieties of Religious Experience,[7] Santayana contends that religions persist because they provide responses to moral demands that are humanly fit: Those that survive are "spontaneous variations" in imagination that meet social and personal needs better than competitors:

There must be some correspondence between the doctrine announced or the hopes set forth, and the natural demands of the human spirit. Otherwise, although the new faith might be preached, it would not be accepted. The significance of religious doctrines has therefore been the condition of their spread, their maintenance, and their development, although not the condition of their origin. In Darwinian language, moral significance has been a spontaneous variation of superstition, and this variation has insured its survival as a religion. For religion differs from superstition not psychologically but morally, not in its origin but in its worth. (*IPR*, 68)[8]

The claim Santayana is making here is this: Religions *originate* in instances of pathetic fallacy, in pure experiences of "affectional facts" where the graceful *consequences* of an event have been confused with its *cause* or causes. That is what makes their origin "superstition." But the upshot of Darwinian natural history is clear: Origination of a historical entity is one thing and its maintenance or development is another. Maintenance or development, Darwin argues, proceeds by way of natural selection. Santayana argues that the selective principle at work in the history of religions is "moral significance."

That claim, because it is so partial, is false. Religions have persisted on the basis of myriad selective factors including economic, political, social, and psychological ones (like the emotional appeal as well as the political and economic uses of superstition itself), and also because most practitioners think that religious doctrines are true and religious rites effective. What cannot be denied, however, is that "moral significance" has appeared explicitly in the history of religions as a principle of selection and, more to the point, that "moral worth" is the principle Santayana invokes in his own effort to bring about a selective transmission of his own religious inheritance.

"Moral worth," Santayana claims, is the only part of Greek religion that survived "the dissolution of paganism" brought about by the pre-Socratic philosophers, Socrates, Plato, and Aristotle, as well as the part of Christianity that continued beyond the rise of the modern natural sciences, the emergence of critical history, and the recognition of cultural plurality. In both cases, believing in divinity understood as a natural *power* became a weaker and weaker option.

In the classical case, Santayana argues, the more the pre-Socratics developed their analyses of natural processes and the more Socrates and his followers articulated a grammar of ethical discourse, finding divinity in moral and intelligible ideas, the more Greek mythology was "placed in a sad dilemma, with either horn fatal to its life: it must either be impoverished to remain sincere, or become artificial to remain adequate." Full-fledged Greek religion, in fact, did not survive "reflection on the process of nature or desire for philosophic truth." Once the pre-Socratics distinguished cause from consequence, adherence to the traditional gods lost its foothold in cultural life, "incapable of withstanding the first sceptical attack" by critics of polytheism like Xenophanes (IPR, 39). "The reality which the naturalistic gods had borrowed from the elements proved to be a dangerous prerogative; being real and manifest, these gods had to be conceived according to our experience of their operation, so that with every advance in scientific observation theology had to be revised, and something had to be subtracted from the personality and benevolence of the gods. . . . Such is the necessary logic of natural religion" (IPR, 41–42).

To be sure, Santayana maintains, "in the decay of mythology the gods could still survive as moral ideals. The more they were cut off from their accidental foothold in the world of fact, the more clearly could they manifest their essence as expressions of the world of values." Indeed, he claims, this tendency came to full expression with Plato and even more distinctly with Aristotle, who made goodness, to the exclusion of power, the criterion of divinity (IPR, 43–44).

These claims of Santayana's are misreadings of Plato and Aristotle, but they capture his own critical intention with some precision, and inform the variety of paganized Christianity he champions at the turn of the century.[9] On his reading, which is a variant of the dominant literary and academic account of Christianity in his time, Christianity spliced segments of Hebraic religion together with insights garnered from Stoics, Platonists, and Aristotle, and transformed this syncretic construction by making Christ crucified its devotional center and the necessary and sufficient basis of spiritual joy. Christianity took the realistic and historical narrative of the Hebrew Bible, displaced its national covenant with a Christocentric covenant of grace, made Christ's self-sacrificing solicitude the model of spiritual perfection, spiritualized well-being by making it an "impersonal" quality or character of humanity independent of any external or material consequence or reward, and universalized this gospel.

Classical sources had taught Santayana that "what we should do is to make a modest inventory of our possessions and a just estimate of our powers in order to apply both, with what strength we have, to the realization of our ideals in society, in art, and in science. These will constitute our Cosmos. In building it—for there is none other that builds it for us—we will be carrying on the work of the only race that has yet seriously attempted to live rationally," that is, the Greeks (*IPR*, 149).

But the classics were deficient, to Santayana's way of thinking, because they were "innocent of any essential defeat" (*IPR*, 104). Christian sources, to the contrary, taught him that our reach exceeds our grasp; that the life of reason misses the mark its devotees promise to themselves; that the cosmos which reasonable people can build together is "like Noah's Ark floating in the Deluge"; that people's lives fall short of their search for perfect knowledge, virtue, and power; that there is something inalienably catastrophic about the human prospect; that we must learn ways to flourish alone and together, with love or solicitude, ever shadowed by the Cross (*IPR*, 145).

But for Santayana, Christianity also has its corruptions. It does not correct the "hopeless misunderstanding" that poetry, in order to be religion, must deny that it is poetry, so it continues to spawn deception or superstition. The dark side of its message of "definitive redemption" is fanaticism (*IPR*, 72, 104). By pretending to prejudge historical events and by proclaiming a spiritual exclusivism that counts some people out of reach of solicitude, it entrenches itself in narrow and vicious illusions. Protestantism's emphasis on biblical literalism and its reaffirmation of Hebraic exceptionalism (with a hellish vengeance uncommon to the Hebrews) simply redouble Christianity's defiled declension.

Romanticism, in Santayana's view, overcomes some of these difficulties, by construing Christian eschatology as imaginative and symbolic, not realistic; by accepting the responsibilities imposed by the privileges of human self-assertion; by abandoning classical metaphysical projects and turning to the arts and sciences to manage the difficulties that stand in the way of getting what we most desire; and by deserting the Christian quest for immortal bliss in a supernatural world; instead, commending ways to make encounter with the natural world as joyous as possible. These are all cultural revisions to value.

But romanticism, too, carries its own iniquities. On Santayana's reading, at any rate, its promise is vitiated by the cults of personality and power it introduces into the West. To his way of thinking, shaped as it as by Neo-platonic forms of Christian thought and practice, it is *character*, rather than personality, and *significance*, rather than power, that can provide the sense of well-being or meaning that people religiously crave.

Spiritualization, Barbarism, and Emerson

Do these distinctions make sense? Is there any difference that makes a difference between character and personality, or power and significance? To my mind, whatever sense they make surely depends on the context in which we put them. To take a relevant example, one context Santayana uses to explicate character and personality is personal continuity and change. Personalities are constituted by traits or dispositions or beliefs that are variable and modifiable. So it makes sense to note, for instance, that a personality that has maintained continuity and coherence nonetheless has undergone changes in character. The same relation between old and new, continuity and change can hold with regard to power and significance. The difference powers make, the significance exhibited by them, is subject to variation and change.

This, however, is not what Santayana has in mind in *Interpretations*. Here, he aligns himself with a tradition that thinks of personality and power as mortal and incidental, and character and significance as eternal or timeless, a tradition that pins its spiritual hopes on escaping from mortality to something else again. Santayana himself does not contend that people actually *escape* mortality: Everything existential dies. But he does claim that people can discipline themselves to *play at* immortality by performing an "intense contemplation" or "difficult idealization," rising "continually by abstraction from personal sensibility into identity with the eternal objects of rational life" (*IPR*, 88–89).

With this in mind, Santayana pictures personalities *exhibiting* characters and powers *instancing* significance. Moreover, his Emersonian intuition is that "the best things that come into a man's consciousness are the things that take him out of it" (*IPR*, 129). His claim, in part, is that people or personalities live and die but that the characters they exhibit are randomly related to time, detachable, because repeatable, from mortal human being. Also, the powers constituting events come and go, but the significance instanced in their patterns of behavior is arbitrarily related to their existence. "Eternal" characters and significance, on this view, are the things that make historical people and events matter.

More specifically, Santayana's proposal is that the well-being people crave occurs as they become so identified with the characters or the ideals that hold them in thrall, that there is no difference that makes a difference between their personality and that character. On these grounds, it is not, say, Peter, I love. It is "the willingness to live with energy though energy bring pain," which is the character that he exhibited. I may lose Peter, but not the virtue he displayed. It is not Steve, but his tragicomic wit. Again, I may lose the person but not the character. Moreover, if that is the character or the significance with which I identify, then so long as there is any distinction between me and those ideals, I suffer a lack of well-being. But if I "evacuate" myself into this eternal character or that eternal significance, I become the vehicle of goods (if they *are* goods, which remains an open question) that, again, are randomly related to my (or his or our) duration.

This is the Santayana who is fascinated with "Platonic Love in Some Italian Poets"; the Santayana that so appealed to T. S. Eliot, paving the way for the latter's own classic essay on "Tradition and the Individual Talent" and its "impersonal theory of poetry."[10] It is the Santayana for whom the romantic self-expression of poets like Whitman and Browning becomes anathema, the very mark of barbarism, the Santayana who rails against them for singing of themselves rather than surrendering themselves to "the ideal" (and fessing up to the traditions that informed their poetic voices).

Indeed, as Santayana portrays the discipline of spiritualization in *Interpretations of Poetry and Religion*, giving myself up to this or that ideal (for example, "the willingness to live with energy, though energy bring pain," or "tragicomic wit") instead of concentrating on living well with diverse personalities would truncate the activity, because, "compared with the ideal, every human perfection becomes a shadow and a deceit." On the contrary, "the ideal is the union of all we prize in all creatures; and the mind that has once felt the irresistible compulsion to create this ideal and to believe in it has become incapable of unreserved love of anything else" (*IPR*, 77–78). So, for example, Dante's Beatrice becomes a transparent vehicle for beauty, which becomes a neutral transport for love, which instances a consent of being to being in general, which is the activity of God. The discipline of spiritualization thereby pushes itself limitlessly toward divinity.

To be certain, we should never lose sight of the fact that, for Santayana, spiritualization is *an imaginative discipline*, a playing at something that has a profound practical impact. "Nothing in the world," he asserts, obliges us to agree with Platonic poets when they say that

> eternity can no more be separated from beauty than heat from fire. Beauty is a thing we experience, a value we feel; but eternity is something problematical. It might well happen that beauty should exist for a while in our contemplation and that eternity should have nothing to do with it or with us. It might well happen that our affections, being the natural expression of our instincts in the family and the state, should bind us for a while to the beings with whom life has associated us—a father, a lover, a child—and that these affections should gradually fade with the decay of our vitality, declining in the evening of life, and passing away when we surrender our breath, without leading us to any single and supreme good, to any eternal love. If, therefore, the thoughts and consolations we have been rehearsing have sounded to us extravagant or unnatural, we cannot justify them . . . by showing where and how we may come face to face with God. We may well feel that beauty and love are clear and good enough without any such additional embodiments. . . . We can welcome beauty for the pleasure it affords and love for the happiness it brings, without asking that these things should bring supernatural extensions. (*IPR*, 87–88)

But to admit all this, Santayana argues, is to reject nothing more than "the mythical element" in the Platonic discipline of idealization, an unrealistic, symbolic, festive practice that shapes lives by motivating its practitioners, as James would have put it, always to make *more* of their appreciation and affection, turning each experience "to spiritual uses" (*IPR*, 89). This leads Santayana to claim that

> if we take the sights and loves that our mortal limitations have allowed of, and surrender ourselves unreservedly to their natural eloquence; if we say to the spirit that stirs within them, "Be thou me, impetuous one"; if we become, as Michael Angelo says he was, all eyes to see and all heart to

feel, then the force of our spiritual vitality, the momentum of our imagination, will carry us beyond ourselves, beyond an interest in our personal existence or eventual emotions, into the presence of a divine beauty and an eternal truth—things impossible to realize in experience, although necessarily envisaged by thought. (*IPR*, 88)

But even given the imaginative status of "living under the form of eternity," Santayana remains hypercritical of the romantic cults of personality and power that he claims are instanced diversely by Whitman and Browning. In my own view, at any rate, there is nothing gainsaying Santayana's common Western complaint that self-absorption is likely to lead to personal disease and social psychopathology, or his insistence that power per se deserves no celebration, but rather power that matters because it realizes some good. But most of the time, and surely at their best, Whitman and Browning would have agreed.

In fact, I think, the difference between the Santayana who wrote *Interpretations*, on the one hand, and Browning and Whitman, on the other, is that, at their best, "the barbarians" drop the traditional Christian interest in breaking through time to eternity and, with it, the concomitant disciplines of idealization or spiritualization. *Even understood as an imaginative practice, they simply stop searching for any avenue to eternity.* Instead, they find spiritual revitalization in replacing the old articulations of well-being with new ones, which, to be sure, resonate with vital Reformed Christian traditions as well.

Put another way, Browning and Whitman both proclaim the discontinuous character of their worlds, their selves, and their sublime "Good Moments" in a way that Santayana cannot allow or, at any rate, does not admit to accepting, in *Interpretations of Poetry and Religion*. Santayana still wants both the sense of well-being that comes with revision and the continuity leading to fulfillment that he imagines spiritualization brings. Indeed, he wants revision that fosters fulfillment, something new that still provides a way to live under the form of eternity. He wants to replace worn-out supernaturalism with a vigorous religious naturalism, but one that is still very much concerned with self-surrender, submission to "the Ideal," spiritualization, the continuous displacement of more partial passions by more comprehensive ones, eventuating in an imaginative performance of eternal fulfillment.

This predilection for "a sane and steady idealization" on Santayana's part hardly makes him "the Pope of Theory," as Frank Lentricchia currently suggests.[11] But it does lead to his poetic and religious demand for a "total vision" that he cannot find in the "analytic" poetry of "episodes" that Whitman and Browning write (*IPR*, 108, 104). Browning leaves us, Santayana claims, with "passions, characters, persons." Whitman "carries the disintegration further and knows nothing but moods and particular images." Both are barbarians because they regard their "passions as their own excuse for being." They do not "domesticate them either by understanding their cause or by conceiving their ideal goal." They are neither schooled in the traditions that hold them in debt nor capable of reaiming at a new destiny now that those traditions, both classic and Christian, have become dead options. Their "delight is in abundance and vehemence; [their] art, like [their] life, shows an exclusive respect for quantity and splendor of materials" (*IPR*, 108–9).

This is bad but telling criticism, because Browning and Whitman aim for the survival of human goods as much as Santayana does. They write to show what makes the intensity of emotions good and to construe the significance of materials; only, they find what they need on the surfaces and encounters of the characters, persons, passions, moods, and images that history and current life, including present aspirations, provide. They quit searching depths that are not there for an indefinite breadth that is. Browning and Whitman know their traditions, which are their agonies. But by abandoning the quest for poetic fulfillment in the wake of experiential loss and by facing the future with the creative discontinuities of their own poetic powers, they open the texture of destiny to the potential blessings and curses of revision. This, I suggest, is something Santayana still fears in 1900, even as he engages in it.

In fact, with respect to Whitman, Santayana knows all of this, including his own ambivalence. The latter is played out in "Walt Whitman: A Dialogue," written ten years before for *The Harvard Monthly*. In that essay "McStout" bemoans Whitman's dissolute romanticism—"his vague pantheism, his formlessness, his confusion of values, his substitution of emotion for thought, his trust in impulse rather than in experience"—while "Van Tender" defends, indeed praises, "his voice of nature crying out in the wilderness of convention"; his willingness to abandon "theory or a description of things" for "appreciation"; his sense of "sublime justice"; his ability to provoke "the widening of your sympathies, your reconciliation of nature"; his "profound piety that recognizes the life of every thing in nature and spares it, and worships its intrinsic nature"; his ability to "make us feel the fitness, the necessity, the beauty of common things." All these characteristics, Van Tender asserts, make Whitman "a poet of the highest type." For Van Tender, "a barbarism is an annoyance," but one worth sustaining for the receptivity and sense of connectedness that Whitman fosters (*GSA*, 97–104). Surely ambivalent in 1890, Santayana still clearly favors Van Tender's Whitman at that time and, alongside him, the openness to revision that comes through engagement with alien others. Ten years later, the ambivalence is still there, but Van Tender's Whitman is mainly suppressed, overcome by Santayana's concern for Whitman's "terrible levelling," which, he fears, leaves human life not composite but aggregate and, so, uniform rather than excellent.

Santayana's ambivalence concerning revision is further clarified in his chapter on Emerson in *Interpretations*, which I read both as approving a kind of poetic protest that fosters a sense of indefinite natural connectedness and as condemning natural supernaturalism as a lie. The chapter emphasizes what Santayana characterizes as the lasting contribution of American transcendentalism. Emerson, Santayana now openly asserts, is the only American to become a "fixed star in the firmament of philosophy" (*IPR*, 140). He has won his seat through his methodical construal of every element of culture as poetic. His genius now lies not simply in his character, but in his ability to show that the institutions and practices of private as well as social life are all products of the human imagination. Santayana claims that Emersonian transcendentalism is a view that disrupts an old Western hierarchy, reiterated by Enlightenment philosophers, that subordinates the human imagination, as poetry, to science or to human understanding and reason. Emerson rejects this view and turns it on its head, by displaying science, understanding, and reason, along with all the other kinds of thought and activity in which people engage, as imaginative or poetic.

On Santayana's reading, the image of culture that Emerson gives is one that restores poetry to its proper status as the fount of every sort of discourse and distinctively human practice. Previewing Whitman, Emerson's proposal actually democratizes the diversity of cultural languages and styles for the sake of public welfare. Emerson, Santayana now argues, properly construes poetry as an "insurrection from beneath, a shaking loose from convention, a disintegration of the normal categories of reason in favor of imaginative principles." It is poetry that lets people develop their own sense for the beauty of the world into which they have been born; and it is poetry that enables them to create worlds "like . . . young god[s]" (*IPR*, 132). Emerson flees to his woods, not to restore his connection to an old world, but to be "the creator of his own worlds in solitude and freedom." To the tightly conventional minds of his contemporaries" he brings "a breath as if from paradise." His countrymen are "stifled with conscience and he [brings] them a breath of Nature; they [are] surfeited with shallow controversies and he [gives] them poetic truth" (*IPR*, 132–33).

And the Emersonian truth, Santayana claims, is one that simultaneously reflects and guides an entire American epoch:

> His constant refrain is the omnipotence of imaginative thought; its power first to make the world, then to understand it, and finally to rise above it. All nature is an embodiment of our native fancy, all history a drama in which the innate possibilities of the spirit are enacted and realized. While the conflicts of life and the shocks of experience seem to bring us face to face with an alien and overwhelming power, reflection can humanize and rationalize that power by conceiving its laws; and with this recognition of the rationality of all things comes the sense of their beauty and order. The destruction which Nature seems to prepare for our special hopes is thus seen to be the victory of our impersonal interests. To awaken in us this spiritual insight, an elevation of mind which is at once an act of comprehension and of worship, to substitute it for lower passions and more servile forms of intelligence—that is Emerson's constant effort. (*IPR*, 133)

Emerson was surely right, Santayana asserts, to insist on the imaginative character of distinctively human thought and practice. Just as surely, he was right to focus on the ways imagination gave point to an otherwise pointless nature. More particularly, he was right to champion the practice of poetic revision, repairing "to the material of experience, seizing hold of the reality of sensation and fancy beneath the surface of conventional ideas, and then out of that living but indefinite material to build new structures, finer, richer, fitter to the primary tendencies of our nature, truer to the ultimate possibilities of the soul" (*IPR*, 161).

The result, according to Santayana, is Emerson's "topographical" image of a new "cosmic order" that provides a context for the "drama" of human life. Emerson lets literal Christianity go, along with every Christology; he hangs on to an inverted Protestant principle that permits affectional rebirthing of himself and the world when conventions ossify and people are apathetic; and he revises his religious tradition in a way that gives people a thick description of spiritual life. All this makes Emerson eponymous with his age.

But was Emerson right to claim that the imagination is *omnipotent*, according to Santayana? No. The trouble with Emerson is that he remains "the psyche of Puritanism," by portraying Spirit as an engine, indeed, an American-built and -vested engine, pulling the world toward truth and right forever. Emerson, Santayana argues, "inherited the problems and the preoccupations of the theology from which he started, being in this respect like the German idealists, who with all their pretense of absolute metaphysics, were in reality only giving elusive and abstract forms to traditional theology. Emerson, too, was not primarily a philosopher but a Puritan mystic with a poetic fancy and a gift for observation and epigram, and he saw in the Laws of Nature, idealized by his imagination, only a more intelligible form of the divinity he had always recognized and adored" (*IPR*, 138).

By distinguishing tradition from the "reason" that is Emerson's revisioning of revelation, the Concord sage threatens to demolish "the labor of long ages of reflection" (*IPR*, 135). By picturing poetry as a key to metaphysical disclosure, he tries to make us believe that "since the human understanding is something that is human and conditioned, something that might have been different, as the senses might have been different, and which we may, so to speak, get behind, therefore the understanding ought to be abandoned." Reading Emerson, "we long for higher faculties, neglecting those we have, we yearn for intuition, closing our eyes upon experience. We become mystical" (*IPR*, 135). Finally, by maintaining "the national hope and pride of a religious people that felt itself providentially chosen to establish a free and godly commonwealth in a new world," Emerson sanctions the conflation of nationalism and eschatology that signifies American spiritual exceptionalism (*IPR*, 139). Emerson commits three lies: one against historical derivation; one against the immanence of criticism; one against the natural history of nations.

Emerson, Santayana concludes, leaves us with a complex religious vision of the promise and problems of human life, but one that still adds up to a religion of illusions, not the "religion of disillusion" Santayana wants. What is needed, he says, is a religion that suffers neither from Emerson's flight from tradition taken as a source of authority, nor from his worn-out attempt to make direct contact with absolute reality, nor from his infatuation with poetic self-assertion, nor from the self-deceptions involved in identifying his own self, race, and country with God.

The religion of disillusion that Santayana is preparing himself to propose will acknowledge that "the existence and well-being of man upon earth are, from the point of view of the universe, an indifferent incident" (thus giving the lie to any religion that construes humanity, human imagination, or the values that humans hold dear, to be either the masters or the justification of the universe) (*IPR*, 148). It will underscore the responsibility people have to one another to construct their own life of reason, morality, and spirit (giving the lie to any religion that confesses the belief that something or someone else can build it for them). Emphasizing the narrative character of that life, it will provide rituals of piety that link the present to the past as well as disciplines of spirit that link it to a conception of destiny (giving the lie to any religion that severs spiritual life from tradition on the one hand and from material futures that can be imagined and realized on the other). Insisting on the affectional roots of human goods, which are the only goods there are, it will train people in charity, teaching them to appreciate alien individuals and peoples as they understand themselves (giving the lie to spiritual exceptionalism). Finally, it will foster imaginative practices of spiritualization that let people love life in the consciousness of impotence (giving the lie to any religion confessing belief that any power, human or otherwise, can *make* a new heaven and a new earth). This, indeed, outlines the sort of religion that Santayana will propose in *The Life of Reason*, a work he is beginning to draft even before *Interpretations of Poetry and Religion* goes to press.

Lucifer, Hermes, and Christ

Before turning to *The Life of Reason*, however, I want to interpret *Lucifer: A Theological Tragedy* for the light it sheds on Santayana's conception of idealization or spiritualization. Santayana will develop this notion, which involves playing at eternity, when he proposes a discipline he calls "ideal immortality" in *Reason in Religion* (*LR*, 3, 51–73). He will do so in his attempt to naturalize the Christian Platonism he finds so appealing. But in *Lucifer* (in all probability written during his 1896–97 sabbatical leave at Cambridge, where he was studying Plato and Aristotle under Henry Jackson), he calls this practice into question in various ways that will not become prominent in his thinking until he writes "Hermes the Interpreter," as his ultimate "Soliloquy in England," in the aftermath of the Great War.

Three issues are at stake. Are the things that people claim to be divine unified in one being, as the practice of Platonic spiritualization supposes, or not? Is divinity immortal, as that practice also presumes, or not? Is Santayana committed to Platonic spiritualization as preeminent among religious disciplines, or not? *Lucifer*'s answers are strikingly clear. The things people claim to be divine are antinomial, not unified. They are mortal, not immortal. Spiritualization is one among a variety of spiritual disciplines, each of which appeals to different natures or temperaments, but in fact *interpretation*, rather than *idealization*, appears to win Santayana's approval as the spiritual discipline of choice.

How does *Lucifer* go? Why is it a "theological tragedy"? "The time is the present," Santayana writes. "The place is the imagination of this age, so largely given to comparative and historical studies." The characters "lie in the mind of every man whose education has made him heir of both the Christian and the Pagan tradition."[12] Its point, he claims, is "not identical with the sentiments of any one of the characters but lies implicit in their tragic juxtaposition. All spirits are dependent on a latent power, but independent of one another" (*LTT*, xiii).

In the first act, Hermes, the "laughing god" of interpretation (*LTT*, 66), meets Lucifer, whose allegiance to truth and justice have made him rebel against the creator God whose armies he once commanded. Hermes has been sent by Zeus, first among the powers of nature, to exchange greetings with the triune Christian divinity who threatens to displace him. Lucifer falls in love with the winning Hermes, whose sole intention is to understand and to make diverse parties mutually understandable to one another. Lucifer reveals to the messenger that his heavenly revolt occurred when it became clear to him that worshiping the God of creation *as* the God of justice was a lie; creation is indifferent to justice. Knowing that to be desired is to be good, and to be just is to give desires their due, Lucifer had led the angels, embodying actual desires, in an uprising against this deceit. But the angels, having no messenger of understanding like Hermes to foster equanimity, fall into Hell, led by Lucifer's own lieutenant, Mephistopheles, who embodies the arrogant self-assertion instanced by cacophonous desires. When Hermes asks Lucifer to show him Heaven and Hell, Lucifer consents, swearing that "All that is mine I yield to thy control" (LTT, 30).

The second act takes place in the Garden of the Hesperides, where Lucifer introduces Hermes to Mephistopheles, only to have this governor of Hell, self-assertion incarnate, belittle Lucifer's love of Hermesan interpretation. Still, Hermes's nature is irresistible enough for Mephistopheles to reveal his own conflict with Lucifer—willfulness is at odds with justice and finds deceit comfortable—and to accept Lucifer's request to serve as Hermes' guide to the gates of Heaven (which, at this point, Lucifer cannot bring himself to pass through).

The third act, transpiring in Hell, brings the conflict between Lucifer and Mephistopheles to a head. Lucifer has proposed a banquet in honor of Hermes and himself. But Mephistopheles will not let Hermes in, because he is an "enemy of Hell" (LTT, 82). Further, he leads his witches and devils in a revolt against Lucifer who, disgusted by their slavishness, leaves them to their own forsaken fate.

In the fourth act, Mephistopheles and Hermes encounter Saint Peter at Heaven's gate. When Mephistopheles requests their admission to Heaven, Peter, knowing that Mephistopheles's own pride will bar his access, denies Hermes entrance on the grounds that the messenger is neither a son of Adam nor of Christ. Mephistopheles points out that "God receives many that the churches damn" (LTT, 99). Peter agrees, but says that Hermes has "no need of grace. That is a sadder and a higher lot than [his]" (LTT, 101). Eventually Lucifer misses Hermes enough to accompany him into Heaven. But it is not the creator God they eventually encounter; he is absent from every scene in the play. It is Christ, who presumes that the implicit motive for Hermes' venture to Heaven must be to give witness to his Lordship, not interpretation leading to mutual understanding. In any case, Christ claims that now that Hermes has entered the realm of sin and grace, his only "choice must be either to die or to believe in me." He will not greet him otherwise (LTT, 130). But Lucifer's response is telling: The choice is moot; everybody, including Christ, dies. Belief in Christ is "too gross and palpable a fiction" (LTT, 134). Christ, not accepting Lucifer's judgment, tells the rebel that he (the embodiment of spiritualization) is in fact the heart of Lucifer's love for Hermes. The act ends when

Lucifer tells Christ that, if Christ can persuade Hermes that he is Lord, he—Lucifer—will give Christ his allegiance.

But the fifth act is decisive. On Olympus, the gods fear for Hermes' safety; they are curious about the god of Sinai. But Hermes returns, followed by Christ, whom Zeus comically mistakes for his own father, Cronos (the god who eats his own children). Christ holds out the promise of immortality to Zeus in exchange for his heart. Zeus shows no interest, but Aphrodite expresses an affinity, and Hermes—ever understanding—declares his willingness to listen and to "venture" with him. But because his affections are "knit for better or for worse" to his Olympian family, he cannot leave them (*LTT*, 174–75). Christ, a failure in his mission to persuade Hermes to *believe*, curses the Olympians and vanishes. Zeus, stealing lines from Lucretius, undercuts Christ's curse, reminding his own that "we also thought he should not taste of death, but it is fated. Fleeting is the breath that saith: I am eternal. We were born and we must therefore die. Such is the wage of being" (*LTT*, 177–78).

Back on Lucifer's island, Lucifer grieves for the death of Hermes, something that has not yet actually happened. Knowing that the sort of understanding that interpretation permits is eventually just as fleeting as any other natural occurrence, a random incident in an unplanned universe, he takes comfort in "the eternal bitter truth" that is "the essence of [his] lofty mind" (*LTT*, 187).

Here, then, is a play that shows a diversity of spiritual practices—Platonic spiritualization embodied in Christ, allegiance both to justice without deceit and to truth demonstrated by Lucifer, the natural sense of beauty or affection presented by Aphrodite, the dedication to mutual understanding displayed by Hermes. All of these practices are contingent on natural powers at work in the world, especially the powers of human imagination. Indeed, if his own admission is to be trusted, all these practices appeal to Santayana. The tragedy lies not in the mortality of these gods (which, to be sure, is both assured and sad) but in their conflict, a conflict of good with good that can reach no resolution because, identifying themselves as changeless, the gods have no way to affect one another.

The one challenge to this theological tragedy is Hermes the interpreter, whose task it is to transgress the borders that isolate the Olympians from the Heavenly Host, as well as from Lucifer and his fallen rebels, for the sake of mutual understanding. Hermes is like Christ in some extremely relevant respects: He is a mediator of divinity. He is an outlaw god. He is a favorite son of Zeus. He is affiliated with Aphrodite, goddess of love; He befriends Lucifer, avatar of truth, reason, and justice. But Hermes is also unlike Christ in telling ways. Most significant, he is uninterested in breaking through time to eternity, and unconcerned with disciplines formulated to do so. His interest, rather, is in breaking across boundaries that keep figures from taking delight in one another as well as in the lives they have been given to live. He threatens no one with either/ors. He bars no one from anywhere. He demands no evacuation of self, but rather invites the full disclosure of character (or personality). He requires no submission, but rather enjoys the independence of another. He does not judge; he understands; he listens; he learns to appreciate things from the standpoint of alien others. He is the only character in the drama that can play at transformation, who makes a personal difference, and then, not through coercion, but rather through unadulterated appeal.

Hermes, eventually, emerges as a "guide" for Santayana, a model for his own philosophical self-understanding, a way to design the life of the spirit as human comedy, rather than as theological tragedy. But, to all appearances, *Lucifer* drops stillborn from the press, and Hermes plays no explicit role in Santayana's next and clearly most influential set of books, *The Life of Reason*.

5

A PRAGMATIC

LIFE OF REASON

The Age of Interpretation

Hermes the interpreter does not figure in *The Life of Reason*, because Santayana is not ready to give up Platonic spiritualization or its background assumptions; he will not embrace Hermesan understanding as a spiritual ideal until the Great War. But "interpretation" is now Santayana's philosophical signature. *The Life of Reason*, indeed, is an effort to charter the idea that *philosophy is interpretation*; it is Santayana's bid to win people over to the startling assertion that opens up the five volume work: "The age of controversy is past, that of interpretation has succeeded" (*LR*, 1:32). What Santayana has in mind is a reprise of claims he has already made in his work on Lotze, the sense of beauty, and the essays constituting *Interpretations of Poetry and Religion*. Transcendental philosophy is a dead option. The philosopher's task, as Lotze had maintained, is "mediation" among a diversity of parties to cultural dispute, including common sense, social thought, religion, art, and science. But contrary to Lotze, Santayana argues that there should be genuine give-and-take among those communicants. No one of them holds veto power over all the others; nor does philosophy reveal any "special knowledge" authorizing this or that cultural hierarchy. On the contrary, diverse claims are authorized by the "representative" weight they carry, that is, by the extent to which they are "favorable to all other interests and [are] in turn supported by them all" ("WA?," 35). In this vein, he says that "our task is not to construct but only to interpret ideals, confronting them with one another and with the conditions which, for the most part, they alike ignore" (LR, 1:32). Every claim gets a hearing; but every claim is subject to the varieties of critical jeopardy. Here, then, is a civic humanism, a post-Christian republicanism, an account of philosophy that transforms it into intellectual statesmanship, that makes its work cultural reconstruction, and that aims to show, as synoptically as possible, how the institutions and practices of culture can hang together without hanging themselves: "The problem," Santayana declares, "is to unite a trustworthy conception of the conditions under which man lives with an adequate conception of his interests" (LR, 1:28).

The irony is that, with The Life of Reason, Santayana commissions the very movement in philosophy that Dewey and his disciples will quickly come to champion and dominate, and that Santayana will eventually criticize with some severity. Philosophy in The Life of Reason is the kind of inquiry that prepares citizens or their leaders for concrete social or cultural action. It does this by showing how cultural institutions and practices may both constrain and support one another without leaning on anything above, beneath, or behind these human establishments. In this way it makes good on the promissory note delivered by Santayana in Interpretations, underwriting the claim that

> the work of human intelligence [accomplishes] what is commonly believed to be the work of God. The universe, apart from us, is a chaos, but it may be made a cosmos by our efforts and in our minds. The laws of events, apart from us, are inhuman and irrational, but in the sphere of human activity they may be dominated by reason. We are part of the blind energy behind Nature, but by virtue of that energy we impose our purposes on the part of Nature which we constitute or control. We can turn from the stupefying contemplation of an alien universe to the building of our own house, knowing that, alien as it is, that universe has chanced to blow its energy also into our will and to allow itself partially to be dominated by our intelligence. Our mere existence and the modicum of success we have attained in society, science, and art are the living proofs of this human power. The exercise of this power is the task appointed for us by the indomitable promptings of our own spirit, a task in which we need not labor without hope. (IPR, 147)

This is a hair split away from Dewey's later view that "Faith in the power of intelligence to imagine a future which is a projection of the desirable in the present, and to invent the instrumentalities of its realization, is our salvation." The difference is Santayana's Spinozistic reminder that the universe *is*, in the end of the day, indifferent to human desire. The life of reason is the self-assertion of human intelligence, self-consciously "floating in the Deluge" but nevertheless the only engine in the world intentionally at work to make the human spirit flourish. This is *The Life of Reason*'s large idea.

There are four major aspects of this work that I will focus on for the sake of clarifying and criticizing Santayana's religious naturalism: its emphasis on intellectual statesmanship of a distinctively republican sort; its naturalistic view of mind, particularly its epiphenomenalism; its singular kind of pragmatism, which focuses more on institutions than on either theses or methods; and its construal of religion as a constituent of post-Christian republican life, especially its way of distinguishing religious cant from religious virtues. But before I turn to these particular issues, it will be helpful to comment on Hegel's influence in *The Life of Reason*.

Hegel and The Life of Reason

For many of its readers, *The Life of Reason* leaves the deep and lasting impression that Santayana is calling for a return to philosophy as it had been practiced by the Greeks, especially by Heraclitus, Democritus, Socrates, Plato, and Aristotle. Santayana claims, after all, that his variety of civic humanism assumes that Heraclitus was right to picture existence in terms of flux or process and that the atomic, mechanistic terms formulated by Democritus equipped science with a language of explanation that has never been bettered. Hence, "with the flux observed and mechanism conceived to explain it, the theory of existence is complete" (*LR*, 1:17–18). Moreover, Socrates' introduction of disciplines by which to interrogate one's own heart and mind, Plato's idea of the good, and Aristotle's conception of human beings as rational animals living in society with one another furnish the West with a language of moral judgment that remains functionally adequate. There is no doubt, then, that Santayana opts to highlight and recanonize these Greeks.

But with all of Santayana's kudos to the Greeks, I believe it makes sense to interpret *The Life of Reason* as more Hegelian than classical in its preoccupations and problems and that, indeed, Santayana's invocation of the Greeks, and even his clear admiration for Spinoza, are part of a basically Hegelian strategy to get leverage on the failures of the modern philosophical tradition. That tradition, which Santayana pictures in great part descending from Plato and the church fathers, is doubly bound by an avoidable quest to legislate the right ways to think and act by coming into direct contact with the really real. Its ideal of objectivity leaves Western practitioners of philosophy either making finally unsupportable epistemological claims or resting in a radical skepticism that denies the possibility of reasonable life altogether.

Santayana has many critical things to say about Hegel, but he sees him as a precursor who offers an alternative to the quest for objectivity. In this crucial respect, indeed, Hegel is more appealing than any of the Greeks and far more forceful than Spinoza: Hegel's *Phenomenology* can be read as offering a spiritual discourse that accepts the contingency of everything including itself and as locating spirit in the varied efforts of humankind to accept its utter contingency and to find ways of achieving happiness in light of it. Even more to the point, Hegel's *Phenomenology* lets readers abandon the quest for objectivity, because it pictures reasonable people as responsible to one another and as capable of reasonably rejecting outmoded visions without exactly refuting them.

Hence, Santayana will muse in *Persons and Places* that it was Hegel's *Phenomenology of Spirit* and not, say, Spinoza's *Ethics* or any work of Aristotle that "set me planning my *Life of Reason*." He says that "a critical thesis, say, on *Logic, Sophistry, and Truth in Hegel's Philosophy* . . . would have knit my own doctrine together at the beginning of my career, as I have scarcely had the chance of doing at the end. My warhorse would not have been so much blinded and hidden under his trappings" (PAP, 389).

These incidental remarks receive strong support in Santayana's 1902 essay, "The Two Idealisms: A Dialogue in Limbo." There, Santayana presents his version of the differences between good and bad idealism, and points to Hegel as the one modern idealist who came close to exemplifying the good. The very title of the essay is significant in this regard. Characterizing the location of philosophical discourse as limbo set it betwixt and between orders of life, and picturing philosophy as conversation with the living dead—rather than as coming into the presence of some Sacred Idea or Objective or Reality—makes philosophy a discipline for the selective transmission of traditional wisdom. Philosophers find themselves in limbo because they take their inherited thought, and hence their own identity, to be dead. Their task is to revive or resurrect traditional concerns or interests by redescribing their situation in ways that let them cope better or satisfy their interests more completely. Among the moderns, Hegel is so helpful because he was such a "catholic observer of all forms of life and a great student of its higher processes" ("TIDL," 22). These were just the things demanding redescription if "reason" is to be revised in a way that effectively takes the notion away from the theologians and metaphysicians and makes it a function of tradition and practice.

The things that appeal so much to Santayana about Hegel's redescription of things are his thick accounts of human forms of life, his Spinozistic emphasis on the close connections among desire, virtue, and happiness, and his location of all three in articulate institutions of culture. Even if Hegel's writing retains vestiges of the traditional attempt to learn about virtue by encountering being itself, the upshot of his arguments undercuts the old search for an ontology of presence and makes philosophy into a cultural and historical conversation about how to overcome the things impeding the satisfaction of human desires ("TIDL," 9).

Schopenhauer, Santayana argues, scuttles the Western notion of virtue altogether by having virtue consist in "not living at all," utterly ignoring "the joy of fruitful action and of reasonable thought" ("TIDL," 9–10). Besides, Schopenhauer misplaces virtue outside the boundaries of social life, interested only in saving himself from the consequences of caring. Fichte wrecks virtue by making it synonymous with any expression of will and by linking discovery of it to a reduction of the world to some ideal unity. Hegel, to the contrary, sets virtue in the context of social life and articulate reason; he focuses quite precisely on the joy of fruitful action and of reasonable thought; and he ridicules efforts of his compatriots to dissolve their minds adequately enough to discover some epistemologically immediate ground of being. He is at one with those Greeks, like Socrates, who maintain that "the hidden foundations of things have no other dignity or value than that which they acquire by supporting the superstructure" ("TIDL," 19). If he, too, clings to the superstition that being and being good coincide as a matter of fact, he also pictures the life of reason as going on indefinitely in the various institutions of humankind, constantly confronted with the task of reconciling conflicting desires and virtues but "powerless to correct them" once and for all ("TIDL," 27). Hegel, therefore, abridges Western hopes without abandoning them altogether, by championing the self-assertion of solicitous solidarity among people on earth. He betters the classical conception of moral life by accepting its contingent and antinomial character, and by making the members of humankind responsible to one another rather than to something or somebody less contingent and more lawlike.

Hegel makes two mistakes, Santayana thinks. One is to ask "what must exist besides to make possible that which exists already" ("TIDL," 24). To that extent he does not sufficiently revolt against metaphysics and the quest for objectivity. But his focus on the self-assertion of humankind overshadows such mythologizing, because it leaves the message that "it is not the stuff things are made of that concerns us, but the things into which that stuff may be made" ("TIDL," 22). That, of course, is part of Santayana's pragmatic message in *The Life of Reason*. The other mistake Hegel makes is to underplay the joy that is possible in a human world that is contingent and antinomial at any given moment. His picture of things waxes a little too Protestant, suggesting a gospel of joyous suffering.

The Life of Reason, to the contrary, seeks out the institutions and circumstances that permit and even foster festivity for death-haunted creatures. That, in Santayana's rectification by redescription, is what most religious and social rituals, artistic accomplishments, and even scientific explanations are all about. That is what makes the institutions of the modern Western republics worth saving. Their literal aim is to arrange for kinds of conduct that will "perfect natural happiness" (*LR*, 1:3).

The thing that pops out of *The Life of Reason* like a jack-in-the-box is the poverty of philosophy as it has been understood by most Westerners in modern times. Since Descartes, anyhow, philosophers have encouraged the view that scientific method is the key to well-being, and have encouraged themselves to picture their own discipline in scientific terms. Without deriding the importance of science one bit, Santayana takes away its privileged position by showing the ways in which natural happiness triumphs as much through common conversation, social movements, religious festivities and stories, and artistic endeavors as through the explanation, prediction, and control of events. All these things help people manage the difficulties of finitude, the problems of suffering, absurdity, and evil, encounters with the uncontrolled and the uncontrollable, and so all of them are vehicles of joy. "Every solution to a doubt, in so far as it is not a new error, every practical achievement not neutralized by a second maladjustment consequent upon it, every consolation not the seed of another greater sorrow, may be gathered and built into this edifice" of reason (LR, 1:6).

But, from Santayana's vantage point, the schools of modern philosophy positively impede reasonable life. Nineteenth-century idealists and liberal theologians tried to revive the corpse of supernaturalism while their naturalistic opponents, the positivists, aped theology by claiming the same sort of objectivity and looking for the same sort of superscientific knowledge to defend such things. Born of the problems of finitude and of the quest for mortal joy, they have all capitulated to fanaticism, redoubling their effort after forgetting their aim.

Intellectual Statesmanship

Santayana's understanding of philosophy as intimately connected to republican moral and civic concerns is not news from nowhere. I have already noted that, traditionally, Harvard philosophers had been concerned professionally with civic polity. They continued to be, even when James and Royce redirected the profession of philosophy in disciplinary rather than civic ways. Philosophers like James and Royce ended up wearing two hats: one in which they spoke public discourse, the other in which they debated technical issues with colleagues. They used the language of republican statesmanship, the language of leadership bent on forging one commonwealth out of many interests, to characterize their role as public figures.

In part, this professional self-conception had been inherited from previous generations. Ever since the endowment of the Alford Professorship of Natural Theology, Moral Philosophy, and Civic Polity, at least, moral philosophers at Harvard had pictured themselves as formulating social policies. Indeed, they had viewed themselves as sitting in judgment over the various enterprises and institutions of culture, somewhat in the manner of tribunes or magistrates. Although much of their effort had been devoted to the technical defense of theism and Christian conscience, this work functioned as a means of bolstering judicious statements awarding seats of intellectual authority and establishing both the privileges and responsibilities of this or that party to cultural dispute. They had seen their mastery of natural theology and moral philosophy as equipping them with definitive procedures and canons of judgment that let them authorize policies relevant to the public welfare. Francis Bowen, one of Santayana's own teachers, embodied this sort of philosophical tribunal.[1]

Bowen retired after nearly fifty years of service the same year that Santayana became an instructor. But throughout his career, philosophy at Harvard was still invariably captured by the idea that both spiritual well-being and moral life were secure only so long as there was a way for people to describe themselves as standing in an immediate relation to God and/or his creation.[2]

The Alford Professorship provides a key to historical interpretation in this respect. Its three parts were related in a nested way. The formulation of civic policy presupposed a specification of "the moral sense" that directly revealed man's obligations to God. In a polity ordered from the ground up, public security depended upon a display of public virtue, which in turn relied upon the disciplines of personal virtue. This task in turn presupposed a reasonable defense of theism, indeed the sort of theism that provided the right background assumptions for assent to moral sense theory.

In my view, neither of Santayana's most influential teachers and colleagues, James and Royce, ever entirely gave up the quest for the nonhuman ground of truth (Royce) or moral significance (James) that Bowen sought. But both highlighted the republican more than the Christian element in their Christian republican background by emphasizing contributions to community more than original revelation in their writings on moral philosophy (neither making much of Christ as deity).[3]

For example, Royce often compares the office of the philosopher to that of the "great statesman" in *The Religious Aspect of Philosophy* (1885), where he identifies the "warfare of human aims" as *itself* calling into question, or at least confusing, the significance of human life. Royce claims that answering the question whether life is worth living depends, in great part, on successful "reconciliation" of these diverse human aims.[4] But departing from tradition, Royce suggests that philosophers are not so much tribunes as mediators who articulate principles of compromise. They do not issue verdicts but provide disciplined ways for different "interests" to understand one another well enough to settle their own disputes.

Royce assumes that well-being can be reached: "The highest good," he argues, "would be attainable if all the conflicting wills realized fully one another. For then, not abandoning each its own aim, each would have added thereto, through insight, the aims of the others."[5] This line of thinking eventually leads Royce to claim that divinity itself is that ongoing community of republican compromise to which people contribute their best selves.[6]

James is even more emphatic about philosophy as intellectual statesmanship in "The Moral Philosopher and the Moral Life" (1891). There, he, too, pictures the task of the moral philosopher as analogous to that of a republican statesman counseling potentially conflicting parties on how to reach compromise for the sake of public peace or harmony. Indeed, James breaks away from the search for moral objectivity, opting instead to highlight republican solidarity.

Whether a philosopher argues for theistic idealism or not (and, at this point, when he is as Roycean as he will ever get, he is inclined to), James claims that the quest to discover a Moral Law validating the worth of this or that way of thinking and acting is "either an out and out superstition, or else it must be treated as a merely provisional abstraction from that real Thinker in whose actual demand upon us to think as he does our obligation must be ultimately based."[7] In either case, adherence to objective (in the sense of nonhuman) moral truth plays no role in making life worth living. Responsibility to one another in community (including, James hopes, another who supernaturally thinks in some way that includes everybody else's thoughts and who commands their allegiance) provides the larger context in which to reflect about such things.

Here is the heart of intellectual statesmanship, Jamesian style, which will become Santayana's style as well: "Take any demand," James argues,

which any creature, however weak, may make. Ought it not, for its own sole sake, to be satisfied? If not, prove why not. The only possible proof you could adduce would be the exhibition of another creature who should make a demand that ran the other way. The only possible reason there can be why any phenomenon ought to exist is that such a phenomenon is actually desired. Any desire is imperative to the extent of its amount; it makes itself valid by the fact that it exists at all. Some desires, truly enough, are small desires; they are put forward by insignificant persons, and we customarily make light of the obligations which they bring. But the fact that such personal demands as these impose small obligations does not keep the largest obligations from being personal demands.[8]

Indeed, James argues, "we see not only that without a claim actually made by some concrete person there can be no obligation, but that there is some obligation wherever there is a claim."[9] Obligation properly emerges out of shared affections or desires, much as British predecessors like Shaftesbury, Hutcheson, Edwards, and Burke had claimed.

Now James is not just saying, dumbly, "let a thousand claims or obligations bloom." But he is saying "there is no a priori morality, no morality prior to people making one or claiming one." He is also saying "every moral claim is addressed in a social form: To make a moral claim is to make a proposal binding us." I *ought* to help the bag lady across the street, James is saying, just when I as one of us am disposed intentionally to do so. If I say you ought to do this, I am proposing that we dispose ourselves to this intention. Finally, James is also saying something about reciprocal recognition that has consequences for moral thinking and criticism. Here emphasis falls on the term "wherever." He is saying, seek out and recognize claims as proposals for us, where "us" includes the one(s) making the proposal (James wants to add, no matter how nonconforming) and those who hear it; then bring what powers of discernment and judgment you have to bear, and decide whether the claim (no matter how nonconforming) better enables the humankind we know about to flourish than other, competing claims.

For both Royce and James, then, the point of moral life is to realize the federal republican principle, *e pluribus unum*, one out of many. This is the case for Santayana as well. Morality emerges, he asserts, "out of all the extant forces of human nature and [moral effort aims to establish] a perfect harmony among them" (*LR*, 1:23). For all three, social responsibilities emerge out of desires; moral virtues or practices function to satisfy these desires. Despite the different lines of thought each eventually pursues, they all begin with two assumptions about the good life. First, the sole and sufficient reason why something is good is the fact that it is felt to be good. Second, there are many and diverse actual feelings of good. In the face of this pluralistic assumption, the idea of philosophers standing above parties to cultural dispute judging them according to a priori standards seems spiritually and morally repugnant.

Moreover, as Timothy Sprigge has pointed out, this way of thinking carries with it the notion that "someone cannot truly grasp the fact that something is a value for someone without it becoming something of a value for oneself. Such a grasp coincides with imaginative reproduction of the way things look to the other, and this necessarily brings with it the associated connations."

"From this it follows," Sprigge argues, "that the more one grasps the ideal colors in which things look to others the more one will take as one's aim the joint realization of as many of these values as possible in a single harmony. The essential point is that nothing anyone values is condemned as such, only, at most, as the realization of other values."[10]

Santayana puts it this way: To represent an interest "means to intend, as far as possible, to secure the particular good which that particular interest looks to, and never, whatever measures may be adopted, to cease to look back on the elementary impulse as upon something which ought, if possible, to have been satisfied, and which we should still go back and satisfy now, if circumstances and the claims of rival interests permitted" (LR, 3:215–16).

Commitment to this view helps make possible a shift in the philosopher's identity from tribune to mediator or statesman. So, of course, does Charles Eliot's reorganization of the Harvard faculty into autonomous departments and his introduction of an elective curriculum that dismantles the old status of philosophy as culturally preeminent and decisive.

Representative Authority

Here is Santayana's civic republicanism in a nutshell: "The ultimate ideal, in order to maintain its finality and preclude the possibility of an appeal which should dislodge it from its place of authority, must have taken all interests into consideration; it must be universally representative" (LR, 3:215). Santayana expresses particular urgency about maintaining, reconstructing, and in some sense restoring the life of the spirit in his republican culture for two basic reasons. For one thing, it is his view, certainly not uncommon among his colleagues at Harvard at any rate, that people simply do not have any clear vision of the things that bring life joy or make it worth living. They suffer from moral weightlessness and spiritual vapidity as a result. For another, and conse-quently, the ordinances, rules, and rules of thumb that organize personal and social activities are, from all he can tell, disconnected from sources of joy, or randomly related to them. So (as Oliver Alden eventually will put it in *The Last Puritan*) people are left feeling "curiously unreal."

Santayana, along with the rest of his colleagues at Harvard, thinks that philosophers, serving as intellectual statesman, can help resolve this problem. First, they can diagnose the causes of it. Second, they can tackle the difficulty of moral and spiritual diversity attending the particular sort of culture they serve. Third, they can present representative visions of the things that make life worth living and show how the institutions and practices of public and private life can be organized to make them possible.

Santayana, then, plainly couches "interpretation" in a republican idiom. He pictures the sense of duty or the virtues as growing out of, and subserving, a plurality of interests or desires at work in culture. "Virtue" or "duty" do not simply *oppose* or constrain interests or desires. The nature of true virtue, living a genuinely good and happy life, involves representation of the interests and desires extant in "the human commonwealth."

So on the view of philosophy that Santayana shares with his Harvard colleagues, philosophy plays an important social role. It contributes to a better public life by providing some intellectual representation or vision of the things that make life significant for humanity in its plurality; and it gives people the breadth and disciplines of mind to settle disputes over contending interests and desires satisfactorily enough to let justice and public peace prevail.

Philosophy understood this way will inevitably tackle all sorts of technical, theoretical issues. But as the voice of reason, it does not just engage in syllogistic exercises. To the contrary, it shows reason as a form of communicative life (the way, say, Habermas now does), a life that philosophers frankly model. Even at its most contemplative, philosophy is a practice, a way of living well, a way of conversing geared to redound to the benefit of the human community.

As Santayana understands it, at any rate, at the heart of republican criticism is the idea that people should consider themselves responsible and answerable to one another rather than to something transcending the human community. This involves departure from the theological part of philosophy as it had been practiced in an earlier Christian republican United States.[11] Santayana's rendition of philosophy as representative, anyhow, assumes not only that reason is a form of life but also that reasonable life is natural and historical all the way along. Hence the *moral* need, at any rate, to break through the corruptions of time to eternal truth or reason makes no sense. Representative reason demands a sort of immanent criticism. By picturing publicly virtuous life as growing out of shared interests and desires that are originally gratuitous, it places both grace and law in culture, simply abandoning the hopes of orthodox Christians who wait for a gracious God to displace an indelibly fallen world with one in which humankind can truly flourish.

Naturalism in The Life of Reason

Three things make interpretation in *The Life of Reason* postromantic: its naturalism, its pragmatism, and its insistence on religious virtues geared to curb the pretensions of human self-assertion. Like the romantics, Santayana redescribes the varieties of discourse as so many vocabularies imaginatively deployed to express human aspirations, solve human problems, and manage human difficulties. But unlike the romantics Santayana completely rejects any transcendental project in *The Life of Reason*. He characterizes reason as a "form of life" (*LR*, 1:23) constituted by social practices and institutions rather than as a link to some creative ground of being; and he tries to break the back of natural supernaturalism both by ridiculing the idea that humanity is divinity incarnate and by celebrating the memories and aspirations of humankind, rooted as it is in a "world which was not made for [it] but in which [it] grew" (*LR*, 5:85).

The naturalism of *The Life of Reason* emerges out of the "wistful materialism" that Santayana had proposed in *Lotze's System of Metaphysics* in 1889, that he had developed in *The Sense of Beauty* seven years later, and that he had maintained in *Interpretations of Poetry and Religion* in 1900. The major difference is that, in 1905, Santayana increasingly emphasizes the view that social practices and institutions form the natural life of the human spirit. Common sense, society, religion, art, and science each provide habits of mind, heart, and will that hold modern republican culture together.

Thus, as with his earlier wistful materialism, Santayana rejects the notion that philosophy is geared to provide incorrigible "first principles" upon which to build a sure and certain picture of things that will answer the question, What makes life worth living? On Santayana's account, "religion and philosophy are not always beneficent or important, but when they are, it is precisely because they help to develop human faculties and enrich human life. To imagine that by means of them we can escape from human nature and survey it from without is an ostrich-like illusion obvious to all but to the victim of it" (*LR*, 1:273). The natural disciplines of culture make human life worth living, not one of them alone but all of them together. And all of them together constitute a tradition into which individuals are born and bred.[12] The varieties of discourse and practice work well enough without having to rely on any distinctively philosophical standards. Santayana asserts that "the transcendental philosophy, in spite of its self-esteem," adds nothing "essential" to the garden variety of cultural criticisms (*LR*, 1:29). Transcendentalist efforts to *oppose* reason to traditionally informed cultural practices are futile.

The thing that makes such traditions natural, Santayana claims, is their grounding in the contingent interests or affections actually avowed by people. There is nothing necessary or inevitable about traditions. They are chances: contingent, variable, and modifiable forms of life sensitive to the wants and needs, interests and impulses, of the people populating them, living as they do in demanding environments.

The philosopher, then, does not hanker after illusive first principles. Santayana calls himself a "chronicler of human progress." His task is to evaluate how, and how well, important parts of culture contribute to our welfare, and to propose or "plot" ways that things might go better (*LR*, 1:8–9). He estimates "events in reference to the moral ideal which they embodied or betrayed" (*LR*, 5:58). He does so recognizing that his moral standards serve as abbreviations for living human interests, materialized in practices, and also that "under other conditions other ideals, no less legitimate, may have arisen and may have been made the standard for a different judgment on the world" (*LR*, 5:58–59). Indeed, in Santayana's view, such "spontaneous variations" (*LR*, 5:104) might yet happen; they almost surely will; so it is futile to try to "foresee what ultimate form the good might some day take" (*LR*, 5:59).

This proposition about human life and the role philosophers may play in it might depress many people, Santayana suggests, if they are "in the habit of believing in special providences" that extract them from the contingent dangers of nature, or expect "to continue [their] romantic adventures in a second life" (*LR*, 5:89). Such people might well feel, at least for a time, that they had "nothing left to live for" in a world as contingent as the one Santayana pictures (*LR*, 5:90). But a thorough naturalist or "materialist," Santayana advises, "one born to the faith and not half plunged into it by an unexpected christening in cold water, will be like the superb Democritus, a laughing philosopher" (*LR,* 5:90). A naturalist no longer haunted by supernaturalism can find the promise of the world enchanting, without grasping at the straws held out by super-naturalism or metaphysics.

Anybody bred into the older theological or romantic cultures in the West was virtually bound to have a picture of human success or fulfillment that made Santayana's naturalism look bleak. But as Santayana redescribes things, those older cultures held out false pictures of success and fulfillment. "Every solution to a doubt, in so far as it is not a new error," he now claims, "every practical achievement not neutralized by a second maladjustment consequent upon it, every consolation not the seed of another greater sorrow" can be gathered together to articulate a joyful life—one in which the human spirit flourishes (*LR,* 1:6).

To be sure, Santayana's natural world includes "the genuine sufferings of living creatures" (*LR,* 5:90). In fact, it is true that his naturalism predicts "an ultimate extinction for man and all his works." But "the panic which seems to seize some minds at the thought of a merely natural existence is something truly hysterical." It is not "mechanical science that introduced mutability into things nor materialism that invented death" (*LR,* 5:92–93). Naturalists just take cognizance of such conditions without blinking and then urge people to realize that "the reasonable and humane demand to make of the world is that such creatures as exist should not be unhappy and that life, whatever its quantity, should have a quality that may justify it in its own eyes" (*LR,* 5:94).

Santayana's naturalism makes suffering look mean and tries to disclose ways to overcome it. But it holds out no way to overcome misery once and for all. Given the ways of the world, he claims, it cannot because, as he puts it,

adjustments in it are tentative, and much friction must proceed and follow upon a vital equilibrium attained. This imperfection, however, is actual, and no theory can overcome it except by verbal fallacies and scarcely deceptive euphemisms. What [natural historical] mechanism involves in this respect is exactly what we find: a tentative appearance of life in many quarters, its disappearance in some, and its reinforcement and propagation in others, where the physical equilibrium attained in-sures to it a natural stability and a natural prosperity. (*LR,* 5:94)

Santayana's point is this: Well-being occurs, not always, not often, but memorably; and it rests on a long and complex string of sheer historical contingencies, among which the actions and passions of human beings must be counted. But being natural, human well-being cannot possibly be anything other than historically contingent.

Natural Mentality

Philosophers, like John Dewey and A. W. Moore, who otherwise celebrated Santayana's work in *The Life of Reason* as a profound naturalistic reconstruction of moral philosophy, balked at one crucial point. Bent on showing that thought played a indispensable role in the transformation of nature and society, Dewey and Moore could not stomach Santayana's claim that the human mind is a natural "epiphenomenon." They could readily agree that "nature was the sum total of its own conditions" and that "the mind was a part of this complex" (*LR*, 1:103). They could also agree that "consciousness [is] the expression of bodily life and the seat of all its values" and that "thought [is] a link in the chain of natural events" (*LR*, 1:207–8).

Santayana, however, goes on to claim that the human mind understood as *consciousness* amounts to a kind of caused event that has no causal efficacy. Echoing assertions James had made in *Principles of Psychology*, especially contentions about emotions, Santayana argues that "mental transformations are indeed signs of changes in bodies; and so long as a cause is defined merely as a sign, mental and physical changes may truly be said to cause one another. But so soon as this form of augury tries to overcome its crude empiricism, and to establish phenomenal laws, the mental factor has to fall out of the efficient process and be represented there by what, upon accurate examination, it is seen to be really the sign of—I mean by some physiological event" (*LR*, 1:211).

A. W. Moore, in particular, argued that Santayana seems to want things both ways.[13] Santayana, he pointed out, claims on the one hand that "reason" or "intelligence" should be defined as "reflection . . . applicable in action," thus apparently portraying mind as instrumental (*LR*, 1:5). But he claims, on the other, that "thought is nature's concomitant expression or entelechy, never one of her instruments," thereby denying instrumentalism and suggesting that consciousness is not efficacious at all (*LR*, 1:223).

There is no getting around the fact that Santayana's use of terms to consider this problem concerning the relation of "mind" to "body" is vexed and slippery, especially in *The Life of Reason* in which he has not yet distinguished "psyche" or intelligence that is instrumental, from "spirit" or consciousness, which may (but may not) reflect or signal such intelligence without itself being instrumental in any other way.

To my mind, especially in light of the way he links thought to language in *Reason in Science*, Santayana would have been better off distinguishing two kinds of explanations or accounts, one relying on an adequate explication of the intentions, interests, values, and ideas a person has in mind that motivates her to do something; the other relying on a clarification of physiological factors at work in material changes that take place consequent to intelligent behavior. It is not clear to me what is gained by searching for some third explanation that attempts to fit these accounts together, because they have distinctive aims: the telling of personal stories on the one hand and the prediction of cause-and-effect relations that govern the behavior of physiological or physical stuff on the other.

What does Santayana claim about thought and language in *Reason in Science* (in all probability written subsequent, and perhaps consequent, to Moore's criticism)? The most striking thesis that Santayana presents in this book concerns the status of thought (or more perspicuously, the status of thought with intent) and comes in an explication of his expressivism. "The uttered word," Santayana asserts, "produces an obvious commotion in nature; through it thought, being expressed in that its material basis is extended outward, becomes at the same moment rational and practical; for its expression enters into the chain of its future conditions and becomes an omen of that thought's continuance, repetition, and improvement. . . . *Expression makes thought a power in the very world from which thought drew its being*" (LR, 5:180, emphasis added). This is the way that thought comes to matter, that is, the way it makes a practical difference in the world.

While this insight suggests the expressiveness of thought, taken alone it remains unclear whether Santayana is claiming that uttered words express some sort of prelinguistic thought or, to the contrary, that uttered words or languages *constitute* thought. But he clarifies that issue posthaste. Much as James had argued in "What is an emotion?"—that behavioral patterns (for example, crying) constituted the emotions they were said to express (for example, sadness)—Santayana now argues that "*Words underlie the thought they are said to express—in truth it is the thought that is the flower and expression of the language—much as the body underlies the mind*" (LR, 5:181). The "force of language," Santayana concludes, "is just as empirical as the reality of things" (LR, 5:183, emphasis added). It is "an overt phenomenon, linked observably with all other objects and processes" (LR, 5:181).[14]

As an expressivist, Santayana denies (in Sabina Lovibond's words), "the logical priority of thought over the language in which it is made manifest."[15] Thought is inseparable from the language, which is its physical manifestation. Language is therefore not simply a medium for thought; it is false to think of it as an instrument by which to get (presumably) prelinguistic thought from the inside out. There is no prelinguistic thought. Using language is the way thought goes on.

Moreover, in Santayana's view, language or thought is a transmissible convention, a social practice. It is an activity that must be emulated and repeated. In other words, it must be learned, like training in carpentry must be learned. Thought, manifested in language, is embedded in a life that is shared in material ways. It is essentially communicative. Here is Santayana's example:

A thirsty man . . . begs for a drink. Had his petition been a wordless desire it might have been supposed, though falsely, to be a disembodied and quite immaterial event, a transcendental attitude of will, without conditions or consequences, but somehow with an absolute moral dignity. But when the petition becomes articulate and audible to a fellow-mortal, who thereupon proceeded to fetch a cup of water, the desire, through the cry it expressed, obviously asserted itself in the mechanical world, to which it already secretly belonged by virtue of its cause, a parched body. (LR, 5:181)

Thought, in this vision, is inextricably a matter of articulation and audibility between and among social beings sharing the same language in the same environments, and the meaning that this or that thought has is determined through its communicative function or use (though, note well, in Santayana's view, not every communication functions to transform the material and social environments). The thinker is a speaker, and the speaker, first and foremost, is making contact with others in the same speech community.

This explicates Santayana's claim that "the intellect's essence is practical" (*LR*, 5:172), embodied in the social institutions of common sense, politics, religion, art, and science, each and all of which are fundamentally communicative. But does it undercut the epiphenomenalism with which he started?

Not necessarily. Santayana's aim in defending epiphenomenalism is to resist simultaneously two conclusions about "mind." One is that personal conscious-ness or *reflection* does not exist at all. The other is that consciousness is all that exists. Reductive or eliminative materialists claim the former. Idealists claim the latter. His claim is that reflection does indeed exist, but that *apart from its communicative function*, it is powerless as, say, dreams are powerless. In fact it is "dreaming awake." This may strain some intuitions that some people hold about the force of thinking, but it is less unsettling than the views with which it competes.[16]

Just how physical events can cause immaterial, causally inert moments of consciousness is something Santayana never makes clear. But in his own view, he is not equipped to do so. The issue is "a question for the natural sciences to solve" (*LR*, 1:209). Neurophysiologists may clarify how things go in this regard sometime, but philosophers have no special knowledge to add to such an account.

So, to Santayana's credit, it may well be, as John Lachs has put it, that his epiphenomenalism is "the least inadequate solution" available to the mind-body problem, so long as that problem is taken seriously.[17] In Santayana's version of that problem, reflection is a physically engendered, ongoing "*tran-script*" (*LR*, 1:213, emphasis added) of behavior that matters; a *function* of cerebral patterns of behavior that does not transform anything in particular.

As he will eventually put it in his squabbles with Dewey, "For a naturalist, nothing can be substantial or efficacious in thought except its organs and instruments, such as brains, training, words, and books." But the most impor-tant thing to Santayana is this: Thought is *more* than "brains, training, words, and books." "Actual thought," he claims, "being invisible and imponderable, eludes this sort of chase"; actual thought amounts to the apprehension of immaterial things like "names, aspects, functions" ("DNM," 344).

More than anything else, I believe, Santayana's epiphenomenalism is an attempt to explicate not only the *occurrence* of thinking that leads nowhere else in particular (so is not instrumental), but the important role that thinking, understood this way, plays in the experience of human well-being. From moral and spiritual vantage points, Santayana believes, the sort of thought most "worth having" is quite literally the end of power or transformation. This is the point of his saying that "Spirit is useless, being the end of things; but it is not vain, since it alone rescues all else from vanity" (LR, 1:212).

In *The Life of Reason*, Santayana continues to claim that well-being occurs in reflective episodes of consummate joy that *give point* to things, that let people mind about matter, that *symbolize* the meaningfulness or value that existence has for them, that leaves them feeling triumphant rather than defeated or brutalized or just unreal—all in the clear light of their material finitude, their *inability* to transform basic conditions on which they depend, their ultimate impotence and eventual annihilation. This is why he presses his point that "a bodily feat, like nutrition or reproduction, is celebrated by a festival in the mind, and consciousness is a sort of ritual solemnizing by prayer, jubilation, or mourning, the chief episodes in the body's fortunes" (LR, 1:213). That makes thought "essentially practical in the sense that but for thought no motion would be an action, no change a progress; but thought is in no way instrumental or servile; it is an experience realized, not a force to be used" (LR, 1:213–14).

Pragmatism in The Life of Reason

I have already noted that Arthur Kenyon Rogers was right on target when he claimed in 1906 (a year before James published *Pragmatism*) that *The Life of Reason* was the first attempt "to give any systematic expression to that new group of tendencies which, under the name of Pragmatism, or Humanism, is causing a ferment in the philosophical world at the present time."[18] F. C. S. Schiller in England and John Dewey, fast rising as a philosophical star of great magnitude, rather immediately echoed Rogers's view.[19] Horace Kallen, writing in 1911, eventually came closest to the mark by characterizing *The Life of Reason* as an instance of "Epiphenomenalistic Pragmatism."[20] Santayana's presentation of philosophy as republican interpretation, his nontranscendent picture of reason as a form of life, a set of practices and institutions that organized interests in harmonious ways, and his linguistic expressivism combined with his nonfoundationalist construal of knowledge and his epiphenomenalist characterization of spirit or consciousness to make the work pragmatic or humanistic.

Knowledge Is Nonfoundational

Santayana actually waffles between two discrete reflections on knowledge in *The Life of Reason*, one in which he attempts, badly, to naturalize epistemology the way, say, Quine tries to do in *The Roots of Reference* and elsewhere, and another in which he works out consequences for understanding knowledge from a traditionalist starting point. To my mind, both of these considerations are lacking in lucidity. For any philosopher looking to a discussion of knowledge as the heart of philosophy (something for which I do not look), this part of Santayana's work would be sufficient to warrant G. E. Moore's judgment that "this book is so wanting in clearness of thought that I doubt whether it can be of much use to anyone."[21]

The first and most vexing line of thought about knowledge that Santayana introduces places it in the framework of sensations, perceptions, and judgments. The second and less question-begging one makes knowledge a matter of inference from particular reasons to relevant conclusions. The sensation model leaves Santayana preoccupied with how thoughts and things are latched together once they become distinguishable. The most implausible part of his answer to this distinctively epistemological question is his notion that individuals first sense (or perceive) discrete qualities, like hardness, roundness, redness, and sweetness and then, through some sort of mental "chemistry," they sense "concreted" objects, like cherries, out of those characteristics.

This line of thinking, with its metaphors of mental chemistry, is neither good physiological psychology nor adequate sociology of education. It is an effort to rehearse the thinking of children emerging into awareness in an empathetic way. But Santayana gives no reasons for his claims about the priority of discrete qualities in the order of knowledge acquisition, nor any details about the supposed chemistry at work to solidify objects out of their characteristics (but then one is led to wonder how he reasonably could, without falling into incredible talk about some fiction like "mind stuff"). To the contrary, he simply confuses a sound logical point—that things are reidentifiable in terms of their characteristics—with a psychological view that contradicts all the observations suggesting that children learn to identify, say, cherries, long before they develop a capacity to note their discrete characteristics.

Santayana's motive for telling this story about the origin of the link between "ideas" and "things," is not, however, to lay down some rock-bottom ground on which to build the rest of knowledge. In all probability, rather, it is to safeguard a difference between two sorts of discourse in order to ward off any reductive metaphysical materialism and idealism: I think that this is the spirit in which he asserts, for example, that "a quality is recognized by its own idea or permanent nature, a thing by its constituent qualities" (LR, 1:183). The claim is that ordinary objects of observation are "concretions in existence" that fuse together various and changing neutral stuff in repetitive and consecutive ways, whereas qualities are "concretions in discourse" or fictive terms that are practically important as they become indicative of the stuff with which people have to contend.

But, making such assertions, Santayana keeps slipping into the quicksand of phenomenalism. Raw experience, he claims, impresses people with the "sensuous material" on which both "ideas" and "things" depend. For example, he argues, "the perception which, recurring in different objects otherwise not retained in memory gives the idea of roundness, is the same perception which helps to constitute the spatial concretion called the sun" (LR, 1:167–68). On the one hand, such assertions seem to imply that both thoughts and things emerge out of perceptions that are "neutral" as between subjectivity and objectivity (the claim at the heart of James's radical empiricism). On the other, Santayana makes a host of claims, as we have seen, positing a natural, material world existing prior to, and apart from, any imaginative activity or raw experience. He argues at points that "real" material stuff or processes cause perceptions to appear and that these perceptions, which are imaginative or mental, in turn ground knowledge claims. But he argues at other points that real material stuff is just as ideal or as symbolic as the perceptions it is said to cause.

Tangles like this tend to vindicate G. E. Moore's caustic remarks about *The Life of Reason*'s worthlessness. They make it look like Santayana has an interest in classical philosophical disputes about knowledge and being, or mind and "the world out there." But he gives no clear signal about where he stands in this respect. He seems to straddle idealism and realism on the status of material stuff or the world out there, as well as between empiricism and rationalism on questions concerning the justification of knowledge claims. Moreover, while he holds out the promise of showing how thoughts link up with things, his speculations about the growth and development of mentality never establish any answer to questions about how to bridge the chasm between presumptively subjective ideas and objective realities, or how to tell, in any decidedly epistemological way, the difference between fact and fiction.

There is a way to read Santayana's speculations about the natural history of mentality in a better light, however, as critics like Dewey, Schiller, and Rogers actually did. To do this, however, these readers had to deny the importance of questions that inform a good deal of traditional philosophical discussion of knowledge and being, and to excuse Santayana for asking them. Moreover, they had to accept Santayana's thought as turning from metaphysics to culture in the physical universe as well as from the search for foundational knowledge to an attempt to achieve a practically satisfactory and humane understanding of things. Finally, they had to place knowledge in the logical space of reasons rather than sensations and perceptions.

This was possible because the better part of *The Life of Reason* assumes, as had Santayana's previous writing, James's natural historical point of view. Santayana pictures human individuals as situated in distinctive traditions or cultures, which, in turn, are set in physical environments predictable in terms of theoretical entities that scientists are trained to posit.

On this view, the language of material stuff that explains physical experience is no less a language for being explanatory; and the stuff is no less material for being posited indicatively in a language. Every observation a person makes assumes all sorts of principles and protocols of logic and communication that nobody exactly "senses," so it is impossible, except for analytic purposes, to differentiate the basic facts on which classical empiricists hope to ground knowledge. But the categories and standards that people use to organize their understanding of things not only vary but also increase in variability the more intelligence develops. So it is impossible to find a constitutive reason pure or privileged enough to escape critical jeopardy, the way classical rationalists and Kantian critical philosophers want to do.

Sure enough, Santayana claims, "logical forms of thought impregnate and constitute practical intellect," which proceeds *both* by interpreting particular observations in terms of general principles *and* by checking general principles against particular observations (*LR*, 1:176). But "if the common mistake of empiricism is not to see the omnipresence of reason in thought, the mistake of rationalism is not to admit its variability and dependence, not to understand its natural life" (*LR*, 1:177).

Thinking, in Santayana's expressivist version, is not simply spectatorial but active, a dynamic interplay between our "rational expectations," or what we generally believe, and "the shock of experience," or the particular events we observe that confirm or disturb such general beliefs. "The shock of experience can indeed correct, disappoint, or inhibit rational expectation," Santayana argues, "but it cannot take its place. . . . To observe its defeat is already to give it a new embodiment" (*LR*, 1:176).[22] This line of thinking, rather than the just-so story about mental chemistry, informs Santayana's criticisms of canonical figures in the modern Western philosophical tradition, especially Berkeley, Hume, and Kant.

"We may construct," Santayana says, "a theory as disintegrating as we please about the dialectical or the empirical conditions of the experience given; we may disclose its logical stratification or physical antecedents; but every idea and principle used in such a theory must be borrowed from current knowledge as it happens to lie in the philosopher's mind" (*LR*, 5:36). There is no evasion of dogmatism in this weak sense, no avoiding human opinion, no *scientia* that opposes *opinio*. On the contrary, in Santayana's view, our thought is imaginative all the way along: "In imagination, not in perception, lies the substance of experience, while knowledge and reason are but its chastened and ultimate form." Knowledge and reason should be construed, he says, as "forms of imagination happily grown significant" (*LR*, 1:50). There is no escaping the human: Knowledge proceeds dialectically by way of opinion, not by overcoming it.

Efforts to establish unshakably basic facts or more invariant principles and protocols were not only fruitless but typically motivated by malice toward disputed ways of thinking that had functional roles to play. The background assumptions both of a physical world and of a battery of languages to signify human life as part of it were indispensable. Rationalists and empiricists erred "only in denouncing the other and wishing to be omnivorous, as if on the one hand logic could make anybody understand the history of events and the conjunction of objects, or on the other as if cognitive and moral processes could have any other terms than constant and ideal natures" (*LR*, 1:182).

The key to understanding the failures of the philosophical tradition, Santayana argues, lay in the classical and Christian quests for direct contact with reality outside the bailiwick of human conventions. The pretense of escaping human nature, he asserts, "may cause admiration in the schools, where self-hypnotization is easy, but in the world it makes its professors look ridiculous. For in their eagerness to empty their mind of human prejudices they reduce its rational burden to a minimum, and if they still continue to dogmatize, it is sport for the satirist to observe what forgotten accident of language or training has survived the crash of the universe and made the one demonstrable path to Absolute Truth" (LR, 1:273–74).

Reason in Common Sense, read along this natural historical track, commends a radical turn away from the search for nature's own language. Instead, Santayana argues, people should accept the fact that human conventions or traditions of discourse and practice are natural: Human beings are less than half-formed without their ability to signify things and to express themselves in light of their customary practical ideals. Without conventional symbolization, they are more helpless than monkeys.

This does not mean, however, that adequate information is beyond human ken. "Neither the path of abstraction," Santayana argues

nor that of direct and . . . unbiased observation . . . can lead beyond that region of common experience, traditional feeling, and conventional thought which all minds enter at birth and can elude only at the risk of inward collapse and extinction. The fact that observation involves the senses, and the senses their organs, is one which a naturalist can hardly overlook; and when we add that logical habits, sanctioned by utility, are needed to interpret the data of sense, the humanity of science and all its constructions become clearer than day. Superstition itself could not be more human. The path of unbiased observation is not a path away from conventional life; it is progress in conventions. It improves human belief by increasing the proportion of two of its ingredients, attentive perception and practical calculus. The whole resulting vision, as it is sustained from moment to moment by present experience and instinct, has no value apart from actual ideals. And if it proves human nature to be unstable, it can build that proof on nothing more stable than human faculty as at the moment it happens to be. (LR, 1:274)

This prominent pragmatism dwarfs the importance of Santayana's confused and confusing attempt to naturalize epistemology for two reasons: First, it pictures informed activity as resting on a fallible, corrigible, but practically satisfactory common sense—the forms of discourse articulating "common experience, traditional feeling, and conventional thought which all minds enter at birth and can elude only at the risk of inward collapse and extinction" (LR, 1:274). Foundational knowledge is neither available nor required. When disputes arise over this or that belief or set of beliefs, critics may show that and how their conclusions follow from good reasons—reasons not currently jeopardized or impugned by relevant debate; but that is all they need do to settle pertinent issues.

Second, Santayana implies, the way in which discrete thoughts or terms are linked to discrete qualities or things is a very subordinate concern, if one at all, from a pragmatic point of view—a problem hardly ever raised outside the context of the "special" philosophical disciplines bent on escaping from human conventions altogether. The important issue, from this vantage point, is not whether beliefs hook onto things or mirror them, but how beliefs and other patterns of thinking dispose people to make something of their circumstances in light of their interests and desires.

All that knowledge has to go on, Santayana claims, is evidence and inference: We can "look for all the evidence we choose before we declare our inference to be warranted; but we must not ask for something more than evidence, nor expect to know realities without inferring them anew. . . . We cannot cease to think and still continue to know" (LR, 1:77). But if this is the case, then it is "impossible to base science on a deeper foundation or to override it by a higher knowledge. What is called metaphysics, if not an anticipation of natural science, is a confusion of it with dialectic or a mixture of it with myths" (LR, 5:318).[23]

Institutional Pragmatism

Santayana's expressivism, his characterization of reason as immanent criticism, and his nonfoundational view of knowledge give him a strong family resemblance to pragmatists from Peirce and James through Dewey, all the way up to Goodman, Putnam, and Rorty. His squabbles with James and Dewey and his unwillingness to accept the label "pragmatist" have, for too long, obscured this fact.

The most distinctive thing about Santayana's brand of pragmatism is its focus on the life of reason as something constituted by institutions of social practice that harmonize diverse interests. "Reason as such," Santayana claims, "represents or rather constitutes a single formal interest, the interest in harmony. When two interests are simultaneous and fall within one act of apprehension the desirability of harmonizing them is involved in the very effort to realize them together. If attention and imagination are steady enough to face this implication and not to allow impulse to oscillate between two irreconcilable tendencies, reason comes into being. Henceforth things actual and things desired are confronted by an ideal which has both pertinence and authority" (*LR*, 1:268).

We talk about this sort of adjudication or coordination going on individually and privately at times, but whenever we do, we model our understanding of personal harmony on practices that occur publicly, socially, or politically in institutions, for example families, councils, parliaments, courts, or academic seminars. In fact, consonant with his civic humanism, Santayana pictures the life of reason in fundamentally political terms: He claims that his five books are essentially exercises in "retrospective politics" (*LR*, 5:58); that a rational life is a "rational polity" (*LR*, 5:230); and that "representation" or "representative" completeness carries philosophical authority (*LR*, 5:253). The philosopher, Santayana asserts, is parliamentary. He has "the gift of conversation." He does not pretend "to legislate from the throne of Jehovah about the course of affairs" but asks "the ingenuous heart to speak for itself, guiding and checking it only in its own interest" (*LR*, 5:208).[24]

So, in Santayana's view, common sense, society, religion, art, and science—all as subject to variation and modification in structure as humankind itself is—not only embody distinctive passions or interests, but serve to bind one another critically without being bound by anything outside or beneath cultural life. Each institution has proper roles to serve because each has determinable interests to satisfy or difficulties to manage. Each is subject to criticism by the others, so long as those others are construing themselves properly: This is the thrust of his claim that "to rationalize an interest is simply to correlate it with every other interest which it at all affects" (*LR*, 2:118–19). So the life of reason is a process articulated not only by the standards internal to each sort of institution but also by the forms of critical interchange and exchange permitting compatibility among them.

It follows that, while Santayana agrees with Peirce, James, and Dewey that the best way to settle disputes about what counts as reasonable is to reflect on distinctive sorts of activity, his emphasis is somewhat different, because he does not reduce reason either to the overcoming of doubt (Peirce), or to the concomitant sentiment (James), or to the methods of the natural sciences (Dewey). All of these things play a role in *The Life of Reason*. But no one of them is definitive for Santayana; they are each instances or parts of reasonable life. There are other kinds of discord than doubt, other ways to resolve discord than method. For him, living rationally is primarily a matter of avowing and enacting particular forms of life, or institutions, that help to organize many potentially conflicting human desires and interests more or less harmoniously.

Santayana, to be certain, does not mean that institutional life is inevitably rational. Any particular institution can run amok. This happens, for example, when people forget the conventional status of common sense and let it obstruct investigations in the sciences or constrain flights of imagination indispensable to human festivity; or when people let or make governments curb liberal community, or design them as little else besides engines of industry or cruelty; or when fanaticism and superstition corrupt religious life; or when art becomes effete or collapses into nothing more than political propaganda; or when moral reflection leaves people absentminded; or when the life of learning becomes a cultural appendage randomly related to lived experience.

Santayana does mean, however, that living reasonably cannot be reduced to holding some particular web of belief, having some particular feeling associated with overcoming doubt, or maintaining a special method of thinking and acting. The life of reason involves social structures that are neither just cognitive or doctrinal nor simply methodical. The institutions of common sense, society, religion, art, and science or learning and reflection involve many patterns of thinking and practice that are affectional, expressive, and visionary as well as cognitive or doctrinal.

Indeed, in Santayana's view, in some crucial respects every institution of reason including both common language and the highest reaches of science involves departures from method; the life of reason involves explorations, trials by error, and whimsical mental and practical variation (or what Peirce had called "musement"). By no means can reasonable life be reduced to some artificial code of rules and regulations or method of argumentation. In virtually every institution, a crucial quality of reason is the disposition to depart from accepted methods, codes, and norms when such things turn out to obstruct the resolution of relevant problems and the management of persistent difficulties that stand in the way of the good life.

The Goal of Comprehensive Synthesis

It is important to point out that, if *The Life of Reason* is startlingly fresh for its naturalism and its pragmatism, it still exhibits Santayana's allegiance to an older philosophical goal, one embedded in his understanding of philosophical *representation* at this time, namely the ideal he eventually calls (in 1915, when he rejects it) "comprehensive synthesis" ("PH," 99). His aim, he says, is "to do justice to all extant interests," and in that sense he is not only committed to a Socratic free exchange of ideas, but also to the Platonic, and then Hegelian, ideal of universal agreement (*LR*, 1:255). He seeks to conceive "a harmony and cooperation of impulses . . . leading to the maximum satisfaction possible in the whole community of spirits affected by our action" on which everybody can agree (*LR*, 1:256).

Santayana, therefore, does not posture himself as an intellectual statesman representing American, or Anglo-American, or European, or even Western culture. The "we" for which he affects to speak or stand is humankind. He says he aims to be "a mouthpiece for the memory and judgment of his race" (*LR*, 1:2). To be sure, just as he abandons the search for some "absolute reality" on the grounds that it has no "function in the elucidation of phenomena," so he ridicules "a supreme good which was good for nobody" (*LR*, 1:260). The life of reason has to emerge out of "the actual demands of living beings," that is, out of the affections or interests of people with natures "fluid and imperfect." But in *The Life of Reason*, and in Hegel's shadow, Santayana is still seeking "finality," or the "Whole," or the "End," even if it inevitably eludes recognition, much less realization; he still imagines that there is some defensible way to speak authoritatively for humankind (not just in an authorial way to anybody interested in listening and responding critically) (*LR*, 1:260–61).

Even in this respect, to be sure, *The Life of Reason* departs from crucial assumptions traditionally identified with the Western philosophical tradition.

If Santayana still pursues what Milan Kundera has recently characterized as "the dream of paradise, the age-old dream of a world where everybody would live in harmony," he rejects the notion that such harmony depends on discovering (as Kundera has disparagingly put the conceit) that people are "united by a single will and faith, without secrets from one another."[25]

As Santayana pictures it, intellectual statesmanship begins by observing the diversity of conflicting desires—and not simply desires but the traditions of memory, practice, and aspiration that articulate them. Its aim is not to proclaim in a godlike voice the genuine "single will and faith" bonding humankind. Its goal is to suggest ways that the traditions embedded in the modern Western republics can live and let live.

So the philosopher in Santayana's *Life of Reason* still has something to do that is publicly critical: The intellectual statesman plays an important and beneficent part in realizing equilibrium among conflicting interests by suggesting the terms of peace. This suggested peace, inspired "by sympathy and by knowledge of the world, is the ideal, which borrows its force from the irrational impulses which it embodies, and borrows its final authority from the truth with which it recognizes them all and the necessity by which it imposes on each such sacrifices as are requisite to a general harmony" (*LR*, 1:265).

The interesting thing is that Santayana attempts to maintain this allegiance to "comprehensive synthesis" as a post-Darwinian, recognizing that the idea of one "core" human nature, present in both Greek philosophy and in Christianity, and still embraced by the Enlightenment, is dead. "Human nature," he knows, is "merely a name for a group of qualities found by chance in certain tribes of animals, a group to which new qualities are constantly tending to attach themselves while other faculties become extinct, now in whole races, now in sporadic individuals. Human nature is therefore a variable, and its ideal cannot have a greater constancy than the demands to which it gives expression" (*LR*, 1:270).

So his dream does not involve breaking through the appearance of human variability and mutability to some timeless soul of humanity shared across the boards. The sort of peace he thinks "reason" or the intellectual statesman can arrange requires no essential human nature. It requires enough continuity and coherence among the varieties of humankind for the powers of empathy, persuasion, and tolerance to work. Harmony or "moral solidarity" have to be negotiated because there is nothing gluing humanity together that makes it inevitable (*LR*, 1:278). The "bonds" people can find—say in their language, society, religion, art, or science—inevitably count lots of people out; inevitably, more inclusive ones have to be made out of those already found. "Spiritual unity," Santayana said, is not given; it "is a natural product"—a product made by the natural beings that are human (*LR*, 1:282).

Religion among the Institutions of a Republic

How does Santayana interpret religion in the context of his pragmatic life of reason? What makes religion good for the republic he aims to represent? What natural interests does it satisfy? And how does it hang together with other post-Enlightenment republican institutions?

In *The Life of Reason*, Santayana extends earlier proposals for a poetic religion of disillusion born of classical and Christian sources. Religion, he now claims, adds four virtues to republican life: the disciplines of piety, spirituality, charity, and "spiritualizing" practices he calls "ideal immortality." What do they add to the disciplines informing the institutions of common sense, society, art, and science?

As Santayana characterizes them, each of these institutions helps empower people to get what is in their best interests (and all of them overlap to some degree). Common sense, for example, lets people cope with mundane problems in pedestrian ways with some competence. The arts "make life better," first by "establishing instruments for human life beyond the human body, and molding outer things into sympathy with inner values," and finally by giving "free expression" to "the forms of our possible happiness" (*LR*, 5:13, 224–25). The physical and biological sciences posit theoretical entities that let people explain, predict, and, to some extent, control the environments in which they live; history transforms testimony into evidence about what has actually happened.

Social institutions like the family, the country, the state, industry, government, and war secure "the fortunes of particular bodies, natural or corporate" (*LR*, 2:137). They structure hierarchical and segmented orders of realistic power, authority, status, and wealth, by differentiating, for example, parents from children, rulers from subjects, owners and managers from laborers, officers from troops, and alliances from enemies. These social orders are good, Santayana claims, when and as they make secure and help to constitute "liberal life." They become corrupt whenever they transform natural and relative inequalities (for example, smart and dumb, wise and inexperienced, well-trained and mediocre, graceful and clumsy, eminent and normal) into structures of material or psychological domination and degradation. They instantiate reason by providing the material security, nurturing, rearing, schooling, and services required to let a people both treat one another justly and achieve the kinds of individual well-being that "impersonal" excellence—the transformation of "personalities" into "characters"—can bring.

Nothing is more telling about Santayana's understanding of society in *The Life of Reason* than his reflections on democracy and aristocracy. These reflections are, in many ways, deeply flawed by Santayana's failure to give any telling account of distinctively political action. Moreover, to the extent that they are marked by instances of racism, sexism, and classism, they are repulsive to a contemporary sensibility like mine.[26] But there are insights and values to appreciate here that shed light on Santayana's understanding of the role religion plays in civic life.

The first thing to note is that, for Santayana, social inequality is not the worst thing; suffering is. On the one hand, he claims, "it is no loss of liberty to subordinate ourselves to a natural leader. On the contrary, we thereby seize an opportunity to exercise our freedom, availing ourselves of the best instrument attainable to accomplish our ends. . . . So long . . . as by the operation of any causes whatever some real competence accrues to anyone, it is for the general interest that this competence should bear its natural fruits, diversifying the face of society and giving its possessor a corresponding distinction" (*LR*, 2:89–90). Indeed, "there is no greater stupidity or meanness than to take uniformity as an ideal. . . . Grant that no one is positively degraded by the great man's greatness and it follows that everyone is exalted by it" (*LR*, 2:90).

Hierarchical and differentiated structures, accordingly, are central to social and political life. They make up the rules, roles, and relationships realistically required to accomplish the work of socialization, economic productivity, civil or federal services, technological advance, and military preparedness.

With this in mind, along with his view that undeserved suffering is the worst thing, Santayana commends a *social* "aristocracy of talent" and a *political* "timocracy" in which, roughly speaking, government and its services will be run by people who know what they are doing because they have some expertise relevant to the offices they hold. The trick is to develop institutions that combine equality of opportunity with mechanisms for insuring the service of distinguished representative leadership. Ideally, anyhow, in this sort of polity "the services required of each must involve no injury to any; to perform them should be made the servant's spontaneous and specific ideal. The privileges the system bestows on some must involve no outrage on the rest, and must not be paid for by mutilating other lives or thwarting their natural potentialities" (*LR*, 2:113).

But, Santayana warns his readers, actual aristocracies in the Western world are more likely based "on the chances of some early war, reinforced by custom and perpetuated by inheritance," than on ability. "As a rule, men's station determines their occupation without their gifts determining their station. Thus stifled abilities in the lower orders, and apathy or pampered incapacity in the higher, unite to deprive society of its natural leaders," whose authority becomes morally and politically baseless (*LR*, 2:99–100, 122). That makes aristocratic distinction a bad thing. The "thwarting of . . . unequal natures," to Santayana's way of thinking, makes it despicable (*LR*, 2:105).

In fact, Santayana claims, it is just such abuse that has led to political democracy. The principle of political democracy, he asserts, "is not the absence of eminence, but the discovery that existing eminence is no longer genuine and representative" (*LR*, 2:115). Popular enfranchisement—"the people's liberty"—"consists not in their original responsibility for what exists—for they are guiltless of it—but merely in the faculty they have acquired of abolishing any detail that may distress or wound them, and of imposing any new measure, which, seen against the background of existing laws, may commend itself from time to time to their instinct and mind" (*LR*, 2:116).

People do not elect to be born, or the families, polities, traditions, or other material conditions into which they are bred. Even so, universal suffrage may work well enough, in Santayana's view, especially so long as democracies are ordered in representative ways that allow competent, hopefully eminent, deputies to carry out the best interests of the people. But that is the issue: Are "the people" virtuous enough to deputize people in the know? Can they be depended upon to elect leaders who carry representative authority, who not only speak for their mutual and diverse interests, but have the know-how to satisfy them?

Surely, Santayana argues, popular voting is neither identical with nor insures capable representation. Government becomes "representative only by embodying in its policy . . . the people's conscious and unconscious interests" (LR, 2:121). This is something theocracies, monarchies, and oligarchies—all eventually greedy, self-serving, and oppressive—actually failed to do. But to Santayana's mind, modern industrial democracies, fundamentally divided between rich and poor, producers and consumers, and highly and poorly educated—and without effective ways to provide anything close to universal training in the civic virtues—had not fared much better.

Santayana argues that Montesquieu had been right to place virtue at the heart of any republic intending to order itself from the bottom up. Public virtue—a dedication to the common welfare and the disciplines of justice, prudence, courage, and wisdom to make good on the commitment—is all that defends persuasive liberty from the menacing clutches of greed and military coercion.[27] By picturing democratic republics this way, Montesquieu clarified not only how "flattering and profound" experiments in democracy were, "but at the same time how ominous" (LR, 2:136).

No matter whether sovereignty resides in the people or the leaders who emerge out of them, Santayana insists, no society can function realistically or adequately without kinds of social structure that distinguish superiors from inferiors, and that segment populations into social sorts or roles. Social uniformity, homogeneity, and indistinction are not just unrealistic; they constitute a nightmare.

This is important for understanding religion, to Santayana's mind, because imaginative religious practices serve as a counterpoint to the hierarchies, segments, and differentiations of society or "the world." Religions function to bond the very people—even peoples—together whom social structures differentiate and subordinate one to another. They give people ways to understand and identify themselves and others as generically human sharing the same lot, just as social structures give them local, official, and distinctive identities. They let people avow their humankindness. On this view, one of the things that religions have traditionally contributed to republican culture, then, are rituals of cohesion and consensus, rituals that other social institutions do not typically offer, but nevertheless from which they benefit.

The Limits of Assertion and Religious Virtues

To Santayana's mind, however, there is one thing in particular about religious practices, including rituals of cohesion and consensus, that distinguish religions from virtually every other cultural institution: Common sense, society, art, and science are diverse ways of empowering people; they are forms of assertion. Religious practices underscore the limits of human assertion. They serve constantly to remind people of their finitude, creatureliness, and ultimate powerlessness.

Indeed, he claims that religions emerge in the wake of the perception or judgment that the life of reason is eventually vain. This is why he classifies religions as "post-rational." Interests, per se, are "pre-rational" because they constitute distinctively human life whether or not anyone tries to rationalize them through correlation. Reflective, deliberate, and critical policies of every variety naturally emerge out of unreflective desires, perceptions of loveliness, passions, or affections.

But the life of reason, the impulse to harmonize every human impulse in beautiful ways, inevitably falls short of its aim. The human cosmos, as Santayana had put it in *Interpretations*, always floats in a deluge. The practices of language, society, art, and science are all geared to empower people in ways that let them satisfy their desires harmoniously—in ways that will transfigure, as he puts it, a fatal project into a liberal art. But no matter how liberal life becomes, it remains a fatal project. There is no human way to transcend mortality or to avoid dealing with problems of finitude. All the fine arts in the world never cured a human being of inescapable powerlessness. If we have learned anything at all from the past, Santayana contends, it is that life poses questions we cannot answer (hence absurdity), physical debilities we can not fix (hence suffering), and both private and social conflicts or troubles that surpass our moral capacities to handle (hence evil). In a word, human power is severely and inevitably constrained by circumstances that far surpass its management. Religious practices and institutions have clarified this more persistently than any other part of culture. They have brought people "face to face with the mystery and pathos of mortal existence" (LR, 3:4).

In another time, Santayana argues, Western religious institutions and practices had thrived on the notion that people could make contact with a nonhuman, but personal, power that could do for them what they could not do for themselves. Christian believers, at least, had practiced the theological virtues of faith, hope, and charity thinking their destinies lay in the hands of a supernatural power at work in the world who was able and gracefully willing to *overcome* the problems of finitude exhibited in absurdity, suffering, and evil.

Religion, Santayana notes, "would not have been necessary had things responded to our first expectations" (LR, 2:29). But aspiration outruns achievement, reach exceeds grasp; people come to recognize that even their best efforts are shadowed by conceit. The evils that people encounter in themselves and others, the pains they suffer, and the conceptual puzzles that leave them perplexed, all threaten to disorder any humane order of things. Indeed, the more reasonable people are, the more they realize that the ways of the world constantly throttle attempts at human mastery. In great part, then, religious thought and practice mark reason's limits. To Santayana's mind at any rate, religion begins where the self-assertion of human beings leaves off. The discourse and rituals of supernatural redemption and salvation had emerged in the wake of despair over natural potential and in search of relief from natural catastrophe. They were developed, Santayana argues, "under high pressure; in the last extremity everyone appeals to God. But in the last extremity all known methods of action have proved futile; when resources are exhausted and ideals fail, if there is still vitality in the will it sends a supreme appeal to the supernatural. This appeal is necessarily made in the dark: it is the appeal of a conscious impotence, of an avowed perplexity" (LR, 3:33).

To be sure, in Santayana's view, this means that religious people had waxed superstitious when they convinced themselves and others that the life of reason—God's rather than man's—knew no limits and was fundamentally and utterly efficacious. They deceived themselves by believing that God could and would bring about the beautiful life they themselves could never quite construct. Such "faith in the supernatural," Santayana claims, "is a desperate wager made by man at the lowest ebb of his fortunes," and depends either on the pathetic fallacy or vicious intellectualism, both of which transform ideals into powers (LR, 4:299).

To Santayana's way of thinking, the gods that people imagined actually configured their own aspirations in unforgettably dramatic ways. But such figures did not cause themselves or anything else to come into being; nor did they authorize this or that table of virtues and vices. Rather, divine figures made such things strikingly memorable. The legends in which gods played prominent roles gave point to the lives of people living in this or that culture, clarifying their spirit, their attachments, loves, and highest hopes for themselves and their fellows. Religious scriptures were the greatest stories ever told. But, properly understood anyhow, they did not give absolutely accurate transcripts of reality or absolutely infallible instruction in moral life.

When religions had posed as science, Santayana said, they had misplaced man's hope. When religions had articulated their myths and practices as eternally true and right, discounting or ridiculing or excluding the aspirations of other peoples from considerate appreciation, or extinguishing aliens altogether, they had been arrogant, vicious, and cruel:

> It was a prodigious delusion to imagine that work could be done by magic; and the desperate appeal which religion has made to prayer, to castigations, to miscellaneous fantastic acts, in the hope of thereby bending nature to greater sympathy with human necessities is a pathetic spectacle; all the more pathetic in that here the very importunity of evil, which distracted the mind and allowed it no choice or deliberation, prevented very often those practical measures which, if lighted upon, would have instantly relieved the situation. Religion, when it has tried to do man's work for him has not only cheated hope, but consumed energy and drawn away attention from the true means of success. (*LR*, 3:274)

Religions Provide Another World to Live In

According to Santayana, then, commonsense language, social policy, artistic creation, and scientific explanation help empower people to satisfy their desires or to get what is in their interest. They help to structure the world in which people live in realistic ways. Religions, to the contrary, give people "another world to live in" (*LR*, 3:6). Traditional Christianity had been wrong to suggest that religion provides an escape hatch from human nature. But it was right, Santayana argues, in one fundamental respect. In crucial ways, religions are otherworldly—they provide time out from normal social life. If common-sense language and social policy establish the realistic order in which people live, religion offers a way to embark from it. Religion provides a cultural space that is *unrealistic* or festive—space in which people can stretch their imaginations in various ways beyond the confines of their practical and socially regimented lives. Holy days are holidays in which people can depart from their workaday worlds, in order to engage in imaginative activities that discipline them to live triumphantly with finitude.

Santayana, to be sure, is well aware that there are a variety of religious traditions (even if he is, like most other people at the time, highly ignorant of their details). As we have already seen in *Interpretations of Poetry and Religion*, he holds no truck with the movement, prominent among some liberal Protestants, post-Protestants, and "scientists of religion" to find some core religious experience or "religion in general" to hang onto once various superstitious and fanatical beliefs had been rejected.

In Santayana's view, "what religion a man shall have is an historical accident, quite as much as what language he shall speak." But such historical accidents are all that people ever have to work with, and "the attempt to speak without speaking any particular language is not more hopeless than the attempt to have a religion that shall be no religion in particular" (*LR*, 3:5). What makes any religion significant, indeed, is the idiosyncratic bias its "special and surprising message gives to life" (*LR*, 3:6).

A moment's probing, Santayana argues, will reveal that the "core religious experiences" that liberals claim to discover amount to nothing more than "vestiges of old beliefs, creases which thought, even if emptied of all dogmatic tenets, has not been able to smooth away at its first unfolding" (*LR*, 3:6). Redescribing religious dogmas in more general terms does nothing to void their historically accidental and culturally idiosyncratic character.

Both Santayana and his liberal opponents contend that religious superstition and fanaticism are bad things, historically responsible for deceit and atrocity. Both urge people to abandon those elements of religious life that foster these vices. But their diagnoses of the problem and the cures they suggest are radically different.

When *The Life of Reason* appears, for example, James is urging people to curb their religious imaginations, let go of their scriptures, and abandon their rituals and institutions, in order to discover some facts about divinity on which everybody can agree. He is doing so on the (Enlightenment) grounds that religious imagination, scripture, and ritual repeatedly provoke people to butcher one another. Dewey, at the same time, advises readers to engage fully in the democratic practices of their polity and downplays participation in religious disciplines that call for time out from political fervor.

Santayana thinks that these recommendations throw out the baby with the bath water. Religious imagination, literature, and ritual per se are not responsible for superstition and fanaticism. Moreover, their function is not distinctively political. Rather, they institute an "other" world in which people have a chance to learn disciplines of the imagination that let them love life when their finite powers, political and otherwise, have run their course.

What lets superstition and fanaticism run amok, in Santayana's view, is *taking the disciplines of poetic religion realistically*—taking fictive gods for material facts, religious literature for revelations of the really real, religious rituals for artful transactions that overturn the conditions of natural life, and religious institutions as politically and socially authoritative.

Santayana argues that attitudes toward prayer mark the difference a naturalistic reconstruction of religion can make. For supernaturalists who confuse ideals and powers, oftentimes in order to empower themselves at the expense of others, prayer is instrumental, a realistic transaction, "a desperate effort to work further and to be efficient beyond the range of one's powers" (*LR*, 3:40). But for those who accept religious thought and practice as imaginative, prayer is a discipline that weans "the mind from extravagant desires" in order to "teach it to find excellence in what life affords, when life is made as worthy as possible" (*LR*, 3:45). Religious naturalists in any tradition can still pray, but with this difference: They recognize that prayer "will not bring rain, but until rain comes it may cultivate hope and resignation and may prepare the heart for any issue, opening up a vista in which human prosperity will appear in its conditioned existence and conditional value" (*LR*, 3:47).

Piety, Spirituality, Charity, and Ideal Immortality

At every step in *Reason in Religion*, Santayana recommends maintenance of all those elements in religion that underscore the fallibility and finitude, the derived existence, and the responsibility of humankind to itself and its environs. Piety, spirituality, charity, and ideal immortality are each practices that let people identify themselves with historical movements and relationships that transcend the bounds of their own personal lives.

Santayana characterizes *piety* as loyalty to the sources of one's being, ranging from parents to country to culture to the planet and, ultimately, to whatever powers in the cosmos there are that support human life. Disciplines of piety train people to recognize the ways in which all the functions of the human spirit are "heritages and trusts" for which they must be thankful (*LR*, 3:183).

The disciplines of *spirituality*, Santayana claims, have to do with goals rather than with antecedents. If piety emphasizes gratitude and thanksgiving rather than assertive power, spirituality demands self-surrender to ultimate concerns. Its disciplines fortify people with aspiration, with a sense of beauty or divinity or "ultimate purpose." Reading the Hebrew prophets or the psalms, or the gospel narratives, or the lives of the saints, for example, functions to shape up a vision of life divine in this sense. And all these narratives challenge "worldly success" measured as wealth and aggressive power, appealing rather to civic and religious virtues instead.

But in the sort of republic Santayana envisions, the practice of *charity* makes the most significant difference. Without it, he argues, religious piety and spirituality are both subject to corruption. Piety and spirituality secure a sense of joy both by instilling thankful memories, firm allegiances, and exhilarating hopes. But so long as any tradition of piety and spirituality identifies itself as engaged in the *only* proper relationship with the sources and goals of humankind, it suffers from something Santayana calls "the aristocrat's fallacy." Without charity, people avowing a particular heritage and derivation, on the one hand, and a shared sense of ultimate concern, on the other, can forget too easily the variability and mutability of human good (*LR*, 3:214).

In view of the contingency of pious attachments and spiritual paths, Santayana claims, charity becomes the crucial practice for anybody with allegiances to the naturalism, pragmatism, and republicanism he is commending. The virtue of charity, Santayana asserts, amounts to this:

> After adopting an ideal it is necessary . . . without abandoning it, to recognize its relativity. The right path is in such a matter rather difficult to keep to. On the one hand lies fanatical insistence on an ideal once arrived

at, no matter how many instincts and interests (the basis of all ideals) are thereby outraged in others and ultimately also in one's self. On the other hand lies mystical disintegration, which leads men to feel so keenly the rights of everything in particular and of the All in general, that they retain no hearty allegiance to any human interest. Between these two abysses winds the narrow path of charity and valour. (LR, 3:215)

Indeed, in a passage that flags the rhetorical summit of *The Life of Reason*, Santayana identifies charity as the crucial republican virtue. He begins by restating the republican premise that "the ultimate ideal, in order to maintain its finality and preclude the possibility of an appeal which should dislodge it from its place of authority, must have taken all interests into consideration; it must be universally representative" (LR, 3:215).

Recall that to do this, in Santayana's view, means to "intend, as far as possible, to secure the particular good which that particular interest looks to, and never, whatever measures may be adopted, to cease to look back on the elementary impulse as upon something which ought, if possible, to have been satisfied, and which we should still go back and satisfy now, if circumstances and the claims of rival interests permitted" (LR, 3:215–16). Charity is practically necessary because the "texture of the natural world" is constituted by conflicts of interest "in the soul and in society, all of which cannot be satisfied altogether" (LR, 3:216).

In Santayana's view, indeed, it is his insistence on the discipline of charity that most clearly distinguishes his understanding of the life of reason from that of Plato's and his followers. Platonists assumed that the texture of things was nomothetic—that philosophers could break through the appearance of conflict to a given reality that was harmoniously ordered. Santayana now assumes that the texture of things is antinomial, a conflict of interests all the way along. Plato's republic, he asserts, illustrates "justice without charity," where all the constituent interests of social life are presumed to be proportional to one another, but only at the expense of "radical injustice toward every interest" actually not included (LR, 3:218). Santayana's republic, to the contrary, is ordered from the bottom up and disciplined by consideration of any genuine interest. Harmonious order is his aim, not his assumption. It is the sort of promise he thinks people must try to keep, full well knowing its complete realization is impossible.

Santayana points out that Plato's republic pictures things in terms of "us versus them," and therefore makes the disciplines of war and internal prosperity primary. Santayana's picture begins by accepting the particularity of diverse peoples but emphasizes the formulation of policies of "universal solicitude" geared to resolve conflicts without recourse to coercion or war. Plato's republic emphasizes role-specific duties for which every citizen has responsibilities. Santayana's does too, but his religious virtues train people to transgress, imaginatively, "the limits of personal or corporate interests," even to identify and empathize with the affections or values of "rival forms of life" (LR, 3:221). The practice of charity, in particular, imaginatively suspends the sense of civic duty sufficiently enough to appreciate the beauty that alien traditions have, at least for the interests constituting them. So unlike Plato's republic, but quite in line with the aesthetic tradition of spirituality in America, Santayana's *Life of Reason* encourages "admiration and solicitude for what is most alien and hostile to one's self," in order to "co-ordinate felt interests with other actual interests conceived sympathetically, and to make them converge" (LR, 3:221).

Piety brings joy to people by bonding them to the (familial, traditional, and other natural) sources of their lives. It provides kinds of cohesion that link people imaginatively to movements and powers at work in the world before they were born, even before humankind came to be. Spirituality invigorates them by training them to surrender their selves to causes outlasting their own mortal lives, extended indefinitely into the future. Charity opens them up to whatever is lovely and lovable in others who are different. These three disciplines let people escape from the constraints of their own egos and from the rules, roles, and relationships constituting their normal social personalities. By giving people ways to evacuate or sacrifice themselves to the sources and goals that shape them, as well as to alien others that delimit them, the religious virtues discipline them to love "the excellences that life actually affords."

What do the practices of "ideal immortality" add to piety, spirituality, and charity? Santayana argues that dying is both a perfectly evident prospect *and* absurd to people. Its absurdity, he claims, results from the fact that personal identity relies as much on expectation as on memory and current avowals or beliefs. The question is never just Who am I? but (as James's *Principles* had taught him) Who am I to become? Personal practice presumes a future: "Every moment of life accordingly trusts that life will continue" (LR, 3:235). But this trust is inevitably abrogated, so that "a note of failure and melancholy must always dominate in the struggle against natural death" (LR, 3:259).

In Santayana's view, sadness over death is inescapable but despair is not. Orthodox Christians had been wrong to characterize mortal life as nothing but a stain upon eternity. Very much like Nietzsche and the Epicureans, he suggests that mortal life, including the process of dying, can be festive: The religious virtues lead to a sense of ultimate well-being in the face of impotence and, simultaneously, serve as training for death. Accepting mortality, he claims, provides an "opportunity to live in the spirit" that carries felt compensations without in any way relying on superstitions about life after life (*LR*, 3:261). Death surely deletes people from the earth but neither the facts of their experience nor the traditions they carried on nor the ideals to which they devoted their lives. Living in the spirit, he argues, gives people a "double immortality," identifying them with values randomly related to time while alive, and influential as exemplars of diverse characters when dead (*LR*, 3:272).

Spiritualization, Anti-Hebraism, and Personal Idiosyncracy

To my mind, the main thrust of Santayana's case for the maintenance of religious institutions and practices in a naturalistic world is persuasive. Nothing, at least apart from our own memories and hopes, makes religion a necessity. Nonetheless, we may *want* to maintain our religious traditions, particularly for the inheritance, the aspiration, and the exercises in self-criticism that they offer. The virtues of piety, spirituality, and charity articulated and exercised in Western religious communities have added practices to the human repertoire of behaviors that enhance, and for many, complete, a sense of personal well-being, by teaching people how awesome and wonderful their cosmos is, by underscoring the ways in which their identities are inheritances and trusts, by opening them up to the excellences of aliens, and by shaping affections that come into play at wit's end, when self-assertion flails and fails. Piety, spirituality, and charity are not news from nowhere and, while there are a diversity of traditions with distinctive fables and activities that have instructed people in their practice, *without* the institutions of religious communities—scriptures, rituals, and all—they would not have mattered; they would not have made a difference.

But I depart from Santayana's reconstruction of the religious virtues over the issue of spiritualization and the idea of "ideal immortality." Heir to Reformed

Christianity that he was, Santayana's "religious practices" in *The Life of Reason* still aim to sacrifice the idiosyncracies of personality to the divine, that is, to the sources and goals of being this or that person. By doing so, he argues, people became "transparent" vehicles of spiritual significance, practically achieving "immortality" by identifying their mortal personalities with ideals that transcend them, ideals that he claims are randomly related to time.

I think this strand in Santayana's vision accounts, among other things, for his strong (though unexceptionably Enlightenment) anti-Hebraism.[28] In *Reason in Religion*, Santayana faults "the Hebrew tradition" for maintaining material *rather than* spiritual aspirations, claiming that such aims had introduced both superstition and fanaticism into the West.[29] He claims that, unlike the Greeks who recognized the fictive status of their gods, the Jews pictured their god as a material power and his commandments as exclusively proper, and actually hoped that if they kept their promises to him, and bound themselves to his laws (*rather than* opening themselves up to his grace or spirit) it would make a material difference. Naturalistic Christians, he argues, would be better off spiritualizing their vision entirely, sloughing the bad, Hebrew, parts of Christianity's own heritage and, with them, religion's twin vices.

But, quite apart from the fact that Greeks and Jews would not recognize themselves in this self-serving Christian story of spiritual triumph, Santayana's continued commitment to spiritualization hampers his own efforts to naturalize Christianity. On my view of things, at any rate—which, to be sure, is not Christian—it is *just* the idiosyncratic personalities or figures, say, of prophets, saints, saviors, sages, rabbis, and bhoddisatvas that are memorable and worthy of celebration; *just* their distinctive characters that embody the sense of beauty, well-being, grace, spirit, or equanimity in the face of absurdity, suffering, evil, or death. They play such a prominent cultural role because their piety, spirituality, and charity matter, because these practices transform their (storied) behavior and feelings, thereby leaving the world a lovelier place. They matter in ways, thank goodness, not geared to accrue wealth or coercive power. But they still matter—or they are not natural.

On Santayana's own naturalistic grounds, I believe, spiritual life cannot be opposed to material life, because all life is material, including every part that gives life point. The religious virtues matter in ways that other conventional forms of social life tend to suppress. They let people embark from the incessant drive for aggrandizement. They let them devote their lives to understanding and serving others. They assuredly involve meditation on fictive gods and literature. They may establish serenity in extremis. But if we prize these virtues, it is not because they let anybody escape personality; it is because they let them escape, in the term Santayana comes to use in *Realms of Being*, "distraction" (*RB*, 673–735). They are valuable because the personalities who practice them are fruitful, and stretched in ways that lend a modicum of grace both to their own lives and those of others.

In my view, *The Life of Reason* is valuable for its naturalism, for its pragmatism, and for its explication of reason in terms of practices and institutions, including religious ones geared to bond people together in ways that accept the limits of physical, intellectual, and moral capacity. But does it carry the weight of representative authority, as Santayana appeared to hope? Is it a "comprehensive synthesis" or "total vision" that does justice to all human interests at work when it was written? Who knows? How, indeed, could anybody tell? Surely Santayana's intention is explicit. Certainly Santayana tries to hang together many of the major institutions and practices constituting the reasonably prosperous and free sort of republic available in the modern West. But just as surely there are interests, for example, political and economic interests, excluded from serious consideration in the work. And certainly the book had and has critics claiming either that Santayana's vision is inconsiderate, unjust, or not charitable; or that he is guilty of philosophical malfeasance or sloppiness.

But, perhaps more important, in the years following publication of *The Life of Reason*, Santayana himself comes to *abandon* the project of "comprehensive" philosophical representation at work in *The Life of Reason*, on the grounds that it is so much pretense, a mask offering an illusory escape to the critic from his own idiosyncratic voice. In its stead, he fashions a sort of festive criticism that, to my way of thinking, marks one of his special contributions to the naturalistic and pragmatic traditions that he helps to inaugurate; a sort of criticism very much designed to display how people might well learn how to love life—indeed, lives—conscious of their own fundamental powerlessness.

6

FESTIVE CRITICISM

Cambridge Interpretation in the Golden Age

Santayana is no voice in the wilderness when he announces in *The Life of Reason* that "the age of controversy is past; that of interpretation has succeeded" (*LR*, 1:32). Virtually without exception, his Harvard colleagues continue to picture themselves as mediators between or among cultural interests during the first decade of this century. They all think their work is publicly important because it is statesmanlike, because they are engaged in helping diverse social institutions work out cultural compromises.

In particular, James is articulating his essays in radical empiricism (published mainly in 1904–5) and his lectures on *Pragmatism* (1907) in such terms. "The present dilemma in philosophy," he argues, calls for mediation or reconciliation between the "tough-minded" interests of science and the "tender-minded" ones exhibited in literature, social thought, art, morality, and religion. There is no reason to "reduce" science to sentiment or vice-versa, he claims, because each serves different needs in a "world of pure experience" that is neither "mental" nor "material," but "affectional" or qualitative, value-laden, and imaginative all the way along.

Royce, too, is engaged in projects that will lead him to claim, by 1908, that "interpretation is, once for all, the main business of philosophy," on the grounds that the primary philosophical task is to create community where none has existed before. Community emerges, Royce contends, not by controversion of hostile claims, but through a "comparative" or "interpretive" understanding of their positions. In this view, hinted at as early as *The Religious Aspect of Philosophy* (1885), worked out initially in *The Philosophy of Loyalty*

(1908), and more systematically articulated in *The Problem of Christianity* (1913), such mediation makes controversy irrelevant by transforming danger-ously opposed pairs into mutually forgiving ones.[1]

James and Royce continue to engage in the language of statesmanship and to view their interpretation as responsible social criticism until they die. But Santayana changes his mind, or frees it from the bounds set by his one-time teachers and, then, colleagues. Reflection on contemporary material, social, institutional, and ideological conditions, especially during the Great War, leads him to believe that the spiritual impact of interpretive criticism is blunted so long as it is developed solely on the model of intellectual states-manship, federal republican style. It is not that James's and Royce's interpretive options are unappealing, although idealism's day is clearly over and if James's pragmatism holds powerful appeal, his novel "science of religions," announced in *The Varieties of Religious Experience*, is simply stillborn.

Santayana begins to think, more radically, that the force of interpretive criticism is jeopardized when those doing it construe their work as some sort of republican duty. He claims in *Character and Opinion in the United States* (1920) that the language of statesmanship carries with it a "brimstone" sen-sibility, a sense that, unless criticism contributes in some material way to the winning of a new heaven and a new earth, it is decadent or worthless (*COUS*, 53). Employing such language, James and Royce and Santayana himself had gone out of their way to show the rest of American society that philosophers were pulling their civic weight. They had pictured themselves as fundamen-tally engaged in social and cultural policy formulation. But by doing so, Santayana comes to think, they had belied the genuinely expressive, poetic, meditative, and festive character of their vocation.

James's Doctrine of Human Blindness and Practical Worthlessness

Santayana's "brimstone" charge is telling. But it obscures a significant philo-sophical move that James had made to break away from republican officious-ness at the turn of the century. By then, James was already arguing that there are good reasons for reframing interpretive criticism so that it can escape the deadening confines of republican duty. His recommendation had come in the wake of the imperialist escapades executed by the United States in the Philippines, the foreign affair that had provoked Santayana's "Young Sammy's First Wild Oats" (and, in retrospect, the charge that James was a typical American exceptionalist in his anti-imperialism). It had appeared in his talk to students "On a Certain Blindness in Human Beings" (*TT*, 132–49).

There, James had argued that practical interests and social responsibilities made people blind and dead to alien forms of life. Such blindness was, in one sense, normal; in another, it was diseased. It was normal because getting things done required adherence to standards of appropriate behavior that, while focusing attention, also served as blinders. It was spiritually diseased because such adherence kept people from understanding radically different sorts of human experience, much less letting them flourish. In the case of America's invasion of the Philippine Islands, James railed, this human blindness had let Americans think of Filipinos as disposable matter, an attitude which, in turn, had led to what James called the cold-blooded, wanton, and abominable destruction of "the soul of a people who never did us an atom of harm in their lives."[2]

James had continued by arguing that, if the world of practical responsibilities fostered this blindness, it could still be cured. People could unblind themselves to the wants and needs and objectives of others by becoming "irresponsible" or "worthless" as practical beings. If people wanted to catch sight of "the world of impersonal worths as such," that is, the things that made life worth living for humanity plurally understood, they must (in some therapeutic connotation of that term) outlaw themselves from the role-specific duties imposed by practical social life because "only your mystic, your dreamer, or your insolent loafer or tramp can afford so sympathetic an occupation" (*TT*, 141).[3]

Nothing that I have read suggests that James's doctrine of human blindness per se had been formative for Santayana. Moreover, it could be read as varying Schopenhauer's notions of "the world as will" and "the world as idea" that *had* helped to shape Santayana's own views since his undergraduate days. But it is the case that, coincident with James's death and his own departure from the United States, Santayana begins to identify himself as an intellectual tramp, vagabond, or outlaw; to picture the normal, practical conditions of thought as a sort of madness, and to challenge himself to become abnormally sane, that is, practically worthless but contemplatively appreciative of the human spirit in its plurality. To this end, he resigns from Harvard and takes up the pose of a man without a country, hosted by the world, and devoted to spiritual disciplines that, often enough, appear irresponsible to philosophers hoping to command representative or some otherwise privileged authority at the center of society.

Even before Santayana leaves Harvard, however, his own thinking takes a significant turn. Building out from the naturalism, institutional pragmatism, social realism, and poetic religion that he had articulated so far, Santayana makes three remarkable moves. First, he uncouples the language of representative authority from the old quest for comprehensive synthesis. Second, he blurs the line between philosophy and literature by presenting strong poets as philosophical precursors in *Three Philosophical Poets* (1910). Third, in "The Genteel Tradition in American Philosophy" (1911), which turns out to be a sort of American swan song for him, he begins explicitly to wrestle more with the shadow of William James than with Emerson.[4]

Philosophy as a Personal Work of Art

Harvard's philosophy department had a good deal of trouble accepting Santayana's syllabus for a course on "Three Philosophical Poets." Some worried out loud that the course did not fall within philosophy's bailiwick, because it appeared to investigate literature rather than the distinctive problems of philosophy. In other words, they caught the point of Santayana's lectures and took mild offense.[5] Muddying the distinction between philosophy and literature did not sit comfortably with colleagues bent on establishing "representative authority" by providing a "comprehensive synthesis" of all extant human interests (as Santayana himself had tried to do in *The Life of Reason*).

Santayana would eventually explicate the tack he began to take in *Three Philosophical Poets* and "The Genteel Tradition" in his essay on "Philosophical Heresy," which appears in 1915. This piece is even more radical than his last Harvard-based works, rejecting the notion that a philosopher can achieve comprehensive synthesis or representative authority in intellectual matters. In "Philosophical Heresy" Santayana calls into question not only every effort to make direct contact with the really real, but also the sort of intellectual statesmanship exemplified by his own *Life of Reason*. His point is to show that when philosophers make claims and recommendations, they do so on their own authority: They are critics who first muster whatever relevant reasons they have at their command on behalf of their views; then they subject them to whatever adverse criticism comes their way. Philosophers, in other words, may try to become "spokesmen," but they had better do so recognizing that their philosophies are "personal work[s] of art," created to express themselves and available for review and evaluation by others.

The basic assumption in "Philosophical Heresy" is one that Santayana has already promoted for years: Traditional beliefs provide the media or baseline for any sort of critical thinking, including philosophical reflection. The fact that people can discover their own distinctive points of view through self-interrogation and close observation does not detach them from their intellectual inheritance. The Enlightenment prejudice against prejudice, then, is overdrawn. Prejudice per se is unavoidable. The task is to distinguish prejudice that enables critical thinking and prejudice that disables it. Critical thinking lets people review, amend, and selectively transmit the traditions into which they have been born and bred.

From this perspective, the "battle over the Absolute" that had been waged by James and Royce was avoidable, almost beside the point. The important—and usually bad—thing about this or that philosophical view is its departure from "orthodoxy" or from traditionally held beliefs, not whether it is absolutely or just relatively true, objective or subjective. To Santayana's mind, every philosophical view worth discussing is both objective, because it is based on accepted critical observations, and subjective, because it is "personal, temperamental, accidental, and premature" ("PH," 94). Visions or opinions are "philosophical," he claims, when they try to bring about *revisions* in orthodox belief, especially when they try to make wholesale revisions. The context for this revisionary activity, Santayana argues, is just "the current imagination and good sense of mankind—something traditional, conventional, incoherent, and largely erroneous, like the assumptions of a man who has never reflected, yet something ingenuous, practically acceptable, fundamentally sound, and capable of correcting its own innocent errors" ("PH," 95).

In fact, Santayana argues, most of the works that have counted as philosophy so far promote unnecessary errors or avoidable departures from good sense due to some "rebellious partisanship" or some "deliberate attachment to something the evidence against which is public and obvious" ("PH," 95).

"Philosophy," in truth, has been a sort of literature that denies its own literary status, in order to plead the special or privileged character of this or that web of belief.

Santayana is clearly conservative in his judgments about the relative weight to give accepted opinion on the one hand and departures from it on the other. But the point Santayana is trying to make here is *not* that traditional patterns of thinking are inevitably true or even destined to be better than the revisions that impugn them. To the contrary, he admits that traditional "discourse instinctively deviates from the truth, to set forth instead something more manageable, more rhythmical, more flattering" ("PH," 96). Rather, his message is that critical revision is practically necessary only when beliefs become outmoded or counterproductive or when "some scandalous error exhaust[s] people's patience and [stings] them into an eloquence and clearness they never knew before" ("PH," 96).

Philosophers, Santayana suggests, have mainly revised traditional beliefs in ways that cause more problems than their "improvements" are worth, by seeking some special philosophical knowledge outside the bounds of informed opinion. In pursuit of this goal, he asserts, they wax "sectarian" or wane "atavistic."

To Santayana's mind, philosophers are "sectarian" when they take some one part of traditional belief as the key to special truth. Rationalists and empiricists, for example, had jeopardized belief by privileging, respectively, certain principles of thought or certain observations as foundations for distinctively philosophical truth. So had moralists, aesthetes, theologians, and proponents of scientism, each by construing their vocabularies as privileged or revelatory. On the other hand, Santayana suggests, philosophers are "atavistic" when they confuse powers and ideals, endowing the material ways of the world and every culture in it with their own affections, ideals or values. Supernaturalists and idealists, he argues, had deformed orthodoxy in this way.

Santayana asserts, to be sure, that some philosophers had attempted to serve as spokesmen for orthodoxy (in, for example, his own previous work), rather than commit sectarian or atavistic heresies. But these efforts had been self-defeating because they had been tied to a quest for an impossibly complete vision. He now claims, as critical of his own previous pretensions as anything else, that even Aristotle, the greatest synoptic philosopher, had been incomplete, sectarian, and atavistic. His work, for example, had suffered from having no genuine physics, from an inflated humanism, and from a concomitant confusion of material and final "causes."

The only satisfactory option open to those admitting the futility of efforts to step outside corrigible opinion grounded in tradition, Santayana argues, is to confess that "a system of philosophy is a personal work of art which gives a specious unity to some chance vista in the cosmic labyrinth." "To confess this," he writes, "is to confess a notorious truth; yet it would be something novel if a philosopher should confess it, and should substitute the pursuit of sincerity for the pursuit of omniscience" ("PH," 100). Granting this transformed the venerable philosophical aim for comprehensive synthesis into a synoptic view that is inevitably personal.

Santayana's principal proposal in "Philosophical Heresy," then, is to renounce the idea that philosophy is a civic discipline outfitted with standards capable either of measuring all things or mediating among all interests. Because philosophers have craved "totality in their views and authority in their sentiments," they have been comically pretentious, masking "self-expression" or "the composition of an historical artist" with "a public value which it [does] not have" ("PH," 101–2).

Here again, Santayana testifies to a sort of libertarian conservatism: What philosophers propose in the way of synoptic views is rendered on their own authority. But nonetheless, they are not just daydreaming. They do *propose*. They do commend their visions of things to audiences in public ways. So his point is not that philosophical views have *no* public value. To the contrary, he claims that "nothing could be of greater moment in poetry or politics" ("PH," 102). His point is that philosophical visions enter political, social, and cultural space as personal expressions and advice, not as the measure of all things or as an expression of all interests ("PH," 101).

Santayana suggests that if many philosophers had "touched the hem of nature's garment" as other scientists and artists had, malicious ones had articulated their redescriptions of the way things hang together with more vehemence and posturing than most other thinkers. The best philosophers, he argues to the contrary, had been original, poetic, and synoptic without pretending to rely on some special, borrowed authority. They had realized that their views were "proper to some particular genius, which has succeeded in flowering at some particular time and place" (*TPP*, 212).[6]

On this view, what makes philosophy good is neither its comprehensiveness nor its representative character so much as the (Romantic) fact that it embodies, as he will put it in *Three Philosophical Poets*, "the indomitable freedom of life to be more, to be new, to be what it has not entered into the heart of man as yet to conceive" (*TPP*, 212). To Santayana's way of thinking, then, the trouble with the idea of representative authority is moral, not epistemological or metaphysical. It curbs "indomitable freedom." It incarcerates individuals in the descriptions of things wrought by previous thinkers, obstructing their ability to formulate their own novel languages. With that creative freedom, Santayana argues, "goes the modesty of reason, both in physics and in morals, that can lay claim only to partial knowledge, and to the ordering of a particular soul, or city, or civilization" (*TPP*, 212).

This moral criticism signals a very significant tension that is to become more and more pronounced in Santayana's work. As he understands it, philosophy in the West, at least since Plato, has aimed to unlock the key to public harmony or the good society. It has also pursued personal fulfillment. Indeed, mainline Western philosophers have made every effort to show that solutions to the problems of social harmony and personal fulfillment coincide, in, say, *nous* or *agape*, or romantic intuition, or civic republican virtues. This quest to show the overlap between public and private good, surely, has fueled the projects of Harvard's intellectual statesmen seeking representative authority.

But now Santayana is suggesting a possible slip betwixt social solidarity and the sort of personal fulfillment people may experience in solitude; he is suggesting that personal well-being may involve *embarkation* away from normal and traditionally held beliefs, away from consensus *toward* the new creation or the re-creation of personal *difference*.

The point is worth belaboring a little. In *The Life of Reason*, Santayana had sought to show the ways in which the practices and institutions of a viable republic allowed cultural space on its margins for "another," religious "world to live in"—a religious world that acknowledged but departed from socially realistic order for the sake of celebrating generic human bonds. Now he makes the same move with regard to the cultural location of philosophy, suggesting that at least some of its practitioners distance themselves from the work of solving immediately pressing social or cultural conflicts in order to reflect on the predicaments and promises of the human spirit.

In this regard, Santayana's thinking continues to be stereoscopic: On the one hand he insists on the requisite sorts of political, social, and economic organization that let modern republics flourish, because such socialization precedes individuality. But on the other he argues that social order per se does not secure the sense of well-being that comes in the solitary and personal affirmation or avowal of the things that bring joy to fragile human life—hence his emphasis on philosophy as a personal work of art in "Philosophical Heresy."

Canons

But "Philosophical Heresy" still awaits writing in 1910, when *Three Philosophical Poets* appears. One of the things that makes the latter work significant is the way in which it shows Santayana departing from the philosophical canon his colleagues are creating and endorsing. It had been no coincidence that the best Western philosophers had gone out of their way to reread their traditions and to place their own work historically by redrawing the canon in order to highlight their own voices as coherent and persuasive. If, indeed, there was nothing "absolute" with which to compare a philosophical view, there were plenty of other keenly persuasive philosophical views, overlapping, crisscrossing, and diverging in historically telling ways.

Santayana adds his three philosophical poets—Lucretius, Dante, and Goethe—to his own company of precursors at a time when Royce is successfully reconstructing the canon of modern philosophy in order to highlight epistemology and metaphysics as the two distinctive disciplines that philosophy has to offer. Royce's canon—Descartes, Spinoza, Locke, Berkeley, Leibniz, Hume, and Kant—becomes authoritative in most influential philosophy departments in the United States for seventy years or more.[7] Santayana's philosophical poets, to the contrary, get taught in departments of literature and, later, in courses in Western civilization.

For Royce, the line from Descartes to Kant marks progress toward the resolution of fundamental philosophical problems like linking mind to the world and establishing the conditions for any possible experience. For Santayana, Lucretius, Dante, and Goethe confront the problems of human finitude in efforts to show how people achieve the personal well-being they crave. To be sure, their respective naturalism, supernaturalism, and romanticism "sum up all European philosophy" (*TPP*, 4). But they each do so by providing novel ways for people to interpret themselves and their prospects. They each create jarringly different pictures of human joy, the ways to it, and the things impeding it. There is no way to square one with the other or to construe their wisdom as progressive or cumulative. Each gives an epoch its paradigmatic self-image: Lucretius, Santayana claims, epitomizes classical naturalism; Dante depicts and evokes traditional high Christianity; and Goethe clarifies romanticism. People need to recall eponymous poets like these, "superpose" what insights they can from them to develop a synoptic view articulating how things hang together—and hope for an equally creative poet for their own time.

In fact, Santayana argues, on the current scene, people can do no more than hope, because his contemporary culture is in "limbo," betwixt and between a slowly dying romanticism (itself concurrent with the Christian supernaturalism from which it descends) and a religious naturalism that does not hide from its inhuman material conditions, but needs to display, in greater detail than anybody has so far, the spiritual life that is possible in them. No "supreme poet" has yet emerged to give voice to the new age (*TPP*, 215). Indeed, this image of culture as passing through limbo perdures throughout the rest of Santayana's writing: He remains unconvinced that religious naturalism's supreme poet or poets have emerged by the time he dies in 1952.

Nonetheless, Santayana hitches his own writing to this aspiration. In a seemingly incidental remark that turns out to auger the temper of much of his own writing during the next forty years, he calls for an original mind who can do for his own time what Dante had done for high Christendom by fashioning a *natural comedy*:

> Throw open to the young poet the infinity of nature; let him feel the precariousness of life, the variety of purposes, civilizations, and religions even upon this little planet; let him trace the triumphs and follies of art and philosophy, and their perpetual resurrections—like that of the downcast Faust. If, under the stimulus of such a scene, he does not someday compose a natural comedy as much surpassing Dante's divine comedy in sublimity and richness as it will surpass it in truth, the fault will not lie with the subject . . . but with the halting genius that cannot render that subject worthily. (*TPP*, 210)[8]

Unlike the author of *The Divine Comedy*, the poet who writes the natural one will recognize, with Lucretius, that his ideal is not the cause of everything and that only natural things shed light on other natural things. With Goethe (after Spinoza), the new poet will find ways to celebrate the fact that the practices constituting the life of the spirit articulate "perfectly human distinctions and human preferences" (*TPP*, 209) and that "of this universe, man, with all his works, [is] an incident in an incident, and a fragment of a fragment."[9] He will make the Goethean confession that "you are saved in that you lived well; saved not after you have stopped living well, but during the whole process" (*TPP*, 190).

But like Dante (and even Goethe after him), Santayana's new poet will also confess that "grace is needed, besides virtue," that human well-being or "salvation" depends as much on gratuitous "external conditions" or circumstances that people can neither engineer nor earn, as it does on their own behavior (*TPP*, 191). He will claim that graceful life, lovely life, is inseparably "the love of life," and that this affection is "something antecedent and spontaneous. It is that Venus Genetrix which covers the earth with its flora and fauna. It teaches every animal to seek its food and its mate, and to protect its offspring; as also to resist or fly from all injury to the body, and most of all from threatened death. It is the original impulse by which good is discriminated from evil, and hope from fear" (*TPP*, 52).

The thing that makes Dante such an important forerunner, Santayana thinks, was his ability to articulate, in a very fine-grained way, the social habits—unreflectively acquired for the most part and, in that sense, "antecedent and spontaneous"—constituting the virtues and vices in his culture. "Behind mythical and narrow conceptions of history," Santayana asserts, Dante "had a true sense for the moral principles that really condition our well-being" (*TPP*, 90). Far better than either Lucretius or Goethe, Dante displayed how virtues and vices—the Aristotelian virtues of wisdom, justice, temperance, and courage, as well as the theological virtues of hope, faith, and charity; the vices of lust, gluttony, avarice, wrath, pride, malice, envy, vengeance, deceit, indifference, despair, and heresy—practically shaped how his contemporaries viewed their prospects and problems.

Religious naturalism's poet will need to attend to virtues, vices, powers, and dominations in as much detail as Dante had in his time. But "if any similar adequacy is attained again by any poet, it will not be, presumably, by a poet of the supernatural. Henceforth, for any wide and honest imagination, the supernatural must figure as an idea in the human mind—a part of the natural. To conceive it otherwise would be to fall short of the insight of this age, not to express or to complete it" (*TPP*, 134).

Spinoza's Role in Santayana's Canon

Coincident with the publication of *Three Philosophical Poets*, Santayana writes his introduction to *The Ethics of Spinoza*. The piece is decidedly pedagogical but, nonetheless, interpretive in ways that help focus Santayana's turn to philosophy construed as festive criticism. For James and Royce, Spinoza is eponymous with monism. James attacks him, indeed, as the paradigmatic monist, the bad old sort of philosopher who rationalistically deduces philosophical truths about the world from clear and simple first principles.[10] For Royce, to the contrary, Spinoza is the greatest philosopher, before Kant at any rate, to embody absolute (hence, monistic) idealism. Royce applauds Spinoza for recognizing that "the world is one, and so all the things in it must be parts of one self-evident, self-producing order, one nature."[11]

For Santayana's older colleagues, then, Spinoza makes it into the canon of modern philosophy because the monism/pluralism debate is so important for modern metaphysics. So it is remarkable that Santayana's small 1910 portrait of Spinoza is drawn without any reference to this metaphysical debate—or to the problem of the one and the many—at all. To the contrary, Santayana pictures Spinoza as the one modern philosopher who has paved the way for articulating an "orthodox physics," linked up with an "orthodox ethics," without having to engage in any reflection on metaphysical *order* (*PAP*, 234). Rather, he invokes the Spinoza who writes to Oldenburg: "I do not attribute to nature either beauty or deformity, order or confusion. Only in relation to our imagination can things be called beautiful or ugly, well-ordered or confused" (*E*, vii).

This, Santayana notes, is the Spinoza valorized by German romantics like Novalis and Goethe, who poeticize philosophy by perceiving "the relativity of good and evil, and of all human conventions." Spinoza, "not being afraid to confess that the universe is non-human, and that man is relative . . . [accepts] the natural status of all the rest of his being" (*E*, viii). Humankind lives dramatically in an undramatic universe. The whole aim of Santayana's Spinoza is Hebraic and prophetic: to secure "good-will, mercy, and peace among men"

(*E*, xi). By picturing the large facts of nature as nonpurposive, this Spinoza makes goodwill, mercy, and peace primarily a function of the responsibility of one (natural) human to another, rather than to some capital "N" nature back behind humanity: "There is infinite being, no doubt, beyond our human interests and ideals, and, to the contemplative intellect, that being has a certain dignity, because it is great; but its greatness is not moral, its dignity is not human, and to call it 'good' would not be a higher truth but a silly impertinence. The infinite knows no obligation, it is subject to no standard" (*E*, xiii).

So while both James and Royce still attempt to provide a kind of metaphysical deduction for their moral views (I mean the sort of argument that goes "We ought to believe x, the ways of the world being as they are"), Santayana invokes Spinoza as a precursor who circumvents that sort of analysis altogether. Ethics, beauty, sublimity are "anthropological" topics, not theological ones, disclosed by understanding "a matter-of-fact record of the habits and passions of men." Such anthropology, Santayana says, "is not the expression of any ideal; it does not specify any direction in which it demands that things should move. Yet it describes the situation which makes the existence of ideals possible and intelligible" (*E*, xv).

Spinoza, then, becomes a near-perfect bridge figure for Santayana, allowing him to make a smooth transition from intellectual statesmanship to festive criticism. On the one hand, Spinoza vindicates intellectual statesmanship by showing how public well-being is dependent on the ways in which largely institutionalized human interests constrain one another. "The particular ideals of man have a legitimate authority over *him*, in his moral, political, and aesthetic judgments; but it is grotesque to suppose that they have, as the Platonists imagined, any authority over universal nature" (*E*, xx). On the other hand, Spinoza makes room for festive criticism, ironically enough, by fashioning nature or God as nonmoral. Quite precisely because Spinoza claims that "man, with all his works, [is] an incident within an incident, and a fragment within a fragment," he becomes

> well-fitted to chasten and sober all those dogmatists that lay down the law for God out of the analogies or demands of their private experience. When people tell us that they have the key to reality in their pockets, or in their hearts, that they know who made the world, and why, or know that everything is matter, or that everything is mind—then Spinoza's

notion of the absolutely infinite, which includes *all* possibilities, may profitably arise before us. It will counsel us to say to those little gnostics, to those circumnavigators of being: I do not believe you. God is great. (*E*, xxi–xxii)

What this or that philosophical poet can do is donate his own personal work of art, knowing that "when the movement of his life is over, the truth of his life remains." That, for Santayana, is the force of Spinoza's recommendation to see personal life "under the form of eternity." To see things that way is to see them for the difference they will have made. It is, Santayana asserts, "to see them in their historic and moral truth, not as they seemed as they passed, but as they remain when they are over. When a man's life is over it remains true that he has lived; it remains true that he has been one sort of man, and not another. In the infinite mosaic of history that bit has its unfading color and its perpetual function and effect." Doing this, Santayana claims, is expressly festive because, without overcoming inevitable death, it helps to overcome death's "sting" (*E*, xvii).

William James and the Genteel Tradition in American Philosophy

Three months after Santayana tendered his first letter of resignation from Harvard (he would not actually leave his post for more than a year), he delivered "The Genteel Tradition in American Philosophy" to the Philosophical Union at Berkeley, in August 1911. It is useful to read this lecture, now probably his most widely read essay, after his introduction to Spinoza's *Ethics*, and in light of the quest for a voice capable of articulating the natural and human comedy that he had called for in *Three Philosophical Poets*. This voice is the standard by which he measures his American predecessors and contemporaries.

By that gauge, Santayana's lecture presents William James as the strongest or most provocative voice with which to contend, even as he falls short of writing religious naturalism's comedy. The trouble with American culture, Santayana claims, is this: Its moral, religious, and literary ideals are holdovers from other ages and, therefore, no longer rooted in the material affections, practices, and institutions of its people. Philosophy in America is not grounded in the patterns of American life: "America is a young country with an old mentality," its "hereditary philosophy [has] grown stale," and its "academic philosophy" is similarly spoiled (WD, 187).

America's old mentality, Santayana claims, is informed by a "Calvinism" that has been deformed by a "native-born" Emersonian romanticism. The Calvinist had proclaimed (indifferently from both Santayana's "Dante" and his "Royce") "that sin exists, that sin is punished, and that it is beautiful that sin should exist to be punished." The heart or conscience of the Calvinist is "agonized." It is "divided between tragic concern at his own miserable condition, and tragic exultation about the universe at large" (WD, 189).[12] The Calvinist's theodicy placed sinners in the hands of an angry God meting out justice in ways that, appearing arbitrary to people, was really or divinely proportionate and beautiful. Calvinism, in other words, had kept comedy divine and humanity tragic, by placing the triumph of blessedness over suffering or despair outside the ken of human beings, indeed outside the natural world altogether.

This theology, Santayana suggests, had practically suited "early American communities," situated in a "small nation with an intense vitality, but on the verge of ruin, ecstatic and distressful, having a strict and minute code of laws, that paints life in sharp and violent chiaroscuro, all pure righteousness and black abominations, and exaggerating the consequences of both to infinity." But the successful merchant capitalism and militant expansionism that Calvinism rationalized or, at least, complemented, eventually led to the relaxation of "the pressure of external circumstances, and indirectly the pressure of the agonized conscience within," allowing for the change in "high social morality" that Emerson (as well as, for example, Hawthorne and Poe) came to express and embody (WD, 190).

With Emerson, Santayana argues, "the second and native born American mentality began to take shape." Emerson redescribed humanity's problems and promise by letting sin "evaporate" and by construing nature as "all beauty and commodity," pliable to an all-powerful self—particularly an American self—fated to be the willful agent or creator, or the vehicle of creation, of perfectly lovely life. As Cornel West has put it (playing on Santayana's phrasing): "Emerson's theodicy essentially asserts three things: 'that the only sin is limitation,' i.e., constraints on power; that sin is overcomable; and that it is beautiful and good that sin should exist to be overcomable."[13] Like the liberal

American churches he could no longer abide, Emerson truncated Calvinism by locating the beauty of the Calvinist's God in the natural world, by reading his providence into its processes, and by construing transcendental self-scrutiny, self-revelation, and self-assertion as undivided from the heart of divine creation. He divinized the self, sometimes identifying it with private and idiosyncratic genius, sometimes with the public life of the American nation, and sometimes with both.

Emerson's vision suited the wants and needs of a racially and economically circumscribed and militant American middle class (one whose "evaporated sense of sin," I note, also allowed the genocide of an indigenous Indian population, the internal colonization of blacks, and the emergence of policies of worldwide empire or Americanization). In the doing, it became even more explicitly anthropomorphic than Calvinism, by embracing the view that human (American) power knew no genuine limits, no circumstance it could not render lovely in solitary and social ways. This firm natural supernatural optimism was surely anathema to Calvinism but, Santayana suggests, "If you told the modern American that he is totally depraved, as Calvinists actually had, he would think you were joking, as he himself usually is. He is convinced that he always has been, and always will be, victorious and blameless" (WD, 191).

For Santayana, absorbed as much with human powerlessness as with divine hopes, Emerson's theodicy finally left him quaint. Santayana is preoccupied not only with the awesome power of nonhuman forces circumscribing mankind's possibilities, but also with human forces that leave some people empowered and others dominated. So Emerson's vision of (American) good and right marching on victoriously forever simply does not wash. It is neither tragic nor comic enough, confusing humanity, particularly the American people, and divinity the way it does.

To Santayana's mind in 1911, then, Emerson's lasting contribution is not his American religion but rather his transcendental "method" or, better, "attitude." To take this attitude is to have "no system," Santayana claims, but to "covet truth." The way Emerson did that, he asserts, is to return to "experience, to history, to poetry, to the natural science of his day, for new starting-points and hints" by which to flesh out, as Santayana now explicitly puts it, his own "piece of human soliloquy" (WD, 196–99).

Here then, in 1911, we have the picture of philosophy that moves beyond *Three Philosophical Poets* toward "Philosophical Heresy." Philosophy is a personal work of art, the creative imprint that an individual leaves on others. "Soliloquy" is pit against the systematicity found in "professional philosophers," and Santayana—now preparing to distance himself quite theatrically from professionalism—subjects the latter to ridicule:

> [P]rofessional philosophers are usually only apologists: that is, they are absorbed in defending some vested illusion or some eloquent idea. Like lawyers or detectives, they study the case for which they are retained, to see how much evidence or semblance of evidence they can gather for the defence, and how much prejudice they can raise against the witnesses for the prosecution; for they know they are defending prisoners suspected by the world, and perhaps by their own good sense, of falsification. They do not covet truth, but victory and the dispelling of their own doubts. What they defend is some system, that is, some view about the totality of things, of which men are actually ignorant. No system would ever have been framed if people had been simply interested in knowing what is true, whatever it may be. What produces systems is the interest in maintaining against all comers that some favorite or inherited idea of ours is sufficient and right. A system may contain an account of many things which, in detail, are true enough; but as a system, covering infinite possibilities that neither our experience nor our logic can prejudge, it must be a work of imagination and a piece of human soliloquy. (WD, 198–99)

This proclamation, in my view, marks Santayana's more or less definitive self-admission into the company of philosophers Richard Rorty eventually dubs "edifying" rather than "systematic." Rorty suggests in *Philosophy and the Mirror of Nature* that

> on the periphery of the history of modern philosophy one finds figures who, without forming a "tradition," resemble each other in their distrust that man's essence is to be a knower of essences. Goethe, Kierkegaard, Santayana, William James, Dewey, the later Wittgenstein, the later Heidegger, are figures of this sort. They are often accused of relativism or cynicism. They are often dubious about progress, and especially about the latest claim that such and such a discipline has at last made the nature of human knowledge so clear that reason will now spread throughout the

rest of human activity. These writers have kept alive the suggestion that, even when we have justified true belief about everything we want to know, we may have no more than conformity to the norms of the day. They have kept alive the historicist sense that this century's "superstition" was the last century's triumph of reason, as well as the relativist sense that the latest vocabulary, borrowed from the latest scientific achievement, may not express privileged representations of essences, but be just another of the potential infinity of vocabularies in which the world can be described.[14]

Although many interpreters, in my view, have distorted Santayana's writing in ways that make him seem like the essentialist the "edifiers" oppose, by and large his work, at least from "The Genteel Tradition" on, warrants Rorty's claim.

James's New Way to Hope

It is at this point that Santayana introduces James as outflanking the genteel tradition. Indeed, Santayana claims, the brothers Henry and William have broken the shell of worn-out tradition.[15] Henry outwitted the old culture in "the classical way," by understanding it in the superb detail of his novels. But William had learned the lasting lesson of romanticism by taking up its transcendental attitude without hardly ever falling into its idealistic confusions. "Thus he eluded the genteel tradition in the romantic way, by continuing it into its opposite" (WD, 204). He had given his culture a new self-image and a new way to hope, at once Protestant in its emphasis on tensions between well-doing and well-being as well as society and solitude, but abandoning most of the entrenched assumptions of Christian theology and its idealist offspring.

On this view, Emerson had rejected systematicity. But he had made no clear break from the genteel tradition because, despite his happy use of transcendental self-criticism, he was unwilling to accept the utter contingency of the human predicament or the limits of human self-assertion. His "spirit" was still a mechanism of necessity, still the engine that made providential ascent inevitable, still the thing that made "being" work itself out one way.

Santayana pictures James following Emerson's antisystematicity. But while holding onto the Protestant dialectic between righteousness and grace that had marked both Calvinism and romanticism, James drops the ideas of historical necessity or providential inevitability. He accepts the open-textured character of the transcendental attitude. He welcomes spiritual heterogeneity or difference. He champions a Darwinian historicism that asks how things come to be, rather than trying to envision how they will turn out after everything else has happened. He sees human beings as *chances to make things better*, as "concrete endeavors, finite efforts of souls living in an environment which they transform and by which they, too, are affected" (WD, 207–8). Finally, he views divine spirit as a finite and "romantic adventurer" with an undetermined future.

James's brilliance, Santayana claims, lies in his recognition that the "scope," the "duration," and the "quality" of the life of the spirit, whether human or otherwise, "are all contingent," at work in a universe that "is an experiment . . . is unfinished . . . has no ultimate or total nature, because it has no end" (WD, 208). This "radically empirical and radically romantic" way of thinking and feeling, Santayana proclaims, "represented the true America, and represented in a measure the whole ultra-modern, radical world" (WD, 204). Without avoiding the problems of meaning brought on by suffering, absurdity, and evil, James portrayed finite and inconclusive ways to overcome them. Without inflating the powers of human self-assertion, he argued that "intelligence . . . is an experimental act, a form of vital tension," not some "miraculous, idle faculty, by which we mirror passively any or everything that happens to be true, replicating the world to no real purpose" (WD, 206).

If the very heart of comedy was to highlight how mean suffering was and to find and display ways to overcome things that impeded human joy, James's vision was comic. To be sure, James remained alienated from Spinozistic naturalism. He persisted in his commitment to the occurrence of supernatural help in some cases where people were unable to save themselves, so his view fell short of being a "natural comedy." For that matter, he was never able to provide, with much detail, the social practices and institutions, or exercises in solitude, that made a place for grace in the natural world. James's *Varieties of Religious Experience*, to be sure, investigated a plethora of solitary human encounters with deity, and reflected on the social contributions made by such "religious geniuses," whether as exemplars or as social activists. But his "religious experiences" were divine, not natural, comedies. He failed to recognize them as cultural performances.

Nonetheless, Santayana claims, James's construal of the spiritual life in terms of sheer contingency gave people "a new philosophical vista . . . a conception never before presented" and "enticed faith in a new direction" (WD, 210). "Henceforth," Santayana concludes, "there can hardly be the same peace and the same pleasure in hugging the old proprieties" (WD, 211).

Once again, comparisons and contrasts between Royce and Santayana are telling. Just as Santayana is canonizing James for making way for natural comedy, Royce is canonizing him as an American Moses, philosophically condemned to fall short of idealism's promised land, waylaid on the Pisgah of pragmatism. In his 1911 Harvard Phi Beta Kappa Address "William James and the Philosophy of Life," written shortly after James had died, Royce has the last laugh on his friend, the foe of absolute spirit, by describing him as embodying one of its stages. Royce asserts that James's pragmatism is "a form of Americanism in philosophy" that emphasizes the nation's distinctive qualities: energy, practicality, and courage. But Royce also says that James's pragmatism represents "a people that is indeed earnestly trying to find itself, but that so far has not found itself." At best, James epitomizes the "hopeful unrest" of an American Israel wandering through the desert on its way to the promised land. His pragmatism offers too much "chaos" and has to be taken up into that "larger view" offered by absolute idealism, which has an account of spirit triumphant. Royce even suggests that James was on the verge of accepting a kind of absolute idealism in his last works. He would be remembered the world over, Royce asserted, because he had uttered "some of the great words of the universal reason."[16] For Royce, as for the mainline interpretations of "the spirit of American philosophy" that followed his lead, not Santayana's, James was no comic.

James's Shortcomings

To Santayana's mind, James's utterly historical universe provides the broad setting for celebrating the disciplines and joys of spiritual life in the natural world. But James had not taken Spinoza seriously. He "was not naturalistic enough to feel instinctively that the wonderful and the natural are all of a piece," and so he felt obligated to search for the supernatural in religious experience; he kept grace somehow waiting outside the natural world, having to make forays into it (*COUS*, 83). Beyond that, James had three shortcomings, all of which helped to posture himself as an intellectual statesman formulating policies by which to reconcile this or that party to cultural dispute. First (and despite his own "certain blindness" doctrine), James tended to characterize philosophy as a kind of responsible social work, when actually, Santayana begins to assert, it is a disciplined play of mind that demands "time-out" from social judgment and policy formulation. Second, James divided his philosophical "responsibilities" in partly self-deceptive ways, commanding himself to describe "things as they are" on the one hand—utterly contingent, open-textured, and ultimately gratuitous—while making himself find things "propitious to certain preconceived human desires" on the other (and so, in the crucial instance, arguing for supernatural powers that could overcome problems we could not, in a world definitively marked by ultimate human impotence) (*COUS*, 61). Finally and following, he was overzealous in his rejection of the traditional role that "truth" played in Western philosophical discourse, by identifying the truth with currently vindicated opinion.

On the first score, Santayana highlights the difference between a Jamesian pragmatism that always pictures thought as conducive to some particular action, and his own festive view that it is in holidays from work, or in "high moments, when action [becomes] incandescent in thought, that [people] have been most truly alive, intensively most active, and although *doing* nothing, have found at last that their existence was worth while. Reflection is itself a turn, and the top turn, given to life" (*COUS*, 3). Human welfare surely demands social policy formulation and political action. But these things do not inevitably circumscribe personal well-being. Cultural space must be maintained for the contemplation of things that make life worth living, where people can stretch their imaginations beyond the parameters of social policy formulation, and set themselves, at least from time to time, discretely apart from the constraints of political action, so they can discern and celebrate its point.

Especially in a culture shaped by the "perpetual incubus of business" (*COUS*, 189), committed to the "gospel of work and belief in progress" (*COUS*, 211), and under the delusion that business, work, and progress, American-style, offer the one divine way of doing things, Santayana seeks to safeguard the notion of philosophy as a set of disciplines providing "a consolation and sanctuary" where people can dispose themselves to clarifying their ultimate concerns and can contemplate the things that make life flourish (COUS, 93).

But second, philosophy understood this way involves faithfulness to "the hard truth," first, that all of mankind is but an incident in an incident in an unstable universe randomly related to human wish and will; and, second, that *our* tradition, be it American, or Anglo-Saxon, or German, or classically Western, conventionally blinds us from the practices and aspirations of others—ways of being human we can discern if we take the time and trouble to listen and understand before rushing to judgment. At issue, Santayana contends, is the possibility of breaking away from our own preconceived desires, the responsibilities engendered by them, and the judgments descending from them, sufficiently enough to understand the varieties of human being, power, and assertion distinct from our own.

Finally, if people are to maintain allegiance to "the hard truth," then, Santayana argues, James's pragmatic account of the truth is not altogether satisfactory. Here, Santayana was perfectly willing to accept James's view that there is no good reason to develop a *theory* of truth. With James, he could have said that the truth "was nothing distinct from the reality on the one hand, and the ways it may be known on the other."[17] That was the pragmatic force of his claim that the truth "is a question of the identity of the fact asserted and the fact existing" (COUS, 156). He thinks that James's psychological explication of how people link thoughts with things—by substituting terms one for another in propitious ways—evades fruitless epistemological conundrums. Nonetheless, he is convinced that while James gave a satisfactory account of the justification of belief, or how people properly go about making claims on the truth, he thinks his mentor had failed to signal the role that *truth as a regulative ideal* plays in the activities of cognitive vindication. For Santayana, *discovery of fact* (interpreted, to be sure, in vocabularies of human invention) and *telling the truth* are not scholastic pseudoproblems but morally and spiritually indispensable disciplines in a world beset by ignorance and, even more pressingly, lies. So, if and when James let people think that "an idea is true so long as it is believed to be true, or that it is true if it is good or useful, or that it is not true until it has been verified," he was, unwittingly, permitting obstruction of discovery and safeguarding convenient deceit and self-deceit (COUS, 159).

Realism and Pragmatism

Is this a telling criticism? It is surely a persistent one, currently being played out, for example, in the conflicting views of Hilary Putnam and Richard Rorty. It will help to clarify the tenor of Santayana's criticism of James to turn to the current intramural conflict going on between these two realistic pragmatists. Rorty's pragmatism is realistic and Putnam's realism is pragmatic and they tend to converge in a position similar to one occupied by Santayana.

I characterize Rorty's pragmatism as realistic because his efforts to see language as part of the coping behavior of human beings living their way through contingent predicaments, rather than as a mirror reflecting nature as it understands itself, demand a material backdrop. Like Santayana, he not only presumes that there is extralinguistic stuff, or "bits of the universe," that make the solving of problems and the management of difficulties indispensable parts of our repertoire of distinctively human behaviors.[18] He also argues that, so far as arts and sciences have been normalized, evidential truth conditions exist by which parties to dispute may come to presumptive settlement.

I accept Putnam's own characterization of his realism as pragmatic.[19] His three commitments to conceptual relativity, to taking "our familiar common sense scheme, as well as our scientific and artistic and other schemes, at face value, without helping itself to the notion of the thing 'in itself,'"[20] and to the view that such descriptive schemes "reflect our interests and choices,"[21] all point toward an understanding of philosophy as "a study of the comparative advantages and disadvantages of the various ways of talking which our race has invented"—which is both Santayana's and Rorty's pragmatic view.[22]

One way to display an overlap, at least, in their realisms is to say that Rorty and Putnam are both committed to the view that there are material conditions (including material human conditions) we do not just legislate—that "most things in space and time are the effects of causes which do not include human mental states."[23] One way to characterize their common pragmatism is to say that they agree (1) to an account of language that collapses any *metaphysical* distinction between fact and value, though permitting a *phenomenological* distinction between these two things; (2) to a nonfoundational view of knowledge; and (3) to a nontranscendent picture of rationality. They both profess that every human language, including every language used to indicate facts, is valuative, expressing determinable human interests; that knowledge is constituted by sound opinion; and that, when it comes to ironing out disagree-ments, we have no recourse to some science capable of settling all controversy, but only to judgments and methods of arriving at judgments, which, them-selves, might well be placed in critical jeopardy.

Where these two contemporary pragmatists appear to disagree most is over the role that truth plays in human discourse. Rorty has said that "truth . . . is not a profitable topic," and that he follows Wittgenstein's "resistance to the entire cultural tradition which made truth—the successful crossing of the void which divides man from the world—a central virtue."[24] Putnam responds, implicitly anyhow, by saying that "we may come to think of history and politics as nothing but power struggle, with truth as the reward that goes to the victor's view. But then our culture—everything in our culture that is of value—will be at an end."[25] On this view, truth appears to be a central virtue indeed.

But here, I think, it is crucial to characterize the contemporary dispute in the right sort of way if we are ever to figure out what difference, if any, it makes to accept one of these views rather than the other. This is so for a number of reasons. First, to some extent, I believe that Rorty and Putnam are talking past one another. But, second, in another way I think there is a difference here that makes a difference. Finally, I believe that, whatever this difference is, it is important to consider the view that if truth *is* a virtue indispensable to culture, it is, for all that, capable of distracting us from other virtues if we give it more than its due.

Reflection on Santayana's writings may clarify these three issues. This is so because Santayana accepts both a realism and a pragmatism that Rorty and Putnam, on my interpretation anyhow, could share. He both rejects the notion of truth understood as "the successful crossing of the void between man and world," and defends love of the truth as a virtue indispensable to culture. Finally, he attempts to characterize the discipline or virtue of allegiance to the truth within a broader spiritual context that both makes it a practical necessity and curbs its pretensions.

We know that, at least since the writing of his dissertation, Santayana maintained that we are born into material conditions we do not just legislate, or that, having adopted a way of speaking about those conditions, there are facts to be discovered about them. We also know that a brand of pragmatism emerged out of Santayana's wistful materialism, one that claimed, in *The Life of*

Reason, that reason must be characterized as a life articulated and constrained by the disciplines or human institutions of common sense, social practice, religion, art, and science. In Santayana's rendition of pragmatism, reason is constituted by an intricate pattern of human institutions that bind one another within the context of material conditions that are largely out of human control. Reason is *not* simply a set of logical rules, or a list of applicable but abstract principles, protocols, or criteria. It is a life.

Just as significantly, Santayana's mature works reject the distinction between necessity and contingency. In *The Realm of Matter*, Santayana will argue that "In a contingent world necessity is a conspiracy of accidents" (*RB*, 291). Every condition that permits or fosters human well-being is contingent. Any claim to the contrary, he will say, "foolishly parades the helplessness of the mind to imagine anything different" and fuels vicious dogmatism (*RB*, 417).

But Santayana's mature works not only foreshadow some of the disagreements, especially over the role of truth, that now exist between philosophers like Putnam and Rorty; they also place questions about the virtue of truth within a broader spiritual context.

In *Scepticism and Animal Faith* and in *Realms of Being*, Santayana will follow James's lead in dumping an allegiance to truth understood as the virtue that lets people transcend the void separating them from the world. More clearly than James, though, Santayana will attempt to reduce to absurdity the notions on which this putative virtue depends—there simply is no void separating the human psyche and the material world, or break between necessary and contingent truths, or distinction between principles or facts that are given, on the one hand, and formulated judgments on the other. On his view, the psyche is a structure of material behaviors in the world; we might stipulate necessary relations among logical terms or definitions, but the applicability of this or that logic to the ways of the world is a matter of contingent fact; and finally, we could intuit given essences or qualities or functions (like "rocking" or "nausea" [*SAF*, 92]), but only by *withholding* any belief, assertion, or implication whatsoever, not by establishing any *indubitable ground* for knowledge or claims to truth.

From the standpoint Santayana develops, especially after the Great War, the trouble with maintaining truth understood as the virtue letting us link up our presumptively charmed circle of thoughts with an external world—in other words by letting us intuit things or possess them "just the way they are"—is that this discipline is irrelevant to the demands of scientific, moral, and spiritual life. Prefiguring the later Wittgenstein, Santayana's meditations in *Scepticism and Animal Faith*, for example, will conclude, among other things, that "if all data are symbols and all experience comes in poetic terms, it follows that the human mind, both in its existence and in its quality, is a free development out of nature, a language or music the terms of which are arbitrary, like the rules or counters of a game" (*SAF*, 98).

Following this line of thought, Santayana will assert that "all [the] insecurity and inadequacy of alleged knowledge," that is, knowledge construed as a privileged (because literal) intuition of things, is "almost irrelevant to the natural order of the mind to describe natural things." Epistemology understood as permitting a God's-eye view of the world, or even as revealing invariant norms by which to settle any controversy, is a setup for failure, because it is based upon "a false conception of what would be success." "Our worst difficulties," Santayana went on, "arise from the assumption that knowledge of existences ought to be literal, whereas knowledge of existences has no need, no propensity, and no fitness to be literal. . . . It fulfills its function perfectly— I mean its moral function of enlightening us about our [well-being]—if it remains symbolic to the end" (*SAF*, 101–2).

It is, I think, Santayana's insistence that "truth is a moral . . . good" (*RB*, 551), that the function of our allegiance to truth is basically ethical, clarifying both the dangers impeding and the chances for attaining well-being, that establishes the appropriate context for understanding Santayana's criticisms of James, and the dispute between philosophers like Putnam and Rorty over the role of truth in human discourse. Put another way, the dispute seems more a matter of will or courage than one of intellect alone.

According to my way of interpreting them, neither Santayana nor Putnam nor Rorty sees truth understood as the virtue that overcomes the void separating humankind from the world, because for all three of them, truth understood this way functions to solve a pseudoproblem. If anything, allegiance to truth understood this way is a vice—something that Santayana characterizes as a spiritual distraction that actually impedes the realization of human joy by sidetracking us intellectually the way a cramp sidetracks us physically.

Overcoming the void separating humankind from the world *is not a profitable topic*, at least from the vantage points of these philosophers, because there is no such void. And yet, it would be cavalier, I think, to claim that the dispute between James and Santayana, or Rorty and Putnam, is bogus once we make this clarification, because a significant issue still appears to divide the parties.

For Rorty and James, "truth" is just an honorific or eulogistic term we give to the claims that competent people now happen to have, constrained by the relevant conversations they happen to have held. Putnam and Santayana do not deny that opinion alone constrains the course of controversy. But they do insist that our most significant conversations, those that turn on disclosing moral or material circumstances to help settle an issue one way or another, dispose us to reporting what has actually gone on—to searching out some aspect of the truth. The sheer honorific use of the term "true" keeps conversation wobbling between smug quietism and Nietzschean assertion. It eclipses the truth understood pragmatically as describing (in language) the unknown we need yet to discover if we are to get things right—not philosophically right, just right. The cash value of the term "true," understood as *limit concept* (in Putnam's term) or as an *ideal ideal* or *immaterial sort of being* (in Santayana's terms), demands a presumption that there is a gap between whatever we claim to know, now or whenever, and the truth of the matter; between the ways we signify things knowledgeably and the ways we might give a complete description of what happens (in any modality).

The point is that, on both Putnam's and Santayana's view, knowledge claims (of whatever garden variety, because we only have garden varieties) are versions, fragmentary, and capable of indefinite revision. The truth that anchors realism has many faces, each of which constitutes a physiognomy of plural traditions of thought and action. This point accounts for Santayana's disappointment in James's pragmatism. James's "truth"—and Rorty's—appears to discount the (pragmatic) discipline, to play on one of Quine's phrases, of pushing and pulling ourselves toward objectivity.[26] So does James's "radical empiricism" if, as Santayana claims, it is established to permit some metaphysical disclosure. The object of metaphysical disclosure upends allegiance to truth, by suggesting that there is a "view in which truth is contained once for all and without qualification" (*RB*, 536).

As limit concept, "the truth" ironically fixes the presumption that our best current claims, whatever and whenever, are corrigible, fallible, and variable. They are always open to criticism and refinement. In Santayana's view, the distinction between the "essence" of truth and the "existence" of knowledge claims captured the intuition voiced by James in his own time and by Rorty in ours, that we idolize our knowledge claims—we eulogize them—whenever we count them as literally mirroring the way things are. When we do this, we commit what Santayana calls the first false step in philosophy and what Quine would eventually call philosophical "original sin, coeval with the word"— namely, the confusion of sign and object.[27]

Santayana notes that "the truth posited by animal faith, in action or in curiosity, is posited as unknown, as something to be investigated and discovered, and truth in this transcendent sense can never be denied by an active mind," living as it does in utterly contingent material conditions that constitute it no less contingently. "But," Santayana continues, "when animal faith has already expressed itself in conventional ideas, its own further actions find those ideas obstructive. Truth has now been rashly posited as known. An idea, an idol, has taken the place of the god [the strictly ideal ideal] originally and intrinsically invoked by the mind and posited as unknown" (RB, 536).

The truth, then, that critics like Rorty deny is "itself a blasphemy," and in denying it, Santayana argues, they are "secretly animated by the love of truth" (RB, 536). Allegiance to truth remains a central virtue in our culture, according to Santayana. But it is one that not only recognizes that the Platonic quest to capture some intellectual intuition of the whole universe is a vice; it also demands that we recognize how fragile our knowledge claims are and how revisionary we must always be prepared to be, given the variable and modifiable faces of material power that make up our own lives and the environments in which we live.

Allegiance to the truth, in Santayana's view, is clearly a central virtue, the discipline that undercuts the monumental deceit involved in maintaining that our words call themselves or anything else into existence, that our thinking or wishing or willing make things so. But, for this very reason, allegiance to the truth can never stand alone and, just as surely, can run amok.

Sufficient attention to truth sanely fixes the (modifiable and variable) horizons within which we can hope to overcome the things that impede human joy. But, as Santayana wisely notes, "merely being true does not make things worth knowing" (RB, 441). Again, "the real problem is moral; and even if science presents truth more honestly than the humanities, we should still have to ask whether these scientific truths were the most important, and even whether the knowledge of truth is the ultimate goal or good of mind. Frankly," Santayana asserts, "it is not when the mind is free" (RB, 440–41).

When the mind is free, when matters let life be liberal, the point is not simply to pursue the truth, but rather to pursue the good, as Santayana will put it, that our natural world "suggests, approaches, and misses" (*RB*, 833). To be sure, such poetic freedom is "premature, and even criminal, when the psyche is living at cross-purposes with the possibilities of life" (*RB*, 443). But once we have taken sights on such possibilities, we are left to balance our contrary spiritual interests as best we can, with what creativity we have at our disposal.

Santayana's criticisms place James's pragmatism in needlessly bad light, because James made room for truth understood as an "ideal ideal." But James *was* sloppy enough, in matters of truth, to fail to distinguish between the satisfaction of individuals and groups of people on the one hand and the satisfaction of standards of inquiry on the other, thus letting the use of the term "true" remain subject to moral capriciousness.

The Great War and Santayana's Turn to Festive Soliloquy

Santayana's understanding of himself as a philosopher as well as his views took their most remarkable turns against the backdrop of his resignation from Harvard in 1912, his departure from the United States for good the same year, his dramatic separation from philosophy understood as a professional discipline, and, perhaps most especially, the dark cultural shadows cast by the Great War.

That first "world war" bureaucratized, mechanized, and industrialized mass death, making total war—war that knows no boundary lines between military and civilian worlds—an ever present reality. Coming on the heels of a progressivist era, as Paul Fussell puts it, the Great War "was a hideous embarrassment to the prevailing Meliorist myth which had dominated the public consciousness for a century. It reversed the Idea of Progress."[28]

The sense of hope abridged that began to clutch Europe found its signature in an occasional note that Henry James wrote a friend: There, James said that "The plunge of civilization into this abyss of blood and darkness . . . is a thing that so gives away the whole long age during which we have supposed the world to be, with whatever abatement, gradually bettering, that to have to take it all now for what the treacherous years were all the while really making for and *meaning* is too tragic for any words."[29]

It is no coincidence that transformations in theological and philosophical vision arose during this war and its aftermath: Karl Barth's neoorthodoxy, Ludwig Wittgenstein's therapeutic or self-healing criticism, Husserl's "crisis," Heidegger's dramatic return to "being," Dewey's prophetic pragmatism, and the efforts of Russell to salvage the Enlightenment project of grounding knowledge on itself, all signaled a sense for the "insufficiency of reason," and a recognition of the blinding pride from which human self-assertion could suffer. Each of these major twentieth-century philosophers found their new voices in the war that shattered confidence in the culture they had thought they embodied. Santayana's mature religious naturalism emerged at the same moment, as he lived through the war situated, for the most part, in Oxford, England.

Santayana, to be sure, had been warning his audiences for some time that human self-assertion was overreaching itself, that the myth of Progress was full of deceit, that the quest to find some philosophical unification of all of culture led to dead ends, and that people had better abridge their hopes. So while the details of the war horrified him, the fact that it occurred came as no great shock the way it apparently did to Henry James. To him, the Wilsonian slogan endorsing the war to end all wars was a cruel hoax and a sick joke. In his view, "Only the dead have seen the end of war" (*SELS*, 102).

But as he lives in Oxford during his fifties, a privileged and middle-aged bystander to combat, he finds himself clearing his philosophical voice in a new way, one that highlights *soliloquy* more than statesmanship, *festivity* or celebration more than representation, *playfulness* more than utility, *understanding* more than judgment, *comic relief* more than tragic resignation or sublime exultation, *religious discipline* more than academic enterprise, and *confession of faith* more than profession of claims intended to carry authority for everybody. These are the characteristics that lead Santayana eventually to call his philosophy "a discipline of the mind and heart, a lay religion" (*RB*, 827).

In *The Life of Reason*, using the voice of an intellectual statesman and seeking representative authority, Santayana had asserted baldly that "soliloquy . . . is the discourse of brutes and madmen" (*LR*, 1:156). But by 1914 he is writing little else. The coda for understanding the change appears as the last and rhetorically consummate piece in *Soliloquies in England and Later Soliloquies*,

"Hermes the Interpreter," where Santayana finally returns to the subject of *Lucifer's* affection (*SELS*, 259–64).[30]

There, Santayana openly confesses allegiance to the Greek god who bore "news to his father and brothers in Olympus, concerning any beautiful or joyful thing that is done on earth, lest they should despise or forget it" (*SELS*, 264). Hermes, the Western tradition's most prototypical "trickster figure" or "outlaw-savior"—interpreter of gods on Olympus to humans on earth and vice-versa, of the past to the future, of foreigners to one another, of the high in rank to the low and back again, and of individuals to themselves—becomes Santayana's model for cultural criticism. Hermes, Santayana soliloquizes, is "the great interpreter, the master of riddles," the god who "does not preach, who does not threaten, who does not lay new, absurd, or morose commands on our befuddled souls, but who unravels, who relieves, who shows us the innocence of the things we hated and the clearness of the things we frowned on or denied" (*SELS*, 262–63). Hermes' function is to understand, rather than to judge, to arrange for mutual affection and forgiveness, rather than to command. Santayana sets out to do the same, dropping the language of dutiful statesmanship for one of socially irresponsible play.

Hermes is currently known among literary critics as an absolute comic, a socially irresponsible puck who not only stands outside the norms that shape any given society or polity, but finds humorously imaginative ways to invert those norms, to kill authority or privilege with laughter, and to get the lowest of the socially low to smile triumphantly at the passing moments of joy in their lives. His function is liminal, able to cross normal social or cultural boundaries and distinctions because, as Santayana puts it, "he is everywhere at home" (*SELS*, 261). The laughter that he employs to kill or honor undercuts realistic social organization and purpose, bringing into sharper relief certain conditions and characteristics—for example, mortality, but also experiences of mortal well-being, that human beings may share with one another across the boards. Santayana says

> I should not honour him for his skill in riddles if I thought he invented them wantonly, because he liked to puzzle himself with them, or to reduce other people to perplexity without cause. I hate enigmas, and if I believe that Hermes was the inspirer of those odious persons who are always asking conundrums and making puns I should renounce him

altogether, break his statue, turn his picture to the wall, and devote myself exclusively to the cult of some sylvan deity, all silence and light. But I am sure Hermes loves riddles because they are no riddles to him; he is never caught in the tangle, and he laughs to see how unnecessarily poor opinionated mortals befool themselves, willfully following any devious scent once they are on it by chance, and missing the obvious forever. He gives them what sly hints he can to break the spell of their blindness; but they are so wedded to their false preconceptions that they do not understand him, and are all the more perplexed. Sometimes, however, they take the hint, their thoughts catch fire, and insight, solving every idle riddle, harmonizes the jarring cords of the mind. (*SELS*, 264)

Hermes's role, historically, had been festive in two senses: the social havoc that he willfully wrecked took place imaginatively, not realistically, like the havoc in evidence, say, during carnival. Second, the upshot of his antics was meant to be common joy. Hermes employed every trick of irony he could muster to unmask social pretensions in ways that let every party to conflict or hierarchical difference "acknowledge himself beaten and deceived, yet be happier for the unexpected state of affairs" (*SELS*, 141). His function was religious in the sense that he created an aura of communion undergirding the inevitable dissensions and conflicts attending human society realistically viewed. This is the figure that Santayana identifies with at this crucial juncture in his career.

From this sort of critical posture, the intellectual statesmanship that Santayana had learned from James and Royce seemed too participant in the realistic social obligations of national culture to allow for much Hermesan understanding or expression of human community. Intellectual statesmen shaped criticism in ways that communicated the message: THIS IS REALISTIC SOCIAL WORK. As such, Santayana becomes convinced, they impoverished their liberal art by putting on the blinders appropriate to practical responsibility and social duty articulated in its role-specific terms. These constraints had kept both his one-time teachers and influential colleagues (though not equally by any means) from clearly observing, or at least communicating, the expressive or poetic characteristics of their own visions, as well as the festive character that philosophical reflection could take on.

Conventional wisdom had it that the natural sciences, the new social sciences, and philosophy—pictured more and more by the new professional philosophers as the most rigorous science of sciences—proceeded by constraining the role of the imagination in observation. And excessive imagination was condemned as playful, science praised as workaday, in the modern North Atlantic republics preoccupied with keeping noses to grinding stones. But Santayana thinks that excessive imagination, the disciplined ability to let one's imagination *exceed* one's beliefs and commitments, is quite precisely the one thing needed to discern what James had called "the world of impersonal worths" in his essay on "A Certain Blindness." "Moralists," Santayana said, "have habitually aimed at suppression, wisely perhaps at first, when they were preaching to men of spirit; but why continue to harp on propriety and unselfishness and labour, when we are all but little labour-machines already, and have hardly any self or any passions left to indulge? Perhaps the time has come to suspend these exhortations, and to encourage us to be sometimes a little lively, and see if we can invent something worth saying or doing. We should then be living in the spirit of comedy, and the world would grow young" (*SELS*, 137).

So Santayana begins to find attention-getting ways to frame his philosophy with the metacommunication: THIS IS FESTIVE PLAY. In a culture that has become a "mechanopolis," Santayana muses, when every spontaneous faculty and liberal art had been sacrificed to corporate expansion, bargaining, exchange, and imperialist adventure, people too often forget that

> the mind is not a slave or a photograph. It has a right to enact a pose, to assume a *panache*, and to create what prodigious allegories it will for the mere sport and glory of it. Nor is this art of innocent make-believe forbidden in the Decalogue, although Bible-reading Anglo-Saxondom might seem to think so. On the contrary, the Bible and the Decalogue are themselves instances of it. To embroider upon experience is not to bear false witness against one's neighbor, but to bear true witness to oneself. Fancy is playful and may be misleading to those who try to take it for literal fact, but literalness is impossible in any utterance of spirit. (*SELS*, 138–39)

Santayana's presentation of his soliloquies as festive play assaulted the sensibilities of many of his colleagues and students, especially as the new philosophical professionalism emerged, emphasizing the "special problems" of epistemology and the rigorous work that such problems demanded. Indeed, his insistence on it surely contributed to his ultimate neglect by an Anglo-American philosophical community that has never yet been able to take itself with a grain of salt.

The communication THIS IS PLAY is always very tricky, as Edith Kern has pointed out, "introducing elements of irony and distancing into the relationship between sender and receiver" of it that are missing when discourse is straightforward.[31] It was surely tricky for philosophers who tended to pit their own work *against* imaginative play. In fact, it was the playfully ironic and satirical stance that Santayana took toward his own discourse and that of others that set him squarely apart from his peers. It pit his rhetoric of philosophy against the major, contending philosophical movements of his time, including mainline pragmatists who viewed themselves as intellectual statesmen, Bergsonian vitalists who characterized their work as metaphysically revelatory, German postidealists, enthralled by Nietzsche, who appeared mainly to prize the Enlightenment projects of self-assertion, as well as the new technical "scholastics" like Russell and G. E. Moore, seeking to establish universal conditions linking up thoughts and things with utter verisimilitude.[32]

Soliloquies introduces Santayana's readers to the heart of his mature vision. It presents a view of philosophy as a religious discipline by characterizing its interpretations as related to practical thinking the way religious ritual is related to realistic social activities. Recall that, as Santayana understands them anyhow, realistic social structures are hierarchical and organize people into differentiated roles or functions. To his mind religious rituals proceed in ways that undercut such hierarchies and foster a sense of community or communion among its participants.

When a religious ritual begins, there are communications made that indicate that what is about to occur is socially unrealistic, a piece of festivity. The thing that makes it festivity is that it is geared neither to meet realistic social demands nor really to undercut the social world in which those demands get organized and met. It lets people break away imaginatively from constraints set by such social organization. It does so for the sake of establishing the communal joy that comes as people take on the "masks" that help them express their human bonds, living together as untitled creatures who not only recognize the presence of death but rehearse ways of living joyously with it.

Carnival is Santayana's paradigm for such religious festivity, and he goes out of his way to make that holiday central to his *Soliloquies*. The key to understanding carnival lies in appreciating the role that masks play in it, and the same holds, Santayana claims, for festive philosophy. In carnival beggars imaginatively become kings and kings beggars, people put on death masks in order to vitiate, imaginatively, the distinction between life and death and, more generally, perform in theatrical ways that symbolize their self-renewal and their triumph not over the fact of death but over its rule. The performances in carnival provide people with "another world to live in," an imaginative world in which delight, joy, harmony, proportion, and beauty displace common conflict and the shadow of death as the simply disturbing background against which to place humankind. "Masks," in such performances, let people experience a solidarity with one another and a personal sense of triumph that both departs from normal life but affects it by reawakening a felt sense of shared spiritual welfare.

Now philosophers who wished to construe their discipline as realistic rather than imaginative, and as work rather than playful ritual, typically pictured themselves as *unmasking* things in order to discern the realities behind appearance. But this is so much pretension in Santayana's view. Recall his words: "In this world we must either institute conventional forms of expression or else pretend that we have nothing to express; the choice lies between a mask and a fig-leaf. . . . [A]nd the fig-leaf is only a more ignominious mask" (*SELS*, 139). There simply is no way to divest humanity of its imaginative conventions; the task is to invent masks that clarify our tragic predicaments and present comic ways to resolve or dissolve them, letting us enjoy the lyric qualities that help make life significant. In Santayana's view, that is what philosophical practice can accomplish.

It is important to note in this regard that religious rituals come to an end once they have reestablished a sense of joy in things that give point to the complex structures of the workaday world. People who have participated in them go back to their normal routines, revitalized and recommitted to their common inheritances, social practices, and personal aspirations. So too with Santayana's soliloquies. He does not write them to *upend* a normal and socially realistic life of reason. He writes them to provide ritual space for people to take the time and effort required to catch the joys that finitude, conflict, and death too often shadow.

Santayana maintains that the life of reason per se requires no special philosophical discipline because rational interests are capable, at any rate, of keeping sound enough tabs on one another. But, he claims, because realistic social life outruns harmony, it is necessary to enact well-being in imaginative ways. Because the life of reason does not inescapably bring satisfaction to spiritual demands, any more than righteousness and social service necessarily secure a delightful sense of well-being for mortal creatures, people require cultural space to exercise spiritual disciplines that lend their world an aura of grace. If, in *The Life of Reason*, Santayana had championed religion as another, socially marginal, and imaginative world in which to do this, he now places his own philosophical reflections on the same kind of margin.

Santayana's Festivity and Dewey's Reconstruction in Philosophy

Santayana's new characterization of his philosophy in terms of soliloquy, festivity, playful satire and irony, forgiveness, religious discipline, and confession separate his writing from the Deweyan sort of pragmatism concurrently reaching prominence in the United States. From Santayana's perspective, at any rate, Dewey and his followers appear to collapse the difference between philosophical reflection and social policy formulation, leaving too little room for the spiritual disciplines that function to envision and celebrate graceful life. They try to dissolve the distinction between "contemplation" and "action" on the grounds that "contemplation" is an Old World and undemocratic practice geared to keep some parties empowered and others dominated. Santayana thinks otherwise:

> To envision and clearly to discern the Idea of what we are about is the whole of art, spiritually considered; it is all the mind can or need do; and the more singly the spirit is rapt in the meaning and vision of the work, the more skillfully the hand and tongue will perform it. And the standard and criterion of their skill is in turn precisely the same vision of the Idea: for I ask, what makes an action or a feeling right, except that it clears away obstructions and brings us face to face with the thing we love? The whole of natural life, then, is an aspiration after the realization and vision of Ideas, and all action is for the sake of contemplation. (*SELS*, 227)

There are telling differences between Santayana and Dewey over the action/contemplation distinction—over what kinds of practices play what roles in efforts of the human spirit to flourish. But they can easily be overdrawn, because the two thinkers clearly share views that make them both pragmatists very much concerned with the parts poetry and religion play in liberal culture. Dewey ends *Reconstruction in Philosophy* with reflections that echo the thrust of works like *Three Philosophical Poets*, "The Genteel Tradition," and *Winds of Doctrine*. He expresses typical Santayanan liminality when he asserts:

> Poetry, art, religion are precious things. They cannot be maintained by lingering in the past and futilely wishing to restore what the movement of events in science, industry, and politics has destroyed. They are an out-flowering of thought and desires that unconsciously converge in a dis-position of imagination as a result of thousands and thousands of daily episodes. They cannot be willed into existence or coerced into being. The wind of the spirit bloweth where it listeth and the kingdom of God in such things does not come with observation. But while it is impossible to retain and recover by deliberate volition old sources of religion and art that have been discredited, it is possible to expedite the development of the vital sources of a religion and art that are yet to be.[33]

The crisis that marks these "days of transition," Dewey claims, is a spiritual emptiness stemming from the fact that "intelligence is divorced from aspira-tion." Strengthening the bond between them is, indeed, "the task and problem of philosophy."[34] Intelligence and aspiration together make up the "vital sources" Dewey is looking for.

Santayana has said as much before. But where Santayana puts on a farcical mask in *Soliloquies* to dramatize the desperate need to safeguard extrapolitical institutions that celebrate creaturely aspirations or "the love of life in the consciousness of impotence," Dewey's *Reconstruction in Philosophy* prepares for a "New World" variety of moral rearmament, a secular sort of millenialism. He indicts "otherworldly" institutions as all too political, by claiming that they have functioned, in the past at any rate, to sustain a social status quo that *systematically* divides rich from poor, elite from common, and empowered from oppressed.

It is Dewey's contention (as it had been Marx's) that religions have encour-aged displacement of community *from* society, by shunting the practices of community to the margins of culture rather than setting them in its social centers—in its marketplaces, town meetings, schools, and legislatures. Moreover, he claims, philosophy traditionally has been kept in thrall to this sort of theologicopolitical dominance. Only now, in the wake of the hegemony of "The New World," Dewey asserts, can "the inner set of the mind, especially in religious matters, [be] altered" or "opened up."[35] How so? First, through a "transfer of interest from the eternal and universal to what is changing and specific, concrete."[36] Second, through "the gradual decay of the authority of fixed institutions and class distinctions and relations, and a growing belief in the power of individual minds, guided by methods of observation, experiment and reflection, to attain the truths needed for the guidance of life." Third, through setting "great store upon the idea of progress." Fourth, through a Baconian recognition that scientific knowledge is the power people require to get them where they want to go—to overcome "those phases of nature and life that obstruct social well-being."[37]

For Dewey, distinctively religious institutions and practices are part of the "old world," the "closed world," the "fixed world," the world "where the fixed and unmoving was . . . higher in quality and authority than the moving and altering," and where "a limited number of classes, kinds, forms, distinct in quality (as kinds and species must be distinct) [were] arranged in a graded order of superiority and inferiority," in short, "a feudally arranged" world.[38] From his vantage point, traditional religious communion vents frustrations that have been artificially sustained through the avoidable conflicts of unnecessarily hierarchical and differentiated social structures. The inference from this criticism is clear enough: Why not transform religious communion into political and economic community? Why not turn religious contemplation and ritual into an active quest to solve the particular problems of men?

But from the standpoint of *Soliloquies*, Dewey is both tragically idealistic and unrealistic on issues of social and political practice and blind to the *useful* tensions between festive contemplation, which is something individuals do on their own and to themselves, and problem solving, which is social and public.

To be certain, Santayana agrees with Dewey that it is "a verbal mirage . . . to see happiness in fixity. . . . If to be saved were merely to cease, we should all be saved by a little waiting" (*SELS*, 95–96). But the point of festivity, he claims, is not fixity. Festivals, he claims, "mark the events on which . . . existence turns" (*SELS*, 111). "Without such playful pauses and reflective interludes, our round of motions and sensations would be deprived of that intellectual dignity which relieves it and renders it morally endurable—the dignity of knowing

what we are doing, even if it be foolish in itself, and with what probable issue"
(*SELS*, 132).

Simultaneously invoking and challenging Christian tradition, Santayana
claims that the "wisdom of the Cross" does not lie in any strategy to *break
through* time to some sort of fixity, nor in adopting "suffering [as] an end in
itself" nor in any variety of political millenialism, nor in the denial of death,
which is "a fundamental lie" (*SELS*, 98). He asserts, rather, that sanctioning
such attitudes signals varieties of Christian "folly" stemming from either sectar-
ianism or atavism or both.

To his mind, the wisdom of the Cross lies in a personal "knowledge that
existence can manifest but it cannot retain the good." But he separates himself
from any quest for fixity in his insistence that "the good" is as variable and as
modifiable as human nature (*SELS*, 94). "We have broken loose," he claims,
from "the Christian synthesis" that retained a "forced and artificial liberty . . .
reserved for an ascetic aristocracy" that nurtured itself on the mistaken view
that "nature and the gods . . . and man have a fixed character" that is rendered
graceful by a "single solid wisdom" that reveals "a necessary piety, a true
philosophy, a standard happiness, a normal art" (*SELS*, 166–69). Piety, wisdom, moral freedom, and art remain crucial conduits to happiness or well-
being. So does the recognition of repeatable characters or "eternal essences"
that allow people to make sense of themselves and their world. But necessity,
philosophical truth, and iron-clad regulation fall away, along with the "forced
and artificial liberty" that feeds on these things. All of this, for Santayana, now
instances "true vice," or "human nature strangled by the suicide of attempting
the impossible" (*SELS*, 72).

For Santayana, Christ and Hermes become bound together the same way
Lent and carnival are linked:

> The secret of a merry carnival is that Lent is at hand. Having virtually
> renounced our follies, we are for the first time able to enjoy them with a
> free heart in their ephemeral purity. When laughter is humble, when it is
> not based on self-esteem, it is wiser than tears. Conformity is wiser than
> hot denials, tolerance wiser than priggishness and puritanism. It is not
> what earnest people renounce that makes me pity them, it is what they
> work for. No possible reform will make existence adorable or fundamen-
> tally just. . . . The easier attitudes which seem more frivolous are at

bottom infinitely more spiritual and profound than the tense attitudes; they are nearer to understanding and to renunciation; they are also nearer to the Cross. (*SELS*, 97)

But they are also just as near, he finally confesses, to Hermes as to Christ, especially to Hermes' willingness to discern the innocence of the things people hate and the clearness of the things they frown on or deny—which is the disposition indispensable both for festivals like carnival and for philosophers like Santayana bent on understanding, unraveling, and relieving rather than judging, commanding, and threatening.

The Age of Russell

Deweyan pragmatists, intent on social and political reform, were all too earnest and anxious from Santayana's vantage point, but at least they maintained a clear focus on the problems of human finitude and looked for ways to overcome them. More troubling, to his mind, is the dawning "age of Russell," first in Britain and finally throughout the English-speaking world.[39] Epitomized by Russell's *Problems of Philosophy*, that age is marked by a great desire to inaugurate a professional search for *a science of thought* that (as Cartesians and Kantians had hoped in other times) would establish "knowledge . . . so certain that no reasonable man could doubt it."[40] Russell, in other words, inherits the mantle of a modern philosophical tradition that virtually reduces the love of wisdom to the logic of epistemic truth. The search for the "epistemological conditions" bridging the gap between an otherwise charmed circle of thought and the external world is, to be sure, far older than *The Problems of Philosophy*. But that work becomes as influential as any other in stripping down philosophy in the grand style to philosophy understood more strictly *as* epistemology. Whatever Russell may have thought of the work, philosophical communities in England and America received it as a charter for reconstructing philosophy that way. As John Passmore has put it: "The whole atmosphere of *The Problems of Philosophy* is logico-mathematical, in the Cartesian style; Russell sets out in search of the indubitable, of what it is *impossible* to doubt and criticizes our everyday beliefs from that standpoint."[41]

But to Santayana's way of thinking, the whole problematic of philosophy understood this way comically displaces the celebration of spiritual life with a kind of "blind-man's-buff" (*SELS*, 210). Russell's book on *The Problems of Philosophy*, he says, is "admirable in its style, temper, and insight, but it hardly deserves its title; it treats principally, in a somewhat personal and partial way, of the relation of knowledge to its objects, and might rather have been called 'The problems which Moore and I have been agitating lately'" (*WD*, 112). Moore and Russell seem to Santayana to represent thinkers who suffer from "colossal folly . . . keenly excited about not knowing where they are" (*SELS*, 216, 210). "They are really here," he reminds his readers, "in the common natural world . . . and they have only to remove their philosophical bandages in order to perceive this" (*SELS*, 210).

Santayana's message is clear: The epistemological project that Russell's *Problems* epitomizes is diseased. The renewed quest to establish unmediated Knowledge of Reality simply leads to "intellectual cramp" (*SELS*, 216). Philosophy has itself become spiritually *disordered* by blinding its practitioners from their traditional and proper task, which is to celebrate the good life. If the spiritual disciplines of philosophy are to thrive, philosophers have to take off the bandages of epistemology and metaphysics altogether, accept the finite and fallible status of their knowledge claims, and get on with confessing their belief in the things that make life worth living. That, I now hope to show, is what Santayana's *Scepticism and Animal Faith* tried to accomplish, paving the way for the characterizations of spiritual life he wrought, diversely, in such works as *Realms of Being, Dialogues in Limbo, The Last Puritan*, and *The Idea of Christ in the Gospels*.

7

COMIC FAITH

Meditations at the Margins

There is no more provocative or finely drawn piece of festive soliloquy in Santayana's whole corpus than *Scepticism and Animal Faith*, the work that he published in 1923 to introduce his own natural comedy, *Realms of Being*. The book begins with a preface that must have appeared almost adolescent in its satirical playfulness to mainline Anglo-American philosophers now in "the Age of Russell."

Realists and naturalists in the United States generally characterized *Scepticism and Animal Faith* as a definitive statement of Santayana's critical realism. They pictured it as Santayana's effort to provide the epistemological nuts and bolts for the naturalistic ontology that would follow in *Realms of Being*. In particular, they construed it as an attempt to sweep modern philosophy clean of metaphysics by establishing a naturalistic theory of knowledge linking mind to the world.

But, to my mind, this is a weak misreading of *Scepticism*, a book that opens up with Santayana's unforgettably disarming phrase, "Here is one more system of philosophy" (*SAF*, v). He expects his reader to presume not "one more" but one better, something like the final word. Indeed, he expects his readership to judge that if it is just "one more," then it is no better than the rest, another king without any clothes. Thus his second sentence: "If the reader is tempted to smile, I can assure him that I smile with him" because "my system—to which this volume is an introduction—differs widely in spirit and pretensions from what usually goes by that name" (*SAF*, v).

More than likely, his readers were not looking for "pretensions" because, from the vantage point of mainline Anglo-American philosophers in the 1920s, pretension is a disease that epistemology is deployed to cure. But Santayana is calling that usual view a pretension and, moreover, he is admitting that his own philosophical "system" involves pretension. He is pretending, he is playing, he is delivering his festive metacommunication: THIS IS PLAY.

Professional readers at the time require philosophical discourse to be serious and realistic. Indeed, they expect it to displace pretense with a method for coming realistically face-to-face with nature as it understands itself. They turn to works like Santayana's with the hope that they might come away saying, "Yes. Santayana has articulated something we can endorse. He has provided us with a new system of the universe that includes information that has been missing until now about the links between discourse and the world. He has delivered us from the fear of illusion by showing us the conditions that must obtain for knowledge of reality, or the external world, to occur. Now we can become post-Santayanans."

Such hopes are stymied, if not dashed, when Santayana declares in *Scepticism and Animal Faith* that his system "is not mine, nor new," that it is "no system of the universe," that it is "not metaphysical," and that it is "no phase of any current movement" (*SAF*, v–vii). It is none of the things that characterize philosophy understood as fulfilling some realistic social role. It is not a charter that might be promoted or rejected. *Scepticism and Animal Faith*, Santayana asserts, is a confession, an avowal, a way of "cleaning the windows of my soul" (*SAF*, vi–vii). It is original, the way falling in love or getting born is original, but no newer than affection or birth. It is original because it is a stylized presentation of something Santayana is doing to himself, but it is a variation on spiritual disciplines of self-transformation that had instructed individuals for ages. It is not written to offer any new information, like a cosmology or ontology of presence, or a specification of the nonphysical conditions supporting or governing material life. And, though Santayana highlights the fact that it is "formed under the fire of contemporary discussions," he also insists that it is not authored as part of any current philosophical movement (*SAF*, viii).

All the things that professional readers might demand from a modern philosopher—a new authority to admire, a novel redescription of things, a cosmology or a metaphysics, a contribution to some epistemological movement—Santayana renders unto modern philosophy, and departs to a solitary margin of the culture that modern philosophy thinks it serves. There, he presents his public with a book of exercises, not in epistemology, but for a symbolic transformation of identity that functions, religiously, to restore a sense of life-at-first-hand.

Epistemology or Antiepistemology?

In a sense, then, *Scepticism and Animal Faith*, published when Santayana is sixty, announces that his last "system" will be a departure, not simply from this or that sort of modern philosophy, but from modern philosophy altogether. He not only disavows the dominant projects of contemporary philosophers by poking fun at their pretensions, but also implies that his "meditations" should be taken as pretense, as a sort of play.

Read as a contribution to modern philosophy—that is, read without reference to its preface—Santayana's *Scepticism and Animal Faith* seems to make three proposals on behalf of an epistemological doctrine called "critical realism."[1] First, there is a kind of systematic doubt that lets people suspend any and every belief. Second, this systematic doubt results in the contemplation of things that are left to see or note when every belief has been suspended. These things are terms or characters or qualities or essences that are randomly related to time and place. They, rather than first principles or sense data, are indubitable. Third, because these given terms are in contingent relation with existential conditions, no existential claim can be supported by the weight of foundational certainty. To the contrary, knowledge claims are presumptive; beliefs are intertwined with other beliefs all the way along; they do not rest on any rock bottom.

If this line of thinking is sound, then it may be that at least some confessions of personal belief are rendered legitimate through the realization that no sure and certain beliefs or rules for thought and action lie at the bottom of things. Natural knowledge of the natural world is not sure and certain. It is constituted by fallible, corrigible terms that symbolize things without mirroring them. At best, beliefs carry pragmatic necessity, when they are "unavoidably implicated in action."

But taken as a solution to the basic epistemological problem—which is to discover how discourse can be linked up with the external world in a way that will cure people of illusions—Santayana's strategy has been found question-begging by even his most appreciative critics. This is so because his argument does not adequately establish conditions bridging the gap between an otherwise impermeable sphere of thought and the world out there. Santayana fails to show, as Lachs has put it, "the way in which symbols link up with the reality they depict."[2] If we are to solve this epistemological problem, critics like Lachs suggest, then we need something Santayana fails to articulate: We need a theory that lets us "place limits on appropriate symbolization" by presenting us with "criteria by which the adequacy of a symbol may be determined."[3]

But Santayana has already ridiculed the quest for such an epistemological theory in *Soliloquies*, where he calls it "colossal folly," an expression of that "intellectual cramp" that results from philosophers being "keenly excited about not knowing where they are" (*SELS*, 210). It is, as he now puts it in *Scepticism*, the "snare" that philosophy fell into "when, in modern times, it ceased to be the art of thinking and tried to become that impossible thing, the science of thought" (*SAF*, 254).

The function of methodological skepticism in post-Cartesian modern philosophy, currently epitomized by Russell's *Problems*, had been to sweep thinking clean of all but those unshakable beliefs on which to construct presumably indubitable knowledge. But this is not how skepticism functions for Santayana at all. Quite the contrary. In his meditations, skepticism does not lead to indubitable beliefs. It leads to the suspension of any and every belief. It results not in residual truths but in a kind of imagination that Santayana calls "a solipsism of the present moment." It results in a vacant awareness of terms of discourse, like "blue" or "rocking" or "nausea" or "the milky way" (*SAF*, 15). The outcome of skeptical suspension, Santayana claims, even "ceases to be appearance, in the proper and pregnant sense of this word, since it ceases to imply any substance that appears or any mind to which it appears. It is an appearance only in that its nature is manifest . . . a surface form, without roots, without origin or environment, without a seat or a locus . . . an immaterial absolute theme" (*SAF*, 39).

Herman Saatkamp has put it this way: "Santayana's contention is that if we reduce our knowledge to what is actually evident, we may discern an awareness that is infallible and indubitable; but this infallibility and indubitability characterize such a restricted state of consciousness that it cannot be described as knowledge in any form and therefore cannot provide the basis for the reconstruction of knowledge on self-evident beliefs or knowledge claims."[4]

But, to my mind, the thrust of Santayana's point is even stronger. If a state of consciousness cannot be described as knowledge in any form, then it makes no sense to call it "indubitable" or "infallible," because these are epistemic terms of art. Santayana argues that it is possible to suspend all belief and still remain "immediately" aware of "given" essences, logical or aesthetic themes or terms. But the "whats" that are given are, as he had claimed in *Soliloquies*, "something seen in a dream, or *imaginary*" (*SELS*, 229). He reiterates the point in *Scepticism*: The radical skeptic is left in a "realm of immediate illusion" (*SAF*, 34). As illusions or as sheer images, essences per se carry no epistemic weight whatsoever. So that, for Santayana, while the notion of the given is no myth, the idea that the given grounds any sort of knowledge surely is. What makes the given "given" is precisely the immediacy that severs it from cognitive intent, significance, and import.

Ritual

To understand the role that skepticism *does* play for Santayana, it is important to place it in the festive framework for philosophy that he establishes in *Soliloquies*, particularly his piece on "Carnival." *Scepticism and Animal Faith* narrates a ritual process that, like many other similar rites, gets articulated in four segments: first, one in which the playful or imaginative status of the proceeding is communicated (*Scepticism*'s preface); second, one that separates the celebrant from his normal, social sense of self, fraught as it is with particular spiritual disorders (the book's skeptical exercises); third, one that permits an avowal of humankindness that carries with it a renewed sense of well-being (Santayana's confession of animal faith); and, finally, one that restores him to normal social life, feeling spiritually reawakened (his eventual embrace of common sense).[5]

In this scheme, Santayana's skeptical exercises serve to separate him from his normal sense of self and from the particular spiritual discord or "cramp" present in the modern philosophical quest for epistemological foundations. The ultimate skeptic, he says, "concentrated on *not* asserting and *not* implying anything, but simply noticing what he finds" (*SAF*, 16). Such intuitions—for example, "sounds, figures, movements, landscapes, stories" (*SELS*, 230)—are "not elements in knowledge" (*SAF*, 106). They do not "reveal or discriminate any fact." Put another way, the skeptic's "imagination works in a void." It becomes so vacuous of intent, in fact, that the "data" making it up "cease to be illusions cognitively, since no existence would be suggested by any of them." They are not "illusions" in "the bad sense of this word" because they are not falsely taken to symbolize anything existential (*SAF*, 65).

But, even more significantly, Santayana claims that

> a practical man might still call them illusions for that very reason, because although free from error they would be devoid of truth. In order to reach existences intent must transcend intuition, and take data for what they mean, not for what they are; it must credit them, as understanding credits words, accepting the passing vision as a warrant for something that once was, or that will be, or that lies in an entirely different medium, that of material being, or of discourse elsewhere. Intuition cannot reveal or discriminate any fact; it is pure fancy; and the more I sink into it and the more absolute I make it, the more fanciful it becomes. (*SAF*, 65)

But if this is so, then the epistemological use of methodological skepticism to displace illusion with demonstrable knowledge is ruined; the knots tying together the rigging of modern philosophy unravel. "Essences," on this view, are neither the sense-data that British empiricists had looked for nor the basic principles of thought Continental rationalists had hoped to find. On the contrary, they are terms randomly related to questions of knowledge. The realm of essence that the ultimate skeptic discovers can hardly be specified as founding knowledge or as bringing people face-to-face with nature on its own terms. But, Santayana claims, the discovery of essence can serve to set a person free from life at second hand by ritually placing him apart from his own web of beliefs and outside the bounds of structured social life. This, indeed, is the role skepticism plays for him.

Liminality

Mainline epistemologists employ methodological skepticism in an inevitably disappointed hope of securing residual certitude. But the consequence of Santayana's skeptical exercises is ritual liminality, not certainty. It leaves him betwixt and between a spiritual disorder and ritual rebirth. So it is no coincidence that Santayana calls his realm of essence "limbo," and that he speaks of it as tantamount to "intellectual suicide" (*SAF*, 10). For the function of liminal passage in any ritual process of self-transformation is to enact the death of an old self, but also simultaneously to prepare for spiritual rebirth by relieving an individual of some spiritual disorder impeding a sense of joy.[6]

Santayana calls his realm of essence "limbo" because ritually it is poised ambiguously and ambivalently between living and death. "Living Beings," he asserts, echoing Schopenhauer (and, more ironically, James), "dwell in their expectations, rather than in their senses. If they are ever to see what they see, they must first in a manner stop living; they must suspend the will" (*SAF*, 68). When they do so, they encounter a "strange world" that might make a child scream. Santayana says that the essences that people can intuit when they suspend their wills, and inseparably suspend their beliefs, are like "disembowelled objects," or gutted bodies, or "gaunt clothes without bodies"—"not the living crowd that it ought to be, but a mockery of it, like the palace of the Sleeping Beauty" (*SAF*, 71). In fact, "in the absolute present all is specious; and to pure intuition the living are as ghostly as the dead, and the dead as present as the living" (*SAF*, 37).

This is the sort of lifeless awareness that had led William James to distinguish between anaesthetic formal perception—something that characterized acedic or even catatonic mental patients—and full-blooded belief or conviction, which is willful. For people who are caught in the realm of formal perception, James had noted, "everything is hollow, unreal, dead" (*POP*, 2:437). They are "excluded from the life of the affections, harsh and tender alike, and drag out an existence of merely cognitive or intellectual form."[7] They see things without emotion and, inseparably, they are void of conviction: They do not care. Indeed, these had been the symptoms of James's own psychotic depression, an illness he had described as the opposite of nightmare, or as having powers but no motives. James had nearly scared himself to death by enacting solipsism of the present moment. This was the illness that James had tried to overcome by *making himself* live a strenuous life.

But now Santayana is prescribing James's symptoms as an indispensable segment of his exercise in spiritual renewal. James's characterization of "an existence of merely cognitive or intellectual form," Santayana thinks, is more or less correct. So is his view that affectional beliefs shape or structure our normal social lives. But if, as Santayana thinks, it is ritually important to embark away from that structure for the sake of spiritual renewal, then his skeptical exercises provide the requisite *via negativa* to do so. Prescribing James's symptoms provides a fruitful way to slough off conventions about what he thinks he *ought* to believe in order to embrace freshly the things he really *does* believe as a human agent in quest of spiritual fulfillment.

The point of discovering "the given" for mainline philosophers is to establish things that can be known for certain without having to know anything else. But Santayana's meditations turn this expectation on its head. Indeed, his "discovery of essence" exposes the fact that the projects of modern philosophy constitute a double bind by damning people, on the one hand, to the fear of illusion if they do not discover foundational knowledge, while damning them on the other to the same fear when, inevitably, they fail to secure such knowledge. By promising people too much and giving them too little, modern philosophy impedes spiritual well-being. It causes people needless anxiety and waylays them from getting on with the imaginative exercises that may bring them spiritual relief, recreation, and well-being.

From the standpoint of mainline philosophy, epistemology is a cure for illusion. But Santayana suggests that this cure is itself a disease. The way epistemologists attempt to rid the world of the fear of illusion is itself sick because they cannot possibly excise illusion from the given: The given is nothing but illusion; it is a presentation of the terms constituting imagination. Santayana's *liminal* characterization of the realm of essence, however, does overcome the fear of illusion—by reframing illusion in a way that it does not provoke any anxiety.

Instead of trying to expunge illusion and inevitably failing, in other words, Santayana shows a way to excise desperation and fear. Illusions per se cannot be characterized as fearful or delightful, insignificant or significant. What makes them one or the other or some blend of the two, in Santayana's view, is the role they play in our willful lives as natural human beings. For some of them help us to manage our inevitably difficult lives better, some of them cause needless pain and suffering, and some of them, expressing deep ambivalence, do both.

The liminal character of the realm of essence brings this home, Santayana claims, by showing that "just as food would cease to be food, and poison poison, if you removed the stomach and the blood that they might nourish and infect; and just as beautiful things would cease to be beautiful if you removed the wonder and welcome of living souls, so if you eliminate your anxiety, deceit itself becomes entertainment, and every illusion but so much added acquaintance to the realm of form" (*SAF*, 73).

On Santayana's view, epistemology ties up people in spiritual knots by placing them in fruitless double binds. Santayana's guidance through the realm of essence is geared to unbind them and set them free—free from the search for nature's own terms and free to confess their belief in the predicaments and promises held out by human life. His solitary "discovery of essence" subverts the conventions of Platonistic epistemology by exposing the bankruptcy of "the notion that knowledge is intuition, that it must either penetrate to the inner quality of its object or else have no object but the overt datum" (*SAF*, 85). This, Santayana argues, makes the discovery of essence "hygienic" (*SAF*, 80). If philosophers have been discouraged time and again in their efforts to secure immediate knowledge and a corresponding ontology of presence, their despondency does not come from failure so much as "from a false conception of what would be success." Recall Santayana's claim once again: All the "insecurity and inadequacy of alleged knowledge" voiced by epistemologists is "almost irrelevant to the natural effort of the mind to describe natural things" (*SAF*, 101).

But so long as Santayana situates himself in the realm of essence, he remains betwixt and between spiritual distress and well-being. Although critics like Dewey and Hook would charge him with the view that salvation lay in transcending the "problems of men" by entering the fixed world of essences, Santayana explicitly rejects this position, first in *Soliloquies* and then again in *Scepticism and Animal Faith*.

For Santayana, "pure intuition" is cathartic or purgative, not salvific. The realm of essence is constituted by an indefinite catalog of possibilities; it is no place of grace. To Santayana's mind, those who pictured it that way, like certain Indian thinkers, presented an "egotism of the redeemed with which, as with other egotisms, I confess I have little sympathy" (*SAF*, 51). On the contrary, the skeptical entertainment of essences unbinds people from the conventions of modern philosophy. It exposes the fact that when people use terms of discourse to signify themselves in transaction with their circumstances, they deploy them like "the rules and counters of a game." The terms of discourse do not provide "mirror-images of nature." So it follows, Santayana claims against the rising tide of mainstream philosophy in England and the United States, that people "had no capacity and no obligation to copy the world of matter nor to survey it impartially" (*SAF*, 98).

Essences and Antiessentialism

The thrust of Santayana's "discovery of essence" is to disrupt traditional philosophical essentialism, which construes "essence" as the key to necessary or philosophical truth about the ways of the world. Santayana determines, rather, that essence, per se, is unrelated to any cognition, much less necessary truth: As he eventually puts it in his "Apologia Pro Mente Sua": "The relief that I find, when in the presence of facts I can discern essences, does not come, as in religious faith, through trust in any higher facts. It comes through liberation from anxiety, from the need of faith, and from the very problem of knowledge" (*PGS*, 532).

In Santayana's view, essences are terms or characters that play a role in cognition only when and as they signify events that are existential and, therefore, inevitably contingent. They play a role in small "t" truth claims when and as they characterize such events in practically suitable ways.

But, to my mind, holding on to the discourse of essence and "the given" turns out to be more trouble than it is worth. It is important, I think, to recognize five things here with Santayana. First, skepticism does not lead to certitude but, rather, to a suspension of belief or to liminality. Second, it is possible (if potentially conducive to psychosis) for somebody practicing skepticism to fancy "imaginary" stuff in the absence of belief. Third, *reflection* on this sort of fancying can help take off the "bandages" of modern philosophers who are "keenly excited about not knowing where they are" by disabusing them of the notion of immediate knowledge. Fancying may be "immediate" in the sense that it may go on unreflectively. But fancying is not a way of knowing; and, with the kind of fancying Santayana rehearses, it is not even self-reflexive. Fourth, there is a difference between identifying *what* something is and establishing *that* it has actually happened, is happening, or will happen. Moreover, lots of *what* we can identify is only fictitious. Fifth, terms or languages of terms, per se, carry no epistemic, moral, or spiritual freight. It is only as they inform how we think about what we do, who we are, and how things happen that they pull any weight.

But, then, what is the force of calling what we can fancy when we suspend belief "essence"; and what difference does it make whether the terms or characters we then entertain are classed as "given" or made? If "essence" carries neither epistemological nor metaphysical privilege, and for Santayana it does not; if "the realm of essence" that we can discover is "imaginary" or, roughly, as indefinitely extensive as imagination could be, and for Santayana it is; *and* if discourse works more like the rules and counters of a game (which are contrived or invented, even when spontaneous, activities) than a mirror, which is Santayana's claim—then "essence" and "the given" lose all but satirical point.[8]

To be sure, Santayana claims that terms or characters are universal or repeatable and randomly related to time and place, much as "Hamlet" is a character that can be played by this or that actor, here or there (and remains a character even when nobody ever plays "him" any place or at any time in particular). Well it can, so long as we have Shakespeare's play. To claim that "Hamlet" subsists, or essentially is, even all the while or after the play is lost, is disingenuous. The claim suppresses the fact that the claimant, who has the play in mind, is pretending that neither he nor anyone else does, or even needs to. Just so, redness is repeatable so long as it continues to be an English counter—a counter that plays parts in English very similar to ones played by "rouge" in French and "rot" in German. But entertaining "red" and "rouge" and "rot" depends on learning English, French, and German, respectively, which provide contexts for their use. The one is repeatable in English so long as its rules of thumb remain the same, the others in French and in German. But it is needless and hopeless to search for something else subsisting eternally that all of them repeat. Moreover, English, French, and German have their time and place, and "red," "rouge," and "rot" their variations. Santayana knew this. In *Soliloquies*, published one year prior, he had asserted that "the eternal is always present, as the flux of time in one sense never is, since it is all either past or future; but this elusive existence in passing sets before the spirit essences in which spirit rests, and which can never vary; as a dramatic poet creates a character which many an actor afterwards on many a night may try to enact. Of course the flux of matter carries the poet away too; they become old-fashioned, and nobody wishes any longer to play their characters; but each age has its own gods" (*SELS*, 106).

My point here is not to claim that Santayana was really a psychological or linguistic nominalist (like I am). He was not. My point, rather, is that we can admire the hygienic parts of Santayana's skeptical suspension, and even go on to affirm much of his "animal faith," without having to suffer the "intellectual cramps" involved in affirming myths of the given, myths of subsistence, or claims to eternity or timelessness.

Animal Faith

Santayana's skeptical suspension of belief wipes his heart clear of fear because it sweeps away *every* emotional response available to normal human beings. His radical skepticism is, he says, "a discipline fit to purify the mind of prejudice and render it all the more apt, when the time comes, to believe and act wisely." There is, he claims, "nobility in preserving such scepticism through a long youth, until at last, in the ripeness of instinct and discretion, it can be safely exchanged for fidelity and happiness" (*SAF*, 69–70). The upshot of his marginal meditations, then, is geared to be "fidelity and happiness," not a secure critical realism, and not any "egotism of the redeemed" that finds salvation in fixity.

The liminal encounter with "essence" that Santayana dramatizes does not, of itself, bring any sense of well-being. If it dissolves philosophy's quest for certainty, it also leaves people at the mercy of indefinite possibilities, absent-minded, unready still to acknowledge the things that constitute a human life that can be joyful in the face of impotence and mortality. But it is just that sort of acknowledgment that will signal spiritual restoration or recreation. This is what Santayana tries to accomplish in his confession of "animal faith."

If the disciplines of radical skepticism leave Santayana in a limbo of illusions without any identity whatsoever, the practices involved in confessing his animal faith restore his identity—but not identity understood in a socially realistic way. Realistic social identification proceeds by way of differentiation: born in Madrid, raised in Avila and Boston, educated at the Latin School and Harvard, a turn-of-the-century bourgeois, conservative, anti-Hebraic thinker; a philosopher, poet, novelist, playwright, essayist, and critic, this and that position in various distinct communities and sundry social hierarchies. Santayana's confession of animal faith does not lead to an avowal of any of these social distinctions (though it may presume them). It leads to an acknowledgment of his sense of *generic humanity*; it lets him avow the things that allow for a kind of understanding of himself, others, and the world they share, and that let human joy occur.

Santayana's animal faith is not so much a credo or manifesto of belief, then, as it is a confession, an identification with the ways of being that, overlaid or superimposed, form his sense of humankind. He calls these conditions the realms of essence, matter, truth, and spirit, and he argues that they are inevitably implicated in distinctively human action.

Santayana claims that acknowledgment of matter is a must because humans are material forces thrown into material circumstances that are sometimes overwhelming or even lethal to them, but in any case demand accommodation for life's sake, not to mention happiness. Avowal of spirit is indispensable because humans are material forces of a distinctive sort. They differ from other animals by their ability to signify, to lend significance or meaning to their material lives and conditions. *They mind about things that matter.* Indeed, this ability to mind—this ability not simply to perceive or to comprehend but to appreciate, to fear and enjoy, to assimilate and accommodate—is the thing that lets humans take delight in life alone and together, and is basic to well-being. Minding about things that matter makes life something far better to remember than forget, even in the face of inevitable impotence and mortality. Acknowledgment of essence is required, Santayana claims, to stress the imaginative or poetic character of this minding, to clarify the impotence of ideas apart from material being, to emphasize the determinable character of power, and to underscore the indefinite range of possibilities lying outside one's own particular beliefs and commitments (whereas I claim that we can acknowledge all of this without assenting to the "discovery of essence"). Truth is basic, not so much because error is such a great problem but because lying—deceit especially about the power of ideas apart from material being—sits at the root of so much misery, especially the miseries generated by superstition and fanaticism.

This confession of belief, Santayana claims, not only binds him to his kind, establishing a sense of community beneath and apart from all the divisions and dissensions of normal social life, but also gives the latter its ultimate concern or point. In its narrative form, then, Santayana's *Scepticism and Animal Faith* has closer family resemblances to ritual processes evident in religious festivity and meditation than it does to Russell's *Problems of Philosophy*: It presents a solitary and interior passage from distress to spiritual revitalization. It is an exercise in symbolic transformation that functions to diagnose and overcome a disorder impeding human joy—philosophy cramped by practitioners keenly excited about not knowing where they are. Its function is to permit an avowal and appreciation of humankindness. It is a set of disciplines that lets a person exchange the masks of realistic social status—the masks that differentiate one from another—for the mask of undifferentiated human animal. Hence it leads to a sense of community or communion that lends ballast to the structures of social life and, so, may help to displace Nietzschean weightlessness with sufficient spiritual grounding.

This exchange of masks distinguishes Santayana from his own precursors in the aesthetic tradition of spirituality, Edwards, Emerson, and even James. As they had understood themselves, embarking away from realistic social convention to new spiritual birth required an utter and complete unmasking, a barren encounter with really real being (or in James's case, at least supernatural beings), a confrontation with divine power and creativity. So just as Plato may have wished to drive out the poets from his Republic because they knew the secret that the action of "coming face-to-face with being" was itself theatrical, imaginative, and socially unrealistic, a crucial transformative piece of festive performance, so Santayana's predecessors might well have been rankled by his mature confession of animal faith.

Pragmatism, the Pragmatists, and Santayana's Animal Faith

It is well worth noting again, in light of all the bickering that began to occur between Santayana and the leaders of American pragmatism from this time forward, that *Scepticism and Animal Faith* and the many writings that followed all continued to embrace the views that had rendered *The Life of Reason* pragmatic. Santayana simply never abandoned his expressivist view of language, or his nonfoundational construal of knowledge, or his immanent characterization of criticism or rationality. In *Realms of Being*, for example, he continued to focus on problems of human finitude rather than the new "epistemology." He pictured his "realms" as alternative vocabularies with which to manage life's difficulties, not as revelations of the really real. He insisted on the utter contingency and the unexceptionably material character of existence. And he rejected any hard and fast distinction between knowledge and sound opinion. Perhaps most significantly, he transposed "epistemological problems" into moral and spiritual ones, asking how essence, matter, truth, and spirit made well-being both a problem and a natural possibility.

What, then, accounts for the growing rhetorical rift between Santayana and Deweyan pragmatists in the United States? One symptomatic interchange occurs when Santayana criticizes Dewey's *Experience and Nature* (1925) on the grounds that it presents a "half-hearted naturalism"; and Dewey counters by claiming that Santayana's new ontology of matter, spirit, essence, and truth breaks naturalism's back.

Santayana argues in "Dewey's Naturalistic Metaphysics" that a critic can be a naturalist or a metaphysician, but not both; that, while Dewey makes "experience" the primary reality on which everything else depends, a naturalist espouses no "special system at all, but the spontaneous and inevitable body of belief involved in animal life" ("DNM," 343–44). Dewey and his pragmatic followers in the United States, Santayana claims, let a human "foreground" dominate their pragmatic vision. "In nature," he argues, "there is no foreground or background, no here, no now, no moral cathedra, no centre so really central as to reduce all other things to mere margins and mere perspectives" ("DNM," 348). But "the dominance of foreground," he asserts,

> is in all Dewey's traditions; it is the soul of transcendentalism and also of empiricism; it is the soul of moralism and of that kind of religion which summons the universe to vindicate human notions of justice or to subserve the interests of mankind or of some special nation or civilization. In America the dominance of the foreground is further emphasized by the prevalent absorption in business life and in home affections, and by a general feeling that anything ancient, foreign, or theoretical can not be of much consequence. Pragmatism may be regarded as a synthesis of all these ways of making the foreground dominant. ("DNM," 349)

That, Santayana argues, makes Deweyan pragmatism naturalistic by accident, "when, as in the present age and in America the dominant foreground is monopolized by material activity; because material activity, as we have seen, involves naturalistic assumptions, and has been the teacher and the proof of naturalism since the beginning of time." But the point is that "elsewhere and at other periods experience is free to draw different perspectives into which the faithful pragmatist will be drawn with equal zeal" ("DNM," 349). Think of James's supernaturalism.

But despite this (distorted) criticism of "the pragmatic school," it remains clear, even in this essay, that Santayana's own principles of knowledge and criticism are themselves pragmatic, indeed very much like Dewey's, basically vindicating views by asking what specific practices require or preclude; setting "every phase of human imagination . . . in the common world of geography and commerce" ("DNM," 357); making reason an immanent human function, and vindicating discourse by its significance for practice rather than by some presumptive standard of verisimilitude; and perhaps most significant, showing the accidental and optative status of any particular sort of critical discourse.

Dewey counters by arguing, in effect, that Santayana bifurcates humankind from nature in two ways, rendering it unnatural: first, by underscoring a sharp tension between the care-laden varieties of human activity (including discourse) and the careless ways of the universe in which humans live; second, by introducing "immaterial essences" into his realms of being, thereby requiring a sense in which thought plays no transactional role in nature.

This interchange between Santayana and Dewey exhibits fairly weak misreadings on both sides. Dewey "foregrounds" human discourse no more than Santayana does. Santayana is, for the most part, as insistent as Dewey that *it is in the interest of humans to realize how randomly related most of the ways of the world are to human interests.* On the other hand, both Dewey and Santayana maintain that thoughts or feelings, as immediate or actual happenings, as Santayana put it, "simply *are* or *are had*, and there is nothing more to say about them" ("DNM," 353). Along with James's essays in radical empiricism, they both picture such thought going on directly without any "division of subject and object" but rather in the "rapt" (Santayana's phrase) or "consummate" (Dewey's expression) identification of terms.[9]

Certainly Santayana's *epiphenomenalism* differs from Dewey's *interactionism*. That is, his claim that the signs of discourse, as such, make no material difference contrasts with Dewey's brand of instrumentalism. But even in this regard, Santayana never retracts his view that signs become instrumental as communicated. He simply retains the view that characters can be entertained or appreciated without any particular purpose in mind. This hardly makes him an unnaturalist.

This sparring obfuscates, rather than clarifies, deeper issues separating them. Read sympathetically, both are pragmatic naturalists. But Dewey never abandons the picture of philosophy as intellectual statesmanship and, so, attempts to transform it into a comprehensive effort to formulate social policy. In most of his writings (though not without exception), Dewey presents philosophy as a realistic social and cultural activity—as a socially empowering activity—that, at its best, directly subserves the interests of political and economic democracy.

Santayana, to the contrary, suggests in his delineation of "the spiritual life" that characterizing philosophy as social and cultural *policy formulation* leaves some of its most important properties out, including its capacity to *interrupt* social activity, to *suspend* social policy formulation, to provide *ironic distance* from this or that ideological or political commitment, to bring normal social practices to a standstill long enough to *contemplate* the things that bring joy to human life in its plurality and make it worth living. By insisting on these characteristics of philosophical inquiry, Santayana surely carries on the tradition of Emerson's "Man Thinking," Peirce's "musement," and James's insistence on overcoming human blindness by engaging in *practically irresponsible* reflection. But he does so with a clear eye on satisfying what James had called "the religious demand."

Pragmatism and the Religious Demand

The issues separating Santayana from "the pragmatic school" in the United States take on particular interest if we compare him not with Dewey, at this point, but with Dewey's disciple and heir apparent, Sidney Hook. Hook's influential reconstruction of his movement's deepest existential sensibilities, "Pragmatism and the Tragic Sense of Life," offers a crucial text in this regard.

In this essay, Dewey's most influential redactor ostensibly sets out to set the historical record straight. Responding particularly to European émigrés in New York who espouse varieties of logical positivism, Marxism, or existential phenomenology, Hook argues that it has become commonplace to view pragmatism "as a superficial philosophy of optimism, of uncritical adjustment and conformity, of worship of the goddess of success."[10]

On the contrary, Hook asserts, pragmatism is not superficial because it is a method. It is not an expression of conformity because it is, in particular, a method of criticism. It is not concerned with success per se but with settling disputes. Finally, those ungrateful German émigrés are libelous to characterize pragmatism as the Pollyanna of philosophy. This is so because pragmatism is a critical method for settling disputes that arise in open-eyed perceptions of moral discord. In fact, Hook asserts, pragmatism emerges in recognition of inevitable conflicts between good and good, good and right, and right and right. In a phrase that becomes canonical for some, Hook claims that pragmatism is "grounded in a recognition of the tragic sense of life."[11]

Now there is at least one sort of pragmatism about which Hook's claims are quite accurate, and that is Hook's own sort. Ever since the late 1920s, Hook championed the centrality of method in moral and social criticism. He also pictured philosophy as intellectual statesmanship, as a discipline equipped with a method for settling disagreements among contending social interests. Hookian pragmatism, indeed, always amounted to "*analyzing* specific and basic social problems and conflicts, and *clarifying* the issues in dispute with all the tools at one's command."[12]

Throughout a long career—during which he changed his allegiances in political philosophy from Marxism to democratic socialism to federal republicanism—Hook declared that these problems of men demanded constant attention in view of the fact that the human situation is fundamentally tragic. Hook said that James had set the mood and the motivation for pragmatism by noting that "ineluctable noes and looses form part of [life], that there are genuine sacrifices, and that something permanently drastic and bitter always remains at the bottom of the cup."[13]

Now this characterization of pragmatism accords with much that makes it striking. James had gone out of his way to remind the "healthy-minded," believers in Absolute Spirit, and other tender-minded sorts, that life for many was nasty, brutal, and short. So did all the other thinkers who figure prominently in the tradition, including Santayana. They all noted that life hurts, that conflict is abundant, and that intelligence can and should be employed to help overcome discord.

But now, I think, Hook's essay can be read profitably as something other than straight history. Indeed, it makes the history of pragmatism clearer to read "Pragmatism and the Tragic Sense of Life" as part of a lifelong attempt on Hook's part to steer pragmatism one way rather than others. It is true that

Hook was dogged by European émigrés of various philosophical schools who tended to disparage Emersonian/pragmatic traditions. It is true that Hook's critics tended to judge pragmatism without reading its texts. But it is also true that Hook wanted to sever pragmatism from its religious roots and maintain its later Deweyan focus on "the problem of the public."[14] With its traditionally deep religious concerns, pragmatism was far less fixed on the tragic sense of life, alone, than Hook could admit.

I want to suggest, in particular, that Hook was haunted by pragmatism's Protestant past as well as by its comic possibilities. The son of Jewish parents, raised in New York slums, and a champion of a humanism without any particular or any explicit ties to any traditional religious narratives, Jewish, Christian, or otherwise, Hook aimed to wean pragmatism from the sorts of spiritual contemplation out of which it had grown. In "Pragmatism and the Tragic Sense of Life," Hook *opposed* pragmatism to Christianity and suppressed its roots in Protestant concerns. Christianity, in virtually every one of its variations, had presented itself as an alternative to the tragic sense of life. It had proclaimed a Gospel that there was redemption from the drastic and the bitter. The good news was that the Lord had come, bringing joy to the world and inspiring others to help him do it.

Christianity, at its best, anyhow, had not closed its eyes to tragedy. On the American scene, one need only think of Edwards to recall the ways in which figures in the Reformed traditions highlighted the limits of moral capacity with exquisite severity. But the message of the Gospel was salvation—the healing of wounds, the mending of breaks, and the drying of tears. More particularly, and more importantly for understanding the emergence of pragmatism, the Christian Gospel had emphasized the *finitude* and final *impotence* of human-kind on the one hand while characterizing human joy as *gratuitous*—not earned and not engendered by human power alone—on the other. The Christian testament was a proclamation of well-being, but one that insisted that faring well outran human assertion.

According to the Christian pattern of thought bred into the bones of such thinkers as James, Santayana, and Dewey, assertive moral practice was indis-pensable. But human assertion could never be counted on to add up to the joy people sought. People wanted to be at one with themselves, with other people, with the world, and with the powers on which it depended. But they were incapable of simply *making* these things occur.

James had set the pattern that descended from this insight when he had said that what a person craves "is to be consoled in his very impotence, to feel that the Powers in the Universe recognize him and secure him, all passive and failing as he is." As we have seen, he tried to persuade his readers that "the sanest and best men among us are of one clay with lunatics and prison inmates, and whenever we feel this, such a sense of the vanity of our voluntary career comes over us that all our morality appears as but a plaster covering a sore it can never cure, and all our well-doing as but the shallowest well-*being* that our lives ought to be grounded in but, alas, are not." This well-being, he had said, was "the object of the *religious* demand—a demand so penetrating and unassuageable that no consciousness of such occasional and outward well-doing as befalls the human lot can ever give it satisfaction."[15]

Such talk gives no hint of shallow optimism, uncritical adjustment, or the worship of success. But neither does it bind reflection or inquiry by the tragic sense of life. It highlights the Protestant tension between duty and divinity, social differentiation and communion, life together and the soul in its solitude, moral practice and spiritual performance. It reflects a religious demand for a human joy that is far more inclusive than social, political, or moral action can promise to deliver, indeed a joy that helps give these kinds of action their point. This pattern of thinking is highly visible throughout James's writings, as well as in Dewey's, as well as in Santayana's.

Hook's pragmatism embraced moralism outright in a way that James, Santayana, and even Dewey could not do. He articulated a way to "negotiate conflicts of value by intelligence rather than by war, or brute force."[16] But he offered little in the way of reflection on the prospects for human joy in a world historically, and in all likelihood inevitably, beset by the *failures* of conflict negotiation. For the most part, he did not engage in meditation on private and personal discontent or despair, or on solitary paths to happiness. He provided no expression of worship, or of thanksgiving, or of confessions of graceful divinity. Other pragmatists did.

James, Santayana, and Dewey, preoccupied with the prospects of Christian or post-Christian republican cultures, spoke the language of intellectual states-manship for all it was worth. But they were too interested in addressing *the religious demand* to limit reflection to matters of social policy formulation. To be sure they differed when it came to fleshing out appropriate ways in which to explicate this demand and its satisfaction. But they each showed how moral duty fell short of fulfilling life at its best; and they each explored the limits of human self-assertion and the gratuitous character of human life in its most divine episodes.

James's essay on "The Moral Philosopher and the Moral Life" pointed toward *The Varieties of Religious Experience*. Dewey's *Problems of Men* was simply incomplete without *Art as Experience* and *Philosophy and Civilization*. Santayana's *Life of Reason* pointed toward such later works as *Dialogues in Limbo*, *Platonism and the Spiritual Life*, *The Last Puritan*, *The Realm of Spirit*, and *The Idea of Christ in the Gospels*. All of these succeeding works were shaped by intuitions about ways in which the religious demand for well-being extended beyond moral action and concern for social solidarity. Indeed, this fact makes it far more appropriate to link pragmatism as much, or more, with comedy as with tragedy (and as much with creative fiction as with policy).

Here, I want to suggest, there is a telling resemblance between the classic pragmatists and the writers constituting the great tradition in English literature from Austen to Joyce.[17] It helps to picture the originating pragmatists as related to their own philosophical traditions in ways that parallel the response of the British comic writers to their Anglican and Dissenting past. How so? First, and most generally, both took joy as seriously as cruelty. That attitude sits at the heart of comedy rather than tragedy, and it shaped the original pragmatists' reflections on human finitude. Like the comic novelists, they aimed to release thoughtful people from the constraints of worn-out orthodox theologies that dressed up earthly life in the drab colors of depravity, saving the brilliant ones for afterlife. But they also sought to highlight the pretensions of human power all the while discerning happy endings. Put another way, along with the comics, they were very much concerned with celebrating earthbound and mortal mirth, delight, humor, and laughter, rather than some unearthly and ineffable bliss.

The comic vision, as Robert Polhemus has put it, "does not give to suffering and to evil a dangerous romantic grandeur or an inevitable dominance. Instead it makes suffering mean and seeks to transcend it," not through some "final" sublime assertion or courageous indifference, but rather through finite, transitional episodes of fulfillment. Comic faith, Polhemus argues, "seeks something less grandiose and more reasonable than infinite or permanent happiness and blessed immortality: it seeks more joyful life in a lasting world."[18] As I see it, we could replace the term "comic" with "pragmatic" in Polhemus's assertion and come away with just characterizations of the writings of James and Dewey. But this is even more the case with Santayana's books, especially those he wrote in Britain and Europe during the era stretching from one world war through another.

Santayana's later texts serve as the very paradigm for a festive, comic, and pragmatic naturalism, so it is no coincidence that the pragmatists who dissociated themselves from Santayana, and from whom Santayana separated himself, were tragedians like Hook. Moreover, I think it is no fluke that, of all the originating pragmatists, Santayana tried hardest to retain his Christian inheritance in a comic and pragmatic way.[19]

Grammars of the Spirit

To his own mind, I believe, Santayana's magnum opus in this regard was his four-volume *Realms of Being*, published over the course of fifteen years. But in fact, what he gave his readers from the mid-1920s until his death in 1952 is what Kundera has called a *polyphonic performance* on certain basic themes: His orchestration included, for example, a philosophical meditation (*Realms of Being*), a best-selling novel (*The Last Puritan*), criticism of rival voices ("Apologia Pro Mente Sua"), reflections on society and government (*Dominations and Powers*), literary (including biblical) criticism (*The Idea of Christ in the Gospels*), cultural criticism (*Character and Opinion in the United States*), dramatic dialogue (*Dialogues in Limbo*), panegyric ("Ultimate Religion"), autobiography (*Persons and Places*), and satire (throughout), sometimes woven in different books, just as often conjoined together. Each of these writings present grammars of the spirit in a decidedly "eclectic" way. Each virtually demands a readiness to abandon worn-out conventions constricting human joy and its appreciation, an "openness" to untried avenues of well-being, an appreciation of views or acts that place one's own in critical jeopardy, and finally, a willingness not to will when wit has run its course. All of these activities get reiterated, instance after instance, in Santayana's portrayals of spiritual life.

Open Eclecticism

Indeed, open eclecticism is itself a key theme for him when it comes to explicating his understanding of spirituality. Harking back to his 1910 introduction to Spinoza's *Ethics*, Santayana writes in his 1942 preface to *Realms of Being*, that

> my eclecticism is not helplessness before sundry influences; it is detachment and firmness in taking each simply for what it is. Openness, too, is a form of architecture. The doctrine that all moralities equally are but expressions of animal life is a tremendous dogma, at once blessing and purging all mortal passions; and the conviction that there can be no knowledge save animal faith positing external facts, and that this natural science is but a human symbol for those facts, also has an immense finality: the renunciation and the assurance in it are both radical and invincible.[20]

But if this sort of polyphony is itself an exhibition of spiritual vitality, there is something both serious and satirical about the specificity of questions and answers opening up *Realms of Being*, indeed about the very idea of "ontological" realms itself:

> What is this free life of mind? What are the necessary and sufficient themes that may occupy it? What troubles does it suffer from, when do they vanish, and in what then may it find a positive joy? Such are the questions that ultimately concern me in this book. Romantic souls who think that spirit is an unharnessed Pegasus tumbling among the clouds, will find nothing here to their purpose. The great characteristic of the human spirit, as I see it, is its helplessness and misery, most miserable and helpless when it fancies itself dominant and independent; and the great problem for it is salvation, purification, rebirth into a humble recognition of the powers on which it depends, and into a sane enjoyment of its appropriate virtues. Such salvation and rebirth must come by gift of nature, but they are not impossible. (*RB*, xxxii)

Santayana puts these questions and answers sincerely. They shape the rhetorical narrative of *Realms of Being*, *The Last Puritan*, and *Person and Places*, for example, from beginning to end. But at every step in the writing of his ontology, his novel, and his autobiography, Santayana underscores the optional, arbitrary, convenient, partial, posturing, and self-relinquishing status of each of them.

Santayana's commitments to pluralism, historicity, relativity, and good humor sit at the heart of this eclecticism: "The variety of senses in man, the precarious rule of his instincts, and the range of his memory and fancy, give rise in him eventually to some sense of error and even of humour. He is almost able to pierce the illusion of his animal dogmatism, to surrender the claim to inspiration, and in one sense to transcend the relativity of his knowledge and the flightiness of his passions by acknowledging them with a good grace" (*RB*, xiv–xv).

Playing "ontology" straight in the middle part of this century meant attempting to specify the orders of reality in some hierarchical way, to characterize the really real. But, having committed himself to the view that the search for the really real is itself an impediment to human joy, because it sets up an impossible standard of incontrovertibility, Santayana advances both a generalized view about how things hang together *and*, as Morris Grossman has pointed out, holds "it in abeyance as preferred or special." He presents his ontology as a "choice which frames itself in an extended vision of the optionality and arbitrariness of all choices."[21] The realms of essence, matter, truth, and spirit into which he makes inquiry, he asserts, are not "separate cosmological regions, separately substantial, and then juxtaposed. They are summary categories of logic, meant to describe a single dynamic process, and to dismiss from organized reflection all unnecessary objects of faith" (*RB*, 831). They provide the vocabularies he confesses he can not get along without as an individual person, serving properly poetic and religious functions of meditation by positing a "grammar of the spirit" (*RB*, 835); that grammar is "a kind of rhetoric" (*RB*, 90) that expresses the turns his mind has taken "to render articulate the dumb experience of the soul" (*RB*, 853).

On this view, "standard" ontology is a worn-out attempt to escape from the problems of human finitude rather than confronting them in adequate ways. It recapitulates the old wish for omniscience, the yearning to secure well-being by finding a way to think things through in the manner of the gods, to capture nature's self-understanding. But people provide "all the understanding" nature has of itself (*RB*, xix). And "possession of the absolute truth," Santayana suggests, "is not merely by accident beyond the range of particular minds; it is incompatible with being alive, because it excludes any particular station, organ, interest, or date of survey." Indeed, he claims, mind "was not created for the sake of discovering the absolute truth," but rather functions to "increase the wealth of the universe in the spiritual dimension, by adding appearance to substance and passion to necessity, and by creating all those private perspectives, and those emotions of wonder, adventure, curiosity, and laughter which omniscience would exclude" (RB, xiii).

A "single dynamic process" of human life, then, goes on—a process that can eventuate in wonder, adventure, curiosity, and laughter, even a personal sense of safety and peace—but without *leaning* on any truth providing metaphysical comfort, because there is no such truth available. No other pragmatist so firmly accepts the physical character, and hence the utter contingency, of human life, even at its best. But neither does any other pragmatist offer such extensive reflection on the joys available to creatures condemned to living "dramatically in an undramatic universe," or to possessive creatures doomed, inevitably, to possess nothing, and full well knowing it.

In this picture of things, humankind is challenged to meet necessities at every turn, but "in a contingent world, necessity is a conspiracy of accidents" (RB, 291). The crucial point is this: "that not only are all particular truths and facts contingent, but the very categories of fact and truth, like all other essences, if they are exemplified at all, are exemplified unnecessarily and by a groundless chance" (RB, 422). The fact that such categories are "convenient, or even absolutely true in describing the existing world, is a cosmic accident" (RB, 424). So "nature and law are never logically safe. Their antiquity is mere old age, their respectability, limitation. Contingency signed their death warrant at their birth. The sentence may be indefinitely postponed, the time may never come for the execution; yet the guillotine is always ready to drop" (RB, 728). Any claim to the contrary, Santayana contends, "foolishly parades the helplessness of the mind to imagine anything different" (RB, 417).

In such a world, the old vision of fixed mind knowing fixed nature according to fixed principles makes no sense. To the contrary, changing minds know changing nature according to changing beliefs and critical principles. The root of thinking is animal bias, dispositions to welcome or fear, and these dramatic postures, in turn are known for their "zoological variety" (RB, 482). Under such conditions, knowledge is "not truth, but a view or expression of the truth; a glimpse of it secured by some animal with special organs under special circumstances." Knowledge is like "a war-map in which nothing is set down but what touches the campaign of the season." "Far from rendering knowledge impossible," Santayana argues, all the biases of interest pervading human views supply "instruments for exploration, divers sensitive centres and divers inks, whereby in divers ways the facts may be recorded" (RB, 469). Knowledge, then, is no less instrumental than "any language or telescope" (RB, 418). Indeed, knowledge, on these grounds, is a kind of human assertion, a sort of empowerment, offering suitable ways of solving problems that stand in the path of progress toward the fulfillment of diverse aspirations.

But that makes knowledge part and parcel of willful life and, so, an activity that falls short of securing the spiritual well-being that people crave. Knowledge is a sort of power, but not a sort of power that can overcome inevitable human impotence. Obsession with knowledge per se, therefore, does not adequately respond to the religious demand for well-being in the winter light of human finitude.

That demand is quite precisely the one that informs Santayana's scoring of the realms of essence, matter, truth, and spirit. Spiritual transformation dominates its pages from first to last, because its central motive is this: To acknowledge the ways of being that permit spiritual revitalization, the activities that let people who are prone to moral weightlessness, anxiety, and fear in the face of their finitude and death, learn to love life in the full consciousness of impotence. Thus the heart of Santayana's tour de force is neither a description of the universe nor an effort to ground knowledge on itself nor an exercise in the formulation of realistic social policies. Rather, it is "worship" (RB, 62). It is a mode of reflection that can begin "only when we have thoroughly renounced self-assertion and thrift" (RB, 62–63).

Seen "religiously rather than cosmologically," Santayana asserts, his realms of being "may be regarded as a reduction of Christian theology and spiritual discipline to their secret interior source." In particular, he claims, his "analysis transposes the doctrine of the Trinity into terms of pure ontology and moral dialectic" (RB, 845). The Father, he urges, symbolizes matter, or "the assault of reality, in the form of whatsoever exists or happens." Spiritual life begins materially in the midst of things that matter, both for better and worse (RB, 846). Indeed, there is no escaping "the authority of things," so it makes good sense to figure the Father as a King.[22] The Son, Santayana suggests, signifies alternatively essence and truth. The life of the spirit quickens through submission to the truth about the utterly contingent orders of our thoroughly material condition. It takes shape "in matter organized into the form of a psyche" bent on well-being (RB, 850). According to the Nicene Creed, Santayana points out, "all things . . . were perforce created through the Son; and this doctrine which might seem unintelligible, becomes clear if we consider that power could not possibly produce anything unless it borrowed some form from the realm of essence and imposed that form on itself and its works. Power would be annulled before it began to exert itself unless externally distinct and recognizable in its character. The Son is thus an indispensable partner and vehicle for the life of the Father" (RB, 846).

Thus, "revelation comes by the Son." The psyche, which is a structure of material behaviors, makes signification possible and, with it, the imagination of excellence (RB, 853).[23] The Holy Ghost, finally, is a cipher for the human spirit, which is, in turn, a function of psyche. As such "spirit, being the final fruition of existence" from its own point of view, "absolutely needs the other realms to evoke and to feed it" (RB, 852). Far from occurring in any single moment of rebirth, spirit amounts to "the infinity of the renewable" (RB, 853). Its "peculiarity . . . once it exists, is not to be blind and to be eternally ashamed of egotism. Its will is not to will, but to understand all Will; and so without willing any of the ends that universal Will pursues (not even the will to create spirit), it sees the beauty of all those ends, including the beauty of its own impartial but enamoured vision" (RB, 822).

Comedy

I am pointing out here some things that Hookian pragmatists simply could not abide for several reasons. First, they embraced an Enlightenment emphasis on the self-assertion of humankind virtually without qualification. Santayana, to the contrary, suggests that spiritual redemption eventually depends on the suspension of self-assertion.

Second, philosophy for Hookian pragmatists is social policy formulation. Philosophy for Santayana is ultimately "festive, lyrical, rhetorical," providing a "holiday or holy day in a religious sense" (RB, 349, 423). For him, philosophy does not come to "repeat the world but to celebrate it" (PGS, 29). It is an exercise of the imagination, a way of "conversion or *metanoia*, a true education or discipline"—"a discipline of the mind and heart, a lay religion" (*RB*, 778, 827). Philosophy responds to the "question of being born into another life" (*RB*, 804). It provides a gratuitous rupture in the endless rounds of economic, social, and political concerns that quite properly preoccupy people in their workaday lives. It can outfit the soul in its solitude with disciplines allowing for a mortal gladness not encumbered by deception or self-deception.[24]

Third, Hookian pragmatists pictured philosophy as a social labor performed and endured under the conditions of inevitable and ultimate tragedy. It let people bargain and plot with a modicum of intelligence. For Santayana, philosophical meditation is a ritual process—something that solitary individuals do to themselves—geared to redeem them from their "labouring world," society, economy, polity, and all, by bringing joy into it (*RB*, 185). It is a way of letting people momentarily break out "of the shabbiest surroundings in laughter, understanding, and small surrenders of folly to reason" (*RB*, 746).

To prophetic pragmatists in the United States, holding to the dream of establishing a new heaven and a new earth, philosophy understood this way smelled of decadence, especially in view of Santayana's construal of it as a "chance to rise above ourselves, a culmination, a release, a transport beyond distraction" that had no particular "earthly or even . . . moral benefit" (*RB*, 746). Moral benefit—the meeting of social, political, and economic needs— circumscribed the interests of critics like Hook. For Santayana, too, engagement of these problems could never be abandoned, but *solving them might well leave the spirit oppressed or without joy*. American pragmatists placed people under an obligation to reconcile conflicting social policies. Santayana quite sincerely wished them well. But for him, "in the spiritual life, there is nothing obligatory" (*RB*, 65). Spirit is "an act" that, from a moral point of view, is irresponsible and socially marginal, for "the will in spirit is precisely not to will, but to understand the lure and sorrow in all willing" (*RB*, 731). That makes philosophy a free play of the imagination that permits departure from the obligations and duties of normal social life. But the point of it is not to abrogate the moral demands of life together, nor to escape from those demands, nor to avoid them, but to lend them the weight of significance by recalling *why* they concern us—by discerning what is good or lovely or appealing about the beings among which and with whom we live and we move. Spiritual meditation offers a sort of comic relief that highlights or clarifies things that make life worth living by establishing a sense of the beauty, the loveliness, the lovable character, of being in the world, indeed being in the world both with and without us.

So far then, we know this: We know that Santayana's pragmatic animal faith is comic in two ways. First, it takes joy as seriously as meanness. "The young man who has not wept is a savage," blind to the conceit of his own will to power and possession, indeed to the vanities of his kind. But "the old man who will not laugh is a fool," because well-being comes neither with power nor possession (DL, 57). It comes with that "shift in the center of interest" in psyches that, momentarily and from time to time, lets people abandon their abrasive wills, and in that sense evacuate their selves, for a reconsideration of the beauty of beings they are not, of the circumstances that came before them, now support them, and will outlast them, and of the perfections toward which they aspire though never realize.

To Santayana's mind, the old dream of final beatitude is a sham, but spiritual joy is not: "Intermittence is intrinsic to life, to feeling, to thought; so are partiality and finitude. Spirit cannot achieve unity or perfection physically; the living flame must dance. It suffices that its light should fall on things steadfast and true, worthy to be discerned and returned to and treasured; so that though spirit be everywhere halting in achievement it may be always perfect in allegiance. Its happiness must remain volatile and its union with the Good ideal" (RB, 825).

Secondly, then, Santayana's faith is comic because it exemplifies philosophy understood as permitting a festive or ritual process of spiritual transformation geared to displace despair with delight. That alone gives it a family resemblance to exercises in traditional forms of Christian meditation. But, of course, if Santayana's mature vision gives voice to an understanding of spiritual predicament and joyous fulfillment informed by his reading of the Christian Gospel, it is one that few other Christians have shared.

Traditional Christianity and
Santayana's Religious Naturalism

Several things distance Santayana from traditional Christianity. For one, Santayana abandons supernaturalism without remainder: "God, at least for Jews,

Christians, and Moslems, must be a power that is a spirit, and a spirit that is a sovereign power. As I place spirit and power at opposite ends of the ontological scale, and of cosmic evolution, making spirit the fruit and enjoyment of power, but no part of its radical energy, I must be pronounced an atheist in this company" (*RB*, 839). The whole thrust of *The Realm of Essence* is to show the powerless character of immaterial beings like words, ideas, qualities, functions, and forms, apart from their deployment in conduct. The point of *The Realm of Matter* is to show that the only powers around are physical, that indeed the human psyche is a physical form or structure of behaviors, and that spiritual intuition is a consequence of such physical structures. Supernaturalism posits that matter and spirit constitute separable worlds or existential contexts. But a clear upshot of Santayana's meditations is his bald assertion that "there is only one world, the natural world, and only one truth about it; but this world has a spiritual life possible in it, which looks not to another world but to the beauty and perfection that this world suggests, approaches, and misses" (*RB*, 833).

Secondly, Santayana's commitment to the contingency of things in *The Realm of Matter* disrupts Christian pretensions to provide metaphysical comfort, while his characterization of *The Realm of Truth* as providing *no* necessary truths upends traditional quests for metaphysical disclosure.

Finally, Santayana's acceptance of death as the end of life—period, the end—departs from every variety of Christianity understood as an everlasting life insurance policy. Christianity embraced this way is, as he puts it in *Soliloquies*, a "fundamental lie" (*SELS*, 99) because "death, in every instance, is the end of life" (*RB*, 326). There is no way to beat it, though there is a way to overcome the despair that comes from fearing it. There is "no cure for birth and death save to enjoy the interval" (*SELS*, 97) by discerning and manifesting the good without attempting to retain it.

"Death," Santayana asserts, "does not say to life that life is nothing, or does not exist, or is an illusion." What it teaches us, he says, is "merely that life has such and such limits and such and such a course, whether it reflects on its course or not, whether it limits or ignores them. Death can do nothing to our lives except frame them in, to show them off with a broad margin of darkness and silence; so that to live in the shadow of death and of the cross is to spread a large nimbus of peace around our littleness" (*SELS*, 99).

So if Santayana's pragmatic naturalism abandons supernaturalism, metaphysical comfort, metaphysical disclosure, and the denial of death, it does not thereby abandon the idea of Christ in the Gospels or of life lived under the Cross. It does not abandon a Christian understanding of meditational practice, Christian spiritual transformation, or interior pilgrimage. The change of heart enacted in *The Realm of Spirit*, indeed, is an imitation of Christ crucified for the sake of overcoming the things impeding human joy. It is a turning away from distractions that Christianity had characterized as the flesh, the world, and the devil. It is an affirmation, by way of a suspension of self-assertion, of piety, spirituality, and charity. These preoccupations, indeed, make Santayana's comic faith remarkably evangelical.

To Santayana's way of thinking, the things that make people distraught, even in the most promising of material circumstances, are kinds of personal, social, and cultural assertion that obstruct the spontaneity of human joy by chaining them to "the rack of care, doubt, pain, hatred, and vice" (RB, 673). Nonetheless, it is wrong to mistake "the flesh" with physical life itself, "the world" with social institutions at large, or "the devil" with some external malevolent power.

"The flesh," Santayana contends, does not name the physical limitations of spiritual life, which are inseparable from it, nor sexuality, nor any bodily interest per se, but rather "the false promises that nature sometimes gives and then betrays," as for example the promise of perfect health (RB, 676). To be sure, physical misfortune, calamity, or disaster can be mighty impediments to human joy. Far worse, however, are obsessions to avoid or even void physical helplessness. Physically unfortunate people can still practice the virtues of piety, spirituality, and charity. They can experience the sublimity and peace of willing not to will. Physically fortunate people can too. But, if Santayana's diagnosis is sufficient, people obsessed with triumphing over physical limitation cannot. Their cure for finitude is itself a disease.

Then again, to Santayana's mind, "the world" is not tantamount to the "transpersonal machinery of language, custom, and industry" that makes up the body politic along with our own citizenship in it (RB, 693). Rather, it names conditions that occur "when institutions subject the spirit to forced and useless labor, and pledge it to hideous passions" (RB, 694). In other words, "human slavery to labor, war, politics, morality, and imposed religion" make people far more spiritually distraught than physical suffering, when these things cause bifurcation, division, alienation, and conflict (RB, 704).

But finally, if physical and social interests can run amok, the greatest enemy impeding human joy is deceit and self-deceit. It is no coincidence, Santayana suggests, that the devil's nickname is the Father of Lies. Deceit is the enemy within spiritual activity itself, the one vice "internal to spirit" (RB, 718). The experience of spiritual well-being, Santayana asserts, comes in moments of wisdom, facility, and love. But the worst impediments to joy are activities that distort these practices. They are the delusions of omniscience, omnipotence, perfect benevolence, and, perhaps especially, the lie that spirituality itself carries any existential privilege, obligation, or authority. It makes no difference whether somebody identifies omniscience, omnipotence, utter benevolence, or spiritual privilege with himself, his body politic, his economic or social stratagems, or his deities. They are webs of deceit no matter what, arrogations of power based on false pretense.

The Idea of Christ in the Gospels

The idea of Christ crucified in the Gospels is so crucial, Santayana thinks, because it is a figure of divinity that points away from the arrogance of power, away from pretensions to the one right view of things, and away from claims to exclusive or inclusive moral propriety. The figure of Christ points to a kind of self-surrender, a willingness not to will, that accepts the limits of self-assertion, gives humble thanks to the powers on which this life depends, embraces impotence when potentiality has run its course, by discerning the loveliness of things out of our control, and gracefully suspends moral laws when they impede the love of others as they understand themselves. The figure of Christ in the Gospels renounces the projects of omniscience, omnipotence, perfect righteousness, and the fantasy of spiritual *liberation* or disembodiment, in order to display or reveal how to go about loving life in the consciousness of impotence.

"Liberation, as the Christian should desire it," Santayana claims, cannot be "liberation from fortune or domination over it" (RB, 757). Well-being "could not consist in pretending to be independent, that is, in becoming mad" (RB, 759). Christian piety gives thanks to the material sources of spiritual being. Its monarchial "Father" is a fitting, dramatic presentation of the breathtaking, overwhelmingly consistent, brute force—generative, sustaining, and lethal— of material circumstance.

Santayana's Christian spirituality rejects arrogance for aspiration, for a devoted allegiance to the good, both public and private. The practice of spirituality, or "aspiration become conscious" ("UR," 296) already assumes thanksgiving and a humble recognition of the truth, and disciplines individuals to rise above themselves, to give themselves up to their visions of excellence, to stake their lives on their faith, to incarnate goodness. For spirituality, as Santayana characterizes it, is a function that makes human consciousness felicitously double. It is the psychological function, the "second insight," that lets us "identify ourselves not with ourselves" (RB, 741).

Santayana's Christian charity, as he put it in *Dialogues in Limbo*, is "less than philanthropy in that it expects the defeat of man's natural desires and accepts that defeat; and it is more than philanthropy in that, in the face of defeat, it brings consolation" (DL, 139). This charity is a perception and a love of "the possible perfection in all other things," letting people simultaneously take themselves and their own with a grain of salt while appreciating the alien other (RB, 759). Charity understood this way, Santayana claims, brings a sense of well-being by "detaching us from each thing with humility and humour, and attaching us to all things with justice, charity, and pure joy" (RB, 745). This thanksgiving, this hope, this forgiving love, gives point to social policy formulation and makes life, even for the most impotent among us, a little more divine so long as it lasts.

"St. Paul tells us," Santayana notes, "that Christ liberates us from the law, and therefore from sin" (RB, 760). Romantics are wrong, he continues, to construe release from the law as countenancing moral licence, because

> health and morality are not based on spirit, spirit is based on them, and no spiritual insight can abolish or weaken the difference between what nature allows and rewards and what she punishes and condemns to everlasting torments. The point is that spirit, caught in this vice, suffers guiltlessly from that natural disease and corruption; and to rescue that guiltlessness, to rescue spirit from inner madness as well as outward oppression, is the double work of mercy proper to Christian charity. The moral economy of the universe is not destroyed or suspended; rewards and punishments . . . take their natural course; but sins are forgiven because they *ought* to be forgiven, because the suffering they bring to the spirit, *the spirit* never deserved. (RB, 760)

So in Santayana's view, the figure of Christ crucified gives people an adequate symbol of the salvation possible in human life, by displaying a triumphant way to live with the inevitabilities of renunciation, suffering, and death. Such salvation comes by "shifting the centre of appreciation from the human psyche," or the habits of mind that organize our identities and judgments as moral individuals and social beings, "to the divine spirit," or the habits of mind that let us suspend judgment, both of others and of ourselves, "for the sake of understanding" (RB, 761–62). This shift carries with it "a change of heart, a conversion, momentarily real, but relapsing and becoming more or less nominal and merely intended as life goes on" (RB, 762).

In all, Santayana asserts, the practices of piety, spirituality, and charity inspired by the figure of Christ crucified make a place for grace. That is the point of affirming Christian practice in a world without any supernatural powers at work in it. "That spiritual minds should appeal to the supernatural," Santayana said, "is not to be wondered at. Few are courageous enough to accept nature as it is, and to build their spiritual house on the hard rock of the truth" (ICG, 237). That, indeed, had been the trouble with the visions of Emerson, James, and Royce. Each of these precursors had falsely attributed a moral constitution to the universe; each had confused ideals with powers. Each had felt bound to those two irreconcilable responsibilities, "that of describing things as they are, and that of finding them propitious to certain preconceived human desires" (COUS, 61).

In his 1933 tribute to Spinoza, "Ultimate Religion," Santayana urges people to take another tack. He encourages them to "imagine the truth to be as unfavorable as possible to your desires and as contrary as possible to your natural presumptions" ("UR," 282). Then, he suggests, "we may all quietly observe what we find; and whatever harmonies may then appear to subsist between our spirits and the nature of things will be free gifts to us and, so far as they go, unchallengeable possessions" ("UR," 283).

The Question of Santayana's Catholicism

Is there anything particularly Catholic about Santayana's religious naturalism? Santayana himself claims that, while "religion is the head and front of everything" in his writing, his Catholicism "is a matter of sympathy and traditional allegiance, not of philosophy." Nor, he adds, of personal practice: Such activity "would hardly have been possible. My mother was a Deist [who sent him to listen to Unitarian sermons regularly lest "rascally priests" get the better of him]. . . . [Both] parents regarded all religion as a work of human imagination," and he agreed very early on (PGS, 7). But his Enlightenment-intoxicated parents mainly derided religion for being imaginative mumbo jumbo. He did not. As a young person, Santayana says,

> my sympathies were entirely with those other members of my family who were devout believers. I loved the Christian epic, and all those doctrines and observances which bring it down into daily life: I thought how glorious it would have been to be a Dominican friar, preaching that epic eloquently, and solving afresh all the knottiest and sublimest mysteries of theology. I was delighted with anything, like Mallock's *Is Life Worth Living?*, which seemed to rebuke the fatuity of that age. For my own part, I was quite sure that life was not worth living, for if religion was false, everything was worthless, and almost everything, if religion was true. In this youthful pessimism I was hardly more foolish than so many amateur medievalists and religious aesthetes of my generation. I saw the same alternative between Catholicism and complete disillusion, and I have chosen it. (*PGS*, 7–8)

So, if he is to be believed, at any rate, Santayana's religious naturalism is not philosophically Catholic; it is in some sense culturally Catholic. He is surely right in his assessment of his "philosophy." Nearly forty years ago, Donald Williams wrote that Santayana's philosophy "is opposed to Catholic thought in nearly every respect."[25] My characterization of his antimetaphysical pragmatic naturalism corroborates this view. But what about Santayana's cultural Catholicism?

Paul Tillich called Santayana's picture of the legend of Christ in the Gospels Catholic for its emphasis on the disciplines allowing people to imitate, even incarnate, divinity. Tillich argued, only half correctly, that "grace seems to Santayana—in accordance with Catholic thinking—not so much forgiveness as the gift of spiritual power."[26] This assessment is only half true because Santayana's spirituality let people participate in forgiveness. But just as significant, or more, are these views of Santayana's: (1) that *tradition* sets the context for spiritual life, not direct contact with God (or with reason or with nature);

(2) that the *authority* of past wisdom, carried by *institutions*, is not to be denied or evaded, though it is subject to revision in light of fresh considerations; (3) that *festivity*, more than social work, is the hallmark of religion as a cultural institution; (4) that *ritual transformation*, not certitude, helps resolve the fear of illusion; (5) that imaginative and reconstructive *symbolism*, rather than iconoclasm, leads to the revitalization of private and public life; and (6) that *comic joy*, not simply responsible suffering, characterizes the sort of well-being we picture as divine.

All these views are Santayana's. But what is more significant, historically they are associated with the trappings of Catholicism that became de rigueur along with amateur medievalism and religious aestheticism, as Santayana says, in his "generation," which was the era that spawned Anglo-American antimodernism. It did not hurt, in this regard, for Santayana to have come to Boston from Catholic Avila when he was nine. But, Santayana's allegiance to Catholicism readily squares with the antimodernist mood that swept through Anglo-American high culture at just the point when critics began to suspect that modern "autonomy" and "self-realization" schemes suited the brokers of capitalist greed and power far more than they provided either a personal sense of worth or public justice. His emphasis on tradition and authority, symbolism and emotional expression (or pleasure objectified), festivity and ritual, joy and playfulness are geared to counter the vapidity of possessive "self-realization," the emptiness of consumer independence, the sterility of iconoclastic literalism, the drudgery of both corporate and labor worlds, and the burden of relentless rounds of labor.[27]

In this regard, for example, it is noteworthy that, as Santayana is writing his dissertation, and then *The Sense of Beauty*, Yankee antimodernists like Henry and Brooks Adams are valorizing medieval Catholic culture in their efforts to get critical leverage on capitalist commercialism, materialist complacency, and a breathtaking acceptance of conspicuous consumption; G. Stanley Hall is urging parents to expose their children to Catholic ritual to let them experience the robust symbolism and primitive playfulness requisite for any vital culture. Charles Norton's original Dante Society, inaugurated along with Henry Wadsworth Longfellow and James Russell Lowell in 1876 and catering to aesthetically minded Harvard undergraduates by the time Santayana enrolls, by the mid-1890s is luring innumerable acolytes diversely celebrating the Tuscan for his "moral simplicity and sincerity"; for his "high pitch of emotional intensity"; for his "spiritual certainty in an uncertain, excessively tolerant age"; and for his emphasis on "human dignity."[28]

As Santayana is writing *Interpretations* in 1900, popular moralists like Charles Dinsmore are transforming Dante into a strenuous Rooseveltian activist. By 1905, when *Reason in Common Sense*, *Reason in Society*, *Reason in Religion*, and *Reason in Art* make their appearance, a host of cultural commentators are linking up art, ritual, and belief as antidotes to bourgeois banality, taking medieval Catholic culture for a paradigm. Ralph Adams Cram's medievalist fantasies, present in both his architectural and social blueprints designed to exult corporate social hierarchy and stability, Vida Dutton Scudder's Anglo-Catholic socialism, and Henry Adams's *Mont Saint Michel and Chartres*, are but three prominent, contrary examples.

At least through the 1930s and the dawning realization that corporate social "organicism," based in great part on fantasies of medieval Catholic "oneness," could readily go the vicious ways of fascist Italy and Nazi Germany, expressions of sympathy with belated, antimodernist Catholicism abounded in circles of high culture in the United States. For the most part, the forms such sympathy eventually took were trivialized and, themselves, commodified; they blunted whatever critical edge or leverage antimodernism might have had (belated as it inevitably was to be). As Lears puts it, "the social impact of antimodernism . . . helped WASP elites to become a unified and self-conscious ruling-class. Gothic architecture and medieval heraldry provided collective symbols—often with Anglophile overtones—for an emerging national bourgeoisie. Premodern emblems certified modern, upper-class institutions: the metropolitan men's club, the suburban country club, the prep school, the private university."[29]

Had Santayana's religious naturalism been unexceptionally belated, had he found no way to express his own anti-antimodernism by exposing the evasive banality of antimodern characters, his contribution to religious criticism would remain as quaint as Henry Adams's *The Virgin and the Dynamo* and as self-deceived as T. S. Eliot's "Ash Wednesday." But the force of *The Last Puritan*, and other works like *The Genteel Tradition at Bay*, lay quite precisely in disclosing the ineffectiveness of standard revolts against modernist progressivism: Mark Lowe's Wyoming adventures geared to restore the "natural" character of boys; Dr. Bumstead's therapies for neurasthenia at Great Falls; Peter Alden's leisured escape into the Orient and dope; his revolts against the constraints of domesticity and "work"; his son Oliver's similar revolt against domesticity and cities; the allure of preppy athletics and "Lord" Jim Darnley's lavish, almost knightly, homoerotics; Harriet Alden's American exceptionalism; Cousin Caleb Weatherbee's nostalgic and furious effort to recapture a republican Catholic Americanism; Vicar Darnley's near-Coleridgean faith; Rose Darnley's quiet desperation; Mario Van de Weyer's Etonic festivity. All these gestures hurtle headlong toward the trenches, Verdun, and the peace to end all peace at Versailles; and finally toward the mid-twentieth-century option between the greedy, public short-sightedness of the North Atlantic democracies and the orders of personal and political horror brought to pass in Germany, Italy, and the Soviet Union.

Ultimate Religion and the Last Puritan

What Santayana calls "ultimate religion" in his panegyric on Spinoza comes together conflictually with both the high American tradition of aesthetic spirituality and the broad American tradition of spiritual exceptionalism in the figure of Oliver Alden, his *Last Puritan* (1935). Enormously popular in its time, the novel let Santayana perform the view that philosophy was good literature if it was good for anything. To this end, "Santayana" is told by "Mario Van de Weyer" in the book's epilogue,

> now you're not arguing or proving or criticizing anything but painting a picture. The trouble with you philosophers is that you misunderstand your vocation. You ought to be poets, but you insist on laying down the law for the universe, physical and moral, and are vexed with one another because your inspirations are not identical. . . . [W]hen you profess to be describing a fact, you can't help antagonizing those who take a different view of it, or are blind altogether to that sort of object. In this novel, on the contrary, the argument is dramatized, the views become human persuasions, and the presentation is all the truer for not professing to be true. (*LP*, 602)

Santayana characterizes Oliver Alden as the "ultimate Puritan," an Emersonian figure struggling willfully to capture a sense of romantic sublimity, committed to making his life a moral crusade by ever searching out "universal sympathy, understanding, and justice" and daring to give birth to his "own soul." Fictionally a one-time student of Santayana's—"the most gifted of my pupils in my last days at Harvard"—Alden embodies "Puritanism self-condemned" (*LP*, 6). Alden sees himself as suffering from life-at-second-hand, that is, life mediated by worn-out moral conventions and social expectations. He yearns for that "original relation with the universe" that, he has been taught to expect, will restore his life to significance by revealing the ground on which to build a practical sense of identity and vocation. He cannot accept the sort of American spiritual exceptionalism that his mother Harriet embodies. This is so because he has learned from his derelict, free-spirited, and roving father, Peter, that there is a diversity of cultures, each with its own memories, hopes, and practices. Nor can he accept any form of traditional Christianity, because Peter has shown him how its Scriptures are fable and its promise of everlasting life is so much deception and self-deception. Oliver, finally, is open-eyed enough to discern the ways puritanism has rationalized self-aggrandizement and fueled resentment and envy of others who are different. What, then, constitutes his "puritanism"?

Santayana reveals the heart of the novel in an interior scene where Oliver tries to come to grips with his father's apparent willingness to accept the fact that his preferences and decisions are ultimately groundless. Oliver, Santayana writes

> needed comfort. He could find no peace unless he justified his natural sympathies theoretically and turned them into moral maxims. If they couldn't bear the light of day, the test of being made explicit in words, he wouldn't allow them to govern him in the dark. He had broken once for all with his home prejudices. He had vowed himself to universal sympathy, understanding, and justice. To set up Jacob's ladder again would be to restore the moral servitude from which his conscience had so profoundly broken loose; it would be to wall in the infinite and try to live again in a little earthly paradise between four little rivers. The universe wasn't that sort of garden; nor was the human soul that sort of vegetable. Life, for the spirit, was no walk in a paved city, with policemen at every crossing: it was an ocean voyage, a first and only voyage of discovery, in which you must choose your own course. . . . The Old Calvinists, Oliver felt, hadn't been puritan enough; you were not pure at all unless it were for the love

of purity; but with them it had all been a mean calculation of superstition and thrift and vengeance—vengeance against everybody that was happier and better than themselves. They had flattered themselves that at least the Lord loved them: that God had sent down Moses and Christ expressly to warn them of dangers ahead, so that they might run in time out of the burning house, and take all the front seats in the new theatre. And they didn't dare call their real souls their own; wanted to smother them; wanted to find out in some underhanded way, what was the will of God, so as to conform to it, and be always on the winning side. But God had laughed at them and fooled them. There was really no knowing which way the universe would drift. Your hard-boiled moralists were idolaters, worshipping their own fancies and hypnotized by their own words. They had perched on a certain height on the tree of knowledge, had stuck fast at a certain point up the greased pole of virtue. They would climb no farther, and from there they had turned and pecked ferociously at everybody below them and screeched ferociously at everybody above, invoking their hard, dry reason to discredit all that was beyond their own meagre and cruel morality. But this reason of theirs was just *their* reason, their effort to entrench themselves in their limitations. Not only was such a thing useless and in the end impossible, but perhaps in the moral world there was no single pole, no single tree on which heights and depths could be measured, like record tides. Perhaps the ways of knowledge were incommensurable; like different languages or different arts . . . ; and perhaps the kinds of virtue were divergent too, and incomparable. The lion and the eagle were ideal in their way; so were the gazelle and the lark in theirs. Who should say which was better? Better in what sense, according to what standard? In one mood you might say: Better be like Jim Darnley, fleshly, since you are living in the flesh, hard enough, coarse enough, loose enough to feel at home in the crowd. In another mood you may say: No, better be like Mario, refined by nature, clear as a crystal, merry without claims, brave without armour. . . . Or in yet another mood, why not think it better to be as Oliver himself was, burdened but strong; groping but faithful, desolate but proud? It was a foolish debate: free and infinite spirit, in a free and infinite world could never stop short at any point and say: This is truly right, this is perfect, this is supreme.

Perhaps the whole pilgrimage of spirit was the only goal of spirit, the only home of truth.

But what was he saying? A goal? A home of truth? Was there anything here but chaos and a welter, a truth composed of illusions, a home all perpetual unrest? If the spirit of life were really free and infinite, what difference could there be between freedom and madness? The whole adventure of existence became no less horrible than enticing; you had to close your eyes, to stifle your reason, in order to take sides somehow and continue to live. But the one thing Oliver could not do was to stifle his reason and close his eyes. How, then, should he go on living?

. . . But by an entanglement of thought, and by a hereditary prejudice, young Oliver's romantic sympathies were perturbed. He demanded some absolute and special sanction for his natural preferences; as if any other sanction were needed for love, or were possible, except love itself. Love, without that impossible absolute rightness, seemed to him a bewitchment. All life, unless you share it, is evidently a bewitchment, a groundless circling and circling about some arbitrary perfection, some arbitrary dream of happiness, which there is no antecedent reason for pursuing, and no great likelihood of attaining. Not having the key to this secret—the open secret of natural life—his reflection came to a stand. The puzzle was too much for his wits, and useless thinking became a torment. He shook himself together, tossed the hair from his forehead, and ran out into the night air, across the wet fields. Hadn't Hume, too, with less excuse, turned in the end from philosophy to backgammon? (*LP*, 318–20)

The Open Secret of Natural Life

Alden is a classic Emersonian puritan because he thinks of himself as having embarked from sham traditions (his "home prejudices," the morally determinate universe of "Jacob's ladder") for "universal sympathy, understanding, and justice." But he is haunted by his realization (which Santayana embraces) that there is no requisite standard for discerning such things because the ways of knowledge are incommensurable, like "different languages or different arts";

and that virtues are "divergent too, and incomparable." To his mind, the theological (and then, modern philosophical) search for objectivity dead-ends. All that Oliver finds when he makes this sort of effort is "chaos, a welter."

The whole strategy of exiling himself from tradition in order to enter into some immediate relation with the source of joyful life, either understood as something outside himself or as himself, leaves Oliver with the sense of acedia or sloth:

> [A] curious film of unreality and worthlessness now seemed spread over his daily life . . . a fiction to which he condescended, as if he were playing in private theatricals. The characters were assumed, and not very well done; yet you must pretend to be in dead earnest, till you actually forgot that you were not. But for him, a trap door had opened into the cellarage of this world's stage, which other people seemed so strangely ready to tread all their life long as though it were the bedrock of nature. (*LP*, 227)

Given his understanding of the problem of spiritual life and of the traditional options for success in it, he remains damned no matter which tack he takes; damned if he does not embark from tradition and damned if he does; damned if he does not try to encounter "the bedrock of nature" and damned if he does. It is only as and when he is able to jettison the traditional options, only as and when he accepts "the open secret of natural life," that personal contentment in the midst of traditional moral commitment becomes a possibility he can bet his life on.

The thing that distinguishes and distances Santayana's voice from young Oliver's Emersonian one in *The Last Puritan* is what Santayana calls "the open secret of natural life." Young Oliver is blinded to this "open secret," the truth that life, "unless you share it," is a "groundless circling and circling about some arbitrary perfection, some arbitrary dream of happiness, which there is no antecedent reason for pursuing, and no great likelihood of attaining."

Santayana's voice in *The Last Puritan* asserts that the conscious demand to *purify* spiritual life of tradition is itself a tradition. The effort to encounter deity immediately is itself a symbolic and conventional process of personal transformation. The strategy deployed by Emersonian romantics is to find the privileged key permitting a breakthrough from human tradition to direct acquaintance with nature construed as one's own self-begetting soul—a soul that Emersonians picture as the source of joy and meaning unsullied by the motley

"Babel" of human "language" (*LP*, 125). But the strategy leads nowhere because the nature/culture distinction on which it is based is false: The fact is that "human affairs" are "natural phenomena and the whole trouble came from trying to regard them otherwise" (*LP*, 161).

So long as Oliver demands the kind of Enlightenment disenchantment that Santayana rejects, he continues thinking that poetry, in order to be religion, must deny that it is poetry. He is the paradigm critic of *Interpretations of Poetry and Religion*. For him,

there was a sunny and a shady side to the road of knowledge. The sunny side was the study of nature, where all exploration was joyful, and free from evil passion and prejudice. The same was true of mathematics which, if not so sunny as geography or astronomy or natural history, at least was pure from human taint. You were honestly challenged by your problem, and could work your way honestly forward until you came to an honest solution or an honest difficulty. Only non-human subjects were fit for the human mind. They alone were open, friendly, and rewarding. Unfortunately, the human subjects had to be studied too: and here, in history, language, and literature, not to speak of religion—all was accidental and perverse. Perhaps story-telling, just for amusement, might be very well for the theatrical sort of people who liked it; although Oliver himself had never cared much for tales and poetry and things supposed to be funny. . . . But to tell stories and pass them off for the truth—what an extraordinary outrage! The histories and theories which people had composed in their heads did not appeal to him as visions, as incitements to the imagination, which is the way in which they appeal to the humanists who cultivate them; and not caring for them as fictions, it never crossed his mind to mistake them for truths. On the contrary, he instinctively hated them for trespassing on that ground; they were counterfeits; they were rendered malignant by the very fact that they had a subject matter more or less real, which they dared to caricature and diminish and dress up in the motley of particular minds. Yet this subject-matter itself was a sorry affair: a chaos of barbarous and ignorant nations, struggling for a wretched existence and rendering existence doubly wretched for one another. The human world was so horrible to the human mind, that it could be made to look at all decent and interesting only by ignoring half the facts and putting a false front on the other half. Hence all that brood of fables. But this flattering office of poetry and elegance did not redeem them in Oliver's eyes: they were only "frills"; and all such beautifications belonged to the shady side of knowledge. (LP, 114)

For Santayana, things are different because, once again, the Enlightenment option between enchantment and disenchantment is itself a dead option, working off an objectivism that does not work. There are no antecedent reasons for pursuing universal sympathy, understanding, and justice, apart from particular traditions into which people are born and bred. Excellence understood this way emerges out of shared interests articulated in narratives people inherit and pass along amended. There is no supernatural will with which these interests conform. People have chances, indeed they are chances, to *enact* sympathy, understanding, and justice. But they will do so with better humor and far more joyfully the more they are able to recognize that the universality they hunt for is a mechanical rabbit, wound up for a chase that always approaches but just as inevitably misses its quarry. That is what Santayana has "Oliver" eventually learn just before he dies, not in the midst of the Great War he has volunteered to fight in, but in a car accident that is unrelated to any intention he or anyone else in the novel harbors.

What *The Last Puritan* leaves begging, however, is any clear vision of the practical conditions allowing both for the spiritual understanding and the political or social justice that Oliver craves. Santayana lets *The Last Puritan* clarify how exhausted Western culture feels as the Great War draws to a close. But just what spiritual and moral options Westerners have left open to them in 1935, in the midst of worldwide depression and the rise of the mid-twentieth-century totalitarian regimes and the world-resource-raping capitalist democracies, is a subject *The Last Puritan* does not even broach. That, rather, is the theme Santayana pursues in the very last, but hardly the best, of his longer books, *Dominations and Powers: Reflections on Liberty, Society, Government.*

8

STRONG LIBERAL DEMOCRACY

AND SPIRITUAL LIFE

The Politics of Spiritual Life

During the first half of this century, pragmatists like Dewey and Hook pictured democracy American-style as the divine way of doing things, and then urged citizens to pour all the enthusiasm they once may have had for religions, like Christianity or Judaism, into ordering political life from the bottom up. For them, participation in the practices of democratic institutions is the one natu- ralistic upshot of the Western religious traditions most worth saving. On this view, if participation in specifically religious institutions like churches and synagogues motivates citizens to become vigorous participants in democratic politics, well and good. Then such religions can be authorized as conducive to the healthy life of the republic. But that is not very likely from a Deweyan point of view. This is the case, first, because church and synagogue adherents are prone to claim that the beliefs that inform their institutions are not subject to the sort of critical jeopardy that the give-and-take of democratic delibera- tion demands. They claim to provide an unshakable consensus of belief prior to the very deliberations that democrats rely upon to create accord. Moreover, the rituals that largely constitute their religious activities are spiritually excep- tionalist, exclusivist, and divisive, entitling some to full well-being and spir- itually penalizing or anathematizing others. So, the Deweyan argument goes, religious cults are contrary to the democratic task of *creating* community out of diversity. They presume a universal unanimity of will that is prior to politics and cut out people not party to it. But democratic politics takes all comers willing to engage in democratic decision making, which begins in deliberations where consensus leaves off.

Santayana has misgivings about this line of thinking. Most generally, he is unwilling to identify any particular form of political life as divine. More specifically, he criticizes elements of political democracy that, he claims, frustrate activities favorable to both public and private good. As Santayana sees it, preoccupation with equality often undercuts excellence and fosters mediocrity; concentration on universal suffrage repeatedly serves as an excuse for avoiding effective political deliberation, decision, and action. Indeed, even when citizens actually do think, resolve, and execute policy *as* citizens, immersion in politics truncates the kinds of spiritual discipline that go on largely in private, sometimes even in solitude. In fact, like Nietzsche, Santayana tries to unmask ways in which democracy can rationalize cruelty or humiliation in the name of equality, by making personal anomalies that comprise individual distinction appear offensive or pathological.

The question, for Santayana, is not so much whether this or that sort of spiritual life supports democracy. It is not to ascertain "the *social* place and function of religion" (*ACF*, 65). In fact, he turns that issue on its head. For him, the question is whether and how political activities favor spiritual life. Then, too, while Santayana shares the view that traditional supernaturalistic creeds and cults curb critical thinking in deleterious ways and privilege some people at the expense of others, he remains committed to the idea that, naturalistically embraced, religious institutions and the narratives and disciplines that inform them may contribute to both public and private well-being.

But there are important hitches in this disagreement between Deweyan pragmatists and Santayana. It turns out that they are talking past one another in some significant ways. First, the Deweyans champion what Benjamin Barber has recently called "strong democracy." Santayana, to the contrary, criticizes kinds of democracy Barber characterizes as "thin."[1] Deweyans like Barber see democracy as "the way that human beings with variable but malleable natures and with competing but overlapping interests can contrive to live together communally not only to their mutual advantage, but also to the advantage of their mutuality."[2] Santayana, on the other hand, usually construes democracy as uniform adherence to the will of the majority. He attacks it for its illiberal consequences and defends an imperial sort of liberal republicanism.

Second, Deweyans criticize religious practices and institutions on the sound assumption that they are, in all but the most extraordinary cases, super-naturalistic in ways that will hamper participatory politics. Santayana defends religious sanctuaries, rituals, and solitary disciplines on the hope that they will be embraced naturalistically in ways that will contribute both to moral cohesion and personal contentment.

To my mind, the culture Dewey urges us to embrace is worse off for not including the sorts of naturalistic religion that Santayana approves; the society Santayana commends to us is worse off because its imperial liberal republicanism shortchanges the beneficial power of participatory citizenship; and, finally, religious naturalism in a strong liberal democracy is a live and inspiring option, because both are better off linked to the other.

Dewey's Common Faith

Dewey notes links between democracy and spiritual life in a great number of works, perhaps none more succinctly than in *The Public and Its Problems*, where he says that "Democracy is not an alternative to other principles of associated life. It is the idea of community life itself. . . . [It is] a name for a life of free and enriching communion."[3] His Terry Lectures on *A Common Faith*, however, delivered at Yale in 1934, stand as his classic statement on the issues involved in linking politics and religion. There, he identifies religiousness with the intelligent articulation of ongoing democratic aims, institutions, and practices. Faith amounts to a commitment to whatever range of social activities make up democratic community. It is a devotion to the realistic social structures or institutions permitting and fostering the responsibility of people to one another and the care of people for one another. The faithful courageously keep their sights on "the human abode," disciplining themselves to do what it takes to assert and achieve human solidarity (*ACF*, 59). Their aim is not to establish the will of the majority and to demand uniform adherence to it. They are *not* majoritarians or uniformitarians. Rather, their intent is to engage in practices that foster mutual understanding and respect, and that lead to a reconstruction of social arrangements conducive to the public and private well-being of the individuals constituting the community. They are liberal mutualists.

Perhaps most significantly, as Deweyan democrats work toward the resolution of conflicts emerging in the community, they deny themselves the false comfort of some prior and transcendent support or authority for this or that political proposition. Deweyan democrats systematically resist such independent grounds for reaching agreement. As Barber puts it, their process of political deliberation, decision, and action

> equalizes value inputs. It gives to each individual's convictions and beliefs an equal starting place and associates legitimacy with what happens to convictions and beliefs in the course of public talk and action rather than with [some] prior epistemological status. The legitimacy of a value is thus a feature of its publicness, of how it is refined, changed, or transformed when confronted with a public and the public norms which that public has already legitimized through its politics.[4]

Deweyan democrats deny allegiance to some realm or being transcending "the human abode" in order to accept responsibility and solicitude for one another. They continually seek to ameliorate their common lot through the development and use of appropriate political, economic, and social technologies. Their faith is realized in the "radical intervention of intelligence in the conduct of human life" (ACF, 78).

From this social and political vantage point, Dewey argues that the time has come for people to distinguish "religions" from "the religious." "It is widely supposed," he claims (in 1934), "that a person who does not accept any religion is thereby shown to be a non-religious person. Yet it is conceivable that the present depression in religion is closely connected with the fact that religions now prevent, because of their weight of historic encumbrances, the religious quality of experience from coming to consciousness and finding the expression that is appropriate to present conditions, intellectual and moral. I believe that this is the case" (ACF, 9).

The form of this argument should be familiar. It is a variant on the traditional Reformed Christian construal of religious life that distinguishes law from spirit or grace. As the law is fixed and dogmatic and the spirit or grace is open and transforming, so too is Dewey's distinction between "religions" and "the religious."

"A religion," Dewey claims, ". . . always signifies a special body of beliefs and practices having some kind of institutional organization, loose or tight." "The religious," on the other hand, denotes neither a specific institution nor a set body of beliefs nor, for that matter, "anything to which one can specifically point. . . . It does not denote anything that can exist by itself or that can be organized into a particular and distinctive form of existence" (*ACF*, 9–10). Indeed, "the religious" qualifies no "definite kind of experience" that can be marked off from aesthetic, scientific, moral, social, or political activities. This is so, Dewey argues, because "the religious" is "a quality of experience [that belongs] to all these experiences" (*ACF*, 10). What makes any of these experiences religious is a particular *effect*: "Any activity pursued in behalf of an ideal end against obstacles and in spite of threats of personal loss because of conviction of its general and enduring value is religious in quality" (*ACF*, 27).

Dewey, however, not only distinguishes the religious quality of experiences from religions. He also argues that there is no way to bridge the gap between his own democratic faith and "the creeds and cults" of traditional religions (which, by his stipulation, are fixed or unchangeable) (*ACF*, 28). For one, to his mind political affairs and spiritual life are inseparable and continuous, so that religious institutions, which artificially force a split between them, are dysfunctional and vicious. But even more substantively, Dewey recognizes that the very heart of strong participatory democracy is a kind of open and critical deliberation that functions continuously to *transform* a plurality of ways of seeing and judging into shared views and intentions. Many traditional religious people insist that "there is some special and isolated channel of access to the truths they hold" (*ACF*, 29). Democrats, to the contrary, are concerned with fashioning judgments through public discourse the point of which is to create consensus. For them, "there is but one sure road of access to truth—the road of patient, cooperative inquiry operating by means of observation, experiment, record and controlled reflection" (*ACF*, 32). Democracy, as all experience, "in its vital form is experimental, an effort to change the given; it is characterized by projection, by reading forward into the unknown; connection with a future is its salient trait."[5] In democratic deliberation, the prior beliefs citizens bring with them are given. But they are not, as religions are want to suggest, constituted by "an irreducible minimum . . . so fixed in advance that [they] can never be modified." Democratic deliberation is "open and public" (*ACF*, 39). It is also future-oriented because its point is to envision the prospect that *we* desire. Its aim is to create a new (or renewed) consensus about the sort of world *we* want to make for ourselves, about what things count as common goods, about how to facilitate the realization of these things, and also about how to manage difficulties blocking their fulfillment. It is experimental because it does not rest on prior beliefs or the status quo but, rather, engages citizens with one another in ways that permit mutual understanding about the sort of world they want to come to share, in large part by working together first to *see* it, and then to *create* it. Democratic deliberation changes people and their beliefs, transforming "I"s into "We."

So, where strong participatory democracy is the desideratum, what citizens, as citizens, assent to in the way of belief must be yielded by ongoing activities of public deliberation. No belief held independent of public deliberation or prior to it is sacred or sheltered from the give and take of public discourse; every belief that citizens bring with them to public deliberation is qualified by the contingencies of history and, so, by provisionality, fallibility, and corrigibility. What authorizes a judgment is not its prior hold on this or that person. It is not the fact that a majority of people at hand continue to hold it or freshly assent to it. A political judgment is democratically authorized by the way its use helps realize a world that will be good for *us*, whether we be members of a majority or a minority. Democratic responsibility and democratic responsiveness are inseparable.

Many people are quick to criticize Dewey at this point for proposing, incredibly, that citizens park their prior beliefs outside the doors of their Town Halls whenever they enter them for the purposes of competent public, democratic deliberation. But that is not his point or his instruction. Citizens, in Dewey's view, cannot help but bring their prior beliefs with them, *because they are their beliefs; their beliefs make up their identities*. But democratic citizens are not fixed and unyielding interests capable, at best, of bargaining with other inflexible interests in order to secure the best aggregate of private interests. Democratic citizens are social individuals capable of working together to propose and create a common future in which every one of *us* can envision living well. A creed founded on their common deliberations

> will change and grow, but it cannot be shaken. What it surrenders it gives up gladly because of new light and not as a reluctant concession. What it adds, it adds because new knowledge gives further insight into the conditions that bear upon the formation and execution of our life purposes. A one sided psychology, a reflex of eighteenth-century "individualism,"

treated knowledge as an accomplishment of a lonely mind. We should now be aware that it is a product of the cooperative and communicative operations of human beings living together. Its communal origin is an indication of its rightful communal use. The unification of what is known at any given time, not upon an impossibly eternal and abstract basis but upon the unification of human desire and purpose, furnishes a sufficient creed for human acceptance, one that would provide a religious release and reinforcement of knowledge. (ACF, 85–86)

On this view, the religious or spiritual life has a structural role to play in the sort of society that can, realistically, articulate democratic community. Its concern is with the "unification of human desire and purpose" (ACF, 86). The aim of spiritual life is to nurture and extend "the *values* of natural human intercourse and mutual dependence [which] are open and public, capable of verification by the methods through which all natural facts are established" (ACF, 73).

To Dewey's mind, then, "natural piety" amounts to the celebration and reinforcement of "the things in civilization we most prize." Harking back again to the two-covenants tradition, he claims that these treasures "are not of ourselves. They exist by the grace of the doings and sufferings of the continuous human community in which we are a link" (ACF, 87). "The fund of human values that are prized and that need to be cherished," he asserts, are "values that are satisfied and rectified by *all* human concerns and arrangements" (ACF, 82).

Dewey claims that this "natural piety" is the religious function of institutions in a democratic society (ACF, 82). But there is no need for any discrete religious institutions. Families, neighborhood clubs, schools, town meetings, and civic holidays can all see to the requisite celebrations. Hence, "the old dualism between the secular and the spiritual" is overcome (ACF, 74). The cults, rituals, and disciplines articulating "another world to live in" are not simply dispensable. They are vicious because their focus on illusory otherworldly and supernatural powers distracts citizens from the goods "experienced in the concrete relations of family, neighborhood, citizenship, [and in the] pursuit of art and science" that they "actually depend upon for guidance and support." The activities of the traditional religions have not just obscured the "real nature" of natural social values. Traditional religious disciplines have weakened the force of these social values by depreciating them, by regarding them "as dangerous rivals of higher values; as offering temptations to be resisted; as usurpations by flesh of the authority of the spirit; as revolts of the human against the divine" (ACF, 71–72).

For Dewey, then, being religious demands no life apart from "worldly" society, no distinctive spiritual discipline aside from exercising civic virtues, no creedal assent distinct from the consensus that emerges through the open and public deliberations of active citizens. Being religious, he asserts, demands participation in "God." In other words, it amounts to taking a part in the "active relation between ideal and actual" (ACF, 51). The point is to make the world suitable to our ultimate concerns, where the emphasis falls on a democratically mutual us. This is Dewey the unadulterated Enlightenment fundamentalist, asserting that, really, human self-assertion not "confined to sect, class, or race . . . has always been implicitly the common faith of mankind." Only now, he urges, the task ahead is "to make it explicit and militant" (ACF, 87).

But if we are Deweyan democrats, is it really necessary to embrace what amounts to a "melting pot" faith, where the particularities of tradition are peeled off because they are dross? Must democrats abandon the wealth of distinctive practices that help constitute their social and personal identities as Christians, Jains, or Jews, in order to avoid the pitfalls of supernaturalism and militantly to pursue political solidarity? Not, I think, without threatening the sort of terrifying spiritual uniformity Kundera warns us about.

When Deweyan democrats like me enter the public political realm, to be sure, we must do so without any pretense that we come equipped with epistemic or moral privileges bestowed upon us by some source transcending the natural world of society and politics. But if some variant of Santayana's religious naturalism holds appeal for us, this ordinance presents no distinctive problem. To the contrary, often enough we will be motivated to go into public and political deliberation out of moral commitments we have learned in private associations, including our particular religious communities. But more, our lives are not only public and political or, for that matter, moral. They are also private, personal, and solitary, and, where individuals reach for contentment in the midst of moral conflict, they may be spiritual as well.

Santayana's Spiritual Liberalism

Just "as Plato banished the poets," Santayana contends, so Deweyan pragmatists

> would banish Buddha and Christ. It is an old story. Yet the poets and the prophets, in a regimen that recognized the interests of the spirit among human interests, might unintentionally cooperate with the statesman by offering mankind a holiday from the statesman's world; and I think that as mankind is now constituted it would be most impolitic to force the engine to work under still higher and higher pressure, while closing the safety-valves that religion and post-rational philosophy would open towards the non-human. The spirit in man cannot live for man alone, and man is never happier than when the spirit carries him beyond himself. Nor need this non-human *Lebensraum* be any fictitious superhuman sphere. My personal philosophy, so severely blamed for turning its eyes away from human society, is a strict materialism; and this materialism about the universe makes it easier for me to endure and even to enjoy the materialism of the world. (*PGS*, 566)

As Santayana sees it, there is a tension between statesmanship and poetic spirituality that will not go away, unless we "force the engine" and close "the safety-valves" provided by religious or philosophical disciplines, which emerge when people realize that human efforts to construct a world of perfect harmony inevitably come up short. Certainly, Santayana contends, attendance to spiritual life requires political allowance. As he puts it in *Platonism and the Spiritual Life*, just when and where spiritual disciplines will arise and flourish are "evidently questions of mundane physics and politics: it is the world's business to call down spirit to dwell in it, not the spirit's business to make a world in which to dwell" (*PSL*, 38).

Nevertheless, the disciplines conducive to "spiritual liberty" differ from the political activities that allow for them. So "reason," Santayana claims, must be stereoscopic, aiming both for private and public good. "It cannot define or codify human nature: that is the error of militant sects and factions. But it can exercise a modicum of control over local and temporary impulses and keep at least an ideal of spiritual liberty and social justice before the public eye" (*DP*, 382).

So, in opposition to the picture of spiritual life held by Dewey—the sort that identifies spiritual life with the celebration and reinforcement of "the fund of human values that are prized and need to be cherished"—Santayana asserts:

> Spiritual life is not a worship of "values," whether found in things or hypostatized into supernatural powers. It is the exact opposite: it is the *disintoxication* from their influence. Not that spiritual insight can ever remove values from nature or cease to feel them in their moral black and white and in all their aesthetic iridescence. Spirit knows these vital necessities; it has been quickened in their bosom. All animals have within them a principle by which to distinguish good from evil, since their existence and welfare are furthered by some circumstances and acts and hindered by others. . . . These values each society will disentangle in proportion to its intelligence and will defend in proportion to its vitality. But who would dream that *spiritual life* was at all concerned in asserting these human and local values to be alone valid, or in supposing that they were especially divine, or bound to dominate the universe for ever? (*PSL*, 30)

We have, here, a further extension of James's "Certain Blindness" doctrine and the posture of deliberate irresponsibility central to Santayana's soliloquy on "Hermes the Interpreter." The point is this: We are all social beings whose lives are organized, economically, politically, and socially, to realize certain values or to satisfy certain interests that we either create or have learned to accept, and often enough to cherish, as members of a particular tradition or culture. All of this is not only normal but "intelligent" and "vital." It is practically necessary. But at the same time, no matter how potentially inclusive we claim our culture or tradition or society or picture of the human prospect to be, its values (which are our values) and the responsibilities we accept in order to realize them, blind us from the beauty or excellence of other people, things, events, and circumstances that are alien to us. This, Santayana claims, forces a distinction between the activities involved in celebrating "the values we cherish" and spiritual discipline. "It is the essence of spirit to see and love things for their own sake, in their own nature, not for the sake of one another, nor for its own sake" (*PSL*, 93).

To Santayana's mind, spiritual disciplines permit us to be practically irresponsible enough to appreciate what is strange, even hostile to the values we now cherish. He therefore asks pragmatists to admit spiritual life "into their life of reason as an element. . . . If they refuse to do so, it seems to me that rational life in them would itself sink to the pre-rational level. They would be fighting for a closed circle of accidental interests, established by them as absolute and alone legitimate" (PGS, 565). In Santayana's view, people need to come to political judgment time and again. They need to base such judgments on principles of value. So far as they engage in spiritual discipline, however, people need to suspend the practice of judgment for the sake of understanding, for the sake of seeing and appreciating things for their own sake and, when these things are people, as they understand themselves and their circumstances.

On Dewey's view, being religious boils down to social and political responsibility. On Santayana's, the spiritual aspect of religious life, at any rate, demands imaginative suspension of social and political obligation. Pragmatically speaking, in fact, spiritual life is *necessarily* irresponsible in these ways because its function is to cure the blindness that social, economic, and political responsibilities, intelligence, and vitality bring about. Political technology, proper in its own right, and just as *necessarily* demanding social responsibility, *distracts* people from the disciplines that let them discern whatever is lovely and lovable about things they find socially, politically, morally, culturally or existentially alien.

So Santayana insists on highlighting a necessary tension between responsible social and political life on the one hand and spiritual life on the other. His view, which repositions the older Reformed Christian tension between law and grace so that it rests squarely in the culture of the modern Western republics, is the key to understanding the ditch separating him from Dewey on the politics of spiritual life. For Dewey, spiritual life and citizenship are not only inseparable; they are identical. The political task in democracy is a divine process; it is, he asserts, participation "in God." For Santayana, to the contrary, spiritual life and citizenship are intertwined as parts of a form of life; but spirituality requires *time out* from political deliberation and social work: "political zeal, even in the true friends of spirit is not spiritual. . . . The spirit . . . is not essentially learned or social; its kingdom is not of this world" (PSL, 39).

People bent on practicing spiritual disciplines both depend on the goodwill of those societies who suffer them, and can not be bound exclusively by responsibilities of state or political work, which may well have to be suspended for spiritual discipline and discernment to go on.

Vital Liberty

This disagreement between Deweyan pragmatists and Santayana is one way to measure the intensity of Santayana's "radical liberalism," the social position he tries to explicate in *Dominations and Powers: Reflections on Liberty, Society, and Government* (*DP*, 430). Written in snippets over the course of forty tumultuous years in our century (roughly 1910–50), *Dominations and Powers* offers a view of social life that is largely libertarian in its values (cherishing private association, liberty, and individuality), realist in its means (relying on power, law, and force for order), and minimalist in its political temper (embracing tolerance, pluralism, a sharp separation between government and the governed, and a distrust of political action). *Dominations and Powers* is not only Santayana's final statement on the politics of spiritual life, but the last book to be published while he is alive.

The work immediately received a good deal of adverse criticism, a lot of which came from pragmatists like Sidney Hook and naturalists like Sterling Lamprecht and Herbert Schneider. Adrienne Koch summed up their common critical sentiment by warning that

> the reader must be prepared for the paradox of a book on politics that is essentially a-political, and of a liberal imagination that indulges in eccentric judgments about the shortcomings of democratic theory and practice. In place of relevant reflection on the pressing political problems and tendencies of a dramatic age like ours, Santayana broods upon the necessary limitations to which the human psyche is born, and offers an ironic, almost sportive, vision of the relativity of rationality and rightness in human life. The grandeur of the eternal human effort to live by illusions and yet to resign oneself to their ultimate defeat is intimately evoked.[6]

Michael Oakeshott and Alfred Schutz softened that criticism somewhat by placing *Dominations and Powers* in the classical tradition of "episteme politike."

It was, Schutz argued, a theoretical account of human nature and conduct, "which, wisely used, may teach the politician—any politician—where he comes from and where he leads to."[7] Given this aim, "the many reviewers who have reproached Santayana for the lack of understanding of liberalism, of American leadership, of Soviet Russia's policies, for refraining from any remarks about fascism, and so on, have . . . missed the point entirely."[8]

In great part, Santayana's thesis is a familiar one. People are born into natural, including cultural, social, and political, circumstances and eventually seek spiritual well-being. Santayana is fundamentally concerned with clarifying "the causes and the enemies of the beautiful." That concern, he argues, demands a study of "those *Dominations and Powers* in whose train the beautiful lives, and in whose decline it withers" (*DP*, ix). Put another way: "[A]pproaches to harmony appear, here and there for a time, between the formative impulses of life and the balance of ambient powers. It is these vital achievements that essentially interest me; but it is only in passing that I can hope to point to them or stop to describe them. My subject here is rather the circumstances which, in any case, enable these fruits to mature, or perhaps nip them in the bud. I am concerned with the fortunes of potential *Virtues* in the hands of *Dominations* and *Powers*" (*DP*, 2). Here, then, Santayana reiterates his Edwardsean-Emersonian-Jamesian identification of virtuous character and conduct with appreciation, expression, and enactment of "the beautiful," and addresses issues about the natural, social, and political conditions enabling or impeding public and private well-being.

"The first principle of rationality in government," Santayana asserts, "is that it should protect and encourage vital liberty, in whatever quarter or form circumstances render its expression possible in action" (*DP*, 435). This is so, he claims, because "the play of vital liberty is the immediate multiform source of human happiness" (*DP*, 432). Indeed, because vital liberty is variable across cultures and historically mutable, good government is charged with making space for an indefinite range of vital freedoms, an order he characterizes as "spiritual wealth in spiritual liberty" (*DP*, 456).

Vital liberty, to Santayana's mind, is not "vacant freedom," or "the moral illusion of free action without a definite impulse in an existing world" (*DP*, 46). Nor is it the mythical and nonsensical "liberty of indifference," which purportedly exhibits the human ability to choose this rather than that for no reason or motive (*DP*, 53). Both "vacant freedom" and "the liberty of indif-

ference" are absentminded, forgetful that the choices people make are variations on customary affections that they themselves inherit and enact. People
are defined and constrained on the one hand by these inherited, if plastic,
habits of life, and on the other by the material circumstances with which they
interact. "To flourish," Santayana contends, "without feeling any domination
crossing your path is to obey, and thereby to develop, your inmost, freest, most
disinterested powers; your compulsions have become your choices and your
limitations your virtues" (DP, 151).

So much for Emerson's notion that the only sin is limitation. Contingent
limitations join contingent affections to compose the varieties of human well-
being. If there is one sin, it is distraction, or the kinds of diversion that foster
deceit or self-deceit about circumstances and, consequently, about human
prospects. Santayana's moral and religious naturalism demands that,

> in identifying authority with the favour of Circumstances, we deny all
> intrinsic rightness or wrongness to any form of Will or action. The differ-
> ence lies only in the suitability of that impulse to the world in which it
> arises. You have a right to be what you are and to become what you can
> become. To deny this is literally superstitious; it stands aside from the
> vital fact itself, and seems to feel the presence of another impulse spying
> on it and loathing it. Then, infected with this alien Will, the native Will is
> perturbed and hesitates. But the alien Will is a form of primal will just as
> absolute and groundless morally as the native will it detests. And it is
> mere confusion and cowardice to fear to like what you like because
> another person dislikes it. So far, the willful man who says that Might is
> Right is a true man, and rational; yet he would be mindless in the highest
> degree if he meant that all initiatives are equally fortunate. He may always
> do as he likes, but he will seldom get what he wants. He will prove
> himself a fool, in little things and in great, if he persistently pursues what
> Circumstances deny him. Circumstances are indeed changeable and may
> be rendered more favourable by a man's own action; but to that extent his
> action was well-adapted to Circumstances, and rational. (DP, 313–14)

For Santayana, then, as for James before him, "wills" or "psyches" propose
and environments, which prominently include other willful people, dispose.
So there are two authorities that, together "determine the forms and the

rational variations of morals: the *authority of things*, that permit, prevent, reward, or punish our actions, and the *authority of primal Will* within us, that chooses our path and discriminates between success and disaster in our careers" (*DP*, 433).

The Public and the Private

But for Santayana, "psyches" or "wills," as well as most relevant "circumstances," come cultured. What he calls reason in *Dominations and Powers*— "the art of satisfying our compatible inclinations in the midst of our inevitable circumstances"—is largely played out in institutions both public and private (*DP*, 159). Indeed, the fact that private institutions play an indispensable role in Santayana's picture of vitally liberal life cannot be emphasized enough because, as he understands them, they are extrapolitical. For Santayana, "public" or "political" institutions are fundamentally economic, making space for "private" institutions that foster "vital liberty" by training people in liberal arts, including moral and spiritual virtues.

There are three things about Santayana's division of the public and the private that are noteworthy. First, the exercise of citizenship, or participatory political deliberation, decision, and action, is virtually absent from Santayana's characterization of "the public"; in its stead, Santayana places "government" and its "objects." Second, the hallmark of the private realm is voluntaryism, not individualism. Private life is organized in terms of voluntary associations that carry distinct moral and spiritual traditions. Third, some of those private, voluntary associations, like religious and other educational institutions, make room on their margins for spiritual disciplines, including personal ones.

To Santayana's mind, distinctively political activities of the sort Dewey champions play no role, or no particularly good role, in public life. If anything, Santayana pictures uniquely political activity as a domination, as a meddling force that frustrates vital liberty. Why is this so? Why does there appear to be a surd or a monster for Santayana where there is citizenship for Dewey? The approximate answer is this: Santayana contends that governors require kinds and levels of wisdom that ordinary people do not have. They must receive kinds of higher education, especially in economic, organizational, technical, and liberal arts, that most people will never get. Government's task is to provide economic and social management that will be conducive to "spiritual wealth in spiritual liberty." But, Santayana claims, "the people" are not trained to manage; they have not received the requisite kinds of higher education. They require "representation" by leaders who have.

This is not a very forceful argument. If the trouble were simply that people lacked relevant kinds of education, the imperative, though practically complex, would be straightforward enough: Educate them sufficiently to manage themselves and to deputize the specialists among them to help them out when they know they do not know enough.

But in truth, Santayana makes no room for citizenship because he believes that social consensus is properly a private affair and he worries that an active citizenry will breach the bounds of propriety. The institutions of citizenship enable people both to envision a world of common goods and to effect strategies to bring them about. But to Santayana's mind, people *already* belong to communities, primarily religious communities, that sustain their exercise of vital liberty. Requiring them to engage in the *civic* creation of consensus, he worries, is purchased at the expense either of traditional excellence or inevitable conflict "between primal irrational Wills" (*DP*, 433). What it buys, he fears, is either religious warfare or that sort of illusory cultural Esperanto that he warned against when he reminded readers of *Reason in Religion* that "the attempt to speak without speaking any particular language is not more hopeless than the attempt to have a religion that shall be no religion in particular."

This line of thinking previews the second important point about Santayana's distinction between public and private. If vital liberty rests squarely in the private domain, it is not simply an individual affair. The hallmark of privacy is not individualism so much as voluntaryism. For Santayana, the private domain is largely constituted by *voluntary associations*, like families, friendships, clubs, and religious institutions. The liberal tradition that Santayana champions endorses these affiliations because they make available the possibilities of both moral and spiritual life.

Gilbert Meilander recently has put a similar contention this way: There is "a form of the liberal tradition which does not attempt to overcome the tension between politics and ethics, yet does recognize that there is indeed a tension. This form of the tradition claims that the public realm—the political—exists *not* just to support and make possible individual pursuit of private goals and projects, *nor* to foster fraternal solidarity. Rather, the political realm exists to foster *private, social* bonds—to make space for families, friendships, clubs, faiths, neighborhoods."[9]

This kind of view leads to the judgment that *moral bonding*—what both Santayana and Dewey call natural piety—ought not be a political affair but, rather, a matter of private, voluntary avowal and enactment. Indeed, the alternative, as Santayana sees it, is either a deceitful denial of moral and spiritual plurality, or the militant suppression of it by means of majoritarian or totalitarian coercion. For Santayana,

> Government . . . becomes the rational art of minimizing the inevitable conflict of primal irrational Wills against one another and against the forces of nature at large. If government attempts to go further and approve one set of irrational Wills and forbid another, it becomes itself the agent of a particular irrational Will; and instead of speaking for all wills that move in its domains, and showing each the best terms it can make with Circumstances, it becomes itself a particular net of Circumstances hostile to all other wills, instead of wise friend to them all. (*DP*, 433–34)

The problem confronting the "law-giver wishing to establish a perfect society," Santayana writes (in Fascist Italy in 1934), is that "the people" will not "possibly be of one mind; not all can sincerely aspire to the same virtues, or recognize the same hierarchy of excellences. There will not only be sluggishness or error in doing one's part, there will not only be ineradicable vices; there will also be ineradicable virtues and aspirations contrary to the prevalent public ways. The legislator will therefore be assuming the character of an odious tyrant, in respect to these natural heretics and virtuous rebels" (*DP*, 449–50).

For Santayana, the most desirable way to avoid this tyranny is a sort of *Pax Romana* or *Pax Britannia* or, as he will finally commend, a *Pax Americana*, where diverse "nations" or "peoples" preserve their "language and laws and religion under an imperial insurance," keeping their "moral idiosyncracy, [their] speech, dress, and domestic life, side by side with the most alien races" (*DP*, 452).[10]

During the year Hitler becomes *Führer* in Germany, in a gesture that may well signal his agonized conscience contending with its own humiliating, shopworn Christian anti-Semitism, Santayana suggests that the history of the Jews exemplifies the kind of preservation of moral and spiritual integrity that he has in mind. That history, he now says, is

> a most wonderful instance of a people preserving its moral identity for two thousand years without any territorial possessions. Their fate has been hard, and the sentiment they have aroused in their gentile neighbors has not been kindly. The prejudice against them, however, has been religious rather than political; and even the difficulty they have encountered in establishing a "National home" in Palestine was due largely to the fact that their Holy City is also a Holy City for Christians and Moslems, with the two latter in possession, and at first alone disposing of military force. But suppose these circumstances had been different. Nothing then would have prevented the Israelites, scattered all over the world, from maintaining everywhere their religion and language, and preserving in Jerusalem a sanctuary where all the ceremonies of their Law might have been carried out. Round this sacred nucleus of race and religion, a complete body of arts and sciences, manners and domestic laws might have then grown up; and this without army or navy or police or local jurisdiction. It would have sufficed that the common law, in whatever other countries they lived, should have allowed them possession, as private property, of enough land for their synagogues and dwelling-houses: and especially license to educate their children in their own schools, in their own language, up to the highest studies they should wish to pursue. And I do not think a truly imperial authority, preserving a Roman Peace all the world over, would have any reason for denying any nation these moral liberties. (*DP*, 452–53)

On this view, government at its best manages the "preservation" of distinct peoples by licensing their traditional life, but in ways that are geared *literally* not to matter to other distinct peoples who, nonetheless, share in their material lot. This is politics understood optimally as zookeeping, where lions may lay down with lambs, at least so long as each remains sequestered in their own special pastures.

Private Social Bonds and
Individual Spiritual Disciplines

When I turn to Santayana's liberal criticism of democracy, I will argue that the social voluntaryism that he endorses, and which I share, is better configured in the context of democratic practices than under imperial authority. But at this point, it is important to recall the third characteristic of Santayana's public/private distinction: It is insufficient to distinguish the economic and governmental public realm from the private domain of voluntary associations. This is so because, on the margins of the normal orders of traditional social life, at least where political and economic arrangements permit it, and sometimes in defiance of orders to the contrary, individuals can compose themselves, as Santayana puts it, in light of "that unused residuum of life which the animal soul still feels within itself after social institutions and intellectual conventions have hemmed it in" (*DP*, 160). Spiritual functions of psyche become evident in such occasions, he claims, when

> love or intelligence has become self-transcendent, disinterested, and lost in its ideal object. Will, as Schopenhauer would say, has been eclipsed, and the Idea has come forward and filled the stage. But the Idea here is seen, it is lived; so that there is a living intuition, perfectly temporal and human, that brings that essence into the light of day. And this light of day, for the spirit, is pure; it adds no date or place to the eternal form conceived, but sees and loves it for its intrinsic beauty and perfection. In feasting the spirit on this its congenial food, the arts liberate it from what it felt as exile or captivity, and allow it for a moment to be itself. (*DP*, 171–72)

In this picture, government at its best, largely staffed by efficient economic technicians and social traffic cops, frees and authorizes space for voluntary associations, which function as agents of social, moral, and spiritual bonding and discipline. Where those private institutions are genuinely liberal, they provide space on their margins for the kinds of individual variation that Santayana identifies with the spiritual life, the sort of well-being brought about not simply privately but in solitude, through personal disciplines of self-transcending and disinterested love and intelligence.

There are, to be sure, more ways to seek graceful life than Santayana endorses. Recall, for example, current Emersonians like Bloom and Rorty, content only in their agonizing effort to make their "I"s different from all the other "I"s. But whatever judgment is passed on the details of Santayana's specification of the spiritual life, the way he locates it, together with training in moral virtues, in private voluntary associations, is forceful. If Santayana's picture of the private character of moral and spiritual life is compelling, then he obviates two arguments that raged not only in his own time but still go on.

For one, communitarians have argued that either social life in the modern Western republics is publicly grounded in a prior moral consensus that permits little variation, or it becomes spiritually vapid, an anarchic free-for-all, the spoilage of individuals competing among themselves for pecuniary gain. But Santayana is a liberal communitarian of sorts.[11] In his view, anarchic individualism does not define the private domain. Rather, sufficient moral bonding takes place privately, when voluntary associations concerned with training in moral virtues are given free reign. Moreover, Santayana argues, the moment government enforces allegiance to one among the many voluntary associations at hand, "it becomes itself a particular net of Circumstances hostile to all other wills, instead of wise friend to them all."

Secondly, moral critics on many sides have contended that "spiritual life" is so much bourgeois self-indulgence, because it is bound to *disrupt* concern for social solidarity and justice. But remember Santayana's stereoscopic vision focused both on social justice and spiritual liberty. On his view, voiced both in his "Apologia Pro Mente Sua" in 1940 and in *Dominations and Powers*, spiritual life best (even inevitably) grows out of institutions of moral cohesion and discipline: "Spirit, being a psychic faculty, cannot exist without an organ at a particular place and time, with a specific range. It would cease to exist, if it could embrace every view and every preference at once. . . . Piety must never be dislodged: Spirituality without it is madness" (*PGS*, 569, 572).

As Santayana understands it, spiritual discipline detaches individuals from themselves and their world, but "you cannot be detached without being previously attached; you cannot renounce or sacrifice anything significantly unless you love it. And if you withdraw from any action it must not be from timidity or laziness; that would be giving up one vain impulse for another still vainer and more physical." For Santayana, disinterest is a kind of interest, one aversive to personal attachments. The self-transcendence of love or intelligence that Santayanan spiritual disciplines bring about neither destroy moral actions nor, morally speaking, add to them. Rather spirituality "leaves you content to be where you are and what you are" (*PGS*, 571).

Here, Santayana finds instruction in a scene from the *Mahabharata*,

> where two armies face each other with drawn swords, awaiting the signal for battle. But the prince commanding one of the armies has pacifist scruples, which he confesses to his spiritual mentor—a god in disguise— in the most eloquent words I have ever read on that theme. His heart will not suffer him to give the word. And then the sage, while the armies stand spell-bound at arms, pours forth wisdom for eighteen cantos; yet the conclusion is simple enough. The tender prince must live the life appointed for him; he must fight this battle, *but with detachment*. (*PGS*, 571)

But if this is so, the charge that Santayana's variety of spiritual life disrupts moral responsibility is misplaced, unless disciplines that are geared to bring about personal contentment *in the midst* of moral concern and even social and political militancy are ruled morally deficient. To judge them so, from Santayana's point of view, simply underscores the personal resentment and envy that fuel moralists who humiliate individuals artful and lucky enough to achieve and illustrate the personal well-being that satisfies "the religious demand." Certainly spiritual madness is possible, but no more nor less so than moral zealotry run amok. Spiritual madness dismisses social cohesion and the practice of justice. Moral fanaticism enforces militant unity and makes personal contentment look criminal. So much the worse for madness and fanaticism, but not for spirituality or morality.

Dominations and Powers *at Odds with Itself*

Santayana maintains his post-Jamesian pragmatic naturalism in *Dominations and Powers* with the claim that "reason cannot define or codify human nature: that is the error of militant sects and factions. But it can exercise a modicum of control over local and temporary impulses and keep at least an ideal of spiritual liberty and social justice before the public eye." Moreover, he underscores the impact of contingency on political thinking in his reflection that modern natural history and politics have discredited the ambition of the ancients to legislate for eternity. . . . The shattering of the hopes of the ancients, to build a city on a rock and defy the ages, I think has brought a real lesson, a valuable discipline to our pride . . . an old lesson, but ill-learned till now. . . . Instead of being a dead fact, existence is an index: it points. . . . Evolution is not performing any set task, much less a task imposed on it for the greater glory of our prophetic minds. Evolution is evolving; it is unravelling itself as it can. And so are our affections. Nature is well-ordered enough to have produced spirit, yet chaotic enough to have left it free; it is not obliged to copy or to love its antecedents. (DP, 33–34)

Especially in light of these pragmatic characterizations of morality, spirituality, and politics, I want to argue, Santayana's *Dominations and Powers* is a seriously flawed work, for three reasons. First, his recognition of variation and change in human culture is vitiated by his reliance on an anthropology that presumes, unrealistically or repressively, the homogeneity of this or that "people." Second, his allegiance to Lincoln's vision of "government of, by, and for the people" (which, to be sure, is quite satirical) is corrupted both by his nearly complete blindness to the political power of democratic citizenship, and by his ready acceptance of the notion that some "wisdom," independent of political activity, should rule the world. Third, his useful distinctions between public and private goods, and between private social and solitary goods, are spoiled by his failure to clarify how the public, the private, and the solitary can hang together in ways that empower rather than dominate the efforts of people to be their best selves, both together and alone.

Museum Culture and a Peaceable Kingdom

For all Santayana's insistence on the contingency of things, the historicity of traditions, and the variability of cultures, his portrayal of social life at its best remains all too fixed and inflexible. His "politics as zookeeping" is part of a larger cultural anthropology. In the end of the day, he fails his openly stated preference for an "open architecture." He cannot quite wean himself away from the judgment, or hope, that a reasonable human order makes a place for everybody and keeps everybody in place. "In the end," Santayana argues, "what reason can do best is to disinfect existence as far as possible of illusion, pride, and wanton militancy, and for the rest to accept the natural diversity and inconstancy of Will, only moderating its fury; as can be done by fostering, in due separation and harmony, all possible contrasting virtues, which never would hate one another morally if they never conflicted materially" (*DP*, 333–34). The trouble with this judgment is this: Santayana fails to point out that, on its own grounds, naturally diverse societies never would appreciate one another's traditions, practices, and aspirations unless they participated in material institutions allowing or requiring them to do so.

Santayana's highest aspiration in *Domination and Powers* is for a peaceable kingdom, where *tolerance* among diverse peoples is both fostered and enforced. But the price he pays for his kingdom is all too high, and its purchase too shopworn and mediocre. The price, wittingly or unwittingly paid, is virtually no intermural life together among "special societies," and no Hermesan "border-crossings" from one to others and back again. What is purchased is what Renato Rosaldo has called an "art museum" picture of culture at its best, where special societies stand "alone as [aesthetic objects] worthy of contemplation . . . separate and equal."[12]

This sort of tolerant polity is more or less blind and deaf to the things that make different peoples particularly different. It is not formed by people who appreciate alien others as they understand themselves; it is constituted by presumably monolithic peoples who know their station and mind their own ethnic business. Tolerance, taken alone, leaves the many just that: many. It marks a failure of nerve, particularly, for any polity committed to the principle embodied in the motto of the United States, *e pluribus unum*. It is essentially a device, as Barber has pointed out, by which one people can rest assured that others will be restrained, or self-restrained.[13] That curtails any benefit it might have for public well-being. It deadens rather than vitalizes the possibilities of interaction among the many. It blinds one from another rather than leading to mutual enlightenment. It suggests only three options for developing relations among a diversity of peoples: Either one possesses the others, or is possessed by another, or each is neatly sealed off from the others. So it truncates the life of reason that Santayana himself champions; it abandons the virtue of charitable justice he himself proposes; and it undercuts the possibility of spiritual discernment he prizes above all else.

So it should come as little surprise that *this* Santayana, full of genuine admiration for the moral and spiritual integrity of Judaism as a "special society," for example, is also unabashed in his declaration that, even in the United States, where "language and culture are no longer distinct for the Gentile and for the Jew, something else still separates them. The true virtue and the supreme pleasure of the Jew were always a closed book for the Gentile; and the true virtue and supreme pleasure of the Gentile are a closed door for the Jew" (*DP*, 361).

Moreover, if unscalable walls separate diverse sensibilities according to this picture, "sensibilities" are themselves homogenous and fixed. The fabled "Jew" and equally mythic "Gentile" displace indelibly variable, modifiable, and fluid patterns and processes of life with cartoon cutouts.

Here, it seems to me, Santayana confronts Santayana, and one must ask the other: Hermes, traveler, where are you? Hermes is not the god of tolerance but of mutual understanding; not the god of static difference but of dynamic interaction; not the god who professes that it takes one to know one, but rather the god who figures out ways to celebrate one another's heritages, current practices, and aspirations; the god who learns more about himself along with others by listening to them. The figure of Hermes, boundary crosser, works comfortably in cultures "put into motion," to use Rosaldo's trope. Hermes is tailor-made for a social world in which even evolution evolves (which is any social world, no matter how hard guardians try to stop history). But Hermes becomes inert in the kind of minimalist and patronizing liberal regime that Santayana proposes in *Dominations and Powers*. Hermes is met there by a conservative liberal nearly as platitudinous as the neighbor in Robert Frost's "Mending Wall" who "will not go behind his father's saying" that "good fences make good neighbors."[14]

Santayana's cultural and social analyses have not caught up with his insight that human affections unravel themselves as they can, not obliged to copy or replicate their antecedents. Had he viewed culture and society as emerging out of such affections, he might have said of the *varieties* of *changing* and *variable* traditions that they are *indices* that *point*, not dead structures that entomb, or cages that display. He might have highlighted ways in which both religious and other special communities, enacted through their diverse membership, improvise ways of maintaining strong affiliation, discipline themselves in ways that permit personal contentment, and simultaneously are able to interact passionately with "outsiders" civilly, privately, and personally.

But instead, Santayana notes how "special societies" in the United States, for example, Negro and Catholic societies, "thirst to become in some way segregated and distinguishable"; and he speculates, for instance, on ways the American "black population . . . will know how to develop its own institutions in the places where it congregates and where it might govern itself to advantage" (*DP*, 361–62).

Santayana's point about the importance of moral and spiritual bonding cannot and should not be denied. Blacks and Catholics, among other groups in modern Western democracies like the United States, surely do hunger for ways to maintain the integrity of their traditions and, at least through the procedures permitted voluntary private associations, to govern themselves in the places where they congregate. But we live in a culture where many Catholics *are* blacks, and vice versa, and belong voluntarily to other private societies as well, like families, clubs, alumnae groups, sisterhoods and brotherhoods, unions, social movements, and political parties. Indeed, we participate in a society where, as Alexander Nehamas puts it,

> Foreignness, in fact, starts within the skin itself. Persons . . . are networks of beliefs, attitudes and desires. But these form various clusters which need not all be consistent with one another; and each one of these clusters connects the same person to a variety of different groups whose identity cannot be easily separated from that of the individual in question. One can be Greek born, American educated, a Spanish citizen, a philosopher who spends more time with literature than science but admires science nonetheless, a late twentieth-century male, a reluctant bourgeois, and much more besides. We can be, and we are, foreign to ourselves. Everything we are and in respect of which we change has, in different degrees, effects on the nature of the groups to which we belong; and changes in these groups, in turn, affect the nature of the individual who consists of their interrelations.[15]

But the force of this sort of sensibility, which is illustrated by Santayana's life and informs a great deal of his moral and religious naturalism, becomes virtually blunt in *Dominations and Powers*.

The diverse cultures in which people participate are not museum pieces but lifeways. Their practitioners lead lives together, often enough as one person, not always smooth-sailing, too often rendered frenetic or even desperate by a consumer-capitalist economy, but nonetheless largely reasonable, improvising techniques to negotiate the disparate worlds they pass through daily, trying to balance their multiple inheritances, identities, and aspirations just the way that Nehamas (or his figure) does. In a culture "ineradicably" plural, moral anarchy or chaos is not the only alternative to staying at home and latching the shutters. This is the case, at any rate, when each and all of the institutions of moral and spiritual bonding and training in which people participate sufficiently overlap to offer them *better chances* for spiritual liberty and social justice. But then, surely, the issue becomes this: How do public institutions of social justice hang together with private institutions that foster spiritual liberty?

Santayana would have been better off, to my mind, had he returned to the line of thinking he started to develop in *Character and Opinion* about "English Liberty in America" to address this issue. There, he had appreciated "the spirit of free co-operation" or "liberty in democracy" at work in the United States, especially its "personal basis, its reserve, its tenacity, its empiricism, its public spirit, and its assurance of its own rightness" (*COUS*, 194–95). Private institutions, like the family, neighborhood associations, and schools, linked up with public ones, like a judiciary that protected constitutional rights, maximized "mutual adaptation," and permitted "polyglot peoples" to go their diverse cultural ways (*COUS*, 196). America was encumbered neither by church nor aristocracy (as England was). Its very plasticity demanded more cooperative liberty than its Mother, England, ever afforded its own. Its political order was "a harmony woven out of accidents, like every work of time and nature, and all the more profound and fertile because no mind could ever have designed it" (*COUS*, 231). Because it demanded that "no interest . . . be carried so far as to lose sight of the rest," it allowed for "variety and distinction of character" without rancor. This, to be sure, was workable only where there was unanimous consent to fundamental mutualism (or processes of "perpetual compromise"), but that was what the "constitutional religion" in a democratic republic amounted to (*COUS*, 228, 198). Inimical to "absolute liberty," or the primitive freedom to do whatever somebody wanted, "English liberty in America" was long-winded and reasonable, moving "by a series of checks, mutual concessions, and limited satisfactions" (*COUS*, 216). This picture of democratic political order could have been developed by Santayana in ways that suited both his pragmatism and his commitment to spiritual liberty. But he dropped it in favor of imperial liberalism by the time he finished writing *Dominations and Powers*.

Santayana's Imperial Liberalism

Truth to tell, although Santayana invokes social justice along with spiritual liberty as the goods that drive his vision of "liberal universal empire," he appears to be at a loss when it comes to showing what social justice looks like, or how it works in *Dominations and Powers*. (He had been more acute in this regard in his reflections on charity in *Reason in Religion* written nearly a half-century before; and then again when he had written "English Liberty in America," for *Character and Opinion in the United States* in 1920.) In *Dominations and Powers*, good government amounts to public management and "if any general domination is to be established and successfully maintained over mankind, it must needs be in the name of physical necessities and physical conditions" (*DP*, 454). Administration of national or international affairs should be confined to the economic sphere and constrained by "the authority of things" (*DP*, 457). By force of law, undergirded by police action, government separates the nations, and then distributes the economic wherewithal (which it presumably has the wisdom to specify in due proportions) for them to attend to their own distinctive moral and spiritual traditions.

So, then, Santayana continues to endorse a kind of liberal republicanism that is timocratic, traditionalist, and, at its best, imperial the way the Roman and British empires had been. But this shows just how satirically Santayana endorses Lincoln's precept, "government of the people, by the people, for the people." If Lincoln had stressed participation by *the people* at every point in his threefold maxim, Santayana mainly suggests public ways to constrain them. He construes Lincoln's "of" to be "a calm, objective genitive implying, if anything, that the people [require] a government" (*DP*, 396). "The People are the *object* on which government is exercised" (*DP*, 402). The exercise of government is a practical necessity in view of inevitable conflicts of interest.

Government is a mechanism of material control or constraint that equips a society with the requisite material powers to "sanction verbal laws by force" (*DP*, 429).

"Government by the people," on Santayana's reading, actually undercuts the possibility of participatory democracy. Championing *representative* government, he urges government by the people's more knowledgeable deputies, appointed by dint of expertise. Ordinary citizens do not serve as representatives of and for one another. Rather, the people can be said actually to govern themselves, Santayana claims, when "the members of their government form part of that people and govern in its name and by its acquiescence" or "consent" (*DP*, 403, 418). Without such consent, which may be secured by universal suffrage, civic republicanism is a sham. But political economies are best governed by deputies who are trained in requisite and relevant arts and sciences and are realistically informed about the circumstances favoring or impeding their exercise.

Finally, Santayana's "government *for* the people" turns on serving the people's interests. But on his view, the people's moral representatives should know better what those interests are than the people themselves, who are all too often blinded by shortsighted "desires," often enough manufactured by consumer capitalists, genuinely to attend to "interests." Under the best of circumstances, "wisdom" rules for the people's sake the world over: Leaders trained in the arts and sciences see for the people and judge for the people, on the basis of a separate wisdom unshared by the people themselves. They have oversight capacities that the people do not. If, occasionally, "the people" formulate and execute their own policies without delegation, such moments are "few and brief," and "the natural dichotomy between the government and the governed returns with its moral friction and mutual discontent" (*DP*, 405).

A good government, to be sure, is itself a sort of constraint or domination, certain to frustrate some vital powers. But, Santayana insists, it is the lesser of three evils, permitting more exercise of vital liberty than anarchic individualism on the one hand and totalitarian uniformity on the other. It is a representative government, a government militantly committed to representing the "true interests" of all its people. These "true interests" are determined by two sets of "natural forces," subject to great variation and at best loosely fitting one another, the "primal will" of a people and the "circumstances" that both permit and constrain the exercise of that will. But apparently the people themselves are unequipped to know their own will and circumstance.

Knowledge of these things, Santayana forewarns, is inevitably fallible, corrigible, and, at best, virtual. Political claims about the natural interests of "the people" and about the circumstances fulfilling them or not, are subject to critical jeopardy as a matter of course. Indeed, Santayana claims, things could not be otherwise, given both the "natural diversity and inconstancy of Will" and changing circumstance (DP, 333).

Indeed, Santayana goes on to argue, it is the fallible and corrigible quality of political judgment, along with antinomial pluralism, that makes the quest for unanimity vicious, as practiced either in communist Russia or in the United States, where "commercial imperialism" enforces uniformity. Unanimity is a "militant demand intolerant of the generative order of nature" (DP, 350), a "biological error" based on two mistaken assumptions: "that human nature in all men is essentially similar, and that consequently mankind should not fully develop its vital liberty without coming to a unanimous vision of the world and a cooperative exercise of the same virtues" (DP, 351). To the contrary, "human society offers but a special instance of such a plastic reaction of living matter to whatever extent circumstances permit it to reach any of its perhaps endless potentialities, all different in their direction, and capable of realizing incomparable forms of virtue or beauty" (DP, 351). Unanimity ignores "its own extreme relativity" by denying the value of "all other possible perfections" (DP, 351–52).

The Criticism of Democracy

The twin fears of private anarchy and public uniformity, then, drive Santayana's criticism of democracy. Human society, Santayana claims, is an inorganic composite without any presumptive vital (physical or metaphysical) unity. Societies do not feel or think; only people do. Society is physically "a concourse, not an organism." The "will" of any society or people is pluriform, variable, and historical, articulated in terms of moral and religious traditions that are subject to piecemeal reform. Any truly "morally representative authority" is authorized by, responsible to, and aims to bring about "the existence, welfare, and safety" of a diverse people, or diverse peoples, who voice, at best, a modest and overlapping consensus, one that makes for "mutual respect without mutual assimilation or envy" (*DP*, 375).

The trouble with "spontaneous democracy," Santayana claims, is that it is a revolt against the very idea of tradition, a revolt that fails to generate any representative moral authority. For him, the original American colonies and, then, American pioneers, exemplify "spontaneous democracy" or democracy "unintended and unopposed." The American colonies, for instance,

> breathed independence and individuality, religious and political, at the same time feeling confident of their vocation and ability to grow rich and to save their souls with none but divine guidance. Their zeal for democracy had a political root also in their Protestantism. They remembered the revolt of their kinsfolk in the old country against ecclesiastical and royal despotism, and against landlords; and this sense of ancient grievances was kept alive by daily defiance of all barriers that might block a man's way in his private enterprise, especially so long as experience proved that the more successful each man's enterprise was the more favorable paths it opened to the enterprise of others. (*DP*, 346)

The most striking thing about this characterization, however, is that there is nothing particularly democratic about it. Santayana's "spontaneous democracy" emphasizes "independence," "individuality," rebellion against religious, monarchial, and economic "despotism," "private enterprise," and some sort of individuated salvation. These are the characteristics of eighteenth-century liberalism; they all celebrate individual liberty. But where are the things that make for democracy? Where are citizenship; universal suffrage; participatory political deliberation, decision, and action; the creation of a public consensus about public goods; the civic virtues required for such creativity? They may turn out to be there, but only so long as they work to secure private good or gain; only so long as they are instrumental to liberal individualism.

Indeed, Santayana suggests, "absolute democracy" is really "instrumental democracy" that has fallen in love with itself, fanatically redoubling its efforts to secure political and social equality after it has forgotten its aim, which is liberty (*DP*, 350). This sort of democracy, Santayana claims,

> demands acquiescence in the Will of the majority and in the ways of the average man. The liberty that it would leave to the private mind would be

a derisive liberty. For we should be invited to make our way through the uncharted spaces of vacant possibility; yet in reality, unless we participate in some specific human enterprise, we shall be simply drinking the winds. . . . Liberal society is therefore compelled to form all manner of voluntary private societies to replenish the human vacuity of its political life; but these private societies, being without power or material roots, remain ghostly and artificial. (*DP*, 354)

But this understanding of "absolute democracy" makes *the will of the majority* its hallmark, and uniformity with that will its illiberal consequence. Once again, this sort of polity is fundamentally at odds with social and political democracy, which calls not for an *aggregation* of individuals but for the *composition* of a community. As Barber points out, majoritarianism is a tribute to the failure of democracy; it is, rather, "an attempt to salvage decision-making from the anarchy of adversary politics."[16] Democracy aims at circumventing majoritarianism. As pragmatic democrats understand it, political deliberation begins in conflict and works *toward* a flexible consensus based on mutual understanding. Majoritarianism undercuts the mutualism that allows this sort of democracy to work.

Democracy understood in this pragmatic and naturalistic way demands a new self-description of the public, one that "resists the idea that conflict is intractable."[17] Instead of merely bargaining over conflicting interests, and then aggregating the results, it calls for political institutions that foster a sort of mutual understanding among its citizenry sufficient to warrant decisions geared "to create a common future in which every citizen can envision himself or herself living—and living well."[18] The form of its political disputes, as Barber puts it, "is not 'I want' versus 'you want' but 'I want' versus 'we will.'"[19] The issue is always whether realizing this or that proposal will be good for us, good for the community that *we* constitute and hope to build and live in together.

To go about making political decisions this way neither demands nor particularly fosters mediocrity or uniformity. The intention behind these political activities is to create a way of living into the future that is hospitable to social and psychological pluriformity as much as political unity. It is an attempt to organize a life where the disciplines allowing both for social justice and personal excellence become more accessible, not less. More than anything else, the *equality* at stake in this sort of democracy is equality of opportunity to participate in political decision making; to speak and to be heard with empathy and respect in the course of political deliberation by the citizenry itself.

But Santayana considers none of this. For him, "absolute democracy" amounts to the sort of majoritarianism that equates equality with mediocre uniformity. Democracy, at best, must be "restricted," limited to an equitable distribution of material necessities and to the organization of space for the "preservation" of private associations which foster both moral cohesion and solitary spiritual disciplines. Even then, democrats will be faced with the quandary that

> a man cannot serve two masters. If at bottom we respect only the organized core of society and of the mind, we shall despise the idle play of individual fancy around it, and call it a waste of energy, dissipation, and fireworks. We shall also regard as selfish and demoralizing any disposition to live one's own life, absorbed in interests which the public cannot share. If on the contrary we truly love only play of mind and the liberal arts, we shall regard as a necessary evil this hard nucleus of material being and human convention round which we are condemned to gyrate; and we shall constantly ask ourselves whether so much matter, so much labour, so much organization, interference, morality, and monstrous official dullness are really necessary. In lighter armour and in a fresher air we might be more alive while we lived, and perhaps even live longer. (DP, 354)

The irony is that there is no difference that makes much difference between this "restricted democracy" and Santayana's own "universal liberal empire," save for the fact that what the majority does in the one, guardians do in the other. In either case, people "are condemned to gyrate," because a fundamental disequilibrium remains between public "management" and the moral and spiritual life that goes on strictly in private. In both "restricted democracy" and "liberal empire," according to Santayana, "voluntary private societies replenish the vacuity of . . . political life" (DP, 358).

Civics, Morals, and the Spiritual Life

No doubt Santayana's vision of "two masters" has force. This is so because, all too often, public and private realms in liberal representative democracies like ours (or liberal empires like his) hang together roughly the way that public housing, food allocation centers, public health services, waste disposal crews, and police forces link up with poetry writing, Shakespeare festivals, church services, yoga classes, history lessons, and college seminars on the virtues: badly.

The fact that this is so is deeply troubling and deserves attention. But the fact that we are able to register this distress and give it our attention suggests that our political life together need not be vacuous or merely a matter of public management. Indeed, in spots, it actually is not empty or just bureaucratic. In places, citizens do come together to talk through common concerns (for instance, the threat of cigarette smoking to the health of members in the community); to propose initiatives (for example, the prohibition of smoking in facilities open to the public); to reach consensus on them or, short of accord, to put them to a vote; and, if passed, to see to their enforcement. Activities like these begin with recognition of a common problem; they proceed through discussions that demand efforts at mutual understanding, that call for citizens to think of themselves as community members, and to ask how they will create a common world less threatened by things impeding human joy (for example, by smoke-related cancer and heart disease). These activities are public, but they are not empty of vital liberty. Rather, they help create vital liberty, *as citizenship*, by stipulating its civic particulars. They are not merely exercises in bureaucratic management. Rather, they define civic values that community members share and hope to realize. They work out social justice from de-tails, not on the basis of "wisdom" transcending, or independent from, the political process but, rather, on the basis of whatever persuasive arguments citizens can bring to bear on the practical issues at hand. They only happen occasionally. It is up to us to make them happen more often and more comprehensively.

Santayana was right, to be sure, to stress the limits of public policy formula-tion and to underscore the importance of private voluntary forms of associa-tion. He was right, for the most part, to suggest that "the liberal life of play, art, affection, and worship" goes on, and should go on, privately, in families, friendships, and faiths, rather than in Town Halls (*DP*, 357). He was right to emphasize the fact that these institutions of liberal or spiritual life in the private realm flourish within a political order that permits them. Finally, he was right to argue that granting this permission is tantamount to taking away any coercive power of the state to *make* citizens "volunteer" for one, or even any, association among many.

But he was wrong to imply that there is *nothing* liberal about public or civic life. Think of the *spiritual wealth* he missed out on by failing to investigate the liberal arts of democratic deliberation, so very much dependent on the mutual understanding he prized; by declining to reflect on the exercise of *civic* piety, charity, and spirituality, fortifying public memory, hope, and respect for the outsider; and by resisting the possibility of creating, even expanding, civic bonds of affiliation and affection, by turning toward the stranger, even enemy, in disinterested love and intelligence.

The imperial imposition of tolerance among a diversity of peoples each with its own voluntary forms of association might work, but only by *making* the public and political realm vacant and bureaucratic, and only so long as each "nation" *unrealistically* remained content or resigned to play dead. Surely the mutualistic row that democrats aim to hoe is a lot tougher, both in the short and long run, confronting difference aiming for reciprocal appreciation and for the detailed practical transformations ensuing from it. But at least arranging for such appreciative diversity democratically *enacts* itself as it goes.

Indeed, then, Dewey's democracy and Santayana's religious naturalism are each better off linked to the other. Without attempting to pull epistemic or moral rank, and without transforming moral and spiritual habits into metaphysical powers, Santayana's naturalized religions may count prominently among the private voluntary associations that go a long way toward fashioning the moral and spiritual lives of a democratic citizenry.

Strong liberal democracy *does* put certain constraints on practitioners of religion. As Rorty puts it, thinking of Jefferson, democratic citizens "must abandon or modify opinions on matters of ultimate importance, the opinions that may hitherto have given sense and point to their lives, if these opinions entail public actions that cannot be justified to most of their fellow citizens."[20] But so much the better for Santayana's charitable justice, which is the bulwark that stops the monsters of spiritual corruption that he identifies, fanaticism and mysticism.

Democratic public policy formulation is not coextensive with the moral training people receive in their families, schools, and religious traditions. In a strong liberal democracy, public deliberations are provoked by particular and detailed problems and difficulties affecting all of "us"—problems that call for necessary public actions. Its questions take the form, "What shall we do when something has to be done that affects us all, we wish to be reasonable, yet we disagree on means and ends and are without independent grounds for making the choice?"[21]

The moral bonding and training that go on in private voluntary associations both contribute virtues to political life in a democracy and may be transformed in particular ways by the public actions that result from democratic decisions. But the field of virtues is broader than politics; it is relevant to actions public, private, and personal, necessary, optative, and spontaneous. Training, say, as a family member, a companion, a team player, a colleague, a corporate worker, or a congregant demands habits that overlap with civic virtues without working identically the way they do. Families, affectionate liaisons, sports clubs, colleges, businesses, and religious institutions all have their occasions that are *like* town meetings, but if any of these associations *become* town meetings, they also become laughable, sad, or terrifying.

Moreover, the moral bonding and training that goes on in private voluntary associations is not coextensive with the disciplines people learn, or make up, to deal with their aloneness. Writing or reading Wallace Stevens's "Notes Toward a Supreme Fiction," for example, may rehearse a way to achieve the sort of disinterested love and intelligence that Santayana claimed might bring personal contentment. So, too, might reciting Kaddish. But doing such things weaves together practices mostly unlike initiating a public resolution, caring for children, hitting a sacrifice fly ball, working more and harder without increases in pay, giving useful criticism to a fellow teacher, or telling the Passover story to ourselves and our children.

Moreover, there is no single way to order these activities hierarchically without begging questions. We may assert, with Barber and Rorty, that democracy is "lexically" prior to voluntary associations and solitary disciplines because its procedures license them politically. But this simply suggests that, politically, politics is prior. We may also assert that families, friends, and religious life are more valuable than civic activity because they provide the wherewithal to achieve a modicum of moral bonding and spiritual liberty— but only from the standpoint provided by these associations. Finally, we may say, with Kundera, that the most precious thing of all is the inviolability of solitary life, but only from a spiritual point of view. There simply is no one standard against which to measure these standards.

But as citizens in a strong liberal democracy we may lean our public interest in mutualism, our private social interest in moral bonding, and our solitary interest in spirituality against each other supportively. As I see it, if and when we will to do so, we are maintaining a culture that lets the least among us not only do well, but be well. The "authority of things" holds the ultimate hand in this inevitably tragicomic card game. In the end, we are only able to hope that the cards things now conceal are flush enough.

EPILOGUE

Santayana's Legacies and His Eclipse

Whatever happened to Santayana? What has become of his interest in pragmatic naturalism and the life of the spirit? And, finally, for those of us who currently embrace pragmatic naturalism and continue to take religious institutions, narratives, and rituals seriously, where could we go from here?

To begin with, let me survey, broad compass, the passing of Santayana's influence. By the time Santayana died in 1952, his role among American philosophers, critics, pundits, and poets had become fairly diffuse. His place among philosophers, fair to say his home community if anything was, is most telling. Institutionally, Columbia's philosophy department defined its mission in terms of Santayana's life of reason "from Butler to Edman."[1] And, through Dean F. J. E. Woodbridge, John Erskine, and others, Santayana's sensibilities helped to form Columbia's much imitated (now much contested, sometimes maligned) core course in Western civilization. But philosophical naturalists, perhaps especially pragmatic naturalists, had simultaneously eulogized and buried Santayana by 1944, in the pages of Yervant Krikorian's cooperative manifesto, *Naturalism and the Human Spirit.* Moreover, that book, the very name of which conjured up Santayana's philosophical endeavors as much as anyone's, soon fell on deaf ears. Within a decade, the philosophical crowd involved in Krikorian's project became identified as "old guard," when professional philosophy in the United States took its linguistic and symbolic logical turns in the 1950s: In this regard, Quine's *From a Logical Point of View* (1953) may serve handily as a bench mark.

What led to Santayana's eclipse among the pragmatic naturalists? I have given various reasons for interpreting *Realms of Being* as a text in pragmatic naturalism. I have shown it to be a pragmatic text on four grounds. It abandoned metaphysics and epistemology for reflection on the promises and problems of human finitude. It focused on philosophy, the arts, and the natural sciences as alternative vocabularies for signifying the human predicament, rather than as providing some revolutionary science of sciences or foundational theology. It accepted the contingency of things all the way down. Finally, it construed knowledge as the kind of thought that equips people with the facility to get around the world, whether it is described physically, historically, politically, culturally, morally, or spiritually. But nobody, including Santayana, construed *Realms of Being* or its author as belonging to pragmatism understood as an American intellectual movement.[2] Some influential interpreters, Dewey in fact, even found it inappropriate to call Santayana a *naturalist* after *Realms of Being*, although I have tried to show that Dewey's reasons for impugning his naturalism were not adequate.

By the mid-1940s, certainly, various things divided Santayana from pragmatism and distinguished his naturalism from its most influential proponents in the United States. To begin with, both pragmatism and naturalism became names for quasi-political movements, constituted by public intellectual figures to engage in scholarly disputes for intellectual ends. These parties of discourse, with their overlapping constituencies, not only took public postures that they identified with their philosophies. They also took philosophy to be a crucial component of political technology; it was the thing that tied statesmanship all together ideologically by providing the requisite holistic or synoptic vision. As such, pragmatists and naturalists were very much concerned with battling for, and winning, the minds of "the people." As with most such projects, irony and comic self-criticism were not just muted. They were absent. *Naturalism and the Human Spirit* was deadpan.

David Hollinger has shown the ways in which pragmatism, during Dewey's heyday, was a multilayered movement. Construed as party to professional philosophy, it was a commitment to particular views on truth as warrantability and on meaning as use. But publicly and more comprehensively, pragmatism was something else. The pragmatism that appeared, for example, in the pages of Herbert Croly's *New Republic* was a militant Americanism of sorts blended together with a belief that scientific method or inquiry, accessible not just to professional scientists but, somehow, to everyone, could solve basic cultural and social problems in a naturalistic and pluralistic universe. During the

1930s and 1940s, the mainline pragmatists claimed over and over that scientific method could accommodate the world to humane aspirations in ways other "methods" could not. Scientific method could prevail especially, so popular pragmatic discourse asserted, in an American culture underpinned by the ideals of voluntary action, free enterprise, public virtue based on personal conscience, and democratic processes of decision making.[3]

"Naturalism" in the United States was just as multilayered as "pragmatism," and just as self-consciously partisan in its efforts to win the world over to "scientific method" as the way to stabilize and develop culture at its best—that is, democratic life, American-style. If some "naturalists" stood opposed to Deweyan pragmatism, for example Morris Cohen, out of an allegiance to realism and an antipathy to historicism, this made little difference at the level of public discourse.[4] Krikorian's celebrated collection of essays by naturalists both pragmatic and realist demonstrates this.

Both American pragmatists and naturalists, then, pictured their movements as communities of discourse with deep national allegiances. Santayana, to the contrary, was more like the Wittgenstein of *Zettel* than any other contemporaneous American-trained philosopher. There, Wittgenstein would say that "the philosopher is not a citizen of any community of ideas. That is what makes him a philosopher."[5] As *Scepticism and Animal Faith* and *Realms of Being* had made clear, for Santayana, philosophy was primarily a set of practices he used to work on himself. These practices involved him in *imaginative departures* from the pressing circumstances and practical responsibilities of political technology. The point of philosophy was not primarily realistic social intervention, change, or reform. Philosophical disciplines stood apart from and, indeed, opposed the role-specific duties of structured social life.

By now, indeed, it should come as no surprise to learn that in his own contributions to Paul Schilpp's Library of Living Philosophers volume on *The Philosophy of George Santayana*—his preliminary "General Confession," and his critically responsive "Apologia Pro Mente Sua"—Santayana characterized philosophical discipline in religious terms that undercut the notion that philosophy had an important role to play in political technology. For him, he noted, religion "is the head and front of everything" in philosophy (*PGS*, 7). His vocation had always been, and remained, "philosophically religious" (*PGS*, 24), concerned with "deliverance" of the spirit (*PGS*, 13). As such, it "suspend[ed]" normal social routines (*PGS*, 27), in order to engage in certain sorts of "confessions" (PGS, 28). Statesmen employed political technology to deal with regular social habits, and contended with crises that disrupted the normal. The point of statesmanship was to foster or return to normalcy. Philosophy, to the contrary, offered mankind "a holiday from the statesman's world" (PGS, 567). It was an exercise in consecration set apart from the concerns of social engineering (PGS, 570). It offered a sort of relief for its practitioners from specific social rules, roles, and relationships, actually countering them with other personae, ones that did "not come to repeat the world but to celebrate it" (PGS, 29).[6]

In all of this Santayana maintains the view of philosophy as festive criticism that he had developed in Soliloquies and had exemplified in his books since the early 1920s. It made him, as I have tried to show, quite self-consciously peripheral from the standpoint of realistic social concerns. Indeed, it made him a somewhat ridiculous figure to the American naturalists who, as young thinkers haunted by idealism and more orthodox theologies, had turned to The Life of Reason to provide both a provocative and inspiring alternative. For them, the idea of philosophy as intellectual statesmanship was still crucial; the idea of philosophical views as central to sociopolitical life was unexceptional; the idea of philosophy as a discipline geared to make realistic differences in the arrangement of social, political, and economic structures was taken for granted.

Assumptions like this led to the image of Santayana presented by John Herman Randall, Jr., in Naturalism and the Human Spirit. Noting that Santayana's Life of Reason had been largely responsible for getting naturalism off the ground as a philosophical movement in the United States, Randall also made it clear, in 1944, that Santayana no longer captured the attention of that community. Santayana was "the Moses of the new naturalism, who discerned the promised land from afar but still wanders himself in the desert realms of being" (NHS, 363). From Randall's vantage point, Santayana appeared as both founder and traducer of the philosophical community destined to win a new heaven and a new earth.

It is no coincidence that Randall's characterization of Santayana was couched in Exodus rhetoric. This is the case because such talk had been the traditional way of calling to mind America's divine mission since before the seventeenth century. While the pragmatists and naturalists of the first half of the twentieth century never issued jeremiads in any strong literary or ritual sense of the term, they did couch a good deal of their public pronouncements in jeremiadic words, not only suggesting that the processes of social life in America were divine, but recalling the biblical language of covenant, exodus, and promised land in order to do so. As Charles Frankel pointed out, Dewey and his followers, particularly, saw their "view of democracy as continuous with the Puritan notion that in America a City on a Hill was being built for all the world to see."[7] Dewey's *Freedom and Culture* (1939), for example, looked forward to a transformation of the "geographical New World" into "a New World in the human sense," and construed this drama as a conflict between an Old World of privilege and oppression and a New World of "cooperative democratic freedom."[8] Well within the American jeremiadic tradition, his message was simultaneously self-critical and self-congratulatory, making whatever democratic consensus America had come to through democratic methods the very standard by which to measure the prospects for humankind.

Now Santayana had great respect for the United States. Indeed, his respect grew during the last decade of his life as he came to observe that, among the national powers contending for world hegemony after the Second World War, the United States would probably do the best job of simultaneously defending and realizing the ideals of the Western republics. To his mind, the United States had the right affections, and could provide the power, to safeguard the "cooperative English Liberty" he had praised in *Character and Opinion*. In principle, at any rate (the pressures of market expansion to the contrary), the United States remained committed to letting a plurality of cultures maintain their traditions in some coherent way.

But to claim that the combination of affection and power in the United States compared favorably with other options, especially the Soviet Union, did little to vitiate Santayana's commitment to the view that cultural antinomialism was inescapable: One culture's power inevitably involved another's domination. The satisfaction of one culture's wants and needs was bound to frustrate another's (and oftentimes, thank goodness). That being the case, Santayana reasoned, there simply was no politically harmonious or divine way of doing things. It was deceptive and self-deceptive to equate some political process or other with the course of providence. For that matter, given a plurality of cultures and countries with conflicting intentions, there was no *general* way of being responsible to one another, much less to some objective divinity standing apart from humankind, that could resolve relevant differences. Political responsibility was so context-dependent that it simply was not possible to think up a priori rules for it in advance (a point James had made years before in "The Moral Philosopher and the Moral Life"). This line of thinking implied, for example, that constitutions were historical documents, codifying traditional intentions that were subject to ongoing historical variation and modification. No polity was divine, but some were "sane," because they safeguarded and fostered both moral representation of diverse peoples and let the "vital liberty" of spiritual life—itself extrapolitical—go on (*DP*, 367). Political life demanded scrupulous attention to procedural justice. But, as Santayana saw it, there was nothing *methodological* about it.

I have noted already that the pragmatists and naturalists during the days of Dewey's cultural hegemony saw things differently: They claimed that scientific method had everything to do with a smooth-running democracy. Scientific method, they argued, was the glue that would bind people together responsibly and realistically in an otherwise rough-and-tumble world.

If Santayana is to count as a pragmatic naturalist, as I have been commending, then he must surely be construed as articulating a pragmatism without scientific method. That, indeed, had been the clear message of *Scepticism and Animal Faith* in 1923, when he had noted that philosophy had fallen into a snare "when in modern times it ceased to be the art of thinking and tried to become that impossible thing, the science of thought" (*SAF*, 254). It remained his message all the way through *Dominations and Powers*.

The point here is not that Santayana rejected the pragmatic notion of politics as experimental because he surely did not. Nor is it that he rejected reasonable observation, or the accumulation of relevant information, or the exchange of constituent's views, or the relevant use of expertise as basic to good government, because these views (that can wax either populist or wane mandarin) sat at the heart of his celebration of timocracy. The point is that Santayana, like James half of the time, and like Dewey when he was talking to other philosophers in conversations that the public would not overhear, did not privilege the methods of the natural sciences when it came to issues of political import.

On Santayana's view, any and every critical means available to a culture's constituents—art or science or technical rule of thumb—ought to be deployed for the good of the people at hand. The thing that made any of these activities critical was not only an openness to revision, and not only the extent to which they let a culture understand itself, but also the capaciousness they allowed a people, the breathing room—what George Kateb has recently called the "moderate alienation"—individuals and private communities require to push off in their own spiritually idiosyncratic directions.[9]

Compared with the stance Santayana took against scientism, virtually every contributor to *Naturalism and the Human Spirit* engaged in what Morton White would eventually dub "methodolotry."[10] So, for example, in the opening salvo of that manifesto, Dewey had identified the enemy, "antinaturalism," as constituted by thinkers who "operated to prevent the application of scientific methods of inquiry in the field of human social subject matter. Antinaturalism has prevented science from completing its career and fulfilling its constructive potentialities" (*NHS*, 3). Naturalism, Dewey said, amounted to "respect for scientific method . . . [the] systematic, extensive, and carefully controlled use of alert and unprejudiced observation and experimentation in collecting, arranging, and testing evidence" (*NHS*, 10). Dennes and Lavine agreed, stressing "objectivity" more than Dewey had: The import of naturalism was its insistence on "continuity of analysis," or "the resolution to pursue inquiry into any set of phenomena by means of methods which administer the checks of experimental verification in accordance with the contemporary criteria of objectivity" (*NHS*, 184–85). And Hook bemoaned the "new failure of nerve in Western civilization" (exhibited in the United States, he thought, by Reinhold Niebuhr and Paul Tillich). What were the telltale signs of this new cowardice, according to Hook? They were "a loss of confidence in scientific method and . . . various quests for a 'knowledge' and 'truth' which are uniquely different from those won by the processes of scientific inquiry" (*NHS*, 40).

From this standpoint, Santayana was pictured as not really counting as a naturalist. As Randall put it, Santayana had "known little and cared less about the living currents of scientific thought" (*NHS*, 363); "scientific methods and procedures in any technical sense have meant nothing to him; and the revolutionary changes in fundamental scientific concepts our generation has witnessed have left him untouched" (*NHS*, 364).

This was a caricature from two angles. First, Santayana was very much touched by the revolutionary changes in psychology that James had brought about and, through James, influenced by Darwinian historiography as well.

Second, it is true that he had not read deeply in any science apart from James's *Principles*, but it remains unclear just how comprehensively any of Krikorian's naturalists or pragmatists, besides Ernest Nagel, had done so.

Moreover, Santayana had maintained what could be described alternatively as a weak scientific realism or a pragmatic endorsement of scientific inquiry since he had written his dissertation. Without embracing scientism (which, on his grounds, would be philosophical heresy), he simply assumed that the findings of competent natural scientists ought to be accepted as knowledge about the physical world, which was the only world.

In any case, as I have already noted, almost as soon as it was published, Krikorian's *Naturalism and the Human Spirit* seemed rather quaint to leading professional philosophers in the United States, who now pictured Clarence Irving Lewis's *Mind and the World Order* (1929) as the only pragmatic work worth discussing anymore, because of its Roycean emphasis on the centrality of symbolic logic to philosophy as well as its effort to warrant Russellian principles and "problems of knowledge" on pragmatic grounds. Dewey's crowd and Dewey himself were nearly as embarrassing as Santayana to the young philosophers who followed Lewis's lead, like Quine, Nelson Goodman, Wilfrid Sellars, or Hilary Putnam. If these philosophical giants of their time (which is my time) eventually helped to rescue varieties of pragmatism, they did so in analytic, ascetic, and logically exhaustive styles foreign to James, or Santayana, or Dewey.

What about Santayana's influence among religious thinkers? For the most part, Santayana's religious ideas fell between stools. If he was too religious for most naturalists, he was too pragmatic and naturalistic for virtually all prominent American religious thinkers. His "ultimate religion" was taken seriously by a few neoorthodox Protestant thinkers like H. Richard Niebuhr. This was so because Santayana's relentless disclosure of contingency aided Niebuhr's construal of the radical character of human responsibility "in absolute dependence."[11] Somewhat ironically, Santayana's religious thinking proved less significant for unorthodox religious naturalists like Charles W. Morris, whose "Maitreya" in *Paths of Life* was very much like Santayana's "Hermes" in *Soliloquies*, and like Roy Wood Sellars, whose *Religion Coming of Age* mimicked Santayana's early and perduring insistence on the cultural, historical, and institutional formation of religious life.[12]

Santayana's ideas about religion were simply too naturalistic, and his religious ideas too Christian (and too anti-Hebraic) for Jewish reconstructionists like Mordecai Kaplan, whose God turned out to be a natural *force* of salvation at work in the world (making Kaplan some sort of pantheist).[13] Kaplan, to be sure, succeeded where other self-described religious naturalists failed, by launching a full-fledged institutional movement in the 1930s that, though small, still thrives. The Protestant religious empiricists at the University of Chicago did not try or, even, want to try to get an institutional program going. Henry Nelson Weiman, Bernard Eugene Meland, Bernard Loomer, and Shirley Jackson Case all remained essentially metaphysical, searching (as Case put it) for "a capacity for peering behind the veil of material existence to catch fresh glimpses of spiritual reality."[14] Whiteheadean process theologians were (and are) not all that different in this respect.[15]

By and large, the only religious thinkers to capture broad cultural attention outside the churches throughout the 1950s were the two writers Hook berated in *Naturalism and the Human Spirit*. H. Richard Niebuhr's more famous brother Reinhold continued to contribute to cultural conversation with, for example, *The Irony of American History* (1952). Likewise, Paul Tillich provoked interest in the wider culture with *The Courage to Be* (1952) and *The Dynamics of Faith* (1957). Armed with the conceptual commitments of his Augustinian-Lutheran tradition, Reinhold Niebuhr developed a political vision similar to *Dominations and Powers*, in its realism and in its rejection of the philosophical underpinnings of liberalism. But Niebuhr felt no discernible compulsion to grapple with Santayana. Paul Tillich insisted on the symbolic status of any specification of divinity, much as Santayana had. But both of these thinkers remained supernaturalists: Niebuhr's God was a power who helped those who could not help themselves, as James's gods had been at the turn of the century; and Tillich's "God beyond God" remained nonspecifically supernatural, grounding religious metaphors in a source pictured (beyond pictures) as really real, that is, as nonmetaphorical. Moreover, if neither Reinhold Niebuhr nor Tillich was influenced by Santayana, their students, in turn, read him in no traceable way.

What about novelists, poets, and critics? Surely Santayana was to be found in John P. Marquand's New England satire, *The Late George Apley: A Novel in the Form of a Memoir*, published one year after Santayana's own satirical "Memoir in the Form of a Novel," *The Last Puritan*, went to press in the United States.[16] But Santayana haunted no other major novelist. As to Santayana's own poetry, if Mark Van Doren could claim that Santayana's sonnets "have remained American classics" in *American Poets 1630–1930* (1932), when they were barely half a century old, his verse was written out of American anthologies after that.[17]

Wallace Stevens's "To an Old Philosopher in Rome" and Lowell's "For George Santayana 1863–1952" memorialized Santayana in perceptive and evocative ways. Stevens took virtually all the alloy out, leaving readers pure gold when, meditating on his mentor dying in the Clinica della Piccola Compagna di Maria, he wrote:

> The sound drifts in. The buildings are remembered.
> The life of the city never lets go, nor do you
> Ever want it to. It is part of the life in your room.
> Its domes are the architecture of your bed.
> The bells keep on repeating solemn names.
>
> In choruses and choirs of choruses,
> Unwilling that mercy should be a mystery
> Of silence, that any solitude of sense
> Should give you more than their peculiar chords
> And reverberations clinging to whisper still.
>
> It is a kind of total grandeur at the end,
> With every visible thing enlarged and yet
> No more than a bed, a chair and moving nuns,
> The immensest theatre, the pillared porch,
> The book and candle in your ambered room,
>
> Total grandeur of a total edifice,
> Chosen by an inquisitor of structures
> For himself. He stops upon this threshold
> As if the design of all his words takes form
> And frame from thinking and is realized.[18]

And Lowell surely captures the pointed comedy of an apocryphal self-portrait when he has his sometime "unbelieving, unconfessed and unreceived" correspondent say (as Bertrand Russell reportedly once said of Santayana's views): "There is no God and Mary is his Mother."[19]

More significantly, while Lowell's *Lord Weary's Castle* develops Santayanan themes only coincidentally, some of Stevens's greatest poems bear the marks of deep engagement with Santayana's ideas. Just to take notable examples, Stevens's "The Comedian as the Letter C" (1922), "The American Sublime" (1935), "Notes Toward a Supreme Fiction" (1942), "Final Soliloquy of the Interior Paramour" (1950), and "A Mythology Reflects Its Region" (1955) all sustain Santayana's skepticism and animal faith, along with his natural designs on joy accompanying the recognition of complete contingency and eventual powerlessness.

More than a handful of significant literary and cultural critics, and a fairly broad range at that, trickled out reflections on Santayana's writing and career for nearly thirty years, including (chronologically) Robert Bridges (1920), Owen Barfield (1921), Carl Van Doren (1923), J. B. Priestley (1924), Archibald MacLeish (1925), Ludwig Lewisohn (1932), Desmond MacCarthy (1932, 1936), Q. D. Leavis (1934), Henry Seidel Canby (1937), John Crowe Ransom (1937), Eliseo Vivas (1940), Edmund Wilson (1945, 1946), Max Eastman (1951, 1952, 1953, 1959), Corliss Lamont (1951), F. R. Leavis (1952), Robert Lowell (1953), and Lionel Trilling (1956).[20]

If Barfield and MacCarthy had identified Santayana as the best living literary critic in the English-speaking world, to my mind, the most perspicuous assessment of the bunch was the essay by Trilling. Trilling's " 'That Smile of Parmenides Made Me Think' " put his finger on the materialism that repelled many of Santayana's critics, especially in the United States.

As with all such appraisals, to be sure, Trilling's came from somewhere and had its direction firmly in mind. He criticized Santayana from a position on the literary critical map triangulated by Keats, Arnold, and Freud. His view was preoccupied with personal perfection or fulfillment, but shunned solitude for domesticity; and it waxed un-Emersonian in its judgment that circumstances and the truth about it were fundamentally careless of the human prospect.[21] The " 'tension' or 'ambiguity' or 'irony' " in Santayana's writing that both antagonized and lured commentators, Trilling suggested, served "to remind us that there is a special intellectual satisfaction in admiring where we do not love, in qualifying our assent, in keeping our distance," because that was the sort of critical stance Santayana himself expressed.[22]

Trilling said that if Americans could not like or trust Santayana because they judged him "all too elegant, all too cultivated, all too knowing, all too involved with aesthetic values," their judgment was mistaken. Santayana, he noted, had been severely critical of aestheticism, had complimented the arts and sciences in the United States for really knowing how to do things, had called for the sort of communicative reason befitting democratic republicanism, and had been eager to see America develop its own traditions.[23]

On Trilling's diagnosis, what really bothered Americans about Santayana was his frank admission—accompanied by an empathetic, "we're in this boat together" sort of smile no less—that humankind was condemned to live dramatically in an undramatic universe. That notion put something of a damper on James's adventuresome, untamed federal republican universe open to some sort of human-superhuman cooperation and completion. For Santayana, Trilling pointed out,

> the world is matter, and following the laws of matter. The world is even, he is willing to say, a machine, and following the laws of its devising. The world is not spirit, following the laws of spirit, made to accommodate spirit, available to full comprehension by spirit. It allows spirit to exist, but this by chance and chancily: no intention is avowed. And the world, we may go on to say, is Boston to the boy from Avila; the world is the Sturgis family to the young Santayana—not hostile, yet not his own, not continuous with him. It is, as he says, his host, and he must have reflected that the word implies not only a guest but a parasite.[24]

Americans, Trilling said with magisterial insight, feared Santayana along with "his dreadful knowledge of the abyss." That knowledge was the hard rock on which Santayana built his pragmatic life of the spirit. In terms simply too acutely right to paraphrase, Trilling concluded: "The knowledge of the abyss, the awareness of the discontinuity between man and the world, this is the forming perception of Santayana's thought."[25]

Trilling's Santayana urged people to take up a spiritual attitude that, to my mind, is a live option because it neither hides from the startling disconnection that exists between the ways of the universe and the interests that people have—sun death is still among the cards—nor forecloses comic celebration; thus "if we are in a balloon over an abyss, let us at least value the balloon. If night is all around, then what light we have is precious. If there is no life to be seen in the great emptiness, our companions are to be cherished; so are we ourselves."[26] After Trilling, however, American critics made nothing more than quotational use of Santayana's writing, rather than publicly engaging, analyzing, or agonizing over it. Americans still have a great deal of trouble with the sort of comic naturalism Santayana devised.

Political critics? After a brief flurry of reviews of *Dominations and Powers* (including learned essays by Schutz and Voegelin), hardly any political pundit in the United States and very few political theorists, aside from an aging Walter Lippmann and Russell Kirk, took Santayana's political reflections seriously.

Indeed, if any professional intellectuals have kept strands of Santayana's project in play up through the present they have been cultural anthropologists, first Ruth Benedict and now Clifford Geertz. When Benedict retired from the presidency of the American Anthropological Association in 1947, she listed *Reason in Religion* (and by implication, all of *The Life of Reason*), *Three Philosophical Poets*, *Soliloquies*, *Character and Opinion*, and *Platonism and the Spiritual Life* as classics in her field, shaping her intellectual self-understanding *as* a cultural anthropologist as much as anything.[27] Clifford Geertz owes much to a bevy of precursors, but surely his essays on common sense, ideology, religion, and art (and, I'd wager, eventually science) as "cultural systems" reflect the influence of *The Life of Reason*.[28] But do Geertz's students, for example, Renato Rosaldo, find Santayana's ideas important? They certainly do not make his work recommended or required reading on their syllabi, or note him in their writings, even epigrammatically.

Danto's "Santayana and the Task Ahead"

In 1963, Arthur Danto recognized that many philosophers in the United States were moving "forward into old territory with fresh techniques." On the heels of reading Wittgenstein in English or hashing out their own arguments against the dogmas of empiricism, especially logical empiricism, "analytical" philosophers were recapitulating "the intellectual crisis which Santayana helped overcome," breaking through "to a view of things not dissimilar to the one he achieved." Finding that the verifiability criterion of meaning did not warrant itself, so that nonverifiable sentences were not automatically meaningless, many philosophers began to argue that "the meaning of sentences is bound up with their use." Indeed, they began to appreciate the ways in which "sentences have different logics in different forms of discourse and in connection with different forms of life" and, by so doing, rendered philosophy as capacious as

Santayana's *Life of Reason* had made it, with just its emphasis on the centrality of social or cultural practices articulated institutionally.[29] Danto urged those analytical philosophers who exhibited this new "catholicity and circumspection, [this] breadth and virtuosity," to resuscitate the study of Santayana. Contemporary philosophers "might come to recognize Santayana not merely as a precursor but a guide. . . . [H]is writings might be charts, drawn by a congenial temper, of the varieties of utterance once more validated as fit for philosophical examination. They might, indeed, be taken up and given, as all important philosophical work must finally be, the status of contemporaneity. Whether or not this will in fact happen, no one can say. Philosophy must determine its own history, revitalizing whom it will."

Philosophers did not even reply to Danto's invitation to take Santayana seriously as contemporaneous (though outside professional philosophy, Geertz was fast at work on some of the tasks at issue).[30] They went to other parties and, in 1991, Santayana's philosophical revitalization has not occurred. Where philosophers, like Richard Rorty, have returned to classical pragmatists for contemporary engagement, they have looked to James and, even more, Dewey.

No philosopher, indeed, has pursued the new pragmatism with more philosophical power and panache than Rorty. So the fact that Santayana's name appears on Rorty's vaunted (or infamous) short list of figures on the periphery "of the history of modern philosophy" who, "without forming a 'tradition,' resemble each other in their distrust of the notion that man's essence is to be a knower of essences," makes Santayana's relative *absence* from Rorty's writings all the more striking.[31] Santayana is important to Rorty for his "reflections on philosophy in the new world," and in that regard, Rorty claims, he has "two singular merits. First, he was able to laugh at us without despising us—a feat often too intricate for the native-born. Second, he was entirely free of the instinctive American conviction that the westering of the spirit ends here—that whatever the ages have labored to bring forth will emerge between Massachusetts and California, that our philosophers have only to express our national genius for the human spirit to fulfil itself."[32]

These are insights that find great support in the pages of this book. What Rorty's comment misses about these virtues, however, are their practical moral and spiritual links. Santayana's spiritual discipline, his self-imposed ordinance to appreciate the innocence of the things he hated and the clearness of the things he frowned on or denied, is more than matched by his concern to subject the things he naturally loved to critical moral jeopardy and by his ironic stance toward any "final vocabulary," any animal faith, most especially his own.[33] Ironism surely demands self-criticism. It does not abide spiritual exceptionalism of any sort. And if it looks for no theoretical underpinnings for itself, it still encourages an active understanding and appreciation of the excellence or beauty of others who are different, even radically so. If spiritual exceptionalism runs the risk of humanly executing a divine comedy grotesque in its tragic, or simply vicious, consequences, Santayana's natural comedy at its best is tailor-made, to the contrary, to block arrogance, foster a just estimate of pluriform humanity, demand self-criticism, and make room both for joy and responsibility.

Joy and Responsibility

Joy and responsibility, indeed, are the two large ideas around which Santayana and I spin or, better, reweave our respective webs of belief. In fact, as I read them, the same could be said for every contemporary pragmatic naturalist I read closely, for example, Rorty, Putnam, Stout, West, Gunn, Poirier, Bloom, Barber, Kateb, and Walzer. For philosophers and critics like these, there is a life of the spirit, a life concerned with public and private good, social and personal well-being, virtue and happiness.

Some of these naturalists may not, or may no longer, link up their concern with joy and responsibility with the religious or spiritual traditions of their parents or grandparents. Some of them do. Willy-nilly, that is "the whence" from which those large ideas descend into contemporary American culture. Indeed, religious traditions are more than the source of the focus on joy and responsibility. This is so because religious traditions persist in our culture, recalling individuals and communities to the disciplines of personal and public good.

True enough, simply because secular liberal institutions in the United States grew out of practices that were once distinctively religious does not necessitate the maintenance of those old traditions now—any more than the current practice of medicine demands preservation of the astrology or the doctrine of God's signatures out of which it grew. Like every other party to cultural conversation, either religious traditions pay attention, and are paid attention, as they go, or they become both deaf and dumb.

But if we are pragmatic naturalists who accept the sort of liberal materialism or nonreductive physicalism that Santayana proposed—the sort that, updated, is prepared to say, along with Rorty, "that every event can be described in micro-structural terms, a description which mentions only elementary particles, and can be explained by reference to other events so described"—we also recognize that, here, we are making claims about the good uses of a language, the better to execute human practices.[34] Indeed, we are making comparative judgments about the relative merits, say, of physiology or folk psychology or, perhaps, a variety of religious narratives. The merit we accord to any of these languages depends on their connections with the particular behaviors we hope to exhibit. So whether or not we keep using this or that language depends on what good or bad it does compared with others, on how well it works for what, and on what its limitations are. Finding out (somewhere down the line) that physiology works well to correlate brain states with behavior and, so, to predict the latter on the basis of the former, does not entail that physiology is literally true while talk about minds or consciousness or beliefs or desires is metaphorical, because physiology and folk psychology are both poetic, both made up, and, for the foreseeable future, both will have their uses. Finding out that a particular sort of religious discourse or practice has led as much to self-aggrandizement and cruelty as to just relations among people, comfort for the afflicted, and a sense of personal excellence or equanimity ought to motivate the relevant practitioners to distance historically, refine, recontextualize, or drop the bad parts and enhance the force or appeal of the good ones, thinking up new variations on old themes as well as radically new twists along the way.

For pragmatic naturalists like me, people do not have beliefs and desires that are variable and modifiable. Rather, what makes people people *are* such beliefs and desires. People are born into traditions of discourse and practice that stock not just the broad outlines of their identity, but most of the particular details. I asserted early on that I hoped to find a way to maintain both moral or political commitment and appreciative openness; both the ability to judge and the capacity to suspend judgment in order to understand; both the power to assert and the graciousness to accept; both a sense of ideological assurance and the talent to subject my ultimate concerns to critical jeopardy. I seek an aptitude to sustain equanimity in the midst of moral or political combat; enough attachment to be able to defend, to struggle, to provoke and to be inflamed on behalf of human solidarity; and enough detachment to listen to my opponent, to consider the contrary custom, to seek the means to split our differences in ways that redound to the benefit of our mutuality; also enough disengagement to embark, to separate, to find my own direction, to found my own way, and to imagine yet again.

But I didn't devise these precepts. I inherited them as a Jew, as a liberal, as an Emersonian, as an affectionate Jamesian, as an admirer of Santayana, as a cosmopolitan American, and as an adherent of democratic republican ideals. Do these lifeways hang together? Well, if I am not severely self-deceived, they are the ropes that rig me.

For me, figures like Micah and Isaiah and Amos inform my sense of social criticism along with Paine, Thoreau, Niebuhr, King, and Havel. Stevens, Dickinson, Chuang Tzu, Primo Levi but, even more, Job and Koheleth are my teachers when it comes to learning equanimity and the knack for letting go. If Locke and Jefferson and Madison show me the liberal political arts of separation that provide sufficiently open spaces for such things as freedom of conscience or religious liberty, a free press and speech, free markets, self-determination rather than predetermination, and, most significantly, "individual and familial freedom, privacy, and domesticity" to thrive, Exodus provides the basic paradigm for my understanding of political life.[35] For me, politics is still basically playing out the Exodus story of oppression, liberation, covenant, and self-determining social solidarity. If free universities provide time out for meditation on things that are important, either because they make life worth living or because they obstruct well-being, the historical descent from Shabbat to sabbaticals still rings true.

Emerson, Whitman, James, Royce, Santayana, and Dewey mine the treasures of a culture that fosters the rejection of bad conventions on the basis of moral self-scrutiny, the courage to live experimentally, persisting in one's own direction, and, most preciously, the agility to erase "all mean egotism" by surrendering one's self to the needs of others, and even more, to the possibilities for living well that others, who are radically different, offer like gifts to my imagination.[36] But along with the Emersonians, there is Hillel, reminding me that if I am not for myself, who will be, but if I am only for myself, what am I, and if not now, when; and there is Rabbi Tarphon, counseling: It is not required of you that you complete the work, but neither are you free to desist from it.

Harold Bloom claims that "America, like Hellenistic Alexandria . . . is an eclectic culture, of which [American Jewish writers] are a part. The Jewish writer's problem here and now does not differ from the Hellenistic or American *belatedness*, from the anxiety that we may all of us just be too late."[37] How is it that American Jews are belated, according to Bloom? He says: "Everything called Judaism today essentially is antiquarian, insofar as its intellectual content exists at all. Of course, that same sentence would be valid if the word 'Christianity' were substituted for 'Judaism,' and as valid again if the name of many academic disciplines were the substituted words."[38]

There is something all too apocalyptic and bald-faced about Bloom's diagnosis (which is high-handed at least and, maybe, just mistaken in light of revisionary work that includes his own recent commentary on *The Book of J*). Judaism is what people who ascribe Jewishness to their beliefs and desires, their texts, and their practices, are arguing about right now. The same holds for Christianity, philosophy, literary criticism, democracy, and all the other historiographic forms of life that deny closure to themselves by expecting the sorts of revision and reform that are based on considerate attention to voices yet to be heard, needs yet to be cared for, customs yet to be appreciated, and styles of life lying around the unimagined corner.

Santayana's disciplines of piety and spirituality and charity, Royce's community of memory and hope and interpretation: These forms of life together and life alone, these religious traditions, are critical guy wires to the past, to the future, and to alien others who deserve consideration and solicitude—including the kind of help that comes by leaving people alone—simply because they are there and, being there, make claims on us.

Time was when Western religious traditions relied on notions of essential humankindness and, more, eternal being, to *talk about* our gifted inheritances, our aspirations, and our connections and disconnections with others not ourselves. That we now have reasons to think it *better* to talk about debts, pledges, endeavors, and bonds as idiosyncratic and variable natural contingencies, rather than as things timelessly hard-wired into the ways of the world, results from propitious revisions in thinking and invites further reform.

Whether or not we respond to these invitations, to my mind, is strictly a sociological and pragmatic issue: It depends on us, on the determination we have, and on the imaginative turns we give to life when courage falls short of winning the day, and we find ourselves meditating on wit's end.

NOTES

Chapter 1

1. See Rogers, *Dial* 38 and 40. Paul Conkin is the exception. See his *Puritans and Pragmatists*.

2. See Levinson, "Santayana's Contribution to American Religious Philosophy," "Religious Criticism," "Santayana and the Possibility of Secular Spirituality," "Meditation at the Margins: Santayana's *Scepticism and Animal Faith*," "Santayana's Pragmatism and the Comic Sense of Life," and "Santayana and the Many Faces of Realism."

3. James was on Santayana's side of this fence—hence, paradigmatically, his definition of religion as "*the feelings, acts, and experiences of individual men in their solitude, so far as they apprehend themselves to stand in relation to whatever they consider the divine*" (*VRE*, 34). But James, too, was belittled by later pragmatists, as needlessly concerned with solitude, which they tended to picture as either pathological or misanthropic.

4. Dewey, "The Need for a Recovery of Philosophy," p. 69.

5. Once again, James was closer to Santayana in this regard than later pragmatists. See his "On a Certain Blindness in Human Beings," in *TT*. Indeed, I will try to show in chapter 6 that Santayana posits principles very close to James's "Certain Blindness" doctrine when he turns to "festive criticism."

6. The quote is from Perry's review of Santayana's *Character and Opinion in the United States*, *Dial* (May 1921): 578, but is an early rendition of a charge repeated many times by various other pragmatists.

7. Dewey, *Art as Experience*, p. 195.

8. But compare *LR*, 2:121, where justice to all extant interests constitutes good government.

9. Clebsch, *American Religious Thought*, p. 89.

10. James, "Introduction to *The Literary Remains of the Late Henry James*," p. 63. Also see Levinson, *The Religious Investigations of William James*.

11. Dewey, *Art as Experience*, p. 348. For further exploration of the Reformed Christian backdrop for understanding pragmatism, Dewey, and Santayana, see Levinson, "Religious Philosophy."

12. The phrase is Emerson's, and is one measure of the distance between Santayana and his intellectual grandfather. See Emerson, *Complete Works*, 6:219.

13. Kundera, *The Art of the Novel*, p. 11.

14. This is a paraphrase of the general thesis of Storr's *Solitude*.

15. Rorty, *Contingency*, pp. xiii–xiv. I say "something" right because Rorty's account of "the private" is too narrow, leaving out of consideration things like friendships, families, and voluntary associations.

16. West, *The American Evasion of Philosophy*, p. 228.

17. Polhemus, *Comic Faith*, p. 23.

18. If Kenneth Burke counts, then he and Horace Kallen are the exceptions to this generalization.

19. Quoted in Gunn, *The Culture of Criticism*, p. 82.

20. Gunn, *The Culture of Criticism*, p. 82.

21. West, *The American Evasion of Philosophy*.

22. West, "Subversive Joy," p. 165.

23. Rorty, *Contingency*, p. 87.

24. Rorty, *Contingency*, pp. 24, 23.

25. Poirier, *The Renewal of Literature*, pp. 182–233.

26. Rorty is reflecting on Philip Larkin's claim to this effect. See *Contingency*, p. 24.

27. Poirier, *The Renewal of Literature*, p. 231.

28. Blumenberg, "An Anthropological Approach to the Contemporary Significance of Rhetoric," p. 447.

29. Kundera, *The Art of the Novel*, p. 159.

30. Stout, *Ethics after Babel*, p. 181.

31. Ibid., p. 183.

32. Kundera, *The Art of the Novel*, p. 233.

33. Ibid.

34. Stout, *Ethics after Babel*, p. 212.

35. Ibid.

36. Eco, *The Name of the Rose*, p. 598.

Chapter 2

1. See Flower and Murphey, *A History of Philosophy in America*, 2:373. For an earlier version of the same claim see, for example, Perry, "Santayana," p. 72.

2. Santayana contributed an essay to the volume that was received as the manifesto of the critical realists, and his doctrine of "essence" was the subject of much debate among that party of philosophers. See his "Three Proofs of Realism," in Drake et al., *Essays in Critical Realism*. I argue in chapter 5, below, that there is no evidence that Santayana cooperated with this philosophical party as such and that his essay, as

distinguished from the others in *Critical Realism*, satirized epistemology rather than contributing to it.

3. See Fredricksen, *From Jesus to Christ*, p. 72.

4. Ibid., p. 74.

5. Here, I follow Clebsch's *American Religious Thought*.

6. Fiering, *Jonathan Edwards's Moral Thought*, p. 137.

7. Edwards, *The Nature of True Virtue*, p. 99.

8. Whicher, Spiller, and Williams, *The Early Lectures of Ralph Waldo Emerson*, p. 273.

9. Hughson has made the point that Santayana's sense of beauty departs from every sort of supernaturalism, including the romantic's natural supernaturalism, in *Thresholds of Reality*, chap. 2.

10. Here, I am following Bercovitch's characterization of American spiritual exceptionalism in *American Jeremiad*.

11. Ibid., pp. 105–6.

12. See T. S. Eliot, "Ash Wednesday," in *The Complete Poems and Plays*, p. 65. See also Lears, *No Place of Grace*, for an incisive account of the burdens placed on American culture by the rise of consumer capitalism and its cult of self-realization, as well as the ingenious but ultimately unsuccessful efforts by many critics to oppose these constituents of "modernity."

13. See Bender, "The Cultures of Intellectual Life."

14. See Morison, *Development of Harvard University*, pp. 234–37, 287–89.

15. For Santayana's own account of his Harvard studies, see *PAP*, chaps. 13–16. The Harvard Archives holds documents recording Santayana's enrollment and grades in various courses.

16. Kuklick, *The Rise of American Philosophy*, interprets the emergence of philosophy as a disciplinary, as distinguished from civic, profession. The Harvard Archives holds correspondence concerning Santayana's Walker Fellowship and his faculty appointments.

17. "The Problem of Will in Its Relation to Ethics: A Junior Forensic" was first published in the *Harvard Crimson*, 25 February 1885, supplement 2–4. It has been reprinted in Lachs and Lachs, *Physical Order and Moral Liberty*, pp. 3–8. "The Ethical Doctrine of Spinoza" was first published in *Harvard Monthly* 2 (June 1886): 144–51. It has been reprinted in *The Idler and His Works*, edited by Daniel Cory, pp. 74–86. "The Optimism of Ralph Waldo Emerson" is held in the Harvard Archives and reprinted in *GSA*, 71–84. The Harvard Archives holds all the *Lampoon* and *Harvard Monthly* issues that contain cartoons, drawings, and essays by Santayana.

18. This threat, for example, provided both pretext and context for Royce's *Religious Aspect of Philosophy* (1885). It had also been the dramatic motive for arguments that James presented in such essays as "The Sentiment of Rationality," (1879), "Rationality, Activity, and Faith," (1880), and "Reflex Action and Theism," (1881), eventually edited and collected in *The Will to Believe*.

19. The fact that Santayana signed this essay "Victor Cousin" is telling in this regard, for that French philosopher (1792–1867) had attempted to square empirical finitude with metaphysical infinitude by combining just the sort of Scottish realism that had prevailed at Harvard up through the early works of Francis Bowen, with the sort of post-Kantian idealism that Bowen, Palmer, Royce, and the early James had come to maintain.

Chapter 3

1. See Murphey, "Kant's Children: The Cambridge Pragmatists."

2. See Royce, *William James and Other Essays*, for the claim that, before James and after Edwards, Emerson was eponymous with American moral philosophy.

3. See James, *The Will to Believe*, p. 64.

4. Incidentally, Santayana's "alternative" is remarkably similar to Hilary Putnam's construal of pragmatic realism in, for example, *The Many Faces of Realism* and *Realism with a Human Face*. Both philosophers suggest that, at points, Kant seems willing to drop the notion of "the thing in itself": When he does, he is left without any clear reason to make a transcendental turn, and can account for both science and sentiment as natural ways of thinking that stand in need of no supernatural or metaphysical or transcendental sanctions. See my discussion of realism and pragmatism in chapter 6 for interesting parallels between Santayana and Putnam on truth. The parallels with Strawson, *Skepticism and Naturalism*, are also quite strong.

5. See Santayana's letter to Henry Ward Abbot, dated 5 February 1887, where he says that "a man's stock of experience, his inalienable ideas, are given facts. His reason for holding on to them is that he can't get rid of them" (L, 18).

6. Strawson, *Skepticism and Naturalism*, p. 38.

7. Ibid., p. 51.

8. Ibid., p. 52.

9. Ibid., pp. 52–53.

10. Ibid., p. 61.

11. For Royce's view of philosophy, see Kuklick, *Rise of American Philosophy*, pp. 370–85.

12. See *The Letters of William James*, 1:336–37.

13. Ibid., p. 236.

14. "The Present Position of the Roman Catholic Church," pp. 658–73.

15. Two full-length studies of Santayana's aesthetics appeared in the 1950s. Arnett, *Santayana and the Sense of Beauty*, made some headway toward establishing Santayana's "sense of beauty" as a moral or spiritual concern. But Arnett's work failed to show how *The Sense of Beauty* emerged out of a tradition of aesthetic spirituality, or how Santayana adopted Jamesian principles of psychology in an effort to naturalize that tradition. Singer, *Santayana's Aesthetics*, pictures Santayana's "sense of beauty" as relying on an

untenable notion of epistemological immediacy. I disagree, on the grounds that psychological immediacy—something that Santayana invoked—is not tantamount to epistemological immediacy. Psychological immediacy amounts to things people believe go without saying. Epistemological immediacy, to the contrary, refers to belief purported to be basic in the sense that they are noninferential. In any case, Singer makes no reference to the historical context in which Santayana wrote *The Sense of Beauty*, nor to any of his precedents in the tradition of aesthetic spirituality.

16. It is also true that *The Sense of Beauty* was published in the spirit of the new disciplinary turn that philosophy was taking at Harvard. It was geared to communicate the message that Harvard philosophy counted aesthetics as one of its subdisciplines, and had a faculty member who was diligently working out the relevant theory. In *Persons and Places* Santayana recalled that he was "expected and almost compelled" to construct some distinctive theory. The conventions of the new professionalism placed great importance on having a specialty. Although he claimed that he had no "clear notion of what 'aesthetics' may be," he had agreed to give a course in it in order to "define my status" (*PAP*, 393). He had then written out his lectures in the form of a book that could be submitted as part of the materials making up his case for promotion to assistant professor. Apparently Santayana had difficulty placing his manuscript with a publisher until Barrett Wendell, a friendly colleague in English, arranged for Scribner's to take it. After the book appeared, Santayana received his promotion, though, again apparently, not without humiliation from President Charles Eliot, who found him peculiar, a dandy, a man unwilling to serve on committees, an aesthete, and "unnatural," that is, most probably homosexual.

17. See *POP*, 2:1058–97, for James's theory of emotions. Many critics, for example Danto (in his introduction to *SB*), read Santayana as indebted to Schopenhauer on this point. Surely *both* James and Santayana were influenced by Schopenhauer's characterization of normal intelligence as emotional or aesthetic. But just as surely, they were indebted to Shaftesbury, Hutcheson, Edwards, Burke, and Emerson on this score.

18. See *POP*, 2:1235, 1264–65, for James's acknowledgment of the sense of beauty as an emotion. Also see James's "The Place of Affectional Facts in a World of Pure Experience," in *Essays in Radical Empiricism*, for *his* sense of indebtedness to Santayana's *Sense of Beauty* on this point.

19. See James, *Essays in Radical Empiricism*, pp. 69–77.

20. Santayana's effort is hampered by his on-again, off-again reliance on a phenomenalistic theory of perception that is espoused at the time by Royce and, less solidly, by James. See Royce, *The Religious Aspect of Philosophy*. James's *Principles of Psychology* assumes phenomenalism sometimes, but also characterizes "sensation" as an abstract rather than as a basic term, calling sense-data phenomenalism into question. See Levinson, *Science, Metaphysics, and the Chance of Salvation*, pp. 38–41, for an interpretation of James's claim that "no one ever had a simple sensation by itself." Santayana asserts, in particular, that "modern philosophy has taught us to say [that all the elements of the perceived world] are sensations" that somehow get glued together by

association into single percepts and, then, that they get "attached" to names (*SB*, 29). Beware the locution "modern philosophy has taught us"! It almost inevitably introduces some just-so story about the building blocks of knowledge that uses language Santayana will eventually abandon. There is little need to introduce a phenomenalistic rendition of cognition in *The Sense of Beauty* except to parade disciplinary spit and polish. It stands in stark contrast to the Jamesian view of mentality as a holistic process on which Santayana relies; and it makes no sense in light of Santayana's declaration that aesthetic experience precedes the division of things into the subject/object dualism on which phenomenalism depends.

21. This characterization of the sense of beauty as a "survival" of some primitive mentality may cut two ways in Santayana's culture of inquiry. From a Darwinian standpoint, the notion of survival was closely associated with functional importance. The Darwinian presumption was that if some part of an organism survived, then it must meet some need or demand adequately enough to get transmitted historically. On the other hand, Darwinians admitted the occurrence of nonfunctional "vestiges" that survived as well. Was Santayana claiming that the sense of beauty was functionally important or a vestigial throwback? Both. When metaphysicians like Lotze construed the sense of beauty as disclosing metaphysical reality, it was vestigial. When naturalists like James construed the sense of beauty as grounding lived experiences in "affectional facts," it was functional. For an incisive account of Darwin's theory of "survival," see Gheselin, *The Triumph of Darwinian Method*.

22. See *SB*, 13, and "WA?."

23. Bromwich, "From Wordsworth to Emerson," p. 204.

24. Gadamer, *The Relevance of the Beautiful*, p. 47.

25. Ibid., p. 130.

26. Quoted in Bloom, *Poetry and Repression*, p. 184.

27. Hughson, *Thresholds of Reality*, p. 75.

Chapter 4

1. But see James, "Philosophical Conceptions and Practical Results," pp. 346–47, for his romantic claim that "Philosophers are after all like poets. . . . [B]oth alike have the same function. . . . They give you something to go from. They give you a direction and a place to reach."

2. Clendenning, *The Letters of Josiah Royce*, p. 378.

3. Royce, *The World and the Individual*, 1:4–5.

4. For an interpretation of this effort, see Levinson, *The Religious Investigations of William James*, esp. pp. 71–167.

5. Stout, *Ethics after Babel*, p. 165.

6. Geertz, *The Interpretation of Cultures*, pp. 87–125.

7. Indeed, James had already established a Darwinian account of social and cultural history in "Great Men and Their Environments," in *The Will to Believe*.

8. For an analysis of James's use of Darwin in *Varieties*, see Levinson, *The Religious Investigations of William James*, pp. 74–90.

9. To be fair, Santayana does condition his claim about Plato being a "mythologist of the Ideal" by noting that both Plato and Aristotle obscured their view that goodness was the exclusive criterion of divinity by attempting "to connect (more or less mythically or magically) their own Socratic principle of excellence with the cosmic principles of the earlier philosophers" (*IPR*, 66).

10. Eliot, "Tradition and the Individual Talent."

11. Lentricchia, *Ariel and the Police*, p. 105.

12. See Santayana's anonymous review, signed "H.M.," in *Harvard Monthly* (July 1899).

Chapter 5

1. See Morison, *Development of Harvard University*, for information about the Alford Professorship. See Kuklick, *Rise of American Philosophy*, for an interpretation of Bowen relevant to this discussion.

2. To be sure, the vision of philosophy as intellectual statesmanship republican style is, in some sense, as old as Plato. But its more specific precursor is the civic humanism that first developed as the Atlantic republican tradition that Pocock has brought to life so brilliantly in *The Machiavellian Moment*. See Wood, *The Creation of the American Republic*, for the best current introduction to republicanism in the United States. See also Shalhope, "Toward a Republican Synthesis."

3. The following discussion expands an interpretation of intellectual statesmanship in Harvard's "golden age" philosophy department originally presented in Levinson, "Religious Criticism."

4. Royce, *The Religious Aspect of Philosophy*, p. 126.

5. Ibid., p. 145.

6. The fact that deity is social is one of the main points highlighted in Royce's Gifford Lectures, *The World and the Individual*. Social deity becomes utterly republican in *The Problem of Christianity*.

7. James, *The Will to Believe*, p. 149. The relationships between James's claims in "The Moral Philosopher and the Moral Life" and those he made ten years later in *The Varieties of Religious Experience* are easy to find confusing. In the earlier piece, James rejects moral absolutism and the search for some invariable Moral Law or Moral Lawgiver. In the later piece, James concludes that there are supernatural powers at work in the world that can transform despairing people into saintly ones. But James never construes these "supernatural powers" as providing "objective" grounds for adjudicating any or every

dispute over what constitutes moral obligation or, for that matter, over what constitutes human joy.

8. Ibid.

9. Ibid., p. 148.

10. Sprigge, "The Distinctiveness of American Philosophy."

11. For an overview of the distinctively republican character of the "intellectual statesmanship" present in Harvard's philosophy department at the turn of the century, see Levinson, "Religious Philosophy."

12. Santayana's explicit emphasis on "tradition" as providing parameters for criticism comes in his 1904 Oberlin Commencement Address, originally printed in the *Oberlin Alumni Magazine* (October 1904), and now available in *GSA*, 109–20.

13. See Moore, Review of *The Life of Reason*, pp. 211–14.

14. It is surely true, as Sprigge has pointed out in *Santayana*, that Santayana never articulated a full-blown philosophy of language. But here, just as certainly, we have a philosophy that characterizes thought *as* language.

15. Lovibond is discussing Wittgenstein, and expressivism more generally, in *Realism and Imagination in Ethics*, p. 23. But the characterization fits Santayana's claims in *Reason in Science*.

16. Santayana does not contend with two other views of the relation between mind and body that were available in his time. "Interactionists" contended that minds and bodies were distinct entities or processes, but that they were in some sort of causal relation. "Parallelists" contended that minds and bodies were distinct entities or processes, each of which set up causal chains which, at no point, affected the other. I agree with Lachs's claim, *George Santayana*, p. 144, that "interactionist dualism is incompatible with well established facts of science, and the unconnected parallel development of consciousness and the physical world strains all credulity."

17. Ibid.

18. Rogers, in *Dial* 38 (May 1905) and 40 (February 1906).

19. See Schiller, *Hibbert Journal* 4 (1906): 462–64, 936–40; and Dewey, *Science*, n.s., 23 (1906): 223–25, as well as *Educational Review* 34 (1907): 116–29. Dewey said the work was "the most adequate contribution America has yet made—always excepting Emerson—to moral philosophy." Hartley Burr Alexander rightly called the work a piece of "Hellenistic Americanism" that competed with both realism and transcendental idealism, praising Santayana for his "Protestant spirit, the resentment of magniloquent discourse, the insistence that philosophy shall be directly relevant to life as life really is," in *Bookman* 22 (1906): 527. MacLennan praised Santayana for articulating a humanistic, instrumentalist conception of knowledge in the *American Journal of Theology* 10 (1906): 161–64. G. E. Moore, true to form, was totally unsympathetic with the project. See subsequent discussion.

20. Kallen, "Pragmatism and Its 'Principles,'" pp. 632–34.

21. G. E. Moore, *International Journal of Ethics* 17 (January 1907): 248–53. Open

ridicule followed this claim. Indeed, it is unclear whether Moore thought *The Life of Reason* was a piece of bad philosophy, or no philosophy at all.

22. Stout, *Ethics after Babel*, p. 131, siding with colleagues like Schneewind and Levi, clarifies the point this way: Epistemic criticism involves "the dialectical interplay between beliefs about specific cases and beliefs of a more general form, in a continuing process of refinement and revision. . . . The most powerful argument on behalf of any principle . . . is that it has repeatedly survived exposure to intuitions about special cases."

23. As I interpret *The Life of Reason*, the main thrust of Santayana's account of knowledge is already antiepistemological in the sense that it sidetracks efforts to establish epistemic conditions permitting linkage between thoughts and things. But I think Santayana would still wobble between epistemology and antiepistemology at least until he wrote his *Soliloquies*; and, surely at this point in his career, he still clung to the notion that philosophers had a hand in showing people where epistemic thought came from and how it developed. In this regard, chunks of *Reason in Common Sense* read like exercises in "naturalizing" epistemology, similar in purpose to more recent efforts by, say, Roy Wood Sellars, Morris Cohen, Ernest Nagel, Wilfred Sellars, and Willard Van Orman Quine. My own view is that the just-so stories about the development of knowledge presented by Santayana in *Reason in Common Sense* dead-end when, quite rightfully, he throws up his hands and admits, on the one hand, that the physiology of knowledge is a "question for the natural sciences to solve" (*LR*, 1:209) and, on the other, that the conditions of inquiry as a full-fledged practice are social.

24. In this respect, Santayana stands as precedent for the Rawlsian claim that "what justifies a conception of justice is not its being true to an order antecedent to and given to us, but its congruence with our deeper understanding of ourselves and our aspirations, and our realization that, *given our history and the traditions embedded in our public life*, it is the most reasonable doctrine *for us*." Rawls, "Kantian Constructivism," p. 519.

25. Kundera, "Afterword," p. 233. Kundera, it should be noted, rightfully identifies this dream with the "sunny" side of totalitarianism, or the thing that makes hell attractive to many people.

26. See chapter 7 for a more complete estimation of Santayana's political thought, especially his criticisms of democracy.

27. This picture of the relations holding among aggressive power, virtue, and liberty was part of the stock jeremiad voiced by republicans against wealth and coercion since the beginnings of the United States. See Wood, *Creation of the American Republic*.

28. For a superb overview of the role "Hebraism" came to play in Enlightenment thinking descending from Christian theology, see Manuel, "Israel in the Enlightenment."

29. This "Hebrew tradition," to be sure, is a figure in a Christian morality tale, not Judaism as traditional Jews typically understood it. In traditional Judaism, there is no matter/spirit difference that makes a difference: Spirit matters, or it isn't. Moreover, in

both biblical and rabbinic Judaism, there is no sharp grace/law or spirit/word distinction either. As Jews see these things, there could not practically be one without the other.

Chapter 6

1. See James, *Pragmatism*, pp. 9–26; James, *Essays in Radical Empiricism*, pp. 21–44, 69–78; Royce, *The Philosophy of Loyalty*; and Royce, *The Problem of Christianity*, p. 297. There is reason to believe that James's characterization of pure experience as "affectional" or aesthetic, rather than subjective or objective, was indebted to Santayana's thinking in *The Sense of Beauty*. See *Essays in Radical Empiricism*, pp. 72, 110.

2. See James, "The Philippine Tangle."

3. James, *TT,* p. 25. It is worthwhile noting that even prior to James's formulation of the doctrine of human blindness, Santayana had written two plays in the late 1890s, both of which were published only posthumously, that pursued links between "practical irresponsibility" and understanding on the one hand, while ridiculing philosophy construed as statesmanship on the other. See "The Marriage of Venus," in which the goddess embodying the sense of beauty is portrayed as characteristically irresponsible, and "Philosophers at Court," in which Plato's statesmanship is subjected to ridicule on grounds of pretentiousness. Both plays were published in Santayana, *The Poet's Testament.*

4. It is important to note that, even as Santayana is leaving the United States, he is still being interpreted by colleagues and students as a pragmatist. See, for example, Horace Kallen's "Pragmatism and Its 'Principles.'"

5. See memoranda concerning the course in the "correspondence file of the Department of Philosophy" housed in the Harvard Archives.

6. Santayana identified Socrates and Hume at their best, and had already identified Emerson and James, as embodying philosophy as a personal work of art.

7. See Royce, *The Spirit of Modern Philosophy*, and Kuklick, "Seven Thinkers and How They Grew."

8. Santayana alternates "natural comedy" with "human comedy" in his interpretation of Goethe. See *TPP*, 143.

9. This last quote actually comes from Santayana's introduction to Spinoza's *Ethics*, written concurrently with *Three Philosophical Poets*. "The secret of what is serious in the moral of Faust," Santayana asserts, "is to be looked for in Spinoza" (*TPP*, 189). Goethe's "'poetic intention' [is] altogether Spinozistic" (*TPP*, 192).

10. See James, *Some Problems of Philosophy*, p. 71.

11. Royce, *The Spirit of Modern Philosophy*, p. 60.

12. Compare Santayana's claim (*TPP*, 210) that "in Dante's spheres there could be no discord whatever [hence, tragic exultation]; but at the core of them was eternal woe

[hence, tragic concern for misery]." For references to Royce's conscience as agonized in this Calvinist way, see Santayana, *COUS*, 100–120.

13. See West, *The American Evasion of Philosophy*, p. 17.

14. Rorty, *Philosophy and the Mirror of Nature*, p. 316.

15. In the view Santayana expressed here (which I think is false), Walt Whitman had escaped the genteel tradition altogether, but he stood so far outside it that he was incapable of enticing it in a new direction, the way the Jameses did. In my view, the ways in which Whitman provoked Santayana himself led to important revisions in American traditions, especially American conceptions of democratic culture and democratic individuals.

16. See Royce, *William James and Other Essays*, pp. 1–45.

17. See James, *The Meaning of Truth*, p. 158.

18. Rorty, *Consequences*, p. xliii.

19. See Putnam, *Realism and Reason*, p. 225, and *The Many Faces of Realism*, p. 17.

20. Putnam, *The Many Faces of Realism*, p. 17.

21. Ibid., p. 37.

22. Rorty, *Consequences*, p. xl.

23. Ibid., p. 5.

24. Ibid., pp. xliii, 35.

25. Putnam, *The Many Faces of Realism*, p. 71.

26. Quine, *Word and Object*, pp. 5–8.

27. Santayana, "On the False Steps of Philosophy," pp. 145–74. Quine, *Ontological Relativity*, p. i.

28. Fussell, *The Great War*, p. 8.

29. Ibid.

30. Recall that "Hermes" appears, already in 1899, as the most sympathetic character in *Lucifer*, quite precisely because he embodies the festive criticism and understanding to which Santayana now devotes himself.

31. Kern, *Absolute Comedy*, p. 30.

32. For Santayana's criticism of Bergson and the new British scholastics, see *WD*, 58–154. For his criticism of German idealism and postidealism, see *Egotism in German Philosophy*. Many interpreters have taken the latter work to be propaganda inspired by the Great War. While Santayana was surely repulsed by the apparent links between idealism and nationalism (whether German or British or American), the fact remains that "egotism in German philosophy" had been a topic of interest at Harvard for over fifty years, where, for example, Francis Bowen had repeatedly criticized it. I do not interpret *Egotism* as one of Santayana's major works, though it permits interesting comparisons between the American pragmatists, Hegel, and Nietzsche.

33. Dewey, *Reconstruction in Philosophy*, p. 212.

34. Ibid., pp. 212–13.

35. Ibid., pp. 39–40.

36. Ibid., p. 47.

37. Ibid., pp. 48–51.

38. Ibid., pp. 54–55, 60.

39. The epoch is named by Quine in "Remarks for a Memorial Symposium," p. 1.

40. Russell, *The Problems of Philosophy*, p. 7.

41. Passmore, *A Hundred Years of Philosophy*, p. 230.

Chapter 7

1. This, indeed, has always been the standard way to interpret *Scepticism and Animal Faith*, all the way up through the works of Lachs's *George Santayana* and Sprigge's *Santayana: An Examination of His Philosophy*. According to Sprigge, for example, Santayana wrote *Scepticism* because "he thought that the philosophical climate of his time was such that an ontologist must begin by disposing of all sorts of epistemological objections to his enterprise" (p. 30). In my view, *Scepticism* was epistemological in the weak sense that it presented a characterization of knowledge. But it was anti-epistemological because it opposed attempts to discover generic and unshakable grounds on which to base indubitable knowledge claims.

Santayana, to be sure, had contributed "Three Proofs of Realism," to the manifesto of the critical realists, Drake et al., *Essays in Critical Realism*, pp. 163–86. But his "proofs" were garden-variety attempts to vindicate the notion that we live in a world that, for the most part, is unaffected by our thoughts about it (making him a "realist"), a world that our thought signifies but does not mirror (making his realism "critical," rather than "naive" or "direct"). The fact that Santayana went out of his way to declare himself part of no movement in *Scepticism* is relevant. The book mocked both philosophy understood as the sort of social movement that issues manifestos and philosophy understood as centrally focused on "the problem of knowledge."

2. Lachs, *Animal Faith and Spiritual Life*, p. 209.

3. Ibid., p. 211.

4. Saatkamp, "Some Remarks on Santayana's Scepticism," p. 138.

5. This makes Santayana's view of ritual a precursor to the one developed by Turner in *The Ritual Process*.

6. See Santayana's *Dialogues in Limbo*, which presents yet another, brilliant rehearsal of the ritual process Santayana undergoes in his effort to overcome the "moral cramp" that the projects of modern philosophy cause, just as old theological superstitions had.

7. James, "What Is an Emotion?," p. 175.

8. Note, in this regard, Santayana's claim, made in the preface to volume 7 of the Triton Edition of his works, that his choice of the term *essence* "and my whole presentation of this subject, were perhaps unfortunate" but that there had been "a clarifying and satirical force in the discrimination of essences." *The Works of George Santayana*, 7:xii–xiii.

9. Though unlike James, neither tended to slip back into idealism by suggesting, as James had at times, that such "pure experience" provided a privileged key to understanding the universe.

10. Hook, "Pragmatism and the Tragic Sense of Life," p. 171.

11. Ibid., pp. 170, 172.

12. Ibid., p. 173.

13. Ibid., pp. 171–72.

14. Dewey, *The Public and Its Problems*, p. 208.

15. James, "Introduction to *The Literary Remains of the Late Henry James*," p. 62.

16. Hook, "Pragmatism and the Tragic Sense of Life," p. 190.

17. Again, I rely heavily, at this point in my argument, on Polhemus, *Comic Faith*, for my view of the great tradition in British literature from Austen to Joyce.

18. Ibid., pp. 22–23.

19. There is some precedent for characterizing Santayana's sense of life as comic. See, for example, Kallen's "The Laughing Philosopher." Kallen notes that once Santayana "traversed the Dark Night described by Saint John of the Cross . . . the warfare of the satirist gives way to the peace of sympathetic humor, the tragic sense of life to the spirit of comedy" (p. 29). Both McCormick, *George Santayana: A Biography*, and Lyon in his introduction to the new critical edition of Santayana's *Persons and Places* oppose the interpretation I present. The former presents no incisive sense for the pragmatic tradition from, say, James to Rorty. The latter characterizes Santayana as more tragic than comic, suppressing Santayana's characterization of his own work as satirical, joyful, and Hermesan, and as providing a modern and naturalistic analogue to Dante's *Divine Comedy*.

20. Let me note that the best commentary to date on *Realms of Being*, Sprigge's *Santayana: An Examination of His Philosophy*, accepts Santayana's own explicit rejection of the title "pragmatist." Certainly, if the Santayana who wrote *Realms of Being* is to be counted as a pragmatist, his variance from other philosophers in that family must be noted, as I attempt to do in this book.

21. Grossman, "Reality Revisited: The Controlled Ambiguity of Santayana's Realms," p. 131.

22. See the dialogues on "Autologos" and "Self Government," in *DL*, 58–123, as well as the chapter on "Monarchial Theism" in *The Idea of Christ in the Gospels*, pp. 175–84, for Santayana's characterization of the human inescapability of material power.

23. In an incisive reflection on Santayana's use of the Nicene Creed in *Realms of Being*, Kerr-Lawson argues that Santayana's effort to transpose the second person of God into his own ontology turns out to be "unconvincing," because it "does not bear on the notion of spiritual discipline" so that "much of the vitality of the notion of Christ is lost here." I agree. But Santayana would not have agreed, because he maintained a fairly strong distinction between personality and character, which I cannot accept, even after he pledged allegiance to Hermes. See Kerr-Lawson, "Santayana's Ontology and the Nicene Creed," pp. 26–32.

24. This is the lesson that Oliver Alden, the ultimate puritan, eventually learns, as he escapes the officious world of his Bostonian ancestry to seek a spiritual contentment that all but eludes him. See Santayana, *LP*. The break from statesmanship to philosophical festivity also becomes evident in Santayana's autobiography. See, particularly, "A Change of Heart," in *PAP*, 417–29.

25 Williams, "Of Essence and Existence and Santayana," p. 41.

26. See Tillich's "Christianity without Paul," p. 412.

27. The following cultural contextualization of Santayana's Catholicism is entirely based on Lears, *No Place of Grace*, pp. 142–215.

28. See Lears, *No Place of Grace*, pp. 155–59.

29. Ibid., p. 301.

Chapter 8

1. Barber, *Strong Democracy*, p. 4.

2. Ibid., p. 118.

3. Dewey, *The Public and Its Problems*, p. 148.

4. Barber, *Strong Democracy*, p. 136.

5. Dewey, "The Need for a Recovery of Philosophy," p. 23.

6. Koch, "Political Recluse," p. 20.

7. Schutz, "Santayana on Society and Government," p. 222. See also Oakeshott, "Philosophical Imagination," p. 578.

8. Schutz, "Santayana on Society and Government," p. 222.

9. Meilander, "Individuals in Community," p. 9.

10. See "The United States as Leader," the penultimate chapter in *DP*, 456–61.

11. For reflection on liberal communitarianism, see Cladis, *Individuals in Community*.

12. See Rosaldo, *Truth and Culture*, pp. 43–45. My understanding of social analysis throughout this chapter is greatly indebted to Rosaldo's work.

13. Barber, *Strong Democracy*, p. 18.

14. Frost, "Mending Wall," p. 48.

15. Nehamas, "A Touch of the Poet," p. 114.

16. Barber, *Strong Democracy*, p. 198.

17. Ibid, p. 135.

18. Ibid., p. 207.

19. Ibid., p. 200.

20. Rorty, *Objectivity, Relativism, and Truth*, p. 175.

21. Barber, *Strong Democracy*, pp. 120–21.

Epilogue

1. See "The Department of Philosophy," in Minor, *The Bicentennial History of Columbia University*, p. 145.

2. It is noteworthy that, in *PGS*, Santayana was still characterizing his work as "a sort of pragmatism." See p. 14.

3. See Hollinger, "The Problem of Pragmatism in American History," pp. 88–107.

4. See Hollinger, *Morris R. Cohen*.

5. Wittgenstein, *Zettel*, p. 455.

6. See also Santayana, "On the Unity of My Earlier and Later Philosophy," p. viii.

7. Frankel, "John Dewey's Social Philosophy."

8. Dewey, *Freedom and Culture*, p. 174.

9. See Kateb, *Hannah Arendt*, p. 182.

10. See the epilogue to White, *Social Thought in America*, p. 253.

11. See Niebuhr, *The Responsible Self*, pp. 113–14.

12. See Morris, *Paths of Life*, where Santayana is figured as neo-Aristotelian. Santayana plays no role, indeed he makes no appearance, in Morris's *The Pragmatic Movement in American Philosophy*. See also Sellars, *Religion Coming of Age*.

13. See Kaplan, *Judaism as a Civilization*, p. 152, where Santayana is noted, along with Tertullian, Newman, Chesterton, Belloc, the Royalist French Catholics, and Nathan Birnbaum, for his defense of "orthodoxy."

14. Case, *The Christian Philosophy of History*, p. 175. Dean, *American Religious Empiricism*, tells the story, analyzes the claims, and endorses the projects of the religious empiricists at the University of Chicago Divinity School during the mid to late twentieth century.

15. See Levinson, "Religious Philosophy," for a relevant discussion of Whitehead and his followers.

16. Marquand, *The Late George Apley*.

17. See Saatkamp and Jones, *Checklist*.

18. Stevens, *Palm*, p. 373.

19. Lowell, *Life Studies*, pp. 51–52.

20. See Saatkamp and Jones, *Checklist*.

21. Trilling, "'That Smile.'" West, *The American Evasion of Philosophy*, clarifies the un-Emersonian character of Trilling's work.

22. Trilling, "'That Smile,'" pp. 154–55.

23. Ibid., p. 156.

24. Ibid., p. 160.

25. Ibid., pp. 160–61.

26. Ibid., pp. 162–63.

27. Mead, *An Anthropologist*, pp. 465–67.

28. Geertz, *Interpretation of Cultures* and *Local Knowledge*.

29. Danto, "Santayana and the Task Ahead," pp. 437–40.

30. The exceptions prove the rule. Sprigge, Lachs, Saatkamp, to take the most noteworthy examples, engage Santayana's work as contemporaneous. But their work has not caused any contemporary philosophical *movement* the way, say, Rorty's work on Dewey has.

31. Rorty, *Philosophy and the Mirror of Nature*, p. 367.

32. Rorty, *Consequences*, p. 60.

33. Rorty devises the notion of "final vocabulary" in *Contingency*. See especially pp. 73–74, where he says that they are "the words [people] employ to justify their actions, their beliefs, their lives. These are the words in which we formulate praise of our friends and contempt for our enemies, our long-term projects, our deepest self-doubts, and our highest hopes . . . the words in which we tell, sometimes prospectively and sometimes retrospectively the story of our lives." I see no difference that makes a difference, assuming the historicist and nominalist character of such vocabularies, between Rorty's "final vocabulary" and Santayana's "animal faith."

34. Rorty, *Objectivity, Relativism, and Truth*, p. 114.

35. See Walzer, "Liberalism and the Art of Separation," p. 317, and *Exodus and Revolution*, pp. 133–49.

36. See Kateb's brilliant characterization of these personal traits in "Democratic Individuality," pp. 342–58.

37. Bloom, "Pragmatics of Jewish Culture," pp. 114–15.

38. Ibid., pp. 117–18.

BIBLIOGRAPHY

For works frequently cited in the text, see the list of abbreviations in the front matter.

Alexander, Hartley Burr. Review of *The Life of Reason*, by George Santayana. *Bookman* 22 (1906): 527.

Arnett, Willard E. *Santayana and the Sense of Beauty*. Bloomington: Indiana University Press, 1957.

Barber, Benjamin. *Strong Democracy: Participatory Politics for a New Age*. Berkeley: University of California Press, 1984.

Bender, Thomas. "The Cultures of Intellectual Life: The City and the Professions." In *New Directions in American Intellectual History*, edited by John Higham and Paul Conkin, pp. 181–95. Baltimore: Johns Hopkins University Press, 1979.

Bercovitch, Sacvan. *American Jeremiad*. Madison: University of Wisconsin Press, 1978.

Bloom, Harold. *Poetry and Repression*. New Haven: Yale University Press, 1976.

————. "The Pragmatics of Contemporary Jewish Culture." In *Post-Analytic Philosophy*, edited by John Rajchman and Cornel West, pp. 108–26. New York: Columbia University Press, 1985.

Blumenberg, Hans. "An Anthropological Approach to the Contemporary Significance of Rhetoric." In *Philosophy: End or Transformation?*, edited by Kenneth Baynes, James Bohman, and Thomas McCarthy, pp. 429–58. Cambridge, Mass.: MIT Press, 1987.

Bromwich, David. "From Wordsworth to Emerson." In *Romantic Revolutions: Criticism and Theory*, edited by Kenneth R. Johnston, Gilbert Chaitin, Karen Hanson, and Herbert Marks, pp. 202–18. Bloomington: Indiana University Press, 1990.

Case, Shirley Jackson. *The Christian Philosophy of History*. Chicago: University of Chicago Press, 1943.

Cladis, Mark. *Individuals in Community: Durkheim's Communitarian Defense of Liberalism*. Stanford: Stanford University Press, 1992.

Clebsch, William. *American Religious Thought*. Chicago: University of Chicago Press, 1972.

Clendenning, John, ed. *The Letters of Josiah Royce*. Chicago: University of Chicago Press, 1970.

Conkin, Paul. *Puritans and Pragmatists*. Bloomington: Indiana University Press, 1976.

Danto, Arthur. "Santayana and the Task Ahead." *Nation*, 21 December 1963, pp. 437–40.

Dean, William. *American Religious Empiricism*. Albany: State University of New York Press, 1989.

Dewey, John. *Art as Experience*. New York: G. P. Putnam's Sons, 1934.

———. *Creative Intelligence: Essays in the Pragmatic Attitude*. New York: Holt, 1917.

———. *Freedom and Culture*. New York: Capricorn Books, 1963.

———. "The Need for a Recovery of Philosophy." In *On Experience, Nature, and Freedom*, edited by Richard Bernstein, pp. 19–69. Indianapolis: Bobbs-Merrill, 1960.

———. *The Public and Its Problems*. New York: Holt, 1927.

——— *Reconstruction in Philosophy*. Enlarged edition. Boston: Beacon Press, 1948.

———. Review of *The Life of Reason*, by George Santayana. *Educational Review* 34 (1907): 116–29.

———. Review of *The Life of Reason*, by George Santayana. *Science*, n.s., 23 (1906): 223–25.

Drake, Durant, Arthur O. Lovejoy, James Bissett Pratt, Arthur K. Rogers, George Santayana, Roy Wood Sellars, and C. A. Strong. *Essays in Critical Realism: A Cooperative Study of the Problem of Knowledge*. London: Macmillan, 1920.

Eco, Umberto. *The Name of the Rose*. New York: Harcourt, Brace, Jovanovich, 1983.

Edwards, Jonathan. *The Nature of True Virtue*. Foreword by William A. Frankena. Ann Arbor: University of Michigan Press, 1960.

Eliot, T. S. *The Complete Poems and Plays*. New York: Harcourt, Brace and World, 1950.

———. "Tradition and the Individual Talent." In *The Sacred Wood: Essays on Poetry and Criticism*, pp. 47–59. London: Methuen, 1920.

Emerson, Ralph Waldo. *Complete Works*. Edited by Edward Waldo Emerson. 12 vols. Boston: Houghton Mifflin, 1903–4.

Fiering, Norman. *Jonathan Edwards's Moral Thought in Its British Context*. Chapel Hill: University of North Carolina Press, 1981.

Flower, Elisabeth, and Murray Murphey. *A History of Philosophy in America*. 2 vols. New York: G. P. Putnam's Sons, 1977.

Frankel, Charles. "John Dewey's Social Philosophy." In *New Studies in the Philosophy of John Dewey*, edited by Steven M. Cahn, pp. 3–44. Hanover, N.H.: University Press of New England for the University of Vermont, 1977.

Fredricksen, Paula. *From Jesus to Christ*. New Haven: Yale University Press, 1988.

Frost, Robert. "Mending Wall." In *Complete Poems of Robert Frost: 1949*, p. 47. New York: Holt, Rinehart, Winston, 1949.

Fussell, Paul. *The Great War and Modern Memory*. New York: Oxford University Press, 1975.

Gadamer, Hans-Georg. *The Relevance of the Beautiful and Other Essays*. Edited by Robert Bernasconi. Cambridge: Cambridge University Press, 1986.

Geertz, Clifford. *The Interpretation of Cultures*. New York: Basic Books, 1973.

———. *Local Knowledge: Further Essays in Interpretive Anthropology*. New York: Basic Books, 1983.

Gheselin, Michael T. *The Triumph of Darwinian Method*. Berkeley: University of California Press, 1969.

Grossman, Morris. "Reality Revisited: The Controlled Ambiguity of Santayana's Realms." In *Two Centuries of Philosophy in America*, edited by Peter Caws, pp. 128–34. Totowa, N.J.: Rowman and Littlefield, 1980.

Gunn, Giles. *The Culture of Criticism and the Criticism of Culture*. New York: Oxford University Press, 1987.

Hollinger, David. *Morris R. Cohen and the Scientific Ideal*. Cambridge, Mass.: MIT Press, 1975.

———. "The Problem of Pragmatism in American History." *Journal of American History* 67, no. 1 (June 1980): 88–107.

Hook, Sidney. "Pragmatism and the Tragic Sense of Life." In *Contemporary American Philosophy*, edited by John E. Smith, pp. 170–93. New York: Humanities Press, 1970.

Hughson, Lois. *Thresholds of Reality: George Santayana and Modernist Poetics*. Port Washington, N.Y.: Kennikat Press, 1977.

James, Henry, ed. *The Letters of William James*. 2 vols. Vol. 1. New York: Atlantic Monthly Press, 1920.

James, William. *Essays in Radical Empiricism*. Critical edition by Frederick H. Burkhardt, Fredson Bowers, and Ignas K. Skrupskelis, with an introduction by John J. McDermott. Cambridge, Mass.: Harvard University Press, 1976.

———. "Introduction to *The Literary Remains of the Late Henry James*." In *Essays on Morality and Religion*, critical edition by Frederick H. Burkhardt, Fredson Bowers, and Ignas K. Skrupskelis, with an introduction by John J. McDermott, pp. 3–63. Cambridge, Mass.: Harvard University Press, 1982.

———. *The Meaning of Truth*. Critical edition by Frederick H. Burkhardt, Fredson Bowers, and Ignas K. Skrupskelis, with an introduction by H. S. Thayer. Cambridge, Mass.: Harvard University Press, 1975.

———. "The Philippine Tangle." *Boston Evening Transcript*, 1 March 1899.

———. "Philosophical Conceptions and Practical Results." In *The Writings of William James*, edited by John J. McDermott, pp. 345–61. New York: Random House, 1967.

————. *Pragmatism*. Critical edition by Frederick H. Burkhardt, Fredson Bowers, and Ignas K. Skrupskelis, with an introduction by H. S. Thayer. Cambridge, Mass.: Harvard University Press, 1975.

————. *Some Problems of Philosophy*. Critical edition by Frederick H. Burkhardt, Fredson Bowers, and Ignas K. Skrupskelis, with an introduction by Peter H. Hare. Cambridge, Mass.: Harvard University Press, 1979.

————. "What Is an Emotion?" In *Essays in Psychology*, critical edition by Frederick H. Burkhardt, Fredson Bowers, and Ignas K. Skrupskelis, with an introduction by William R. Woodward, pp. 168–87. Cambridge, Mass.: Harvard University Press, 1983.

————. *The Will to Believe and Other Essays*. Critical edition by Frederick H. Burkhardt, Fredson Bowers, and Ignas K. Skrupskelis, with an introduction by Edward H. Madden. Cambridge, Mass.: Harvard University Press, 1976.

Kallen, Horace. "The Laughing Philosopher." *Journal of Philosophy* 61 (1964): 19–35.

————. "Pragmatism and Its 'Principles.'" *Journal of Philosophy, Psychology, and Scientific Methods* 8, no. 23 (November 1911): 632–34.

Kaplan, Mordecai M. *Judaism as a Civilization*. New York: Macmillan, 1934.

Kateb, George. "Democratic Individuality and the Claims of Politics." *Political Theory* 12, no. 3 (August 1984): 331–60.

————. *Hannah Arendt*. Totowa, N.J.: Rowman and Allanheld, 1983.

Kern, Edith. *Absolute Comedy*. New York: Columbia University Press, 1980.

Kerr-Lawson, Angus. "Santayana's Ontology and the Nicene Creed." *Overheard in Seville: Bulletin of the Santayana Society* 8 (Fall 1989): 26–32.

Koch, Adrienne. "Political Recluse." *New Republic*, 10 September 1951, p. 20.

Kuklick, Bruce. *Josiah Royce: An Intellectual Biography*. Indianapolis: Bobbs-Merrill, 1972.

————. *The Rise of American Philosophy*. New Haven: Yale University Press, 1977.

————. "Seven Thinkers and How They Grew." In *Philosophy in History*, edited by Richard Rorty, J. B. Schneewind, and Quentin Skinner, pp. 125–39. Cambridge: Cambridge University Press, 1984.

Kundera, Milan. "Afterword: A Talk with the Author." In *The Book of Laughter and Forgetting*, translated by Michael Henry Heim, pp. 229–37. New York: Penguin Books, 1981.

————. *The Art of the Novel*. New York: Harper and Row, 1986.

Lachs, John. *Animal Faith and Spiritual Life*. New York: Appleton-Century-Crofts, 1967.

————. *George Santayana*. Boston: Twayne Publishers, 1988.

Lachs, John, and Shirley Lachs, eds. *Physical Order and Moral Liberty: Previously Unpublished Essays of George Santayana*. Nashville: Vanderbilt University Press, 1969.

Lears, T. J. Jackson. *No Place of Grace: Antimodernism and the Transformation of American Culture 1880–1920*. New York: Pantheon Books, 1981.

Lentricchia, Frank. *Ariel and the Police: Michel Foucault, William James, Wallace Stevens.* Madison: University of Wisconsin Press, 1988.

Levinson, Henry Samuel. "Meditation at the Margins: Santayana's *Scepticism and Animal Faith.*" *Journal of Religion* 67, no. 3 (July 1987): 287–309.

———. "Religious Criticism." *Journal of Religion* 64, no. 1 (January 1984): 37–53.

———. *The Religious Investigations of William James.* Chapel Hill: University of North Carolina Press, 1981.

———. "Religious Philosophy." In *The Encyclopedia of the American Religious Experience,* edited by Charles Lippy and Peter Williams, 2:1189–1206. New York: Charles Scribner's Sons, 1988.

———. "Santayana and the Many Faces of Realism." *Texas A&M Studies in American Philosophy.* Forthcoming.

———. "Santayana and the Possibility of Secular Spirituality." *National Humanities Center Newsletter* 8, no. 2 (Winter 1986–87): 1–5.

———. "Santayana's Contribution to American Religious Philosophy." *Journal of the American Academy of Religion* 52, no. 1 (March 1984): 47–69.

———. "Santayana's Pragmatism and the Comic Sense of Life." *Overheard in Seville: Bulletin of the Santayana Society* 7 (Fall 1988): 14–24.

———. *Science, Metaphysics, and the Chance of Salvation.* Missoula, Mont.: Scholars Press, 1979.

———. "What Good Is Irony?" *Overheard in Seville: Bulletin of the Santayana Society* 9 (Fall 1990): 29–34.

Lovibond, Sabina. *Realism and Imagination in Ethics.* Minneapolis: University of Minnesota Press, 1983.

Lowell, Robert. "For George Santayana." In *Life Studies and For the Union Dead,* pp. 51–52. New York: Farrar, Straus and Giroux, 1969.

———. *Lord Weary's Castle.* New York: Harcourt, Brace, Jovanovich, 1944.

Lyon, Richard C. Introduction to the critical edition of *Persons and Places: Fragments of Autobiography,* by George Santayana, edited by William G. Holzberger and Herman J. Saatkamp, Jr., pp. xv–xl. Cambridge, Mass.: MIT Press, 1987.

McCormick, John. *George Santayana: A Biography.* New York: Knopf, 1986.

MacLennan, S. F. Review of *The Life of Reason,* by George Santayana. *American Journal of Theology* 10 (1906): 161–64.

Manuel, Frank. "Israel in the Enlightenment." In *Religion and America,* edited by Stephen Tipton and Mary Douglas, pp. 44–63. Boston: Beacon Press, 1985.

Marquand, John P. *The Late George Apley.* Boston: Little, Brown, 1957.

Mead, Margaret. *An Anthropologist at Work: Writings of Ruth Benedict.* Boston: Houghton Mifflin, 1959.

Meilander, Gilbert C., Jr. "Individuals in Community: An Augustinian Vision." *Cresset* (November 1983): 5–10.

Minor, Dwight C., ed. *The Bicentennial History of Columbia University.* New York: Columbia University Press, 1957.

Moore, A. W. Review of *The Life of Reason*, by George Santayana. *Journal of Philosophy* 3 (1906): 211–14.

Moore, G. E. Review of *The Life of Reason*, by George Santayana. *International Journal of Ethics* 17 (January 1907): 248–53.

Morison, Samuel Eliot. *Development of Harvard University*. Cambridge, Mass.: Harvard University Press, 1929.

Morris, Charles W. *Paths of Life: Preface to a World Religion*. Chicago: University of Chicago Press, 1942.

———. *The Pragmatic Movement in American Philosophy*. New York: George Braziller, 1970.

Murphey, Murray. "Kant's Children: The Cambridge Pragmatists." *Transactions of the C. S. Peirce Society* 4 (1968): 3–33.

Nehamas, Alexander. "A Touch of the Poet." *Raritan: A Quarterly Review* 10 (Summer 1990): 104–25.

Niebuhr, H. Richard. *The Responsible Self: An Essay in Christian Moral Philosophy*. New York: Harper and Row, 1963.

Oakeshott, Michael. "Philosophical Imagination." *Spectator* 187 (2 November 1951): 578.

Passmore, John. *A Hundred Years of Philosophy*. London: Duckworth Press, 1957.

Perry, Ralph Barton. Review of *Character and Opinion in the United States*, by George Santayana. *Dial* 70 (May 1921): 576–79.

———. "Santayana." *Harvard Alumni Bulletin* 55 (11 October 1952): 72–73.

Pocock, J. A. C. *The Machiavellian Moment*. Princeton: Princeton University Press, 1975.

Poirier, Richard. *The Renewal of Literature: Emersonian Reflections*. New Haven: Yale University Press, 1988.

Polhemus, Robert. *Comic Faith*. Chicago: University of Chicago Press, 1980.

Porte, Joel, ed. *Emerson in His Journals*. Cambridge, Mass.: Harvard University Press, 1982.

Putnam, Hilary. *The Many Faces of Realism*. LaSalle, Ill.: Open Court Press, 1986.

———. *Realism and Reason*. Cambridge: Cambridge University Press, 1983.

———. *Realism with a Human Face*. Cambridge, Mass.: Harvard University Press, 1990.

Quine, Willard Van Orman. *From a Logical Point of View*. New York: Harper and Row, 1953.

———. *Ontological Relativity*. New York: Columbia University Press, 1969.

———. "Remarks for a Memorial Symposium." In *Bertrand Russell: A Collection of Critical Essays*, edited by D. F. Pears, pp. 1–5. Garden City, N.Y.: Doubleday, 1972.

———. *Word and Object*. Cambridge, Mass.: MIT Press, 1960.

Rawls, John. "Kantian Constructivism in Moral Theory." *Journal of Philosophy* 87, no. 9 (1980): 515–72.

Rogers, Arthur Kenyon. Reviews of *The Life of Reason*, by George Santayana. *Dial* 38 (May 1905): 349, and *Dial* 40 (February 1906): 87.

Rorty, Richard. *Consequences of Pragmatism*. Minneapolis: University of Minnesota Press, 1982.

———. *Contingency, Irony, and Solidarity*. Cambridge: Cambridge University Press, 1989.

———. *Objectivity, Relativism, and Truth*. Cambridge: Cambridge University Press, 1991.

———. *Philosophy and the Mirror of Nature*. Princeton: Princeton University Press, 1979.

Rosaldo, Renato. *Truth and Culture: The Remaking of Social Analysis*. Boston: Beacon Press: 1989.

Royce, Josiah. *The Philosophy of Loyalty*. Chicago: University of Chicago Press, 1968.

———. *The Problem of Christianity*. New York: Macmillan, 1913.

———. *The Religious Aspect of Philosophy: A Critique of the Bases of Conduct and Faith*. Boston: Houghton Mifflin, 1885.

———. *The Spirit of Modern Philosophy*. New York: W. W. Norton, 1967.

———. *William James and Other Essays on the Philosophy of Life*. New York: Macmillan, 1911.

———. *The World and the Individual*. 2 vols. New York: Macmillan, 1900.

Russell, Bertrand. *The Problems of Philosophy*. New York: Simon and Schuster, 1912.

Saatkamp, Herman J., Jr. "Some Remarks on Santayana's Scepticism." In *Two Centuries of Philosophy in America*, edited by Peter Caws, pp. 135–43. Totowa, N.J.: Rowman and Littlefield, 1980.

Saatkamp, Herman J., Jr., and John Jones. *George Santayana: A Bibliographical Checklist, 1880–1980*. Bowling Green, Ohio: Philosophy Documentation Center, 1982.

Santayana, George. Anonymous review of *Lucifer: A Theological Tragedy*, signed "H.M." *Harvard Monthly* 18 (July 1899): 210–12.

———. *Egotism in German Philosophy*. New York: Charles Scribner's Sons, 1915.

———. *The Idler and His Works, and Other Essays*. Edited by Daniel Cory. New York: George Braziller, 1957.

———. "On the False Steps of Philosophy." In *The Birth of Reason and Other Essays by George Santayana*, edited by Daniel Cory, pp. 145–74. New York: Columbia University Press, 1968.

———. "On the Unity of My Earlier and Later Philosophy." In *The Works of George Santayana*, Triton Edition, 7:ii–xiv. New York: Charles Scribner's Sons, 1937.

———. *Platonism and the Spiritual Life*. New York: Charles Scribner's Sons, 1927.

———. *The Poet's Testament: Poems and Two Plays*. New York: Charles Scribner's Sons, 1953.

———. "The Present Position of the Roman Catholic Church." *New World*, Boston, 1 (1892): 658–73.

———. "Three Proofs of Realism." In *Essays in Critical Realism: A Cooperative Study of the Problem of Knowledge*, by Durant Drake, Arthur O. Lovejoy, James Bissett Pratt, Arthur K. Rogers, George Santayana, Roy Wood Sellars, and C. A. Strong, pp. 163–84. New York: Macmillan, 1920.

———. *The Works of George Santayana.* Triton Edition. 14 vols. New York: Charles Scribner's Sons, 1936–37.

Schiller, F. C. S. Review of *The Life of Reason*, by George Santayana. *Hibbert Journal* 4 (1906): 462–64, 936–40.

Schutz, Alfred. "Santayana on Society and Government." *Social Research* 19 (1952): 220–46.

Sellars, Roy Wood. *Religion Coming of Age.* New York: Macmillan, 1928.

Shalhope, Robert E. "Toward a Republican Synthesis: The Emergence of an Understanding of Republicanism in American Historiography." *William and Mary Quarterly*, 3d ser., 29 (January 1972): 49–80.

Singer, Irving. *Santayana's Aesthetics.* Cambridge, Mass.: Harvard University Press, 1957.

Sprigge, T. L. S. "The Distinctiveness of American Philosophy." In *Two Centuries of Philosophy in America*, edited by Peter Caws, pp. 199–214. Totowa, N.J.: Rowman and Littlefield, 1980.

———. *Santayana: An Examination of His Philosophy.* London: Routledge and Kegan Paul, 1974.

Stevens, Wallace. *The Palm at the End of the Mind: Selected Poems and a Play.* Edited by Holly Stevens. New York: Random House, 1972.

Storr, Anthony. *Solitude: A Return to the Self.* New York: Free Press, 1988.

Stout, Jeffrey. *Ethics after Babel: The Languages of Morals and Their Discontents.* Boston: Beacon Press, 1989.

Strawson, Peter F. *Skepticism and Naturalism: Some Varieties (The Woodbridge Lectures 1983).* New York: Columbia University Press, 1985.

Tillich, Paul. "Christianity without Paul." *Nation*, 12 October 1946, p. 412.

Trilling, Lionel. "'That Smile of Parmenides Made Me Think.'" In *A Gathering of Fugitives*, pp. 153–67. Boston: Beacon Press, 1956.

Turner, Victor. *The Ritual Process.* Ithaca: Cornell University Press, 1966.

Walzer, Michael. *Exodus and Revolution.* New York: Basic Books, 1985.

———. "Liberalism and the Art of Separation." *Political Theory* 12, no. 3 (August 1984): 315–30.

West, Cornel. *The American Evasion of Philosophy: A Genealogy of Pragmatism.* Madison: University of Wisconsin Press, 1989.

———. "Subversive Joy and Revolutionary Patience in Black Christianity." In *Prophetic Fragments*, pp. 161–65. Grand Rapids, Mich.: Eerdmans, 1988.

Whicher, Stephen, Robert Spiller, and W. E. Williams, eds. *The Early Lectures of Ralph Waldo Emerson.* 3 vols. Cambridge, Mass.: Harvard University Press, 1959–71.

White, Morton. *Social Thought in America: The Revolt against Formalism*. Boston: Beacon Press, 1957.

Williams, Donald C. "Of Essence and Existence and Santayana." *Journal of Philosophy* 51 (1954): 31–41.

Wittgenstein, Ludwig. *Zettel*. Berkeley: University of California Press, 1970.

Wood, Gordon. *The Creation of the American Republic, 1776–1787*. Chapel Hill: University of North Carolina Press, 1969.

INDEX